The Sense of Art

Philosophy of Education Research Library

Series editors
V. A. Howard and Israel Scheffler
Harvard Graduate School of Education

Already published

The Uses of Schooling
Harry S. Broudy

Educating Reason: Rationality, Critical Thinking and Education
Harvey Siegel

Thinking in School and Society
Francis Schrag

Plato's Metaphysics of Education
Samuel Scolnicov

Accountability in Education: A Philosophical Inquiry
Robert B. Wagner

The Teacher: Theory and Practice in Education
Allen Pearson

Liberal Justice and the Marxist Critique of Education
Kenneth A. Strike

The Sense of Art

A Study in Aesthetic Education

Ralph A. Smith

Routledge

New York   London

First published in 1989 by
Routledge
an imprint of Routledge, Chapman & Hall, Inc.
29 West 35th Street
New York NY 10001

Published in Great Britain by
Routledge
11 New Fetter Lane
London EC4P 4EE

© 1989 by Routledge, Chapman and Hall, Inc.

Printed in the United States of America

Library of Congress Cataloging in Publication Data

Smith, Ralph Alexander.
    The sense of art: a study in aesthetic education/Ralph A.
Smith.
       p. cm.—(Philosophy of education research library)
    Bibliography: p.
    Includes index.
    ISBN 0-415-90089-1
    1. Art—Study and teaching. 2. Aesthetics—Study and teaching.
I. Title. II. Series.
N85.S65 1989   89-31205
707—dc19   CIP

British Library Cataloguing in Publication Data
Smith, Ralph A.
    The sense of art: a study in aesthetic education.
    I. Title
    111'.85'07

ISBN 0-415-90089-1

For my mother and sister and
in memory of W. D. S. and J. C. S.

Contents

Acknowledgments   ix

Introduction: Building a Sense of Art   1

1   Art in Cultural Context   7

2   Art in Philosophical Context   30

3   Art in Educational Context—
    The Concept of Aesthetic Criticism   48

4   Examples of Aesthetic Criticism   69

5   Teaching Aesthetic Skills   99

6   Toward an Art World Curriculum   124

7   Issues: The Two Cultures and Policy   146

8   Issues: Ideology and Postmodernism   163

Appendix I   Aesthetic Experience   184

Appendix II   The Art World and Aesthetic Skills:
               A Context for Research and Development   202

Appendix III   A Unit on Teaching Aesthetic Criticism   219

Notes   253

Index   275

Acknowledgments

Some of the ideas and topics in this volume were first explored in lectures, journal articles, and monographs which I am happy to acknowledge here. Chapter 1 is essentially the substance of the first Italo de Francesco Memorial Lecture "Art, Society, and Education" presented at Kutztown State University in 1974, and later published in *Art Education* 29, no. 6 (October 1976), 4–9. The discussion of aesthetic experience in Chapter 2 draws heavily on *Aesthetic Education in Modern Perspective,* which was the Dean's Lecture for 1985 of the College of Fine Arts and Communication at Brigham Young University. Portions of Chapter 3 and Appendix II are from a number of articles I've written about Monroe C. Beardsley over the years, namely "Teaching Aesthetic Criticism in the Schools," *Journal of Aesthetic Education* 7, no. 1 (January 1973), 38–49; "The Aesthetics of Monroe C. Beardsley: Recent Work," *Studies in Art Education* 25, no. 3 (Spring 1984), 141–50; "The Artworld and Aesthetic Skills: A Context for Research and Development," with C. M. Smith, *Journal of Aesthetic Education* 12, no. 2 (April 1977), 117–32; and "The Government and Aesthetic Education: Opportunity in Adversity?" with C. M. Smith, *Journal of Aesthetic Education* 14, no. 4 (October 1980), 5–20. The discussion of Joseph Novak's educational theory in Chapter 5 was first advanced in "Concepts, Concept Learning, and Art Education," *Review of Research in Visual Arts Education* (now *Visual Arts Research*) 11 (Winter 1979), 7–12. The tracing of the two cultures debate in Chapter 7 was first presented in "The Two Cultures Debate Today," *Oxford Review of Education* 4, no. 3 (1978), 257–65, while the analysis of policy was discussed in "Justifying Policy for Arts Education," *Studies in Art Education* 20, no. 1 (1978), 37–42, and "Formulating a Defensible Policy for Art Education," *Theory into Practice* 23, no. 4 (Autumn 1984), 273–79. The analysis of ideology in Chapter 8 had its origins in "Ideology and Aesthetic Education," *Journal of Art and Design Education* 2, no. 1 (1983), 7–14 (published by Carfax Journals Oxford Ltd.); "Ideologies, Art Education, and Philosophical Research," *Studies in Art Education* 24, no. 3 (1983), 164–68; and "The Relations of Art, Ideology, and Aesthetic Education," *Journal of Aesthetic Education* 15, no. 2 (April 1981), 5–16. My views on postmodernism were first presented in "Why

Art Must Be Defended," an unpublished lecture given while serving as Distinguished University Visiting Professor in the Graduate College and Department of Art Education at Ohio State University in the summer of 1987.

For permission to quote some of the longer passages in Appendix I, I thank the following: Martinus Nijhoff, Boston, for permission to quote from Władisław Tatarkiewicz, *History of Six Ideas,* 1980, trans. Christopher Kasparek; Andrea Reynolds, for permission to quote from Arthur Conan Doyle, *The Complete Sherlock Holmes,* n.d., Vol. I; Doubleday, New York, for permission to quote from Morton D. Zabel, ed., *The Art of Travel: Scenes and Journeys in America, England, France and Italy from the Travel Writings of Henry James;* Princeton University Press, for permission to quote from Guy Sircello, *A New Theory of Beauty,* 1975; Phi Delta Kappa for permission to quote from Stanley Elam, ed., *Education and the Structure of Knowledge,* 1964.

Finally, I am indebted to Israel Scheffler and Vernon Howard, the codirectors of the Harvard Philosophy of Education Research Center for their encouragement, to C. M. Smith for her professional editing skills and much else, and Marsha May who at times must have thought that the typing of revisions would be interminable.

Introduction: building a
sense of art

This book presents a theory of aesthetic education that addresses the needs of the current moment in society, culture, and education. These needs prescribe the revitalization of the capacity for genuine judgment in the society, the reaffirmation of the ideal of aesthetic excellence in the culture, and a commonsensical ordering of our thoughts about teaching the arts in the schools.

The first need, to reclaim judgment, derives from the unprecedented pluralism of contemporary belief. Such pluralism is responsible not only for much of the confusion, paradox, and contradiction of modern life but also for a growing paralysis of human judgment and will. This observation has been made by a number of cultural critics, and the conclusion they draw is surely correct: we must first understand what is happening before the mind can once more be free to entertain beliefs and to act in light of them.

Reaffirming the ideal of excellence involves a reawakening of historical memory and the celebration of human artistic accomplishment. Historical recollection provides the inspiration if not always the model for new acts of creation and engenders pride in human achievement. The current alternatives—the questioning of our inherent humanity, the radical skepticism regarding the possibility of knowledge and understanding, the lowering of the level of culture in both serious and popular art—lead to the abyss. The task is to remember what human accomplishment has been so that we might regain a sense of what it can once more be.

Rediscovering and reappreciating the artistic masterworks of the past also helps us to understand and assess the role of aesthetic accomplishment in our own experience and judgment of works of art. An understanding of the distinctiveness of art has become necessary in view of one of the dominant thought-clichés of the day—the belief that works of art are inescapably ideological and have no independent aesthetic value. This belief reduces art to its function in a nexus of political, economic, and social relations and disregards the type of interest persons typically take in art: an aesthetic interest.

The reconstitution of judgment, the recollection of artistic accomplishment, and the restoration of the idea of aesthetic value to the assessment of art all depend on ordering our thoughts about the sort of aesthetic learning we want for the young. The character of such learning will in turn ultimately affect the kind and quality of a society's culture.

The educational response of this volume to the needs just mentioned asserts that aesthetic education should consist of the development of a sense of art in the young that disposes them to value excellence in art. "Excellence in art," as I use the expression, means two things: the capacity of artworks at their best to provide worthwhile experiences and the manifold of the aesthetic qualities and meanings from which this capacity derives.

It follows that the major tasks of a theory of aesthetic education are to provide arguments for formally cultivating a sense of art and to indicate how this might be done through schooling. Lest the phrase "the theory of aesthetic education" sound too ambitious, I should say that it implies nothing more than a coherent set of ideas intended to provide guidance for practice in ethically appropriate ways.

To prepare the ground for a discussion of distinctively educational questions, Chapter 1 places art in cultural context and describes current attitudes toward art from historical, cultural, and philosophical vantage points. It relates more closely than is typically the case critical debate in the larger society to thinking about aesthetic education.

Chapter 2 discusses art in philosophical context and draws on modern aesthetic theory for accounts of the kinds of worthwhile experience that art at its best is capable of providing. This chapter sets out two of the three master concepts of this essay—the work of art and aesthetic experience—while Chapters 3, 4, and 5 discuss the third one, aesthetic criticism. In reviewing the work of a number of theorists I perform a task I've set myself on other occasions, that of indicating the relevance of a range of disciplines to the basic problem areas of aesthetic education. Central to the discussion of aesthetic criticism are the ways in which a sense of art directs and animates aesthetic experience. Since the possession of an effective sense of art is a function of having learned appropriate aesthetic skills, I also provide an account of aesthetic concept and skill acquisition.

The principal theoretical work of the essay having been presented, Chapter 6 outlines an approach to an art world or excellence curriculum, while Chapters 7 and 8 examine various persistent issues in the field of arts education. The essay concludes with three appendixes: one that develops a more detailed discussion of aesthetic experience than could be undertaken in Chapter 2, another that provides a context for research and development in the teaching of aesthetic skills, and a third that suggests a model for preparing a unit on aesthetic criticism.

The book's contents suggest the audience for which it was written: mainly teachers of arts in the schools and those who train arts educators, officials employed in the cultural services field, and the general reader interested in learning something about the relations of art, society, and education.

Given the character and composition of these diverse audiences, I have tried whenever possible to recast technical discussion into nontechnical language with a view to making ideas more accessible while avoiding their oversimplification. In the nineteenth century Matthew Arnold called such efforts at rephrasing and dissemination the humanization of knowledge. He believed that thought should be made effective outside the clique of the learned and cultivated without sacrificing its standing as the best knowledge of the time. Arnold, in turn, was invoked by Lawrence A. Cremin in his characterization of the genius of American education.[1]

The commitment to the humanization of knowledge partly explains the approach I have taken in this book. I have been less concerned to produce a work of original scholarship than to effect a synthesis of what others have helpfully said on the subject. This stance stems from a conviction that we are in greater need today of a systematic roundup of useful ideas than of the kind of creativeness and originality that on closer inspection turns out to be little more than conventional wisdom. Too often purportedly new paths reveal themselves to be well trodden. Hence my effort owes less to modesty than it does to the adverse judgment I have passed on much contemporary writing on arts education. The field of arts education, like many others, is afflicted with what the editor of a journal in aesthetics called the "don't look back" fallacy, that is, authors' delusions of novelty sustained by ignorance of what has been written. In this connection, I prefer to recall an eighteenth-century maxim, which holds that true originality consists not in saying new things but in clarifying and reconciling long-established and well-known truths.

A few remarks are in order about some terms that recur in this essay. "Aesthetic education," as I use it, usually functions as a general label that loosely refers to whatever goes on in the name of arts education. In this respect, "arts education" and "aesthetic education" are often interchangeable. When not used in this general sense the term stands for a separate subject or area of study and its peculiar concepts, skills, and contexts, especially those most pertinent to developing a sense of art. In making the term aesthetic central, I follow the lead of others who have written about art and arts education from the eighteenth century to the present. I further exploit a number of the term's meanings.

There is first of all the association of "aesthetic" with a special point of view, mode of attention, interest, or experience which a number of theorists think outstanding works of art are eminently suited to arouse and sustain at a high pitch of intensity. This capacity is often called a work's aesthetic value and the experience occasioned aesthetic experience. The term aesthetic thus suggests the perception and contemplation of things rather than their creation—looking, listening, or reading rather than making—which is congenial to my purpose. Since successful works of art in all mediums of the visual, literary, and performing arts are capable of inviting and prolonging aesthetic interest, the term is also featured in discussions of the functions the arts have in common. To be sure, important differences among the arts limit the applicability of the commonality thesis. Yet, as Jacques Barzun[2] has pointed out, there are fruitful analogies among the arts that contribute significantly to our understanding. The unity of the arts is thus not a wholly discredited idea. Finally, since aesthetic topics and questions are usually addressed by philosophers in a branch of philosophy known as aesthetics, the term aesthetic further brings to mind an area of scholarly inquiry that has importance for our thinking about the nature of aesthetic education.

When referring to "aesthetic education," then, we may associate the expression with the aesthetic perception, experience, and judgment of the arts (with a sideward glance at the aesthetic appreciation of other things), with the arts in general (or art with a capital A), and with philosophical aesthetics (with a sideward glance at scientific aesthetics or the empirical study of the arts). For my purposes these associations of the term "aesthetic" are felicitous rather than limiting.

The decision to make the term aesthetic and related concepts central may arouse skepticism in light of the searching analyses to which a number of aesthetic concepts have been subjected in recent years. Critics have claimed that the notions of aesthetic attitude and aesthetic experience do not bear close scrutiny and are far too vague to be of any theoretical or practical use. That precision is difficult, if not impossible, to achieve in describing human actions is of course true. Thus it is not surprising, and is indeed to be expected, that concepts attempting to capture a distinctive form of experience should prove especially troublesome to define. Yet neither the diligent wielding of Occam's Razor nor the iconoclasm or dismissive attitude of some writers have been successful in dislodging the notion of aesthetic experience, one of the core concepts of aesthetics. John Hospers, himself a skeptic regarding the significance of several aesthetic concepts, has remarked that the term "aesthetic" entered the language for a reason and is therefore not likely to be easily dispatched, and a cluster of new books and articles reveal a continuing interest in the concept. Indeed, I believe that writers who try to discern a distinctive strand of experience known as aesthetic are contributing to an understanding of human rationality itself.

Difficulties of definition notwithstanding, this essay understands a work of art to be a humanly fashioned artifact that has among its characteristics a capacity to occasion in qualified percipients a high degree of aesthetic experience. Aesthetic experience affords by different turns a special kind of enjoyment, stimulation of the mind, insight, and institutional efficacy. There are, in other words, varieties of aesthetic experience, and it is one of the aims of this volume to reconcile ostensibly different points of view. A theory of aesthetic education would doubtlessly be more elegant if it were informed by a single conception of art. But as Israel Scheffler[3] has remarked, an eclectic character is likely to be a feature of most theories of practical activity. The task is to avoid unrestrained and unprincipled eclecticism.

CHAPTER 1

Art in cultural context

> In art the times are out of joint, saturated
> with the trivial and the corrupt; there is
> an enormous need for the critical intelli-
> gence to devote itself to this paradox—
> to explain, unmask, and diagnose in such
> a way as to work toward a reconstruction
> and a purification. Great criticism is al-
> most by definition a recall to order and to
> value.   *Albert William Levi*[1]

A theory of aesthetic education does not require a problematic context in order to justify the study of the arts in the schools. Art is a unique human achievement and teaching about it can be defended on the grounds that regardless of other tasks set for schooling, one of its major goals must be to induct the young into what Ernst Cassirer in his classic *An Essay on Man*[2] termed the circle of humanity—expressions of humanity that include not only language, myth, religion, history, and science, but also art. Art is thus an important component of culture and should be integral to fashioning any human career. Jacques Barzun[3] has likewise asserted that we teach the rudiments of art because art corresponds to a deep human instinct the expression of which is enjoyable. But this does not suffice as an educational justification; there are many human instincts the satisfaction of which is pleasurable that do not merit consideration in the process of formal education.

Curriculum decision makers, then, need additional reasons for taking art seriously. Just what kind of human attainment is art? Is it really as important as science, history, and religion? Is art simply a source of enjoyment or does it also constitute a form of knowledge? Just what is the deep human instinct that art satisfies? And in view of the great variety of things that pass for art today, is it even evident what constitutes art's rudiments? Still further, are school administrators and policymakers to understand by "art" what typically goes on under the rubric of art education in today's schools? If so, they would be obliged to endorse the overemphasis on "coloring, polishing, and playing" at the expense of the serious study of art that John Goodlad discerned in his observations of the educational practices of schools.[4] What, moreover, are we to make of the many contradictory statements we hear about art—that art, for example, is both a revelation and a deception, both purposeful and purposeless[5]—or of the ease with which the art world can accommodate, say, Caravaggio's *The Martyrdom of Saint Matthew* and Frank Stella's *Thruxton 3X* within the category of painting?[6] Indeed the confusing face of so much contemporary art has prompted a number of writers to describe the public's relation to art today as one of anxiety.[7] Accordingly, educators cannot rest content with simple declarations of art's value. Closer attention than ever must be paid to the justification question, to making a convincing, well-supported case for teaching art. In doing this, they must look beneath the surface manifestations of the art world where an enormous diversity of objects and activities create uncertainty about the nature, meaning, and value of art. Being part of the problem, the art world cannot be relied on for guidance in the formulation of a theory of aesthetic education. Educators must therefore try to penetrate to the roots of the current anxiety and confusion.

Special problems are also posed by the democratic ethos and certain of its internal contradictions. On the one hand, a democratic society grants all persons the right to develop the human potentialities implied in Cassirer's conception of humanity, and these include capacities that are actualized best during aesthetic experiences of works of fine art. On the other hand, modern democracies have never been on easy terms with the life of high culture. Democratic societies have not adjusted well to the fact that the artistic treasures of the cultural heritage were produced for the most part under conditions controlled by privileged classes; and they have found it difficult to reconcile the desirability of rewarding and encouraging artistic accomplishment with the elitism that allegedly inheres in such acts of recognition. The modern democrat's division of mind about the value of culture is largely attributable to the difficulty of finding a proper place for excellence and its pursuit in an egalitarian society. This condition also helps us to understand why outstanding artists and intellectuals are expected to display the "common touch"— it enables persons to resolve their ambivalence about the uneven distribution of talent among the human lot.

Ambivalence about excellence also explains the hesitancy with which we often approach the task of policy-making for arts education. We want children to study what is worthwhile, but we do not want to foster exclusivity or, worse, create the impression that learning is remote from the lives of young people; so we recommend the study of popular along with high culture (though the latter generally receives short shrift). Everyone shares a tacit conviction that most things can be done well or poorly, that this is particularly true of the creation of art and makes art criticism possible. Yet recognizing the achievements of some persons means withholding recognition from others; egalitarians cavil at such an unequal outcome and therefore contrive to award some sort of prize to everyone. Moreover, we know that Western civilization is the repository of unparalleled cultural achievement. But our sensitivity to other cultures and a desire to be fair suggest that while Western culture may still deserve a place in the curriculum, it should not be given pride of place. In an excess of reverse ethnocentrism, some multicultural educators go even further and say that Western values and achievements are inherently inferior to non-Western ones. A misconceived egalitarianism in concert with strong tendencies toward sentimentalism and subjectivism can then prove a hindrance to formulating a substantive theory and policy for aesthetic education.

Yet this is only part of the story. For the democratic ethos can also be understood as accommodating critical decisiveness, a commitment to reason and rationality, and the promotion of excellence. Happiness, identity, and self-cultivation can be pursued without going to the extremes of self-indulgence, narcissism, and cloying sentimentality. Similarly, the undeniable presence of a subjective dimension in all knowing does not rule out the possibility of making rational, objective judgments. And there is an egalitarianism that realizes the importance of authority, status, and excellence in the lives of men and women.[8] Ultimately, it is these sterner features of the democratic ethos to which we must appeal in our attempt to frame a theory of aesthetic education.

The foregoing remarks suggest the need for gaining a broader perspective on the current moment in cultural and educational affairs. For instances of such encompassing views I turn to the insights of several of our most trenchant observers, beginning with the late Lord Kenneth Clark's reflections on the relations of art and society and then moving on to the critical writings of Jacques Barzun, Harold Rosenberg, Clifton Fadiman, and Monroe C. Beardsley.

Kenneth Clark: The relations of art and society

In "Art and Society,"[9] an essay rich in commentary on the conditions of life that affect the production and appreciation of the arts, Kenneth Clark presents three generalizations, the first of which is that throughout Western history works of art have typically been made by a minority— creative artists—for a minority—persons of wealth and political or ecclesiastical power—in order to celebrate the value system of the ruling minority in question. Clark emphasizes, however, that works made by a minority for a minority were often accepted by the majority with a sense of approval and involvement. Work thus produced Clark unhesitatingly calls the art of an elite, but he stresses that by virtue of a meaningful and comprehensible symbolism such art often appealed as well to the general public. Records abound from the societies of ancient Greece, the Middle Ages, and the Renaissance that describe the population's awareness of and response to art. Ordinary citizens were often seriously interested in the awarding of artistic commissions and followed work in progress with anticipation. And it was not uncommon for finished art objects to be carried aloft in ceremonial processions through the city streets. The account of events in Siena that attended the completion of Duccio's great triptych the *Maestà* in 1311 is a representative and often cited instance:

On the day when it was brought to the Cathedral, the shops where shut and the Bishop decreed a solemn procession of a large and devout company of priests and friars, accompanied by the nine Signori and by all the officers of the Commune and all the populace; and one by one all the most worthy persons approached the picture with lighted candles in their hands and behind them came the women and children in devout attitudes. And they accompanied the said picture to the Cathedral, marching in procession round the Campo, as is the custom, while the bells sounded the Gloria, in homage to so noble a painting as this is. And they remained all day praying and gave many alms to poor persons, praying to God and his Mother, who is our patroness and with her infinite mercy defends us from every adversity and evil and preserves us from the hands of traitors and enemies of Siena.[10]

A society like that of Siena, observes Clark, needed art, had faith in its value, and thus strongly supported the social position of those who created it. This prompts Clark's second generalization (or what he calls a "historical law"): that a healthy and vital relation between art and society exists when the majority of individuals feel that art is absolutely necessary to confirm their beliefs and to inform them about matters of enduring importance, chiefly issues surrounding the fate and destiny of human existence. Art was able to assume a place of such significance in the lives of ordinary people of previous eras because its compelling images made manifest the invisible world of the spirit. We know what these symbols, images, and iconographies were in the great ages of art; we find them in the pediments and reliefs of the Parthenon, in the portals and stained-glass windows of Chartres Cathedral, in the Paduan frescoes of Giotto, in Michelangelo's Medici Chapel, and in the paintings of Delacroix and Constable, by whose time images of nature had largely supplanted those of God, the Virgin, and the Saints as carriers of import. Each set of symbols or style of artistic statement revealed in its distinctive way the networks of belief and custom characteristic of the society in which it was created. Such symbols and statements therefore performed a crucial function in maintaining strong ties between art and society; they were emblems of social cohesion. Clark ascribes a sacramental character to art of this kind: it expresses the nonmaterial or spiritual strivings of a period.

The sacramental function of art is central to Clark's third generalization: that the spiritual life of a society must be vigorous enough to insist on symbols and images that speak to that society's deepest needs and aspirations; correspondingly, no great social art can be based on physical sensations and material values alone. When artworks are mere luxury items that cater to idiosyncratic individual tastes, art fails to contribute to general enlightenment and a split develops between art and society.

In brief compass, then, here are three historical generalizations about the relations of art and society: art has in large served elite interests while appealing to the majority; art has been most effective as a social force when it has successfully conveyed important beliefs about human existence and its destiny; and art has import only when it transcends physical sensation and material values. Do these generalizations throw any light on our current cultural situation?

Clark is confident that the strivings of human nature have not substantially changed and that persons still hunger for compelling images that express and confirm their nonmaterial aspirations. The heroic materialism of the modern era has not extinguished the needs of the spiritual life. The important difference between the present and past ages is the loss of integrative beliefs which lend themselves to expression in persuasive images. An era dominated by science and humanitarianism has yet to find cogent symbols that command universal acceptance. Science thrives mainly on exactitude of statement and its appreciation is restricted to a tiny elite educated in its abstractions; this severely limits its appeal. Egalitarian humanitarianism, on the other hand, finds it difficult to reconcile itself to the fine arts which are of necessity the products of conditions it considers elitist. The surface symptoms of these underlying cultural divisions are the "humanism versus positivism" debate and the "elitism versus populism" controversy in the arts that center on the relative claims of "high" and "popular" culture. It is as if in the modern age a set of integrating beliefs has been replaced by an imagination of radical uncertainty which ascribes no redemptive value to the arts. In this connection, the image of the dynamo that Henry Adams proposed as the emblem of the modern era was no match in potency and appeal for the image of the Virgin in earlier religious periods.[11] Nor does it seem likely that the computer can serve the needed unifying and humanizing function. Furthermore, though nature lovers and environmental theorists might want to argue the point and present images of nature as counterexamples,[12] it remains true that our cosmpolitan society has difficulty revering nature in the way the nineteenth century did; knowledge of the fouling of nature with toxic wastes and industrial detritus inhibits aesthetic and spiritual communion with nature's beauties. Finally, the prospect for any one image (of sight or sound) commanding universal assent is sharply attenuated not only by the vacuum of belief which such an image would have to transcend, but also by the ubiquity of competing images that clamor for attention, each in its turn tending to nullify the effects of the others.

In short, the conditions of modernity enfeeble the human spirit and frustrate the search for something that answers to deeply felt needs. As one consequence, the artist finds it necessary to engage in a quest for identity, for a meaningful role, for a secure place in society. This is a lesser concern of the artist's counterparts in the sciences and other, more practical endeavors where the acknowledged social importance of an occupational field facilitates and reinforces career decisions. But what is the proper career for an artist today: portrayer of the beautiful, interpreter of life, social and moral critic (perhaps ideological advocate), technical experimenter, shaman, trickster, or simply supplier of market demand? (This last function was suggested by a report that some professional art schools are now designing courses to help young artists, still in their twenties, to cope with instant success in the marketplace.)[13] Some of the problems posed by the conditions of modernity for the contemporary artist are, I think, well reflected in an anthology assembled by an artist in the 1970s.[14] The collection begins with an essay on the aesthetics of highly rationalized activities (systems aesthetics) and concludes with one upholding the role of the artist as shaman or high priest. In between are recorded various stances that reflect constantly changing attitudes toward art and the artist's role. The point of this observation is not to denigrate contemporary artists but to describe their dilemma and the complexities of the artist's station in an age that expresses great uncertainty about the nature and function of art and to recall the difficulties this situation presents for a theory of aesthetic education.

But could not the conditions just identified also be characterized as portending cultural health? Could not the searching and questing, even the anxiety and ambivalence we observe in the art world be signs of vigor and creative energy? Certainly we live in a time of unprecedented excitement about matters relating to art, as reflected in ever-rising attendance at cultural events and increased purchases of artistic artifacts—a development that two sociologists have characterized as the third American revolution, a revolution of cultural consumption.[15] Yet while interest in art is a precondition of aesthetic perception, it does not guarantee that aesthetic experiences will occur. Furthermore, the public's acquiescence in just about everything made and promoted in the name of art could as easily be a sign of malaise, as evidence of choices and decisions made on false grounds. What, moreover, is a public apparently eager and hungry for aesthetic experience to make of an art that intentionally offends and mocks the very idea of art as a source of spiritual nourishment? It was Clark's belief that "the majority of people . . . really long to experience that moment of pure, disinterested, non-material satisfaction which causes them to ejaculate the word 'beautiful,' " a kind of experience that "can be obtained more reliably through works of art than through any other means."[16] The mode of art known as anti-art, however, heaps scorn on such a belief. If Clark is right about what most people still expect from art, it is clear that not all contemporary art is capable of satisfying this basic human instinct. And so we are compelled, with as much wise assistance as we can find, to do some sorting out; we must try to distinguish those works that have potentially humanizing effects from those that do not. We will not be helped by the fact that the vast institution of art and culture now often called the art world does not, with rare exception, encourage discrimination, which is an indication that its constituents have lost the will and capacity to judge. Clark seems to have realized this. Though not oblivious to the efforts of those in cultural institutions who endeavor to make works of art accessible and to encourage the cultivation of cultural interests, he nonetheless says: "But how little we know of what we are doing."[17] Clark recommends that healthier relations be built between art and society by expanding the numbers of those who create and appreciate art without sacrificing artistic integrity. He hopes that communication between art and audience might thus be restored. Like most of the writers discussed in this chapter, however, Clark is better at analysis than prescription.

Jacques Barzun: Reconstituting judgment

If Clark canvassed the whole of art history for generalizations about the relations of art and society, Jacques Barzun, a cultural historian and critic, surveys the last 150 years and thus helps to narrow the field of vision.

In *The Use and Abuse of Art*,[18] the annual Mellon lectures of 1973 presented at the National Gallery of Art in Washington, D.C., Barzun states that his intention is to describe Art (with a capital A) as a force in modern society and its effects for good or ill on human life—a task similar to one he had set in examining the role of science in society. Barzun presents a bleak prospect that many would regard as no prospect at all or take little comfort in. He sees no healthy relations between art and society emerging from the current cultural situation and believes that we are witnessing the liquidation of that cultural estate the foundations of which were laid in the Renaissance 500 years ago. Consolation may be found only in the realization that something new will ultimately grow from the ruins of what we have known. Far from being in the middle of a mere cultural recession we have entered a dark age that will continue until substantial changes occur in social, intellectual, and artistic life.

Behind Barzun's prognosis is an understanding of modern life and art that reveals not only the range and depth of his scholarship but also his finesse in exposing cultural folly. His interpretation goes like this.

With Clark, Barzun assumes that artistic images are not created for amusement. Art, he thinks, is the expression of a power that can significantly shape thought and feeling; it is thus subject to abuse. One form of abuse is the great diversity of functions society has assigned to art, and this is one source of the confusion in our thinking about cultural matters. Cultural institutions, however, often conveniently disregard this pluralism of function when they acknowledge only art's benign or redeeming potential in their efforts to employ it toward benevolent ends. But it is difficult to square this tendency with the ways in which artists themselves frequently view their works. Many of them produce what has come to be called anti-art, which denies art's beneficent effects and strips it of practically all human significance. In their zeal to bring about art's demise, creators of anti-art systematically dismantle the very idea of art. An effective tactic is to reduce art to a mere sensuous stimulus or a pun, to play havoc with the seriousness and profundity of high art. Barzun, using a typical dialectical method—an if-then mode of reasoning that he invites his readers to share—points out the dilemma this diminution of art presents: "If," he writes, "modern man's most sophisticated relation to art is to be casual and humorous, is to resemble the attitude of the vacationer at the fair grounds, then the conception of Art as an all-important institution, as a supreme activity of man, is quite destroyed. One cannot have it both ways—art as a sense-tickler and a joke is not the same art that geniuses and critics have asked us to cherish and support."[19]

Nor, Barzun goes on, can art's benign character continue to be taken for granted once we recognize another major trend in modern art: its revolutionary mission in ushering in a new social order. Even when art's purpose is not overtly revolutionary it may still act as a social and moral critic and produce unsettling results. The truth is that art in the contemporary era has seldom pursued wholesome or conciliatory objectives, preferring instead to vent anger toward society and its institutions, most of all toward the commercial middle class or bourgeoisie, which has had to bear the brunt of artists' animosity.

Barzun locates the origin of the currently pervasive adversarial disposition of artists in the writings of the eighteenth-century German thinker Friedrich Schiller. At approximately the same time that Schiller was publishing his *Letters on the Aesthetic Education of Man* (1795), he also wrote an essay that is usually translated as "On Naive and Sentimental Poetry" but which, Barzun thinks, should be translated as "On Primitive and Self-Conscious Poetry." In this essay Schiller expressed the thought that genius is the only savior in a divided world which has increasingly succumbed to a self-conscious and instrumentalist cast of mind. Since, however, the task of genius is to extend into the human realm the freedom and harmony found in nature, genius rejects a calculating mentality in favor of feeling and spontaneity. While genius as described by Schiller is intelligent, modest, and sincere, it is never *decent*. Modernized, says Barzun, this means that genius can never be middle class or bourgeois; and this conviction, he thinks, has provided the animus for the war between artist and society from Waterloo to last week. Once again, this battle has been raging for about 150 years during which art has gradually come to supplant religion as the principal monitor and judge of moral life and society.

An interesting aspect of this 150 years' war, however, was the victory gradually gained by artists over the enemy, the detested middle class. The bourgeoisie began to purchase the work of discontented artists and installed it in private and public collections. The effect was to celebrate and legitimize the new artistic values. It was, however, as if such toleration proved intolerable to artists, for they next shifted their hatred of society to art itself, or at least to the idea of art. Thus commenced the abolitionist phase of modern art, during which the idea of art as destroyer received currency. Harold Rosenberg termed this abolitionist phase the de-definition and de-aestheticization of art.[20] In often quoted essays, which capture Barzun's characterization perfectly, Rosenberg described how with the skill of a diamond cutter modern artists split away the vital components of art one by one; first to go was subject matter, then drawing, then composition, then color and texture, and eventually flat surfaces and the artifact itself, on which everything else depends. The artifact of art was in effect displaced by the concept of art.

Of relevance here is that in systematically altering the shape, look, and substance of art, modern artists self-consciously abjured its elevating potentialities. Along with the traditional ideal of high art and its humanistic function, abolitionism jettisoned the image of man reflected in such art. The only conclusion to be drawn, says Barzun, is that artists no longer find man to be interesting thematic material. The human condition no longer deserves being ennobled in art, is not even worth having art's mirror held up to it. The individual's career and destiny, of which John Dewey and so many othes wrote, do not seem to matter anymore. The notion that art invigorates and enhances life, that it makes life livelier, loses credibility. In one respect, Barzun is saying that the predominantly adversarial disposition of modern man is mainly the product of the informal aesthetic education he has received at the hands of artists and their apologists over the past century and a half. Thus even while it communicated its most negative and destructive message, art remained the preeminent teacher of ways to think and feel about the self and its proper relation to society. As a result, the antagonistic mentality fostered by much contemporary art has turned lovers of art into haters of the world: the world doesn't measure up.

The muddy river of modernism mapped by Barzun wended its way through a number of side channels for, once again, pluralism is a central fact of contemporary culture. In their various poses as redeemers, revolutionaries, and abolitionists, artists did not confine themselves to a singular style. Some of them adopted the stance, jargon, and methods of science and, as a result, imported scientism into the production of art. We read, for example, of artsts "solving problems" in "artistic laboratories" in which "aesthetic experiments" are conducted. As in scientific research, artistic teamwork may take precedence over individual effort. Yet Barzun cautions that if art's powers are abused when art is asked to take the place of religion, so they are ill used when art imitates science; he calls therefore for a separation of roles and functions.

An age that mixes incongruous domains, that closes avenues of response between artists and audiences or trivializes their relationships, and that also confuses artists regarding their identity and role—such an age, Barzun suggests, is unlikely to muster the resolve needed to disentangle its disparate elements and restore harmony; the notions of art as redeemer and as destroyer cannot produce a synthesis. Such an age is more likely to retreat from the cultural field and try to start anew. The difficulty is to find a way to proceed, to rebuild confidence and instill fortitude in a period lacking belief and will. Like Clark, Barzun is more adept at analysis than he is at recommendation, and he acknowledges the futility of trying to predict the future. But Barzun is convinced that a fundamental precondition of any significant change is the reconstitution of judgment, which always implies choice and commitment. We will not, he thinks, be able to build a new civilization before we have fashioned a different type of personality. Demoralized and disoriented—bombed as it were out of his cultural senses—the contemporary individual has lost the capacity for genuine judgment; the ground must therefore be prepared for the evolution of a new man, a belief that is, of course, fraught with educational implications.

Even allowing for the limitations of the lecture format Barzun adopted and for the necessity of condensing mountains of historical facts into a few coherent generalizations, his critique of art as a force for both good and evil is a powerful stimulus to attempts to redefine cultural and educational relations. The problems for aesthetic education generated by the 150 years' cultural war in the larger society are precisely what the theory of aesthetic education presented here addresses. Any such theory, however, must go beyond broad historical and cultural generalization to a more concrete consideration of another pervasive feature of modern life, namely, the effects that the media of mass communication are having on the art world. Given the belief of many that the communications media bear greater responsibility for the shape and quality of things to come than formal schooling itself, the magnitude of this impact should not be surprising. In turning our attention to this new power, we are narrowing our field of vision still further.

Harold Rosenberg: Artworks and packages

What happens to art when it enters the media system? In a number of essays, notably in *Artworks and Packages* and *Art and Other Serious Matters*,[21] the late Harold Rosenberg, who was a cultural as well as an art critic, focuses on the period from the end of World War II to recent years, during which art has been irresistibly drawn into the media system. Rosenberg was exceptional among modern writers on culture for his insight into artistic consciousness, the problems faced by artists in contemporary society, and the effects of the social environment on creative work and attitudes. He was particularly concerned to understand and record the struggle of artists to resist the forces that threatened to deprive them of their freedom. He was also persuaded of the value of artistic expression as the last bastion of genuine individuality. I bypass the debate on his interpretation of action painting and his political sentiments and concentrate on his discussion of art and the media.

In "Art and Its Double" Rosenberg asserts that "today, every artist lives under the pressure—and enjoys the advantages—of changes wrought in the conditions of aesthetic culture, and in art itself, by the mass media,"[22] or the "media system," as he calls it, by which he understands the network of forces that brings artworks into conformity with society's mechanisms and the imperatives of production and distribution. So far as consequences for the visual arts are concerned, the principal characteristics of the media system are its globalism, mass output and sales, and the conditioning of response. Globalism effects the transformation of the peculiarities of individual works of art into a new format that lends itself to quick and easy conveyance around the whole world (like Coca Cola). The relative ease of transportation and communication and the existence of a potential world audience create an expanding market the requirements of which artists try to meet with works (like prints) that lend themselves to duplication and facilitate portability. Moreover, as the demand for art increases, the criteria for assessing art become quantitative. "The number of times an artist is mentioned and his work reproduced or shown becomes the measure of his importance. Circulation is in itself a merit beyond discussion."[23]

Globalism thus fosters the mass production and duplication of recent art and mass reproduction of work by old masters. This vast proliferation of art objects has led to the discouragement of distinctions between the original and the copy and has forced the reproduction into a schizophrenic existence as the ghost of its original. Under such circumstances, art becomes an "anxious object," and a "tradition of the new" is born, to use two expressions popularly associated with Rosenberg's writings. Works of art, in other words, subjected to Hollywood and Madison Avenue promotion techniques, become fodder for the media's insatiable appetite. All art becomes popular art. This applies even to genuinely traditional art that gets reinterpreted in renovated contexts in order to accommodate contemporary interests and styles of art consumption. Works of the old masters are no longer exhibited as objects demanding prolonged contemplation and study but as objects to be casually viewed by an art public that is essentially on the run. (It is reported that museum visitors spend an average of five seconds in front of each work.)[24] To trade on the title of a publication series that came out a while back, the media system makes art simple.

The unremitting pressure of the media system helps to explain certain acts of ostensible vandalism committed by artists which have achieved

a measure of notoriety. An early example was Marcel Duchamp's defac-
ing a reproduction of the *Mona Lisa* by painting a moustache on it.
Rosenberg sees in the mustachioed *Mona Lisa* an attempt to counter the
media's domination of art by converting one of the media's characteristic
products, the reproduction, into an original work of art (the work eventually found its way into a museum). According to Rosenberg, Duchamp's
aim was to restore artistic consciousness in the face of the media's
relentless reach and to recover the artist's initiative against the automatic
processes of mass society. As Rosenberg puts it, "Only the pressure of
new creations *against* art as it has been defined keeps art from merging
with the media and allows works to survive for an interval as art."[25] The
efforts of contemporary artists to de-define art are thus explained as acts
of desperation, as a struggle to save art in some form from media
encroachment.

Although Rosenberg brings sympathetic understanding to artistic expressions that might otherwise be too hastily dismissed as bizarre and
outré, he also emphasizes the continuing need for criticism. It is important to judge when artists have made genuine creative decisions and
when they have indulged in mere gesturing. (Of course, by the time
Monty Python's Flying Circus has taken hold of the mustachioed *Mona
Lisa,* posturing has turned into buffoonery.)

To reiterate, in Rosenberg's description of the cultural context of art
today, art is seen as submitting increasingly to the imperatives of marketing and distribution. This means that art should be easy to disseminate
and easy to absorb; thus is art transformed into the package. The basic
features of a media package are reliability of production, standardization
of quality, convenience in delivery, and ease of communication—all
characteristics vital to a market economy. But what is art as package,
and how does art get packaged? Two aspects under which to consider
the packaging process are the changes in the traditional role and function
of the art museum and the media's effect on quality in the avant-garde.

If we ask, says Rosenberg, who really defines art, the standard reply
has been the history of art, the physical embodiment of which is the art
museum. Art is what goes into the museum and what goes into the
museum is art. Artists fully understand this status-conferring capacity
and thus keep their eye on museums. (Of course, any definition of a
museum today must include "museums without walls" as well, that is,
the ever-expanding domain of portable works and reproductions.) Until
approximately the mid-twentieth century, the definition of art favored
by museums was determined by the excellences of traditional works of
art, by the masterpieces of the cultural heritage. Works were granted
admission and acknowledged as art when they bore sufficient similarity
to approved cases. Ruled by the strong hand of the past, the museum
consequently came to be looked on as a tomb or graveyard, a dark
repository of relics. The museum thus rivaled the church or temple as a

place for contemplation in an increasingly loud and frenetic society. Today, Rosenberg believed, the museum still performs its status-conferring function, but it has come under new management with a different operating policy. No longer a quiet refuge in which visitors may engage in unhurried aesthetic experiences, the museum has in effect become an educational, community, distribution, and public relations center, one role growing out of the other. Likewise, the modern museum has replaced traditional academic art history as judge and definer of art with the more voguish conceptions of art its staff now prefers. "Art manufactured for the art museum," says Rosenberg, "enters not into eternity but into the market."[26] Perhaps we may say that museum officials, like the natural scientists of C. P. Snow's description, now have the future more than the past in their bones. No longer content to preserve, study, and exhibit the treasures of the past, the new museum creates trends and reputations and in this respect rivals the creativity of artists. As mentioned, even when museum exhibits are devoted to art from the distant or more recent past, works are displayed in ways and with interpretive and explanatory appurtenances gauged to make them more suitable to popular consumption. In a parallel development, works once regarded as second-rate— as dryly academic or sentimental and obvious—are now dragged from vaults and storage chambers and proclaimed to possess special relevance for the modern temper. More often than not, however, works of this kind must rely for their appeal not on any intrinsic qualities but on having somehow been made newsworthy, at least for a moment.

When art is valued for its novelty and exhibits are treated mainly as news events, the museum becomes a link in a communications chain of majestic proportions, replete with all the techniques of media technology. Or, to project another image, the cloister is transformed into a midway thronged with crowds skimming and scanning their way through the museum's galleries and vending places. Viewers, moreover, feel no need for sustained contemplation since handbooks, catalogues, and tapes tell them all they could care to know. Hence Rosenberg conceives of the modern museum as a cog in the global system of the new, as "a mechanism of communication dedicated to audience-building" and engaged in "synchronizing art production and distribution with the rhythm of the cultural commodity market and its insatiable demand for 'revolutionary' innovations."[27] If the museum goes completely hip, says Rosenberg, the only identifiable difference between art and the media will be the size of the audience to which art appeals. In this respect Marshall McLuhan was correct: art becomes media. One need only consider the plethora of catalogues, reviews, interviews, videotapes, films, human-interest stories, biographies, lectures, personal appearance tours, and so forth, generated within and about the art world. The exhaustibility of the supply of traditional, modern, and contemporary art, however, makes it necessary that avalanches of new imagery be produced constantly, which means that there is less and less time to distinguish powerful and compelling work from pseudo art. Any distinctions tend to fade, a trend, we may suggest, that is exemplified in the careers, reputations, and especially the legacies of the late Andy Warhol and Liberace.

Artists swept into the distribution patterns of the global system of the new are hardly able to sustain the mission of an avant-garde: continually to challenge and resist the packaging of art. Perhaps, says Rosenberg, it is repeating the obvious to point out that acquiescence in market demand in cultural matters corrupts artistic imagination and renders it a scarcer human resource than ever before. Mass art exemplifies the standardization and rationalization of aesthetic elements, genuine art their creative combination and expressive power; one is guided by formula, the other nourished by uncertainty and discovery; freshness is foreign to the former, while the latter thrives on it. To reiterate, the characteristic accomplishment of the media system is the package, art's double in which art has trouble recognizing itself. When the avant-garde submits to the command of the media system, its creativity becomes attenuated and serves the merely fashionable. The story of the fashionabilization of the avant-garde is sketched in Rosenberg's essay on the avant-garde in *Quality: Its Image in the Arts*,[28] edited by Louis Kronenberger. It is a tale of how in a relatively short period of time banal impoverishment came to be preferred to the imaginatively articulate.

It is perhaps only fair to add that Rosenberg's emphasis is more closely associated with only one position in a current critical debate. That dispute centers on the relative significance to be accorded to either of two tendencies in modern art. The first trend ran its course from about 1850 to 1950 and extended from Manet and the Impressionists to the Abstract Expressionists of the mid-twentieth century. The second tendency dates from roughly that midpoint and is notorious for the happenings, anti-art, and other varieties of so-called postmodernist art. Hilton Kramer[29] thinks that the first tendency deserves far more attention than it has received because the artists associated with it felt under an obligation, however unconsciously, to work their way through artistic tradition in order to create new aesthetic values. Conversely, the second trend attempts to effect a radical disjunction with the past. The dispute is sometimes said to turn on the respective virtues of modernism (the first tendency) versus postmodernism (the second tendency), although that vastly oversimplifies the situation. We shall have to live through a period of rather intense critical controversy and turmoil before the issues will be more clearly understood. Meanwhile, the big news from the art world continues to be the astronomical prices paid for both traditional and modern works of art (as of this writing, over 50 million dollars for a Van Gogh painting is the record).

Clifton Fadiman: Multiplificty and diffusion

Given the nature of this essay, an extension of Rosenberg's discussion into concerns more proximate to the educational domain would now seem called for. In "Communication and the Arts: A Practitioner's Notes,"[30] Clifton Fadiman, a humanistic educator in the best Arnoldian sense, evokes Plato's criticism of the popular educators and poets of his time as a prelude to an examination of the effects of mass forms of communication on contemporary mind and sensibility. His objective is similar to Barzun's and Rosenberg's—to describe mass communications as a social force and trace its consequences for the life of a society. Fadiman came to the realization, of special importance in this context, that the mass media owe much of their impact and effect to the ways in which signals increasingly approximate the forms of art—that media communications are in effect popular forms of poetry, fiction, and drama.

Fadiman believes that we are living through a transitional period in history more dramatic and throughgoing than that which marked the passage from a hunting to an agrarian economy. Where human communication is concerned, this era of transition has substituted mass signals for the traditional forms of soliloquy and dialogue in which persons voice their thoughts or speak to others in such groups as the family, neighborhood, church, and school. We are beginning to realize the consequences of this substitution; it has resulted in a competition among signals, and those signals ill adapted to multiplication and diffusion are silenced in the struggle for survival, their messages lost. Since the majority of the population now receive their information about the world from television and turn to it and other mass media for entertainment during much of their leisure time, the nature of the uses and abuses of television must become the subject of serious study.

By and large, says Fadiman, commercial television regards audiences more as potential customers for advertised products than as recipients of the cognitive content of a message or appreciators of its aesthetic form. This much is common knowledge, but it does account for the importance attached by television producers to *multiplicity* and *diffusion,* the two principal traits of mass communication networks. To reach, captivate, and retain audiences, media artists have fashioned what is in effect the paradigmatic form of all mass communication—the television commecial. Whatever the "genre" of a television program—news, political speeches, entertainment, even talk shows—it is replete, says Fadiman, with the characteristics of advertisements: reports of news events are trimmed down and dressed up and reality is presented in an accessible guise with suitable visuals, music, and rhetoric. Neither genuine communication nor knowledge, however, results. More often, Fadiman claims, mass communications picture forth "what is not"—an expression borrowed from the Honyuhnms in *Gulliver's Travels* who had no word for telling lies. Hence mass communications media do not lend themselves to conveying the complex meanings of events or to detailing their consequences. Fadiman discovers no evil design behind all this nor any conspiracy bent on manipulating the masses. Media form, he believes, is a product of our social system and of the nature of broadcasting technology. "Bias" in mass communications is thus technological and dramatic before it is liberal or conservative.

To be sure, this picture is overdrawn. Fadiman knows that truth-telling sometimes occurs in the media—in the news, in documentaries, in genuine drama—and that not everything is reduced to mere imagery. Like the other writers discussed in this chapter, he aims at highlighting major developments and fundamental changes in the channels of communication that inevitably affect the ways people take reality and compose their view of the world. We deceive ourselves, moreover, if we think we can choose to use or not to use the media. Being ubiquitous, they will be used. Our days and nights will be flooded with communications, regardless of whether anything truly important happened during a given time span. This is also true of the nonelectronic media. Fadiman conjectures that even if absolutely nothing occurred during a twenty-four-hour period, the London *Times* would still print a full edition the next day. Hence Fadiman's commandment: "Thou shall not send each other too many messages." There is also Fadiman's law, which holds that "the integrity of a signal varies inversely with the complexity of the signalling device" and has as a corollary the assertion that "an original communication of high value may gain rather than lose in effectiveness if forced to encounter resistance."[31] The inherent logic of mass communications, however, militates against both Fadiman's commandment and his law; mass signals are designed to be received with minimum difficulty and the constraints placed on broadcasters are impediments to genuine communication. Fadiman tells of the progressive loss of freedom he experienced as he moved from classroom teaching into radio, film, and then television work.

How do mass communications affect the nature of art and of learning? One needs to keep in mind that television has devised a novel dramaturgy derived mainly from the design of television commercials. This dramaturgy manifests itself in simple, uncomplicated, easily comprehensible pictures of the world. Whatever is learned is absorbed effortlessly. But when fast and smooth transmission of content becomes the primary concern of pictorial presentations, the principle of artistic osmosis—that is, the idea that works of art have to pass through the barriers of time, prolonged critical scrutiny, and perhaps initial misunderstanding—is rendered irrelevant. As a consequence, media artists are constrained by new sets of criteria that set severe limits on their creative imagination; they become mere technicians compelled to obey the law of accelerating invention. Yet even in its debased and trivialized state, dramatic form is a power to be reckoned with. As Raymond Williams[32] once remarked, for better or for worse dramatic form now rivals traditional forms of knowledge transmission.

To be sure, there was a time when Williams, for whom the proper employment of the media is central to furthering the cultural revolution of the modern period, believed that appropriate media policies could bring about more participatory democracy and thus assure people of a greater role in shaping their own destinies.[33] John Dewey expressed a similar hope.[34] But we are far from having produced what Dewey called socially responsible artists of the mass media whose mission would consist of interpreting the significance of major events for the population. Society has yet to evolve from the Great Society into the Great Community, and the slowness of this process is one reason for Williams's having reluctantly abandoned an evolutionary in favor of a more revolutionary stance.

There are convergences, then, in Rosenberg's and Fadiman's analyses of the imperatives of the mass media system. The problem the communications media pose for building healthy relations between art and society is twofold: how to use the media to best advantage toward understanding and broadening access to art; and how to rescue art's autonomy in the process, either from subversion by the media system or, to anticipate the next section, from subservience to ideology.

Monroe C. Beardsley: Relevance and autonomy

The problem of salvaging art's autonomy is one that preoccupied the writings of the late Monroe C. Beardsley. One of the most influential American philosophers of art since Dewey, Beardsley is associated with a philosophical project to recall aesthetic theory and criticism to the study and assessment of the art object itself. He believed this project necessary in light of a tendency in theorizing about art to overemphasize biographical, psychological, and historical interpretations of art. The concepts of aesthetic value, aesthetic experience, and aesthetic criticism, which are central to Beardsley's aesthetics, will be discussed in greater detail in the next chapter. Here I want to draw attention to an essay, "Art and Its Cultural Context,"[35] in which he acknowledges an imbalance in his previous work. He redresses it by explaining what he came to see as the central task of modern aesthetic theory:

> The fundamental task of the philosophy of art in our time . . . is that of providing a coherent and judicious account of the relationships between

the arts and the other components—or segments—of culture. It is to mark out the special sphere of artistic activity, duly recognizing the peculiar and precious character of its contribution to the goodness and significance of life, while understanding art as one strand of social interaction, explaining its inherent connections with other central functions, practices, and institutions that make up a society. This theoretical task has as its practical analogue that of finding ways of preserving and enlarging the capacity of the arts to play their distinctive and needed roles in promoting the quality of social life, protecting them against the enormous political and economic forces that constantly threaten to control, distort, repress, or trivialize them.[36]

Something has already been said about the forces that threaten the exercise of genuine artistic imagination, and the need to reserve unto art a special and distinctive role in human life has been mentioned. With Beardsley's essay, we move to the issue of how coherently and judiciously to concepualize healthy relations between art and culture. There have, of course, been numerous attempts to delineate such relations, but most of them fail to satisfy Beardsley's criteria of coherence and judiciousness, not to mention cautiousness. Many examinations of cultural phenomena are too sweeping or reflect the desire either to impose a grand theory or to engage in ideological axe-grinding.

In "Art and Its Cultural Context," however, Beardsley neither aims at sweeping generalization nor indulges in special pleading. Rather, he wishes to show how, on the one hand, Marxist analysis, anthropological inquiry, and linguistic studies, including semiotics, all cast doubt on the distinctiveness of art and its characteristic function and how, on the other, careful analysis might deal with the difficulties encountered in trying to identify art as a separate entity and activity in society. How does Beardsley proceed? One is tempted to reply, in such model philosophical fashion that one learns as much from his method of reasoning as from his conclusions.

From Beardsley's remarks quoted above it is apparent that his dialectic will move both toward and away from the work of art; that it will consider art's distinctive character and properties as well as its relations to other things, concentrating for a time on art's autonomy and then on its relevance. In what follows I pass over the latter in order to focus on Beardsley's account of the distinctiveness of art. Always careful to clarify strategic terms, Beardsley defines "culture" as a society's modes of activity and entities which feature both causal competencies (problem-solving as a means-end model) and conventional ones (adding character or meaning to activities through conventional rules). The making of works of art involves both kinds of competencies, but the key question turns on the relation in which aesthetic modes of cultural competence and their entities stand to the other modes of competence and their entities.

Beardsley, an admirer if not a devoted student of Dewey's philosophy, recalls that the central theme of Dewey's *Art as Experience*[37]—restoring the continuity between works of art as objects affording refined and intensified experiences and the experiences of everyday life—appeared to recommend a balance but in actuality shifted emphasis to the quotidian end of the continuum. Beardsley thinks that this imbalance in Dewey's aesthetics stems from a failure to distinguish clearly enough the theoretical differences between aesthetic experience itself and activities like installing artworks in museums or playing music in concert halls. Although activities of the latter kind take place in a specialized and not an everyday environment, they do not necessarily involve a disjunction. Rather, they are, as Beardsley's definition of culture implies, continuous with the entities and competencies of culture. (This is merely one instance of Beardsley's ability to shore up conceptual weaknesses in Dewey's aesthetics.) The task then is to discern the special role art plays *in* society and how this role can be kept from being submerged in art's manifold connections and dependencies.

The ground has now been prepared for a brief sketch of Beardsley's critique of several determinisms—political, social, linguistic—which all tend to deny that art is unique and has a special role to play in society. Beardsley regards the beliefs of Terry Eagleton, a British writer and one of the foremost Marxist analysts today, as amounting to an excessively bold definition of art. Eagleton, who stresses the importance of historical concreteness and political progressiveness, questions reference to traditional aesthetic considerations in estimating the significance of works of art. "But what does 'aesthetically superior' *mean,*" asks Eagleton, "if not such things as [quoting Lukács] 'more profound, authentic, human, and concretely historical'?"[38] Since Eagleton seems to consider his criteria applicable to art in general and not just to literature, Beardsley wonders whether Eagleton would not stand corrected if we mentioned, say, classical ballet, whose cultural significance is certainly not negligible but which seems to have little to do with political movements or historical processes. However Eagleton might answer, his writing represents the common drift of much current Marxist thought: works of art have value only insofar as they advance political purposes. The Marxist writer Umberto Barbaro fares little better under Beardsley's philosophical scrutiny, although the work of Stefan Morawski, according to Beardsley, indicates that a Marxist perspective does not have to be reductionist in the extreme.[39]

Marxism is not the only position suppressive of art's special character and independence. Anthropological inquiry, though it sometimes sees art as a mirror passively reflecting the life of a society, usually yields to its holistic, totalizing instincts and weaves art and artistic activity tightly into the culture's fabric of common values and functions. Beardsley points out, however, that extreme forms of configurationism, superorganicism, and functionalism are no longer fashionable. Fieldwork in African and American Indian cultures particularly has shown these groups to be more variegated than was previously supposed and to make provision for individual creativity that is allowed to stand apart from otherwise shared activities. To illustrate this point, Beardsley quotes M. a M. Ngal who, reporting on the creation of fiction in African oral cultures, writes that "beneath stereotyped formulas jealously retained by the conservatism and conformism of each generation, there occurs a true labor of creativity that is not the work of an anonymous community or of associations due to pure chance but rather the product of the active dynamism of the individual genius."[40] Holistic views of societies are thus beginning to give way to descriptions that stress differences as well as similarities among a culture's entitites and competences. Nor can socialization fully explain instances of rebellion against or deviation from social norms. Man, the social animal, is not a completely socialized creature. Individuals can occasionally distance themselves from culture while remaining part of it (which is what the late Lionel Trilling had in mind when he called his essay on Freud "Beyond Culture"[41]).

With these differences among the elements of culture in mind, says Beardsley, we can begin to form a conception of art that sees it as developing along independent and autonomous lines while still maintaining important connections with other cultural components. Art's independence and autonomy can be discerned best in an impulse to change that is generated by demands and needs arising within art itself and not imported from the social environment. Such changes carry the seed of renewed creativity. Initially, depending on its value structure, society may either resist or encourage them. Yet in time an awareness of the governing artistic conventions will grow in any society and dissatisfaction or boredom with them will then support the emergence of new ones. All this can happen while other parts of the culture remain relatively stable.

Beardsley reserves the bulk of his essay for an examination of semiotic theories of culture, which he faults, first, for attempting to reduce all aspects of culture to signs and semiotic functions and, second, for disallowing both the distinctiveness of art and its special humanizing role. To support his first objection and to suggest the limitations of semiotic theory, Beardsley analyzes Clifford Geertz's explanation of a Balinese cock fight and finds that not all features of that event can be reduced to signs. There must, Beardsley concludes, be underlying nonsemiotic conditions on which signs depend and which are relatively unaffected by the meanings assigned to them. Beardsley thus claims to have found cracks in the semiotic picture of reality; culture is not a seamless sign. But even if works of art are in some sense semiotic, or we are willing to regard them as such, the second of Beardsley's doubts is not completely erased. In an indirect reference to the writings of

Nelson Goodman, Beardsley remarks that we might well know how characters function in a symbol system and even acknowledge that characters tend to symbolize in specialized ways in works of art, but still not have learned what it is that art characteristically contributes to human welfare. The question of the difference art makes in human lives is typically Beardsleyan. The notion of serving a human purpose, of making a change in people's lives, is among the central themes in his writing.

This humanistic function is also one that allows him to specify the distinctiveness of art. While there are, of course, different sorts of objects that serve different needs, Beardsley distinguishes between works of art and technical objects. The latter allow us to cope and survive in a world that is often indifferent or hostile to our strivings. But works of art satisfy the need to feel at home in the world; they make the world not only more habitable but also friendlier. By putting on shows, as it were, in virtual time and space (to borrow a Langerian concept), art permits us to create and contemplate expressive qualities that are in a *special* way the mark we make on the world around us, for expressive or aesthetic qualities are uniquely *human* qualities and contributions to the world. Thus Beardsley writes: "In creating works of art we humanize the earth as we can in no other way, we warm it for ourselves, make it a place where we belong, far more fully and significantly than technical objects can do." But, he goes on to say, "individual artworks cannot carry out this function, cannot serve in this unifying, reconciling way, unless we grant them a measure of independence and autonomy, a sphere of influence all their own, in which they can be respected as individuals. We have to approach them in something like a suppliant mood . . . if they are to realize their potentialities and serve us well in their fashion."[42] Perhaps there is no more fitting tribute to art's humanistic mission than to say that art both embodies and celebrates man's effort to find meaning in an indifferent world. The accent on human welfare also makes such a position particularly pertinent to the theoretical foundations of aesthetic education. It lends a deeper and more generous significance to aesthetic appreciation.

Summary

In concluding this brief survey of critical opinion, all that remains to do is to provide a more explicit indication of its relevance to building a theory of aesthetic education. If we take it as the central task of such a theory to provide a context that makes teaching for response to art feasible in a time of great uncertainty about the nature, meaning, and value of art, then we may acknowledge that the writers discussed in this chapter have spelled out some of the problems and made clear why we need to address them. Kenneth Clark shows how dramatically the relations of art and society have changed over history, Jacques Barzun just how drastically over the past 150 years. Harold Rosenberg and Clifton

Fadiman then point out the challenge to building healthy relations between art and society posed by the new reality of the media system and its global commitment to the new, not to say by that system's characteristic product, the art package, which now stands as the chief rival to the work of art. Hence any effort to establish a wholesome connection between art and society, or to construct a new context of response to art, must come to terms with the all-engulfing media system. There is reason to believe, however, that the art package conceptualized by Rosenberg is more closely related to the technical object of Beardsley's description than it is to the work of art, and it is Beardsley's contribution to make us aware of this difference by recalling the traditional or characteristic function of art in forging a satisfying human career, that is, one with shape, meaning, unity, and significance. Art, at least at its best, communicates a sense of the truly worthwhile, whereas the package conveys "that which is not." A theory of aesthetic education will feature this distinction through its emphasis on the humanistic function of art; it will stress the importance for human life of fostering an appreciation of aesthetic accomplishment as the realization of a special kind of human capability. We have now returned full circle to Cassirer's sphere of humanity that includes art.

Given the imagination of despair that pevades thinking about cultural and social matters today, it is worth mentioning that although the critics just discussed tend to confirm the current malaise and to accept it as an understandable consequence of contemporary conditions, they do not accord it permanence. Despite all, Clark remained hopeful; Fadiman has not abandoned efforts to humanize knowledge through the use of the popular media; Barzun's analysis pays homage to the power of ideas to effect change; Rosenberg found in genuine art the possibility of authentic individualism; and Beardsley remained unpersuaded by speculative arguments that art may be inherently dehumanizing. Even George Steiner,[43] who has insistently pressed this latter possibility, believes that there are prospects for humane literacy and that criticism is indispensable to bringing it about.

Granted, then, that inordinate abuse has been inflicted on art in our time, that the complexity and difficulty of art have lost out to the more simplified signals of the media system, that cultural and educational relations have been defined superficially, and that many other contemporary phenomena have seemed to militate against the serious production and appreciation of art, we may still agree with Clark when he says that although we may not know as much as we would like to about what we are doing, we are certainly not wasting our time when we try to broaden access to the arts. For in doing so, we are attempting to help persons satisfy the primal instinct of which Barzun spoke, which Clark hinted at in saying that art answers a basic spiritual need, and which Beardsley specified further as the desire to make ourselves at home in the world and thus to humanize it. The reason this chapter has concentrated on the problems of art in contemporary society has been to establish a genuinely problematic context for a theory of aesthetic education. But such a theory cannot ground itself solely in despair and skepticism; hence the next chapter examines, from the standpoint of modern aesthetic opinion, the kinds of worthwhile experiences that excellent art is capable of providing.

CHAPTER 2

Art in philosophical context

> Art is a simple matter. Consider five
> objects, all familiar at least by proxy:
> Leonardo's *Mona Lisa,* Shakespeare's
> *Hamlet,* Beethoven's *Eroica,* Dante's
> *Divine Comedy,* Michelangelo's *David.*
> Each of these is a work of art, if anything
> is; we would be more surprised if a his-
> tory of the relevant art left them out than
> if it included them. . . . There is really
> no doubt about what these things *are
> for* . . . [T]hey are expected to provide
> worthwhile experiences merely in being
> listened to, looked at, or read. The less
> doubt we have that that is what a thing
> is for, the more confidently we take it to
> be a work of art.   *Francis Sparshott*[1]

No doubt. But it takes Sparshott 684 pages of text and notes to explain
the different conceptions of the worthwhile in our experiences of art that
have been propounded by thinkers from antiquity to the present. What
is ostensibly simple turns out to be complicated and problematic. Yet
since Sparshott's words contain a core of truth, I adopt some of his
language for my purposes even if I cannot follow him in other respects.
That is, I take the general objective of aesthetic education to be the
development of an appreciation of art for the sake of the worthwhile
experiences works of art are capable of providing merely in being contemplated. Recalling the societal demand referred to in Chapter 1 that
requires the reconstituting of judgment, I expand this general aim to
include the development of a disposition to discern and prefer quality in
art. A curriculum for aesthetic education should therefore be an excellence curriculum devoted to the best that has been written, composed,
painted, or sculpted.

If art is as simple as Sparshott asserts it is, then what makes our
experiences of art worthwhile may be said to be equally obvious: it
consists in art's capacity to move and delight, to extend human abilities,
and to inform. Yet saying this is not quite enough. Theoretical problems
arise when we ask about the special ways in which art performs these
functions. Just how do works of art move us emotionally? What is the
nature of the delight they afford? How do they enlarge human potential?
How does art inform, instruct, or teach? What, moreover, are the inherent
values of such states of mind, and in what ways may they affect other
values we also believe to be important? Some of these questions were
alluded to in Chapter 1 and are now subjected to a somewhat more
searching treatment from the standpoint of the branch of philosophy
known as aesthetics.

I believe that those features of art that make the experience of it worth having can be highlighted in a brief review of some of the ideas contained in four contemporary aesthetic theories. Although the discussion to follow will concentrate on a different accent in each of the four positions—on Monroe C. Beardsley's effort to define the peculiar kind of gratification art provides, on Harold Osborne's insistence on art's capacity to stimulate the powers of percipience for their own sake, on Nelson Goodman's emphasis on the character of the understanding art affords, and on E. F. Kaelin's consideration of art's contribution to human freedom and the efficacy of cultural institutions—it will also try to make clear that, collectively, these theories add up to as helpful an account of aesthetic experience as we are likely to get. If it is remembered that aesthetic experience is virtually synonymous with aesthetic appreciation and that aesthetic appreciation is the objective of aesthetic education, the relevance of these four theoretical perspectives to theorizing about aesthetic education should be readily apparent.

Art and gratification: Monroe C. Beardsley

Beardsley's *Aesthetics: Problems in the Philosophy of Criticism,*[2] first published in 1958 and then in a 1981 second edition that contains a postscript of recent writings that bear on his topics, was the most influential work in philosophical aesthetics of the mid-twentieth century. The volume is not only a philosophical synthesis that attempts to clarify a number of aesthetic topics and to formulate a useful terminology for describing, interpreting, and evaluating works of art; it also contains an instrumental theory of aesthetic value that, in addition to influencing Beardsley's analyses of topics and decisions on matters of relevance, also reveals an underlying concern with the role of art in human life. Most of all, the volume is devoted to a systematic examination of the presuppositions of aesthetic criticism and the provision of a philosophical rationale for the kind of literary criticism known as the New Criticism. Because of Beardsley's stress on aesthetic experience, aesthetic criticism, and the role of art in human life, his work has special pertinence for aesthetic education.

The conceptual problem that preoccupied Beardsley more than any other was the question whether there is a kind of human experience that can appropriately be called aesthetic which is not only sufficiently differentiated from other types of experience but is also significant enough to warrant society's efforts to cultivate it. He was particularly intrigued by the likelihood that works of art are objects ideally suited to occasion such an experience, that they are in fact brought into existence primarily for this purpose. This is not to deny that other artifacts and even natural phenomena might possess a limited capacity to call forth aesthetic experiences. Beardsley never took it for granted that he would succeed completely in answering these questions, and he usually expressed some dissatisfaction with his own formulations, as the considerable number of essays he wrote on this topic attest. He also realized that a degree of vagueness will always attach to theories about the characteristics of our interactions with the world and especially about what Abraham Maslow once called the farther reaches of human nature.[3] Those who assess the attempts of others to isolate strands of human experience often expect, unrealistically, greater clarity and precision than a topic permits, and even educators in the arts and humanities are sometimes animated more by *l'esprit de géométrie* than by *l'esprit de finesse*.[4]

Beardsley was aware of these pitfalls. But he also remained convinced that it makes sense to speak of aesthetic value and aesthetic experience and that these not only constitute identifiable aspects of human experience but are in fact interdefined. For, according to Beardsley, the *aesthetic value* of a work of art (or aesthetic object)—that is, its artistic in contrast to its moral or cognitive value—consists in its capacity to induce in a qualified observer a high degree of aesthetic experience. This is what is meant by calling Beardsley's theory of aesthetic value "instrumental": contrary to viewpoints that insist on the intrinsic nature of aesthetic value, Beardsley considers artworks valuable to the extent that they make a positive difference in people's lives.

Although it is convenient here to discuss first the features and then the effects of aesthetic experience as conceived by Beardsley, it should be pointed out that the two are not strictly separable, the latter quite naturally depending on the former. Beardsley's later analyses of aesthetic experience are conveniently collected in his *The Aesthetic Point of View: Selected Essays,* edited by Michael J. Wreen and Donald M. Callen,[5] and some further commentary is provided in his postscript to the second edition of his *Aesthetics.* I shall be referring to these sources in the following remarks.

In an essay titled "Aesthetic Experience," which was written especially for *The Aesthetic Point of View* and probably represents Beardsley's last thoughts on the concept, Beardsley describes aesthetic experience as having at least five features (although he admitted the possibility of there being more or fewer), not all of which need to be present for an aesthetic experience to occur; indeed, only the first is absolutely essential. Thus aesthetic experience is both compound and disjunctive. It is compound in the sense that it is composed of several identifiable features; disjunctive in the sense that although these features do occur here and there in ordinary experience as well, their concentration in aesthetic experience is so pronounced as to set that experience apart from other kinds.

Condensing Beardsley's account of aesthetic experience, we may say that during the aesthetic apprehension of an outstanding work of art the percipient's attention is firmly centered on an object of notable presence whose elements, formal relations, qualities, and semantic aspects are freely entertained. One indicator of aesthetic character in an experience is the percipient's feeling that the work's components are sorting and grouping themselves in appropriate and satisfying ways. While the percipient's attention is thus fixed on the object and the coalescence of its parts into an impression of fittingness, thoughts about past, future, and personal concerns are suppressed in favor of an intense engagement with what is present to the senses. Aesthetic experience thus affords a degree of freedom from the practical worries that normally beset persons. This temporary relief from the ordinary also helps to explain a certain sense of detached affect, or what is sometimes called disinterestedness, that accompanies aesthetic experience. Detached affect does not imply a lack of interest in the object—after all under contemplation are some of humankind's finest accomplishments; rather, percipients subdue mundane preoccupations just enough to be able to achieve a degree of emotional distance. It is this disinterested attention that enables us to remain engrossed in works of ominous or distressing import without being emotionally overcome by such content. Lastly, successful efforts at making conflicting stimuli arrange themselves into formal patterns imbued with expressive qualities and human meaning can be exhilarating; percipients feel as if something has been clarified, as if their experience has consisted of a discovery of new understanding.

To repeat, aesthetic experiences are noteworthy for object directedness; the perception of the fittingness of elements and free participation in making them coalesce into a unified whole; freedom from everyday concerns; detached affect or disinterestedness; and a feeling of active discovery or understanding. These features also make the duality of aesthetic experience apparent: it is both detached and participatory, free and controlled, cognitive and affective.

The feelings and emotions that supervene—and in some cases are scarcely distinguishable from—the features belonging to aesthetic experience are among the effects of that kind of experience. Beardsley suggests, for example, that the aesthetic experience of works of high artistic quality can result in feelings of personal integration and wholeness, of greater self-acceptance, and of the expansion of personality. Beardsley in fact intimates a correspondence among the degree of unified complexity possessed by an artwork; the complexity, unity, and duration of the experience during which it is appropriated; and the integrating and harmonizing effect felt by the percipient. (The same magnitude of consequence, however, cannot be attributed to works that can almost be taken in by a glance, although even in such instances of momentary awareness Beardsley thinks it is possible to speak of a minimally aesthetic experience, even if not in the Deweyan sense of *an* experience.)[6] Most importantly, however, since the feelings and emotional states that correspond to aesthetic experience are positive and desirable, the overall effect of such an experience is a feeling of *gratification,* a distinctive hedonic effect of our participation in works of fine art which Beardsley thought was a more descriptive term than either enjoyment, pleasure, or satisfaction—all terms he had previously tried and found wanting.[7]

To be sure, Beardsley increasingly came to feature more than he had done previously the cognitive aspects of the arts; still his theory is principally a hedonistic one, though not in any simple and crude sense. Aesthetic gratification is not equivalent to a generalized state of feeling well. Nor is it like the enjoyment that attends the informal congeniality of friendly conversation or the excitement of partisan cheering at sporting events. It is in fact but rarely realized in the course of ordinary events. Seldom, says Beardsley, do we enjoy stretches of time during which the elements of our experience combine in just those ways that produce aesthetic satisfaction; when they do the state of being they constitute is one of gratified well-being. We have little reason for disagreeing. How often during a typical day do we experience the stimulation, the sense of freedom, the controlled emotional involvement, the feeling of genuine discovery, the fulfillment and expansion of the self that are the marks of aesthetic experience? Yet this state of mind is a distinctive form of human well-being and therefore an important ingredient in any good and worthwhile life. It constitutes a significant realization of human value. And it is most reliably had through the experience of excellent works of art, that is, through the knowledgeable apprehension of a painting by Raphael, a piano sonata by Beethoven, a sonnet by Shakespeare. Nor does aesthetic gratification depend on a work's uplifting or cheerful nature, for it would be an unacceptable account of aesthetic experience that did not accommodate the great tragic masterpieces.

Beardsley believed that if his theory could stand its ground, it might also go some distance toward resolving a number of problems in the philosophy of art and prove useful in settling certain kinds of practical disputes. For instance, criteria for critical judgment might be derived from the definition of the work of art as an arrangement of conditions intended to lend an aesthetic character to human experience and to draw a gratified response from knowledgeable percipients.[8] The artistic merit of artworks might then be established on the basis of the quality of experience they are capable of providing. On the other hand, our ability to distinguish the aesthetic point of view and its peculiar value from the economic point of view might help disputants decide on the relative merits of, say, building a nuclear power plant on the shore of a scenic lake and leaving the beauty of the area undisturbed for aesthetic appreciation and recreational uses.[9] In another exercise of suggesting some practical applications of his instrumental theory of aesthetic value, Beardsley propounded the idea of aesthetic welfare, with its adjunct concepts of aesthetic wealth, justice, and capacity, which is fertile for formulating cultural as well as educational policy.[10] This concept is discussed more fully in Appendix II.

For present purposes, however, the most important ramifications of Beardsley's conception of aesthetic gratification and his instrumental theory of aesthetic value extend into the philosophy of education or, more precisely, the theoretical foundations of aesthetic education, where they support a humanistic and humanizing conception of art. For those who emphasize the destructive potential of art or doubt its civilizing propensities, Beardsley writes:

> To adopt the aesthetic point of view is simply to seek out a source of value. And it can never be a moral error to realize value—barring conflict with other values. Some people seem to fear that a serious and persistent aesthetic interest will become an enervating hyperaestheticism, a paralysis of will like that reported in advanced cases of psychedelic dependence. But the objects of aesthetic interest—such as harmonious design, good proportions, intense expressiveness—are not drugs, but part of the breath of life. Their cumulative effect is increased sensitization, fuller awareness, a closer touch with the environment and concern for what it is and might be. It seems to me very doubtful that we could have too much of these good things, or that they have inherent defects that prevent them from being an integral part of a good life.[11]

The significance of Beardsley's aesthetics for aesthetic education then is quite apparent; it indicates how the arts enhance human life and provide ideals of human possibility. At a time when developments in the expressive culture have awakened us to the need for restoring more elevated, civilized states of human existence, ideas like Beardsley's should be an urgent priority of policy and deserve a place in any justification of aesthetic education.

Appreciation as percipience: Harold Osborne

"To realize their potentialities and serve us well in their fashion"— the words are Beardsley's, but they could also have been uttered by Harold Osborne, who at the time of his death was the dean of British aestheticians and in this respect Beardsley's British counterpart. Osborne believed that works of art fulfill their preeminent function through their capacity to stimulate and expand direct perception, or what he called the powers of percipience. What is the meaning of percipience? In *The Art of Appreciation*[12] Osborne equates percipience with appreciation and appreciation with aesthetic experience, which he describes in the following way.

Careful introspection about our experience of art reveals it to involve the guiding of our attention over a limited sensory field in such a way that the field's properties are brought into focus according to their own inherent intensities, their similarities and contrasts, and their peculiar groupings. Perception of this kind is unusually full and complete and avoids the narrow focus on practical purposes that is characteristically maintained during our nonaesthetic pursuits. Although aesthetic perceiving, like all perception, qualifies as a cognitive activity and is dependent on knowledge and skills of relevant kinds, the mental attitude assumed during aesthetic experience is in major respects unlike that required for conceptual analysis or the historian's tracing of the causes and consequences of events. Rather, aesthetic experience calls for direct and synoptic vision. To illustrate this contrast: the activities of discussing the antecedents of Picasso's *Guernica* or assigning it a position in Picasso's oeuvre, although they focus on an artwork, are not the same as the direct apprehension of the work's fusion of subject and form; only the latter counts as an act of expressive perception. Yet it should be pointed out that by "direct perception" Osborne does not mean unmediated perception; being cognitive, perception and percipience are not equivalent to instantaneous emotional reaction. Osborne talks about the *way* the viewer orders and interprets the elements of the aesthetic object being contemplated, about what directs an act of percipience and what is being omitted from it.

The kind of rapt attention typical of aesthetic interest also lends aesthetic experience a characteristic emotional color, its mood, Osborne thinks, being one of serenity even when the object under scrutiny has a dynamic character or disturbing theme. This implies that the emotional qualities of a work will not always correspond to the percipient's feeling state. Indeed, because our perception concentrates on the object, our aesthetic interest has less to do with a heightened awareness of our own feelings than with a consciousness of qualities and properties external to ourselves; it is as if we lived for the moment in the objective portion of our phenomenal field of vision. The demands of perceptual awareness and the obligation to see an object as much as possible in its full complexity also tend to discourage the percipient from indulging in idle musings, forming random associations with depicted scenes, and generating feelings that have less to do with the world of the work being contemplated and more with the percipient's personal history. Aesthetic experience, in other words, is remarkable not for its lassitude but for its rigor. Imagination is necessary in order to grasp a work's qualities, but imagination is also held in check. Osborne's emphasis on direct perception also makes it unsurprising that in his account of aesthetic experience appearance takes precedence over material existence; that is, the material base of objects is less significant than the images they project. By their special nature, such images are particularly suited to sustaining the percipient in an aesthetic mode of awareness. Whether the imagery is iconic or noniconic, absorption in it takes us out of ourselves into new worlds, but never into a trancelike state in which ego consciousness disappears completely, for this would involve the risk of losing control over perception and missing the object's sense or import. Osborne acknowledges that percipience—the mind's capacity for direct and complete perception—is exercised in many areas of human life, but he thinks that only works of fine art and their counterparts in nature are capable of expanding percipience to its fullest. At their best, artworks promote the development of the perceptive faculties they activate by challenging these faculties to respond with greater vivacity and a more capacious grasp. A heightened awareness of things perceived during aesthetic experience is thus central to Osborne's theory; persons are more alive, awake, and alert than usual, their mental faculties work more effectively, and they are constantly rewarded with new discoveries. Because aesthetic perception demands a focused effort and differs from ordinary seeing, conceptual analysis, and problem-solving, the skills of aesthetic awareness must be deliberately cultivated.

What Osborne's aesthetics could mean for aesthetic education, and even for education as a whole, should not be difficult to infer. Although teaching the skills of aesthetic appreciation would aim at strengthening the powers of perception for their own sakes, it would also enhance a mental capacity—percipience—that has more general applications and thus serves individuals in other ways. This, however, is not the main thrust of an Osbornean approach to the question of educational justification. To understand what that approach might be, we need to consider Osborne's discussion of the evolution of civilization toward ever-greater opportunities for self-realization.[13]

Osborne's argument is not novel, but it bears repeating from time to time, as it amounts to an appeal for the significant use of leisure. Osborne reminds us that at one stage of evolution human faculties were harnessed almost exclusively to the struggle for survival. This left little time for the sort of detached involvement with objects that we associate with the aesthetic contemplation of works of art. To be sure, the burdens of ensuring mere survival still weigh heavily on much of the world's population, but the long process of liberation from material bondage is producing a state of affairs in technologically advanced societies that, if properly utilized, could usher in a new era of cultural efflorescence. In other words, it is not too soon to ponder the uses and abuses (to retain Barzun's distinction) of leisure time and what they may portend for human life today and in the future.

It is important to realize that the problem of leisure is not one of finding things to do in our spare time, nor even solely of finding something "better" and more refined to occupy ourselves with. For, according to Osborne, the self-cultivation that is possible only with sufficient leisure and that involves the development and expansion of human potentialities for their own sakes has usually supplied the motive and the opportunities for the expression of spiritual needs and aspirations.

Whatever ideology might determine a people's outlook, the liberation from life's material constraints for the purpose of realizing more fully and more freely their humanity has been a near-universal yearning and guiding ideal. Kenneth Clark, it will be recalled, believed that even the members of a predominantly secular society still hunger for moments of nonmaterial satisfaction. This kind of satisfaction is, of course, also available outside the arts, for other capacities—reason, for example—may certainly be cultivated more for their intrinsic worth than for practical application. But the nonmaterial rewards of reason characteristically accrue in the avocational pursuit of philosophy, logic, mathematics, and the theoretical sciences. The exercise of aesthetic percipience in the domain of art has the advantage of being more ostensibly human and responsive to individual needs and purposes; as Beardsley remarked, art makes us feel more at home in the world. For the majority of persons, then, the arts have far greater appeal as leisure-time activities, all the more so because they are dramatic.

Dramatic interest is what the fine arts share with their aesthetically diminished relatives, the amusement arts (to use Osborne's term). Fadiman and Williams have already been cited on the pervasive role dramatic form plays in all of the modern communication and entertainment media, and it is obvious that there is more than enough drama within each person's reach to fill any number of vacant hours. Nor is it the case that amusement values are unimportant and always pernicious. Still, they must be cautioned against, for the baser coin tends to drive out the more precious. Immersion in amusements tends to diminish a person's capacity for the sort of self-awareness that can be obtained through serious art. While the latter energizes the mind, amusement art encourages it to loaf, which is to say that amusement art lacks the qualities Lionel Trilling attributed to literature: variousness, possibility, complexity, and difficulty.[14] The pursuit of the trivial, in other words, represents the abandonment of seriousness by a leisure society. Or to put it yet another way, amusement art provides neither the intensity of aesthetic gratification, the stimulation of intrinsic perception, nor genuine understanding. A society saturated with amusement values will do little to refine to any significant extent the native aesthetic capacities with which all individuals are endowed. On Osborne's account of aesthetic percipience, aesthetic education thus acquires a preventive as well as an enabling mission. To counter the emphasis society places on amusement values, Osborne recommends an extensive education in the skills of percipience.

Finally, it seems only natural that Osborne's concern with the role of percipience in human life and art should have prompted him to define art in respect of this capacity. "Despite all the difficulties of exact definition," he writes, "we regard any artifact as a work of art which is eminently suitable to exercise, extend and amplify our powers of percipience, irrespective of whatever other values it may have."[15]

Art and understanding: Nelson Goodman

There is no doubting the enormous influence Nelson Goodman's work has had on contemporary aesthetics, where his theory has generated a large volume of comment and debate. Sparshott, for example, likened the appearance of Goodman's *Languages of Art*[16] to the shadow cast by a giant rock upon a dreary field, while Howard Gardner opined that overnight Goodman transformed aesthetics into a rigorous and serious domain of study. The rigor and analytic brilliance of Goodman's writings also explain in part the impact his thought has had on art and aesthetic education. His ideas have informed many of the investigations into the problems of teaching and learning in the arts that have been carried forward by educators and psychologists for over twenty years at Harvard Project Zero, of which Goodman was the founder.

Goodman is not concerned with aesthetics exclusively and approaches art via epistemology, which he defines "as the philosophy of the understanding and thus as embracing the philosophy of science and the philosophy of art."[17] This epistemological slant is reflected in his insistence on the cognitive aspects of art, an emphasis that must be clearly understood in terms of what it includes as well as what it does not preclude. Goodman acknowledges, for example, that emotions and feelings are not to be ruled out in our experiences of art and are in fact required for aesthetic experience. But, he continues, "they are not separable from or in addition to the cognitive aspect of that experience. They are among the primary means of making the discriminations and the connections that enter into an understanding of art."[18] Furthermore, "cognition is not limited to language or verbal thought but employs imagination, sensation, perception, emotion, in the complex process of aesthetic understanding."[19] Cognition is thus broadly conceived, but as exercised in art it is not all-embracing. "In contending that aesthetic experience is cognitive," says Goodman, "I am emphatically not identifying it with the conceptual, the discursive, the linguistic."[20] This should help to allay the doubts of those, especially among educators, who shun cognitive accounts of art for fear of just such an identification.

Most importantly, aesthetic experience is necessarily cognitive because it is an interaction with an object or event when the latter is functioning as a symbol. Goodman's main contribution to the elucidation of art rests on his encompassing the arts within a theory of symbolic systems. (In any mention of such systems, one hears echoes of Cassirer's symbolic forms of human culture, but there is a significant difference between Cassirer's scheme and Goodman's, as an informative article by Howard Gardner, David Perkins, and Vernon Howard points out.)[21]

Having located the arts within a general theory of symbols permits Goodman to show what art has in common with other human endeavors. Yet Goodman, as will be realized shortly, also allows for the distinctiveness of art, for the thing that art does better than anything else does. Indeed, Goodman is less interested in what art *is*—for example, a symbol with stable, identifiable qualities of some kind—than in what art *does*.[22] And what art does is to function as a symbol in *distinctive ways*. More precisely, something is a work of art only when it symbolizes in just those ways. This means that "at certain times and under certain circumstances and not at others . . . an object may be a work of art. . . . Indeed, just by virtue of functioning as a symbol in a certain way does an object become, while so functioning, a work of art." Hence, "things function as works of art only when their symbolic functioning has certain characteristics."[23] What are these characteristics? Thus far, Goodman has distinguished five, and he calls them *symptoms* of the aesthetic. The brief synopsis that follows claims only to convey a glimmer of understanding. A more adequate treatment would depend on explaining the specialized terms used in Goodman's theory of symbolization— concepts like reference, along with complex reference and chains of reference; symbol systems; labels; notation, notationality and notational systems; denotation and nondenotational reference; and many more— but such an effort would exceed the scope of this chapter.

1. *Syntactic density,* as a symptom of the aesthetic, marks a condition in which the finest difference in certain respects constitutes a difference between symbols. By way of example Goodman mentions the ungraduated mercury thermometer, where the smallest difference in the height of the mercury column signifies a different temperature, and he contrasts it with a digital read-out instrument that flashes its measurements in sharply separated units.

2. When *semantic density* prevails, symbols are provided for things distinguished by the finest differences in certain respects. Here again the ungraduated thermometer is an example, but so is ordinary English. For although English is not syntactically dense—after all, words are put together into phrases, clauses, and sentences according to definite rules of grammar—it is semantically dense because of the many shadings of meaning and connotation that can be achieved. Pictorial denotation is an instance of a syntactically as well as semantically dense symbol system, "a system such that its concrete symbol-occurrences do not sort into discriminably different characters but merge into one another, and so also for what is denoted."[24] Goodman warns against taking either or both kinds of density as reliable indicators of the aesthetic. We are not to suppose that the aesthetic is more often than not syntactically dense or that the nonaesthetic more often than not lacks semantic density. "Rather the thought is that the syntactically and semantically dense symbols and systems we encounter and use are more often than not aesthetic; that within the aesthetic more often than elsewhere we find the dense."[25]

3. In *relative repleteness,* comparably many aspects of a symbol are significant. Goodman asks us to compare a one-line drawing of a mountain by Hokusai with a perhaps identical wavy line on a chart representing stock

market averages. The only important feature of the chart is the height of the line above the base; variations in the thickness or shading of the line do not matter, "while in the drawing every variation in every aspect of the line does matter. The premium in a work of art seems to be on repleteness; in a diagram on attenuation."[26] Repleteness, then, refers to the fullness of the symbol, to the relatively large number of its features that participate in symbolization.

4. When *multiple and complex reference* occurs, a symbol performs several integrated and interacting referential functions, some direct, some mediated through other symbols and through and across denotational strata or along chains of reference made up of simple links. "A picture of a bald eagle," for instance, "denotes a bird that may exemplify a label such as 'bold and free' that in turn denotes and is exemplified by a given country."[27] Chains of reference of this sort may be among the stronger symptoms of the aesthetic since they are often so unwelcome in other contexts. "Scientific and practical discourse," says Goodman, "verbal or pictorial, normally aims at singularity and directness, avoiding ambiguity and complicated routes of reference. But in the arts, multiple and complex reference of all sorts . . . is common and is often a powerful instrument."[28]

5. The presence of *exemplification* is frequently the most striking difference between the aesthetic and the nonaesthetic. It distinguishes literary from nonliterary texts and serviceable illustrations from works of art;[29] it is also a very difficult symptom to explain.

First of all, exemplification is selective; it involves some but not all of a symbol's features. Goodman mentions the tailor's swatch which, in its normal use, will maintain this relationship of exemplification to a few of its properties—color, weave, thickness—but not to others, size and shape, for example. (Although in another context the same piece of cloth might exemplify a small square or zigzag edges.) Properties exemplified are properties that count. In a painting they would be "those that the picture makes manifest, selects, focuses upon, exhibits, heightens in our consciousness—those that it shows forth—in short, those properties that it does not merely possess but *exemplifies,* stands as a sample of."[30] It is important to keep "standing as a sample of" in mind, for it is one of the characteristics that make exemplification a special case of symbolic functioning.

The second characteristic is *reference,* more specifically, reference that runs counter to the usual path of denotation, which is from the denoter to the denoted. Goodman asserts that reference is what differentiates exemplification from the mere possession of properties; in exemplification, those features that a symbol or artwork exhibits and shows forth it also refers to. Some writers, Beardsley among them, have thought that the possession and display of properties should be enough and that reference adds an unneeded complication. But the case for it becomes plausible once we grant that when some feature is exemplified, that is, functions as a sample, it does call to mind and hence refers to a "label" that applies to it and that would therefore denote it. When a painting exemplifies a color of a certain hue, brightness, and intensity, then in being a sample of just that color it also calls our attention to a label—a word, an entry on a color chart, an object that has the same shade—that could stand for or denote that color. Notice, however, that the property exemplified by the symbol or artwork (the denoted) is primary, while the label that applies to it (the denoter) is secondary. This is what Goodman seems to mean when he says that "exemplification is thus a certain subrelation of the converse of denotation, distinguished through a return reference *to* denoter by denoted" and that reference thus "runs in the opposite direction, not from label to what the label applies to but from something a label applies to back to the label (or the feature associated with that label)."[31]

Symbols, artworks included, can possess properties *metaphorically* as well as literally. How metaphor arises in Goodman's theory need not detain us here (the process requires the transfer of schema of labels for sorting in a given realm to the sorting of another realm).[32] Such metaphorical properties are the ones other aestheticians call human or expressive or emotional qualities. A symphony may convey feelings of tragic loss although it does not literally have these feelings, nor are they the composer's; they are simply feelings the work has metaphorically. Yet by possessing them the symphony can also exemplify or *express* them. Expression is simply another term for metaphorical exemplification. As Sparshott has put it, "if a sad tune expresses sadness, it is metaphorically sad in such a way that the metaphorical sadness is part of its meaning, i.e., our attention is called to the fact that a word like 'sad' could be applied to the work."[33]

A few additional remarks seem indicated about the five symptoms of the aesthetic. First, they are not, as Goodman is emphatic to point out, disjunctively necessary or conjunctively sufficient (as a syndrome).[34] "None is always present in the aesthetic or always absent from the nonaesthetic; and even presence or absence of all gives no guarantee either way. . . . All we have here are the hesitant results of groping toward a more adequate characterization of the aesthetic,"[35] which is probably understating the matter somewhat.

Second, the terms in which these symptoms have been discussed are not necessarily, and need not become, part of the critic's or teacher's vocabulary. Since, as will be suggested later, art teachers operate somewhat in the manner of the art critic, or at least would do well to take the critic as a model, it follows that teachers need not talk about syntactic density, repleteness, exemplification, and the like. As Goodman states, " 'Exemplify' belongs . . . to a theoretic vocabulary that may be used in describing and analyzing the critic's practice. Whether or not the critic uses the terms 'denotes,' 'depicts,' 'exemplifies,' 'expresses,' etc., he concentrates on what a work symbolizes or refers to in one or more of these ways."[36] And so for teachers. What has been said about symbols is not necessarily what gets taught explicitly to students; rather it is part of the teachers' pedagogical knowledge, what they teach *with*.

Third, the five symptoms are "symptoms of aesthetic function, not of aesthetic merit; symptoms of art, not of good as against bad art."[37] In truth, as I point out in Appendix II, one does not discover in Goodman's writing much interest in artistic excellence as such. While the discussions of Beardsley and Osborne were intended to intimate that works of great aesthetic worth would be more likely than works of indifferent value to produce aesthetic gratification or exercise the full powers of percipience, it would probably be a misrepresentation of Goodman's thought if one were to seek a similar correlation between aesthetic merit and such benefits. What good, then, is art as understood by Goodman?

The experience of art is cognitive and hence, like intellectual effort generally, is motivated by a profound need and leads to deep satisfaction. "Neither art nor science," he writes, "could flourish if it did not give satisfaction, or if satisfaction were the only aim."[38] A form of gratification (recalling Beardsley) is therefore among the effects of our interaction with art. Furthermore, symbols—the functioning of which is characterized by symptoms of the aesthetic—"tend to require concentration upon the symbol to determine what it is and what it refers to. Where exemplification occurs, we have to inhibit our habit of passing at once from symbol to what is denoted. Repleteness requires attention to comparatively many features of the symbol. Dense systems, where every difference in a feature makes a difference, call for an endless search to find what symbol we have and what it symbolizes."[39] Concentration, attention, endless search—would it be too much to propose that these (recalling Osborne) also tend to enlarge the powers of percipience?

In Goodman's view, the most important benefit to be derived from art, however, is *understanding,* more precisely, understanding of the world (as distinguished from, for example, self-knowledge or psychological insight). "How an object or event functions as a work explains how, through certain modes of reference, what so functions may contribute to a vision of—and to the making of—a world."[40] And again, less abstractly: "After a couple of hours at an exhibition we often step out into a visual world quite different from the one we left. We see what we did not see before, and see in a new way. We have *learned.*"[41]

There is no question, then, that for Goodman art makes available a good of the highest order which we should make every effort to cultivate. Moreover, since according to Goodman the process leading to the discovery of what a work of art has to offer not only takes time but presupposes training, we may take it that formal schooling is called for. Goodman's account has thus fully answered the requirements for the justification of aesthetic education by indicating both the benefit to the individual and the need for educational intervention.

Art and institutions: E. F. Kaelin

Kaelin, in contrast to Beardsley, Osborne, and Goodman, acquired the accents of his writing from continental existential-phenomenological points of view. The major influences on his thought are Jean-Paul Sartre, Edmund Husserl, Maurice Merleau-Ponty, and Martin Heidegger.[42] Existential phenomenology concentrates on the givens of experience that reside in a person's objective field of phenomenal awareness and in this respect at least can be said to resemble approaches like the ones discussed earlier in this chapter. This overlap of viewpoints has led to some attempts to find common ground between linguistic analysis and phenomenology. Both Beardsley and Osborne, for example, have indicated how phenomenology and existentialism can contribute to analyses of aesthetic experience and how the experience of art in turn offers insight into existential-phenomenological problems.

What is more, although Kaelin's thought is constructed on foundations greatly dissimilar from those supporting the philosophies of Beardsley, Osborne, and Goodman, the effects he attributes to aesthetic experience bear a resemblance to the ones they posit. Indeed, a discovery one makes in comparing and contrasting aesthetic theorists is that their ontological and epistemological differences—that is, the contrasts in their beliefs about an artwork's status, mode of being, and meaning—do not necessarily preclude consonances in the general kinds of benefits they ascribe to art. For instance, Kaelin thinks that works of art are good for the aesthetic experiences they afford, whose worth in turn inheres in the manner in which they intensify and clarify human awareness, a function of what he calls aesthetic communication. Since Kaelin also notes that satisfaction accrues to the percipient who successfully fuses the system of counters ("counters" being surface and depth features) of a work of art, one is reminded of Beardsley on aesthetic gratification. Moreover, Kaelin's view about the capacity of art to intensify and clarify experience might easily subsume Osborne's belief that the preeminent mission of art is to stimulate the powers of percipience. Finally, Kaelin's account of the aesthetic seems equally hospitable to Goodman's stress on the understandings of the world that can be had through aesthetic experience.

For Kaelin, aesthetic experience progresses from origination through unfolding to closure.[43] The first thing he would encourage the percipient of an artwork to do is bracket out (that is, dismiss from mind) a range of irrelevant considerations. This effort of will is necessary to create contexts of significance whose intrinsic values provide the material for immediate aesthetic experience. Attention to the phenomenally given, to the presentational immediacy of qualities, involves perception of what is variously termed matter and form, subject and treatment, and local and regional qualities, all aspects of surface and depth relations. Aesthetic experience is thus animated and controlled by the imperatives of bracketed contexts of significance. The percipient's successful fusion of a work's system of counters results in an act of expressive response that constitutes the consummatory value of the aesthetic experience and signals its closure. Kaelin's term "felt expressiveness" implies a sense of fittingness or appropriateness between surface and depth counters (recalling, incidentally, one of the features of aesthetic experience as described by Beardsley). An example, which I have quoted more fully elsewhere (also see Appendix I), is Kaelin's description of Pablo Picasso's *Guernica*. After pointing out and interpreting the work's semantic and formal features, Kaelin writes: "So interpreted, our experience of *Guernica* deepens and comes to closure in a single act of expressive response in which we perceive the fittingness of this surface—all broken planes and jagged edges in the stark contrast of black and white—to represent this depth, the equally stark contrast of the living and the dead. . . ."[44] What Kaelin terms a single act of expression is, I believe, the same as what Osborne calls an instance of synoptic or integrative vision.

For Kaelin, the point of art is the worthwhile aesthetic experience it provides. Worthwhileness consists both in a work's quality of aesthetic communication and in the exercise of aesthetic perceptual skills and judgment, all of which occur in a context of significance governed by the intrinsic values of a system of counters. It is as if Kaelin, like Beardsley, Osborne, and Goodman, offers his own version of Panofsky's belief that a work of art, whatever other functions it may perform, is essentially a man-made object that demands to be experienced aesthetically. As Kaelin writes, works of art "come to exist only in the experience of persons who have opened themselves to the expressiveness of a sensuous surface and allowed their understandings and imaginations to be guided by controlled responses set up thereon."[45]

Kaelin, along with the other writers discussed here, sees the worth of encounters with artworks in terms of personal benefit to the individual. But he does not rest content with such a formulation and extends his purview to include desirable consequences for society at large. In this he is not alone. Beardsley had pondered the possibility of aesthetic welfare, and Osborne suggested the aesthetic appreciation of excellent works as an antidote to the amusement arts and hence as a means of elevating society's level of culture. Kaelin, however, seems to be saying that a democratic society stands to gain through the aptitudes art can foster and the attitudes it can instill in individuals. Furthermore, such results would be attributable to the special requirements set up by the phenomenological method of experiencing works of art.

When practicing the method of phenomenological analysis a percipient takes his cue from the immediate givens of the artwork and submits willingly to the guidance of the work's context and significance. The percipient approaches the work open-mindedly and tries not to superimpose interpretive or ideological frameworks on it. Aesthetic experience thus demands as well as promotes tolerance or, to use Kaelin's term, a "defanaticized" frame of mind. Aesthetic experience might therefore be considered propaedeutic to some of the virtues needed to sustain a democratic social order.

Yet freedom is also prerequisite for and exercised during aesthetic experience. When an individual relinquishes personal and ideological biases and refrains from forming preconceptions about what an artwork might have to say concerning his relation to self, others, and the world, he allows the perceptually given to communicate freely. This same freedom from prior restraints, however, is enjoyed by the percipient as well. Aesthetic experience as free communication may thus be taken as a paradigmatic instance of freedom, of how persons can in effect choose their futures—an important existential premise—by creating new worlds of aesthetic value and by opening themselves to new possibilities of experience. Art thus serves Being by helping to actualize human powers and potentialities—tolerance and freedom—that benefit both the individual and society.

A justification for aesthetic education responsive to Kaelin's way of thinking might rest on two claims: that aesthetic appreciation (1) enriches the individual by giving satisfaction, sharpening perception, and freely communicating a felt expressiveness and, coincidentally, (2) may help develop in persons attitudes and inclinations deemed desirable by society. Kaelin, however, strengthens the educational case when he interposes the *aesthetic institution* between (1) and (2).

Kaelin addresses this additional element in an essay titled "Why Teach Art in the Schools?"[46] which presupposes the conceptions of art and aesthetic experience just described and concentrates on the institutional question. Institutions give scope to as well as channel human activities. But to keep them functioning efficaciously and benevolently, it is necessary to order "the relations between an individual's impulse to action (of a certain type) and the set of institutions within our society that give form to this impulse."[47] And so for the impulse to art and the institutions that give it form. Institutional theories of art are no longer novelties; the most well known of them are associated with the work of George Dickie and Arthur Danto, whose writings, however, exhibit no interest in education or aesthetic policy. This leaves room for an institutional definition of art framed for educational purposes and provides an opportunity to reap more of the benefits of an institutional account of art than Kaelin believes has been done so far. After briefly reviewing various philosophers' attempts to define art—from Aristotelian essentialism to Wittgensteinian family resemblances to Dickie-Danto contextualism— Kaelin offers his own definition of "artworld" and "aesthetic institution": it is an institution that endeavors "both to permit and to regulate the behavioral patterns constituting the formal practices of producing, criticizing, exhibiting, and appreciating works of art."[48] The basic purpose of the aesthetic institution is to maximize aesthetic value in society. This can happen only when artists produce works of art that are significantly communicative, when critics with a strong historical sense take the measure of these works, and when persons undergoing aesthetic experiences allow themselves to be controlled by the vehicle of perception and are rewarded with aesthetic satisfaction. The importance of such an aesthetic institution is as great as the value society places—or should place—on the arts. For Kaelin that value is high indeed and makes the aesthetic nearly coequal with the scientific institution and similar to it in some respects. Like scientific institutions, cultural institutions are both permissive and regulatory; they encourage maximal pursuit of novel significance and they affect the way new creations come to be appreciated through informed criticism. As in other major institutions, criticism in the aesthetic institution is an effort to exert control over the quality of human thought and action.

The aesthetic institution will operate smoothly and maximize aesthetic value when persons perform their various institutional roles freely and effectively. Efficient performance depends on adequate skills, hence on education. But since all members of society are potentially members of or participants in the aesthetic institution—by attending cultural events, visiting museums, purchasing art objects, and seeking out aesthetic experiences in other ways—they must possess aesthetic skills and the proper mindset to play their parts well; aesthetic education should therefore be available to all. In short, aesthetic education is needed to ensure the efficacy of the aesthetic institution. Thus according to Kaelin the ultimate *social* product of the art world and the aesthetic institution is not works of art so much as "the type of person capable of appreciating works of art with the appropriate critical attitude."[49] Kaelin's writings have thus afforded a new slant on the discussion in this chapter by providing a picture of the individual functioning in society, to be specific, in one of society's major institutions, the aesthetic.

CHAPTER 3

Art in educational context—the concept of aesthetic criticism

> In teaching, we do not impose our wills on the student, but introduce him to the many mansions of the heritage in which we ourselves strive to live, and to the improvement of which we are ourselves dedicated. *Israel Scheffler* [1]

> . . . serious literary and philosophic criticism comes from "a debt of love," that we write about books or about music or about art because "some primary instinct of communion" would have us share with and communicate to others an overwhelming enrichment. *George Steiner* [2]

> . . . in many orders of beauty, particularly those of the finer arts, it is requisite to employ much reasoning in order to feel the proper sentiment; and a false relish may frequently be corrected by argument and reflection. *David Hume* [3]

Such remarks reemphasize the significance of the artistic heritage and the depth of devotion to it that were central to the justification question discussed in the previous chapter. They also introduce new accents: a felt obligation to share aesthetic enrichment and to communicate aesthetic values without willful imposition, and the role that reasoning, reflection, and argument can play in this transmission. While the last chapter indicated how a philosophically respectable case can be made for teaching the arts in the schools, the present one begins the process of showing how such teaching can be both theoretically defensible and practically feasible, an endeavor that will occupy the next two chapters as well.

Scheffler holds that in introducing the young to the cultural heritage we need not consider the principles of understanding we teach to be immutable or innate, only that they are the best we know and that we should be prepared to improve them if possible. He cautions, however, that "such improvement is possible . . . only if we succeed in passing on, too, the multiple live traditions in which they are embodied, and in which a sense of their history, spirit, and direction may be discovered."[4] Far from being mere conditioning or authoritarian imposition, teaching that respects these sentiments helps to define the rational life of both teacher and student and enables them more effectively to shape a human career. In this connection, Scheffler quotes R. S. Peters who states that "the teacher is not a detached operator who is bringing about some kind of result in another person which is external to him. His task is to try to get others on the inside of a public form of life that he shares and considers to be worthwhile."[5] The aesthetic is one such form of public life.

We can now discern the outlines of the problem: how to acquaint students with the aesthetic form of life in a manner that is not only ethically acceptable but also theoretically justifiable and pedagogically promising. The solution I suggest lies in teaching the skills of aesthetic criticism. The remainder of this chapter therefore discusses the nature of aesthetic criticism and makes several critical distinctions. Chapter 4 presents examples of aesthetic critical activity drawn from the writings of a number of critics, while Chapter 5 addresses in greater detail issues involved in teaching aesthetic skills.

The nature of concepts

There are two reasons for inserting a few remarks about concepts at this point. First, a number of aesthetic concepts will shortly be introduced in a discussion of aesthetic criticism and some of their peculiarities pointed out in the concluding portion of the chapter. Second, and of more immediate relevance, the notion of a skill, as in "learning the *skills* of aesthetic criticism," is here taken to be closely allied to that of a concept.

Any mention of "concepts," however, tends to distance those who associate the term with "conceptual analysis," which they regard as among the more abstruse pursuits of philosophers and hence remote from practical and professional concerns. But concepts need not be feared; in fact, they cannot be escaped. This point is well put by H. Gene Blocker in his *Philosophy of Art:* "The world we are aware of is already packaged into conceptual compartments; the world as we are aware of it, therefore, contains a substantial conceptual component. Analyzing these concepts is therefore a way of analyzing the world, at least in the only way we are aware of it."[6]

Still, what are concepts? There is no simple answer. In his *The Opening Mind* Morris Weitz writes that "concepts have been construed as universals, definitions, innate ideas, images, thoughts, conceptions, meanings, predicates and relations, abstract objects, abstracted items, extracted common features, neutral entities, and as habits, skills, or mental capacities."[7] He concludes that the concept of concept is in truth a family of concepts. For the theorist of aesthetic education this presents an opportunity to adopt only those members of the family that are directly relevant to teaching an understanding and appreciation of art; or, in the terminology of this essay, to the development of a sense of art in the young that enables them to engage works of art for the worthwhile experience they are capable of providing.

I intend to settle on one of the options offered by Weitz but will approach that decision somewhat indirectly. Generally, John Wilson reflects my intent when he explains what it is for a student to have grasped the idea of a work of art: he "has something to cling onto; he has the *concept* of a work of art, and he can know what sort of thing to do with cases he has not met before."[8] P. L. Heath states the matter more formally:

> To have a concept "*x*" is . . . (with some exceptions), (*a*) to know the meaning of the word "*x*"; (*b*) to be able to pick out or recognize a presented *x* (distinguish non-*x*'s, etc.), or again to be able to think of (have images or ideas of) *x* (or *x*'s) when they are not present; (*c*) to know the nature of *x*, to have grasped or apprehended the properties (universals, essences, etc.) which characterize *x*'s and make them what they are.[9]

"Knowing the meaning of *x*'s," "being able to pick out *x*'s," "knowing the nature of *x*'s," and "distinguishing non-*x*'s" are as important in aesthetic situations as in others. If we let "*x*" stand for "work of art," then having the concept "work of art" would imply not only knowing the meaning of the term but also being able to recognize, if not universals and essences, at least a characteristic manifold of elements, relations, complexes, qualities, and meanings that make an artwork what it is. To use a phrase common in recent analyses of knowing, the conditions of "knowing that"—knowing that *x* is a work of art—seem to have been met. And this would certainly give the student "something to cling onto."

Yet it is not quite enough; I have therefore chosen the "skill" definition of concept, for the following reasons (which are really not as separable as I make them appear). (1) The idea of a skill has an educationally significant performative component. That is, the student *demonstrates* the possession of a concept by applying it correctly. The teacher takes such exhibitions of "knowing how" as evidence that the concept has been taught successfully. (2) "Skill" furthermore carries connotations of finesse, judgments of fittingness, of "knowing when" to apply a concept as well as a disposition to do so on appropriate occasions. (3) When concept possession is understood as a skill, it also accommodates "knowing with," that is, it brings into play conceptual frameworks or background knowledge that makes the precise and apt exercise of the skill, and therefore use of the concept, possible in the first place. This means that students who employ an aesthetic concept properly in a variety of circumstances can also be assumed to know something about the general category to which it belongs and about the subconcepts it comprehends. (4) Finally, the exercise of a skill should be appropriate not only to specific situations but also to a particular realm or sphere of human experience. Thus, aesthetic skills are most suitably brought to bear at the intersection of two worlds, the world of the work of art and the world of the percipient. Some kind of "knowing where" might therefore be involved as well.

This sketchy treatment of concepts suggests the difficulties that educational theorists and curriculum planners face in the organization of knowledge and activities for aesthetic education. They have to search a range of disciplines for ideas and procedures that can be adapted to teaching in the arts. Decisions have to be made, for example, regarding the order in which concepts are to be presented, the level of sophistication to be aimed at, and the length of time to be spent on the teaching of each concept or skill. These problems are compounded by the number and diversity of the art forms to be taken into account. Consequently the whole task of ordering knowledge for aesthetic learning cannot be addressed adequately here; only a few clues, tips, and illustrations can be offered, mainly in connection with the visual arts. I take it for granted, however, that what can be said about the visual arts applies in principle to the literary and performing arts.

Aesthetic criticism and aesthetic education

A strong recommendation that teaching in aesthetic education should draw rather heavily on the activities of aesthetic criticism does not automatically establish an educationally fruitful relation between criticism and aesthetic education. First of all, probably no generally acceptable account of criticism can be given since there is no consensus on the meaning of criticism either with respect to its logic, scope, rationality, distinctiveness of activities, or even general utility in the aesthetic domain. This is the conclusion of an intensive analysis of the concept of criticism in recent aesthetic theory where it has been the central preoccupation of analytic philosophers. The conception of criticism chosen for purposes of this essay, however, is one that enjoys some support: it is criticism that illuminates works of art *as* art, for their aesthetic value and accomplishment. This definition pointedly excludes some other kinds of criticism,.for example, *ideological* and *cultural* criticism, in which aesthetic value and artistic achievement count for little because of the commitment of its practitioners to different programs and projects.

If a goal of education generally is to enable students to operate in a variety of fields in some approximation of the manner in which specialists in these areas do, then it makes sense to recommend aesthetic criticism of the kind specified as the goal to be achieved in aesthetic education. Enlightened aesthetic criticism hence becomes the model for making sense of works of art, with the proviso, however, that the aim is not a professional but an amateur level of skill. This is to say that the stance of the critic is closest to that of the nonspecialist for whom works of art ultimately exist. The teaching of the concepts and skills of aesthetic criticism to the young can then be justified on the grounds of the congruence of the critic's purposes and methods with the objectives of aesthetic education. By improving their aesthetic understanding, the young will be in a better position to appropriate the significance of art and to realize its potential for contributing to a richer and more worthwhile life.

In teaching the skills and concepts of criticism a few pedagogically useful distinctions can be made. The first is between *aesthetic object concepts* and *critical activity concepts*. "Aesthetic object concepts" refer to the myriad features, properties, qualities, and meanings that can be said to reside in the artwork itself. "Critical activity concepts" encompass the descriptive, interpretive, and evaluative skills with which we explore, understand, and assess works of art.

Critical activity concepts can be further subdivided into the concepts and skills of *aesthetic exploratory criticism* and *aesthetic evaluative criticism*. "Exploratory criticism" consists of efforts to discover through description, analysis, characterization, and interpretation just what is in a work of art that is relevant to it as art and is worth enjoying, contemplating, and admiring. "Evaluative criticism" suggests a stronger judgmental dimension and involves, as part of judgment, the giving of reasons and justifications for assessments. Justifying aesthetic judgments in turn entails centering one's attention once more on the work for further probing in the manner of exploratory criticism; the work is now resurveyed in order to ground the reasons given in support of the judgment.

These distinctions, and others to come, are not hard and fast and certainly not incontrovertible. Although they are not to be thought of as compartments to which we consign the different phases and components of critical activity, they can help the art educator to understand what is happening during an aesthetic response to a work of art and thus make the task of teaching the skills of aesthetic criticism more manageable.

The three accounts of criticism to which I now turn offer more substantial aid to the art teacher. The discussion by Marcia M. Eaton, who is a philosopher of art, is not only an excellent summary of current thinking on the topic of criticism; it also contains a number of felicitous definitions that should prove congenial to educators. Brian S. Crittenden, a philosopher of education, approaches the subject of aesthetic criticism with educational concerns foremost in mind and finds the logic of aesthetic argument directly relevant to fundamental problems of teaching. And Monroe C. Beardsley provides a convenient classification of critical judgments and reasons that emphasizes the role of aesthetic objective reasons.

Marcia M. Eaton: Judgment and shared values

In *Basic Issues in Aesthetics*,[10] Eaton distinguishes interpretation from criticism. By "interpretation" she understands "activity that has as its goal the description or explanation of what a work is—what it means, or what properties or characteristics it has." By "criticism" she intends "the evaluation or assessment of something—in particular judging whether something is good or bad."[11] She is particularly concerned to discover whether there can be correct interpretations of works of art and whether there are facts we can appeal to when attempting to justify our interpretations and assessments. The distinction between interpretation and criticism in Eaton's analysis is comparable to my distinction between exploratory criticism (description, analysis, characterization, and interpretation) and evaluative criticism (judgment and its justification).

In order to highlight certain problems of interpretation, Eaton considers a puzzling case involving interpretation—the many different readings that have been given of Henry James's *The Turn of the Screw*. The story is ostensibly a ghost story, which is apparently how James meant it to be taken; but many readers give a psychological account of it that alters the meaning of the story. Who is right? Is one interpretation correct and others incorrect? And how do we settle such questions?

Much depends, of course, on how certain aspects of the story are understood, described, explained, and interpreted. Indeed, how we describe a work will be largely a function of how we interpret it. Eaton recounts the surprise registered by H. C. Goddard, a literary critic, when he discovered that not only his students but other critics as well disagreed with his reading of the story. To be sure, when Goddard presented his explanation to his students they accepted it. But their acquiescence does not resolve a problem that is fundamental to all critical interpretations: whether Goddard's reading, or anybody else's, can be proven correct or can at least be established as a better reading than those of others. Why, moreover, were Goddard's students willing to change their minds? And matters of meaning aside, how do we determine whether there is any objective basis for saying *The Turn of the Screw* is a good or an inferior work of literature? Eaton's manner of tackling such questions should persuade teachers of art that they ought to know on what grounds they offer interpretations of artworks and whether there is any rational foundation for making value judgments.

In canvassing current aesthetic thinking for views on questions like those alluded to above, Eaton found that in their efforts to justify judgments critics typically appeal to three things: the pleasure a work affords, the facts of the matter, and the artist's intentions. Pleasure, being subjective, can be discounted as a determinant of the correctness of descriptions, interpretations, and assessments of works of art. The artist's intentions, moreover, cannot always be known, and thus their relevance is sometimes difficult to establish. But the facts of the matter—what actually goes on, for example, in *The Turn of the Screw*—should put one on solid footing, and there are theorists who believe that descriptions of such facts can be true or false. Yet it is one thing, say, to describe the governess in James's story as a young woman and something else to describe her as a sexually repressed young woman. Differences like this have convinced some writers that both description and interpretation play a part in efforts to find out "what is going on" in a work of literature; interpretation becomes necessary when description is problematic. Is the young woman really sexually repressed?

When it comes to the interpretation of a work of art as a whole, most aestheticians believe that an interpretation can be no more than plausible, reasonable, and defensible. Yet as Eaton makes clear, a decision still has to be made about which of several interpretations is the most plausible one. She suggests that we will be able to make such a judgment once we have resolved to mean by "interpretation" the formulation of hypotheses about the most general organization and coherence of the elements that make up a literary work (or any other work of art); the best interpretation will then be the most inclusive one. This lends interpretation a larger scope than description enjoys. But interpretation is not limited to the discovery of meaning; it may also attempt to explain how a work achieves certain kinds of effect, say, a quality of freshness, tension, or evocativeness.

Assuming that interpretations and evaluations of works of art can be reasonable and plausible, that is, that we can provide cogent reasons in support of, say, a psychological reading of *The Turn of the Screw* and of an explanation of how the story achieves some of its effects, what role do reasons play in justifying interpretations and assessments? For example, when we assert that a work is good or poor on the basis of the reasons we give, what is the status of the reasons? Notice that it would be circular to claim a work of art is good because it rewards contemplation. We must provide reasons for saying that it is worth contemplating, and these reasons, Eaton states, typically direct attention to a work's manifold of qualities. As she puts it: "Critical reasons *point* to things that can be perceived and at the same time *direct* our perception. . . . [I]f a remark about a work gives us an instruction or suggestion that helps us notice interesting things about the work, then the remark gives us a reason for noticing and appreciating that feature. It gives us a reason for valuing the work."[12]

Another question is whether critical reasons are universally valid. Eaton points out that Jakob Rosenberg in his *On Quality in Art*[13] thinks that artworks are excellent by virtue of such qualities as artistic economy, selectiveness, feeling for the medium, sense for the significant, consistency, inventiveness, intensity, clarity, and expressiveness. Beardsley likewise believes that there are reasons of overarching generality on which aesthetic judgments can be founded, and his approach to this question will be discussed presently. Others, however, are persuaded that it is logically impossible to derive critical judgments from critical reasons. In their view, an aesthetic judgment may inform or enlighten or direct attention to something interesting and worthwhile, but it cannot compel belief. This skepticism about the validity of aesthetic judgments is based on the conviction that aesthetic argument cannot meet the requirements of either deductive or inductive reasoning which, it is claimed, are the only two logical models we have for determining validity. Eaton sets aside these doubts and discounts demands for a logically rigorous conception of aesthetic argument. She thinks that people who live in the same culture and share the same language—as well as some knowledge about art—have enough in common to be brought to the realization that some works are better than others and that reasons can be supplied for singling out features that certify a work as artistically good or poor. In support of this view Eaton quotes Alan Tormey to the effect that what we have in aesthetic argument are "*corroborative* tests, and the *case* for a critical judgment rests on the extent of its acceptance among independent judges. . . ."[14] To secure acceptance for judgments, however, the critic takes care that they and the reasons given for them are formulated convincingly. A good critic knows how to arrange his assessment for scrutiny for others and in so doing will draw on his skills of description, analysis, characterization, and interpretation. Enabling students to make acceptable aesthetic judgments therefore involves making sure that they achieve sufficient proficiency in the use of critical skills.

By *good* criticism Eaton means criticism that "results in a fuller, richer aesthetic experience by ferreting out the aesthetic value of objects and events."[15] This "ferreting out" involves more than pointing out certain features of works and using them as reasons for judging works good or inferior. Especially when a positive assessment of a work's value has been reached, a fuller, richer experience is assured only if students are encouraged to go on looking, to see for themselves how particular qualities contribute to others and how the whole achieves its effect through the interanimation of its elements. Good criticism, that is, leads others to further and more detailed exploration of an artwork; it proceeds from what Steiner called the instinct for communicating an enormous richness, and it answers Scheffler's invitation to take up residence in the mansions of the cultural heritage. In more formal terms, good criticism stimulates others to realize as much aesthetic value as possible. Hence we do not simply acquaint students with what informed opinion has to say about certain works and leave the matter at that. We try to persuade them that learning to appreciate what is worthwhile in art will enhance their lives and be a source of continuing satisfaction. We teach aesthetic criticism on the assumption that those who learn to appreciate and understand art are likely to become lovers of art as well. This hope is founded on the experience of all those who, once having been made acquainted with art of high quality and provided with the skills needed to appropriate its value, seldom express indifference toward it. One conjectures that there might be far less antagonism toward so-called elitism in matters of art if the large majority of persons had actually had opportunities to appreciate the best that has been thought and created. More tolerance might therefore be shown toward those who advocate broadening access to excellence. Unfortunately, the truculent populist is quite often a person who simply never had a chance to learn better. But a more enlightened policy for aesthetic education could change this situation.[16]

We come back then to the notion that a work of art is a human artifact that is usefully understood as something having the capacity to occasion a high degree of aesthetic experience, an experience that is at once gratifying, informative, and enriching. We can make this claim for persons living in the same culture, says Eaton, because they tend to appreciate similar qualities and meanings and to enjoy having them brought to their attention. This interest is initiated early by parents when they point out the qualities of objects to their children and develops into more informed dialogue about artworks and the reading of aesthetic criticism. It may well be, Eaton states, that persons "cannot be *reasoned* into taking pleasure, but we can have *reasons* for believing that things will be pleasurable. Besides being reports of pleasure actually taken (hence the necessity of direct acquaintance), critical judgments also involve assumptions about what other people find delightful (or its opposite)."[17]

Given the capacity individuals have for aesthetic gratification, the reasonableness of critical judgments of art, and the possibility of persons' taking pleasure in similar qualities, Eaton thinks that the habit of mind called aesthetic experience is part of the concept of human rationality. Perhaps no harm will be done if we call such a habit of mind aesthetic rationality, an inclination of mind toward enjoying, making sense of, and judging works of art. Eaton cautions, however, that criticism is helpful only when the persons for whom it is formulated are willing to avail themselves of opportunities for expanding their awareness through further contemplation.

Though Eaton does not discuss educational applications of her views, it should be apparent that her ideas are fraught with pedagogical significance. Like the critic of art, the teacher as critic promises students that by mastering the skills of aesthetic criticism they will be enabled to confront works of art with a degree of self-assurance and to decide for themselves whether their experience of a work has been worth their while. As students cultivate such skills and begin to argue rationally about the values of artworks, the level of aesthetic rationality in the society will rise correspondingly, to the benefit of all concerned.

Brian S. Crittenden: The teacher as aesthetic critic

Crittenden's essay "Persuasion: Aesthetic Argument and the Language of Teaching,"[18] makes a good companion piece to Eaton's; he shares several of her concerns and expands on others. Since aesthetic rationality has already been declared important for the present effort, it may now be said that Crittenden's greatest contribution to the case being developed here lies in the way he argues for the logical respectability of critical discourse.

Before summarizing the most salient points made by Crittenden, I should remark some changes in terminology. Crittenden's general term for aesthetic criticism is "aesthetic argument." Unlike Eaton, he does not distinguish between interpretation and criticism; rather, description and redescription most aptly characterize the critic's activity, although Crittenden has recourse to other aesthetic concepts as well. I mention this primarily to acknowledge the vagaries of aesthetic terms and classifications that grant writers license to stipulate, as I have done, their own working definitions.

The first step in aesthetic criticism and appreciation is careful observation. Crittenden is at some pains to emphasize that, like all seeing, aesthetic perception is "seeing as." The concept of seeing, he asserts, includes that of cognition; theories and other cognitive factors inevitably enter in; hence seeing is inherently concept- and theory-laden. It makes sense to suppose that a person with expert knowledge about an object sees that object, or aspects of it, differently from the person lacking such knowledge. Evidently, then, knowledge can alter what we see.

In seeing of the aesthetic kind, "the focus of attention is on the perceptual features of the object as they relate to one another in the pattern of the whole."[19] In other passages Crittenden talks, without elaboration, about "formal qualities." It is clear, however, that "perceptual features" is to be understood broadly, covering not only visual and auditory but literary properties as well. The critic's taking note of these features is closely related to naming and describing, a task that must be undertaken with care, deliberateness, and seriousness. These are prescribed by what may be called the critic's ethical obligation to the artwork, the nature of which Crittenden makes clear when he cites the critical credo of F. R. Leavis, the literary critic (though the question of whether Leavis himself always honored it strictly must be left aside here):

> The business of the literary critic is to attain a peculiar completeness of response and to observe a peculiarly strict relevance in developing his response into commentary; he must be on his guard against abstracting improperly from what is in front of him and against any premature or irrelevant generalizing—of it or from it. His first concern is to enter into possession of the given poem (let us say) in its concrete fullness, and his constant concern is never to lose his completeness of possession, but rather to increase it.[20]

I inject here some remarks by Lionel Trilling from his Jefferson lecture that in spirit are similar to Leavis's. In commenting on the assault on mind in the modern world, and especially on objectivity, Trilling, with Arnold's words in mind, suggests that objectivity is simply the respect we render an object by trying to see it as in itself it really is; it "is the fullest possible recognition of the integral and entire existence"[21] of something. And we render such respect out of an intellectual obligation and faith that the effort is worthwhile, even while realizing that the structure of mind itself precludes total success.

To return to Crittenden's account, once in complete possession of an artwork's sense, the critic delivers a commentary in which he identifies, classifies, and describes the work's perceptual features in language that is relatively neutral at first but becomes, according to Crittenden, increasingly interpretive. All of this discourse can be subsumed under the headings of description and redescription. Given a complex work of art this process goes through a cycle of redescriptions, each of which has the character of an evaluation. "The judgment eventually passed on the work of art is the final redescription and its appropriateness depends on the 'cumulative effect' of all the intermediate interpretative descriptions."[22]

Three items stand out in the above. First, and incidentally, Crittenden's "final redescription" calls to mind what Kaelin calls "deep description"; both kinds of description have an overall assessment of a work of art built into them. Second, the way Crittenden has explained the progression of critical commentary allows him to claim that just as all seeing is, in a way, "seeing as," so all description contains an element of interpretation; not only that, the interpretive component increases in the course of an aesthetic redescription. Third, and most importantly, Crittenden has now addressed a troublesome aspect of aesthetic or critical judgment: its logical status.

That problem, as Eaton already indicated, is posed by the fact that the verdict on an artwork's aesthetic merit, or lack of it, can be neither deduced nor inferred from the description of the work, no matter how exhaustive and sensitive the latter. A gulf remains between the descriptive and the normative; or so many have insisted. As Crittenden puts it: "Granted the interpretative description, what authorizes us to conclude that the art object is thus aesthetically good or bad?"[23] He answers his own question: there really is no gap to be bridged, no logical authorization to be obtained, no additional connection to be established, precisely because, in his account, the final redescription has emerged seamlessly from relatively neutral and increasingly interpretive and evaluative descriptions as an accumulated evaluation and not as a superadded judgment. Aesthetic argument thus has no separate evaluative phase; after the last redescription, it would be superfluous to ask, "But is it a good or bad work of art?" "Suppose," says Crittenden, "someone agrees that a poem evokes emotions with banal romantic generality. Can he seriously deny, or even wonder, whether in this respect the poem is aesthetically weak?"[24] It should not be difficult for anyone who has read a fair number of aesthetic critiques to think of similar instances in which the way a work of art is being described already anticipates the critic's verdict, and the next section will look more closely at how critical reasons operate.

Although a critic's commentary may often seem to move toward his conclusions with a certain inevitability, Crittenden does not claim that aesthetic argument can be true or false in the sense reserved for deduction and induction. He does insist, however, that we are justified in speaking of the reasonableness of an aesthetic argument and the adequacy or appropriateness of the evaluation. The appeal to rationality is thus maintained. Furthermore, it is reasonableness, adequacy, and appropriateness that guarantee *persuasive power* to aesthetic arguments.

That persuasion would become a highly significant topic for Crittenden could have been guessed from his choice of "redescription" as a major concept, for the critic's going back to the work for yet another rendering of it seems to suggest that the critic is trying to convince someone to take the work in a certain manner. And this is indeed how Crittenden understands the critic's task: the attempt by one observer to get another to agree on how to name and describe relatively neutral elements of a work of art and then to persuade the observer to see these elements as fitting together into one pattern rather than another. The critic may employ a range of techniques designed to impart to the observer whatever knowledge is needed to bring the observer's "seeing as" in line with the critic's. In the effort to persuade, the critic assembles relevant information, explains symbols and associations, renders visible structural and textural relations, and highlights the overall pattern of the whole. As Frank Sibley[25] has stated, in doing all this critics may point out non-aesthetic features in order to clarify aesthetic ones; they may use similes and metaphors, contrasts and comparisons, and repetition and reiteration; and they may augment their verbal performances with nonverbal ones—a sweep of the arm, facial expressions, nods, gestures, etc. But, continues Crittenden,

> It must be stressed that the persuasive nature of an aesthetic argument is not incompatible with its objectivity. On the contrary, the critic is answerable to the real perceptual conditions of the object which he discusses. That is, the object must have those properties and belong to that context of conceptual and other elements which make it perceptible in the way which the critic claims.[26]

This is an extremely important point, for left unqualified, persuasion by itself is suspect. It carries connotations of manipulation, subjective appeal, propaganda, indoctrination—of imposing one's will on others. But unwavering respect for and deference to an artwork's perceptual conditions keeps persuasive argument honest, objective, and hence educationally acceptable.

When can we regard a critic as having argued validly and successfully? Not, according to Crittenden, when the critic has merely managed to get a large number of people to concur with a judgment. For "unless he is directing them fundamentally to the appreciation of the object in its formal qualities and unless the discernible features of the object do support his claims about it, he is not presenting a genuine and valid argument."[27] When the critic's argument is genuine, however, it is also compelling in a way that goes beyond eliciting verbal assent from the critic's audience. "I have tried to argue," Crittenden goes on, "that if the nature of aesthetic argument and evaluation are properly understood, it is not possible for someone to admit the correctness of the conclusion without reflecting this in the way he *sees* the object" (emphasis added).[28] Percipients can thus be said to have grasped the appropriateness of an evaluation only when they see and experience the object in accordance with the evaluation. Crittenden stresses that "it is of the essence of critical judgment that one accepts the judgment as justified as one comes to experience the object in just that way."[29] In other words, the critic's success is certified in the observer's enriched aesthetic experience.

Since, as I said, Crittenden is a philosopher of education, it is understandable that his interest in aesthetic argument was prompted by an educational rather than an aesthetic concern. In fact, the essay on which I have drawn was prepared for a volume, the major purpose of which was to indicate the relevance of a range of aesthetic concepts to an understanding of educational phenomena generally, not just to those associated with education in the arts. Why did Crittenden choose to write about aesthetic argument?

With Scheffler and Peters, Crittenden realized that the educator's role is not restricted to teaching facts, theories, and skills. Teachers also try to make students aware of the value of what they are being taught and of the ways a subject will fit into and enhance their lives. This, however, is done not by factual demonstration but by persuasion. Crittenden thinks that persuasive argument pervades the entire educational enterprise and that anyone who engages seriously in the task of teaching undertakes to persuade systematically. Yet even while seeking to persuade, educators must limit themselves to rational methods. Crittenden's own search for a rational method of persuasion that could serve as a model for educators ended when he had discovered and explored aesthetic argument, for here was a way of persuading that was sufficiently objective and rational for teachers to use. Crittenden therefore concluded that "a careful analysis of the logic of aesthetic argument will provide a clearer understanding of the form of persuasion that is appropriate to the process of teaching and learning."[30] This form of persuasion is probably resorted to many times during a typical day of teaching, but never with more gravity and deliberateness than on those occasions when a teacher speaks on behalf of the educated life itself. Crittenden deserves to be quoted at some length on this topic:

> The educator is involved in initiating others into a distinctive style of life characterized by specific values, attitudes, and ways of proceeding. Because he is convinced that this style of life is worthwhile and because one of its distinguishing preferences is for reasonable rather than arbitrary choice, part of his task as an educator is to persuade rationally those being initiated to see the whole life style of the educated man as inherently valuable for human beings and to choose it as such. . . . In the end . . . I believe he is forced back to depicting as fully as possible the characteristic features of the life style of the educated man and to comparing and contrasting it with alternative styles. It is thus finally a form of aesthetic or critical argument—a judgment not about means but about the total pattern which the component elements form. At this most fundamental level, the norms of rational persuasion for the educator are essentially those of aesthetic argument.[31]

One final observation: the educational significance of aesthetic argument works both ways. "In presenting an aesthetic argument, the critic himself is obviously engaging in a specific form of teaching."[32]

Monroe C. Beardsley: Aesthetic value

Crittenden examined closely the nature of aesthetic argument; Beardsley does the same for the reasons typically used in such arguments. Without giving reasons, says Beardsley, the critic simply renders dogmatic and uninformative value judgments. But what sorts of reasons do critics normally rely on and what kinds of evaluative remarks are actually made about works of art—and which of these are relevant to aesthetic criticism? Beardsley identified critical reasons embedded in a large number of normative statements made about works of visual, literary, and performing art, and in his *Aesthetics: Problems in the Philosophy of Criticism* analyzed the principles at work in them. He further discussed the nature of critical evaluation in *The Possibility of Criticism* and later in the *The Aesthetic Point of View,* edited by Wreen and Callen. I follow here an article written for the *Journal of Aesthetic Education* titled "The Classification of Critical Reasons," which draws on his earlier work on criticism.[33]

In the latter discussion, Beardsley provides samples of critical statements in which critics praise Haydn's *Creation* for its boldness, originality, and unified conception; the finale of Bruckner's Fifth Symphony for its apocalyptic splendor; Pasolini's *The Gospel According to St. Matthew* for its bone-bare simplicity and honest treatment of the life of Jesus; Munch's *The Cry* for its unmatched expression of the Age of Anxiety; and, conversely, judged negatively a novel by Max Frisch because of its excessive detail and overdecoration. In other critical statements, a painting may be commended for being a striking example of the mannerist style, another for the likelihood of its inspiring religious fervor, while still others may receive favorable comment for their forceful condemnation of social ills or the moral uplift they provide. The prices paid for certain artworks are also sometimes taken as indicators of artistic value. Are all such assessments pertinent and justified?

It depends, Beardsley says, on the interest that one takes in an artwork. Since anything so complex as a work of art can be considered from more than one point of view, people may look for different kinds of value in works of art. These values fall into three groups, the first of which is *cognitive* value (see the schematic representation of critical reasons in Appendix II). Persons evince a cognitive interest when they probe works of art primarily for the knowledge or understanding they afford. We know that a work is being praised for its cognitive value when it is judged to be profound, to have something important to say, to convey a vivid image of its era, to impart a significant view of life, and so forth. High cognitive value may ensure an object the status of cultural monument and make it worth preserving, but cognitive value alone is not sufficient reason for saying a work of art is a good one.

The same is true of *moral* value and moral reasons. Music, for example, might reinforce piety and works of literature might strengthen character. Critics have also been known to say that artworks are uplifting and inspiring; that they are effective social criticism; that they promote desirable social and political ends; or that they are subversive. But, once more, "even if all these claims are admitted, they would not properly lead us to say that these works are good works of art."[34]

Having set aside reasons that clearly flow from a cognitive or a moral/social point of view, we are now left with reasons associated with the aesthetic point of view and the quest for aesthetic value. In Beardsley's view, aesthetic value is "the kind of value whose presence and degree we report when we say that the work is good or poor."[35] But reasons adduced in saying a work is good or poor are not relevant simply because a critic has expressed an aesthetic interest in it. Generally, reasons are relevant only when they provide support for the value judgment and also help explain why the judgment is true. Whether a reason is *aesthetically* relevant, however, depends additionally on a theory of aesthetic value. "If we hold . . . that the aesthetic value of an object is that value which it possesses in virtue of its capacity to provide an aesthetic experience, then certain consequences follow. For the only way to support such a judgment relevantly and cogently would be to point out features of the work that enable it to provide an experience having an aesthetic character."[36]

Before moving on to the category of distinctively *aesthetic* reasons, I will mention a few facets of Beardsley's approach that have once again been brought into view. First, he explicitly links his conception of aesthetic judgment to those of aesthetic experience and aesthetic value discussed in the preceding chapter, giving us further evidence of the scope and coherence of his theory. Second, he has formulated a standard for the relevance of reasons: they must both support and explain a judgment. Third, like Eaton and Crittenden, Beardsley is adamant that aesthetic reasons are acceptable only when they point to features in the work of art. Fourth, he has again maintained that relevant aesthetic reasons help explain why a judgment is *true,* which amounts to a much stronger position than that of Eaton and Crittenden (and, I might add, of most other aestheticians) who are content with the reasonableness and plausibility of critical judgments. (Beardsley asks those who say judgments and interpretations can only be plausible why it should be doubted that the reasons for thinking something plausible are true.)[37]

Relevant aesthetic reasons, then, are those that point to properties *in* the work of art. Yet critics are wont to say that an artwork is good or poor because it fulfills (or fails to fulfill) the artist's intention; because it is an example of successful (or unsuccessful) expression; because it is fresh and original (or hackneyed and trite), sincere (or insincere). It is clear that such reasons do not always refer to something found in the work. They point instead either to factors having to do with the artwork's origins, inception, or circumstances of production, for example, the artist's intention, provided it can be known, or his sincerity in creating the work. Or they suggest factors external to the work in other ways, for example, the body of traditional work in comparison with which the work's originality or freshness would be established. Statements about matters like these, that is, about the relations of an artwork to antecedent and external conditions, Beardsley terms *genetic* reasons. Such a reason may explain how a work came to have certain features, but "the genetic reason itself does not explain directly why the work is good, and it is therefore not a relevant reason."[38]

Similarly with *affective* reasons. These refer to psychological and other effects artworks may have on percipients. We infer an appeal to affective reasons when a critic declares that a work of art gives pleasure (or fails to please); is interesting (or dull); is exciting, moving, stirring; is shocking or has a powerful emotional impact. Yet instead of supporting an aesthetic judgment, affective reasons themselves stand in need of explanation: Just what in the work of art is responsible for these effects? Affective reasons then are also irrelevant to aesthetic criticism.

A sizable portion of the statements, reasons, and judgments typically met with in the criticism of works of art has now been set aside. What remain are "descriptions and interpretations of the work itself. . . . When given as reasons, such statements may be called *objective* reasons, since they draw our attention to the object itself and its own merits and defects. These are the reasons . . . that are properly the province of the critic" (emphasis added).[39] Still, objective critical reasons occur in a bewildering variety; hence Beardsley wondered whether further simplification was possible. Somewhat to his astonishment he discovered that these reasons too yield to order. He saw that they are not all on one level; some are subordinate to others. In the end he proposed three basic criteria or general reasons that are supported by relevant critical reasons and under which the features appealed to in relevant reasons may be subsumed. I quote the following dialogue not only to indicate how one of these basic criteria was arrived at but also because it can, I think, serve as an example of the kind of persuasive critical argument Crittenden had in mind.

> We ask the critic, for example, "What makes the Max Frisch novel so poor?" He replies, "Among other things, excessive detail." We ask again, "What is so bad about the detail? Why is it excessive? How does it help to make the work poor?" If he is cooperative, the critic may reply once more: "The detail is excessive because it detracts the reader from those elements in the work . . . that would otherwise give it a fairly high degree of unity," or perhaps, "The detail is excessive because it dissipates what would otherwise be strong dramatic and emotional qualities of the work."[40]

The objectionableness of the detail is explained by an appeal to more fundamental and general principles: that *unity* or *intensity* is desirable in a work of art.

Unity is thus the first of the general criteria. The canon of unity is appealed to when an artwork is judged to be well organized (or poorly organized), formally perfect (or flawed), or to have (or lack) an inner logic or structure or style. Anything that refers to how a work "hangs together" refers to its unity. The second criterion is *complexity,* and we find it implicit in reasons such as these: the work is developed on a large scale; it is rich in contrasts (or lacks variety and is repetitious); it is subtle and finely articulated (or crude). The third criterion is *intensity* of human regional quality ("human regional quality" and the other terms Beardsley assigned to the parts and elements of artworks are listed in Appendix II). Intensity, which we may understand generally as dramatic character, is the criterion invoked by a finding that a work of art is vital (or insipid); forceful and vivid (or weak and pale); beautiful (or ugly); tender, ironic, tragic, graceful, delicate, richly comic, etc.

Objections have been raised that the three canons (or criteria or general reasons) of unity, complexity, and intensity of regional quality are too imprecise and limiting. Beardsley admits that the frequently metaphorical and specialized language used by critics makes it difficult at times to decide what sort of reason we have and where it fits. Yet he thinks he has not forced reasons into categories where they do not belong and that others who apply these criteria with similar circumspection will find them not only sufficiently well defined to be used in this general way but also to have meaning across the arts. What tends to be unifying in a painting is, of course, not identical to what tends to be unifying in a poem or musical composition. Still, Beardsley thinks that critics seem to mean approximately the same thing when they say that one poem or one painting is more unified than another poem or painting.

While the three canons are generalizable in the way indicated, the subsidiary reasons that support them are context-bound. The details found excessive in the Frisch novel, for example, might not detract from another work. Or an arrangement of shapes and colors that lent distinction to one painting might be garish or jarring in another. The basic criteria also differ from subsidiary reasons in always being one-way, that is, pointing to a positive judgment. "Unity, complexity, and intensity of regional quality never count against a work of art . . . but always count in favor of it, to the extent to which they are present."[41] This bold assertion holds up even in cases that appear to contradict one of the canons. On closer examination we realize that a critic who, for example, praises an artwork for its simplicity is not claiming it is good because it lacks complexity. Rather, simplicity in this instance probably refers to a tight, straight-forward organization (unity) or to a clear, immediately discernible human regional quality (intensity). A painting praised for its muted color scheme is not good because it lacks intensity. Instead, its subdued colors may ensure subtlety to the artwork (complexity) or add to the cohesiveness of its design (unity). In short, reasons may sometimes need to be narrowly scrutinized and restated to preserve the one-directionality of the three basic criteria.

One misunderstanding must be averted: from the fact that the three critical criteria are traceable to good-making features of artworks we should not conclude that a work of art must meet, or satisfy to a significant extent, all three before it can be judged good. An artistically excellent work is not necessarily highly unified, complex, and intense, for deficiency in one of the categories may be balanced by strengths in the remaining two. A lack of unity, for example, need not detract from a work that is highly complex and possesses intense regional qualities; a relaxed organization may in fact sometimes underscore these positive qualities. Compensation among the categories has its limits, however. Just as a work of art will never be poor because it exhibits unity, complexity, and intensity of regional human quality, so it is very unlikely ever to be good if it has deficiencies in all three areas.

I have seen the pedagogical merits of Beardsley's classification of critical reasons demonstrated time and again over the years. College-of-education graduate students find the scheme a valuable device for understanding the different kinds of judgment that can be made about works of art and the sorts of reason that can be given in support of them. After some instruction in the use of the scheme, students not only become more thoughtful and rational in their own remarks about artworks, but they also learn rather quickly to discriminate among reasons relating to cognitive, moral/social, and aesthetic values and to discern references to the antecedents, the features, and the effects of art objects. (Just as easily they learn to distinguish among biographical, autobiographical, emotive, and technical criticism, to borrow Peter Kivy's terminology, where "emotive criticism" encompasses what Beardsley calls the intensity of regional qualities.)[42] As a welcome side-effect of the study and application of the critical categories, students develop a deeper appreciation of the relevance of aesthetics to a critical evaluation of artworks as well as to other dealings with art.

A controversial aspect of Beardsley's approach, which I incorporate in my teaching for purely heuristic purposes, is his belief that critical judgments can be true or false. I do not promise that we will ever arrive at the one correct interpretation or evaluation of a complex work of art; it may forever elude us. But as an antidote against an "anything goes" relativism in which so many students are steeped I hold out correctness of interpretation and evaluation as an ideal to strive for, and as a possibility that is, in fact, realized when critical consensus does obtain. It is a strategy that challenges students to persevere in their critical inquiries and not to slacken until they have done the best they can in understanding a work of art.

After what may appear to be a wholesale endorsement of Beardsley's scheme, I now enter a few clarifications and one modification. Some uneasiness may have been caused by Beardsley's having ruled cognitive values and reasons irrelevant to critical judgments of artistic merit, especially since in the preceding chapter the insights and understandings available through art, or the cognitive effects of artworks, were listed among the considerations that justify teaching art in the schools. The impression may have been created that Beardsley divorces the aesthetic from the cognitive realm, that he permits too much to slip through his net of critical relevance, including all and sundry matters cognitive. Some aestheticians take issue with him on this point, and I can appreciate why they do. Morris Weitz, for example, has persuasively argued for the contribution that the cognitive value of a work of literature makes to that work's artistic goodness.[43] And in his later writings Beardsley himself (under the influence of E. H. Gombrich, Rudolf Arnheim, and Nelson Goodman) increasingly acknowledged the cognitive dimension of art and aesthetic experience.[44] We might do well, therefore, to examine more closely what the demotion of cognitive reasons, that is, their irrelevance to critical judgment, does and does not entail.

It does not affect the status of aesthetic perception or percipience as a form of cognitive activity; nothing said on that score has been controverted. Nor has the importance of the cognitive background—the knowledge or apperceptive mass that one brings to aesthetic experience and evaluation—been diminished in any way.[45] I continue to stress, as I have done for twenty-five years, the contributions of art history, aesthetics, and criticism to the teaching of art and to emphasize the significance of several parent disciplines to arts education.[46] I believe that one should engage a work of art with what Arthur Danto calls a rich sense of the art world, by which he means a knowledge of art's theory and history.[47] And I continue to draw on such fruitful and suggestive notions as Harry Broudy's "thinking with,"[48] which derives from Michael Polanyi's "tacit knowing,"[49] and Joseph Novak's theory of assimilation learning (the latter to be discussed in Chapter 5).

In what way, then, might the classification of critical reasons be modified or supplemented? I would assign to cognitive reasons a more explicit function in aesthetic judgment, or perhaps I should say that I would make the function they already have in Beardsley's scheme more explicit. Not, however, by elevating cognitive reasons to the same level as objective aesthetic reasons or even the three categories of general reasons. Rather, cognitive reasons may be mentioned more prominently among subordinate and hence context-limited reasons; that is to say, the cognitive value an artwork is found to have, no matter how great its magnitude, would not by itself be sufficient to secure a positive aesthetic judgment for the work. But that cognitive value could contribute to, or boost, one of the basic critical reasons—most likely complexity or intensity of human regional qualities—that do support a critical judgment directly. Let us suppose a painting is claimed to provide insight into the suffering and hopelessness of nineteenth-century industrial workers. If the work is visually complex, then the cognitive elements add another level of complexity and thus help to support the finding that the painting is good by virtue of its complexity. Or the sympathetic rendering of suffering may augment the work's human regional quality and thus contribute to the criterion of intensity that counts in the work's favor. But cognitive value cannot save a work that has nothing else "going for it." On the contrary, since they are limited by context, the same cognitive reasons that help support a favorable evaluation in one work of art may be assessed against another. For example, a painting that was weak in all the other categories but hammered home its message of hopelessness and suffering with blatancy and obviousness would be found aesthetically wanting and be dismissed for being overly didactic.

Given these emendations, Beardsley's classification of critical reasons may be recommended for its pedagogical worth. Any teacher wanting to convey an idea of critical evaluation would do well to start with his coherent, clear, and comprehensive scheme. I have found nothing in the literature of aesthetics of comparable helpfulness to arts educators. What is more, a teacher may adopt Beardsley's critical categories as a class-room methodology without subscribing to the entire theoretical apparatus from which they evolved—though there would be definite advantages to doing so. One is the scheme's empirical grounding in judgments actually made by critics. And another is the spirit that suffuses Beardsley's entire work. As said before, Beardsley always accorded prominence to the human factor, that is, the benefit and value individuals derive from encounters with art; his thinking should therefore be especially congenial to educators. It is after all the job of teachers to induct the young into domains of human value.

Although my own approach to teaching art has becomne more catholic over the years, I admit at one time to having been something of a "strict constructionist" where critical canons, and Beardsley's aesthetics generally, were concerned. My programmatic intent was to redirect the interest of art educators to the work of art itself, narrowly conceived, as the main locus of aesthetic value. This was done to counteract the overemphasis in the field of arts education on creative and performing activities.

Another very important application of Beardsley's scheme, apart from classroom instruction, should be mentioned. This is the use that students trained in the categories of critical reasons will make of them in their adult lives. It will be recalled that Kaelin, among others, envisions as the ultimate goal of aesthetic education a critically astute citizenry. We want students not only to appreciate art and to walk proudly with their cultural heritage, but also to make informed choices and decisions in the contemporary art world. Beardsley's scheme of critical reasons can help them do that. We live in a contentious and visually oriented age when images, many of them purported to be works of art, often carry the weight of polemic. Our repositories of aesthetic value, our great museums and other cultural institutions, often invite the public to view objects which serve primarily moral/social interests and which are praised by critics for aesthetically irrelevant reasons. It is also quite common today for works to achieve critical acclaim for genetic reasons, for example, the artist's race, gender, or cultural origin, which cannot in themselves establish an artwork's aesthetic merit. We want students to know how to deal with these situations. An aesthetically emancipated person is one who, while perhaps in complete sympathy with the cognitive interests served by an artwork, still demands or conducts an aesthetically relevant critical assessment and is ready to declare a work artistically inferior if it fails to meet relevant criteria.

CHAPTER 4

Examples of aesthetic criticism

> What is distinctive . . . of criticism is
> that it aims to discover those features
> of a thing that call for admiration or
> condemnation. . . . Thus there are two
> levels to the critic's task, each involving
> the other. We ask the critic to give us,
> as definitely as possible . . . *critical
> judgments,* or evaluations of artworks as
> wholes. And we ask for what might be
> called *normative explanations:* calling
> attention to features whose presence ac-
> counts for the thing's being better or less
> good than it might be or than something
> else is—from a certain point of view.
> *Monroe C. Beardsley*[1]

Chapter 3 distinguished aesthetic object and critical activity concepts and divided the latter into exploratory and evaluative skills. These distinctions, though I think they are useful, are somewhat arbitrary, for the possession of aesthetic skills (whether exploratory or evaluative) presupposes a grasp of aesthetic object concepts. A work's sense, after all, is constituted by a work's interanimation of elements, relations, and qualities, and it is this sense that appreciative finesse attempts to detect. More will be said about the teaching and learning of aesthetic skills in the next chapter, but at this point the discussion of aesthetic criticism needs to be made more concrete.

The major purpose of this chapter is thus the discussion of actual examples of criticism. In selecting these examples, I have in general accepted Beardsley's notion of aesthetic criticism as criticism from the aesthetic point of view and art criticism as the aesthetic criticism of artworks. I go somewhat beyond Beardsley, however, by insisting on only one necessary condition for art criticism to qualify as aesthetic criticism: that whatever other values critics may look for in artworks, they must evince an overriding concern with a work's aesthetic features; otherwise it would be difficult to see how they could lead us to recognize an artworks' *artistic* goodness (or poorness). I have therefore taken license to consider different kinds of criticism—for example, historical and psychological criticism—so long as they take an interest in, and lead us to an appreciation of, aesthetic value and accomplishment.

The necessary condition I have set for aesthetic criticism—that irrespective of what other values it may note, there must be a pervasive interest in aesthetic value—certainly seems to have been met by the six critics whose works I summarize in order to convey the nature of aesthetic criticism: Lord Kenneth Clark, Meyer Schapiro, and Leo Steinberg, each an art historian and critic; Hilton Kramer, an art and cultural critic; Stanley Kauffmann, a film, literary, and theater critic; and Richard

Wollheim, a philosopher of art. In their different ways they all pay heed to the principal assumptions, use the concepts, and engage in the typical activities of aesthetic criticism. One consideration that guided the selection of these critical writings was that each, in addition to being an exemplar of aesthetic criticism, also illustrates some point or problem with particular clarity. I will explain briefly. Kenneth Clark's description of Vermeer's *A Painter in His Studio* stands out for the way it directs us to those features in the painting that justify our admiration of it. Meyer Schapiro's discussion of Cézanne's *Quarry and Mont Sainte-Victoire* can be called an exemplification of aesthetic vision itself. One might even say that if aesthetic criticism had not yet appeared in critical discourse, the attempt to describe Cézanne's mature work would have necessitated its emergence. Schapiro also shows how knowledge of art history, of an artist's life and time, and of aesthetic theory can blend in an appreciation of the legacy of one of the giants of modern painting. Leo Steinberg's discussion of the plight of the public for contemporary art and of his own dilemma in trying to come to terms with *Target with Four Faces* by Jasper Johns is fraught with special significance for the teaching of art. His critique was also chosen because Johns's work seems to question, at least at first glance, the relevance of the three master concepts of this volume: the work of art, aesthetic experience, and aesthetic criticism. It is not clear, for example, that the works Steinberg discusses are intended to occasion aesthetic experience or that they lend themselves to aesthetic criticism. Yet I contend that aesthetic criticism is precisely what Steinberg engages in insofar as he grounds his judgment in what can only be called the work's aesthetic features. Steinberg's attempt to deal with Johns's puzzling work also brings us face to face with so-called anti-art and forces us to become more self-conscious about our own critical assumptions, categories, and concepts. We witness such self-consciousness in Steinberg's remark that he found knowledge of the past more of a hindrance than a help in his effort to understand Johns. Steinberg's writing can also serve as a convenient bridge to a basically pedagogical question: How can anything new be understood when one does not possess the concepts with which to approach it? How, in other words, is aesthetic education possible?

Hilton Kramer's evaluation of the artistic achievement of Anselm Kiefer, a contemporary German painter, supplies a good example of a crucial fact of criticism: that an artist whose work has been praised for its strong moral vision must still submit to an estimation of the aesthetic merit of his work. The appeal of Kiefer's moral vision notwithstanding, the critic, thinks Kramer, still has the task of illuminating what it is in his work that leads us to experience it as art. The same observation also holds for Stanley Kauffmann's criticism of Antonioni's film *Red Desert*. Although Kauffmann's principal criteria for judging film are avowedly moral, it is apparent from the way he describes *Red Desert* that the moral value he discovers in the film is inextricably entwined with the film's form and technique. Finally, in Richard Wollheim's critical redescription of Poussin's *The Ashes of Phocion Collected by His Widow* we have an example of what could perhaps be called psychoanalytical aesthetic criticism, for here the interpretation of the pictorial meaning of the *Phocion* painting is based on a demonstration of the interweaving of psychological insight with aesthetic expressive import. On my view, then, Wollheim's psychologically oriented description satisfies the minimal requirement of aesthetic criticism.

Kenneth Clark: Art and energy of spirit

Kenneth Clark's *Looking at Pictures*[2] consists of 16 appreciative responses to Italian, Spanish, Dutch, Flemish, French, and English masterpieces of painting. All are lengthened essays that first appeared in the London *Sunday Times* and are dedicated to Roger Fry, from whom, Clark says, he and his generation learned how much can be discovered in a picture after that first moment of amateurish delight has passed. The essays, in brief, were written for the educated layman or nonspecialist and are intended to bring readers to an awareness of what is artistically unique and admirable about the works selected. Clark also provides some observations on his own method for looking at pictures.

After setting aside conventional myths about intuitively knowing what one likes, Clark talks about the significant increments of understanding and enjoyment that are to be gained from learning how to interrogate a picture. He prefaces his remarks by saying that "the meaning of a great work of art, or the little of it that we can understand, must be related to our own life in such a way as to increase our energy of spirit. Looking at pictures requires active participation, and, in the early stages, a certain amount of discipline."[3]

One of the virtues of Clark's discussion is his description of the typical course of his feelings and thoughts before a painting. He remarks that just as paintings differ in character, so do his patterns of response. But whether he is attracted to a work by its subject, the first sensuous impression it makes, or sometimes knowledge about the artist, on the whole, he says that his feelings "fall into the same pattern of *impact, scrutiny, recollection,* and *renewal*"[4] (emphasis added). A first general impression, which is usually a function of a painting's relationships of tone, area, shape, and color, is followed by a period of careful inspection, for first impressions can often be misleading. During this phase of scrutiny, attention tends to center on such things as color harmonies, the quality of drawing, and ultimately representational aspects (all of the paintings Clark describes are representational). Technical skill when conspicuous may also capture his notice momentarily, but attention soon returns to a search for a dominant motive or root idea from which the picture derives its overall effect.

There is a limit, however, on how long the senses can operate at a high pitch of intensity, and thus attention must constantly be fortified with nips of information. As Clark puts it, "The value of historical criticism is that it keeps the attention fixed on the work while the senses have time to get a second wind." Intellectual preoccupations, in other words, keep the eye unconsciously engaged. Finally, the pattern of responses is completed when the self becomes saturated with the work: this happens when the things of everyday life come to be seen in a fresh and unfamiliar light—when the real world, we may say, is seen in terms of the world of the work, to use Goodman's terminology.

In short, I take Clark's account to be exemplary in confirming both the values of aesthetic experience (Beardsley's object directedness, detached affect, active discovery, etc.) and the techniques and patterns of aesthetic criticism (description and analysis, interpretation, etc.). As for the distinction between exploratory and evaluative criticism, Clark seems to be practicing the former, since his aim is clearly to point out what is worth seeing, aesthetically speaking; the question of the excellence of Vermeer's work is not really an issue. Clark thus provides a model of exploratory criticism for the teaching of aesthetic criticism in the schools, the objective of which, once more, is the cultivation of intense aesthetic experience, or what Clark calls energy of spirit.

Keeping in mind Clark's general pattern of response—impact, scrutiny, recollection, and renewal—I have selected the description of his reaction to Vermeer's *A Painter in His Studio* (c. 1665, Kunsthistorisches Museum, Vienna) to present more concretely a picture of the aesthetic critic in action.[5]

The initial impact of Vermeer's painting on Clark consisted of the highly pleasurable sensations he derived from the painting's quality of light and atmosphere. For example, he likens the rippling and flowing effect of the daylight that falls on the model in the picture and passes over the map of Holland on the wall to "an incoming tide over the sand." And in noticing this quality of light we enjoy "a moment of heightened perception, a simple pleasure of the eye. . . ." Yet that is merely a first impression. (Such qualities, we may say, are comparable to Aaron Copland's first plane of musical listening, the purely sensuous plane of sound, in this instance of a quality of light; or to C. S. Peirce's notion of Firstness that features the qualitative immediacy of things.) Closer scrutiny, however, reveals complicating factors between the model and some of the other objects disposed in the pictorial space, for example, "the swag of curtain, the bizarre silhouette of the painter and the objects on the table, foreshortened almost out of recognition." Paying attention to such details leads us to perceive their relations and prompts the

Figure 4.1. Vermeer, *The Artist in His Studio*, 1665/6. Canvas, 47¼″ × 39⅜″. Kunsthistorisches Museum, Vienna. Marburg/Art Resource, N.Y.

realization that this is in truth how we tend to see things under certain conditions. When Clark attends to details, he also recalls the ways in which other artists have handled them. He is reminded, for example, of Uccello and Seurat, who were similarly fascinated by curious shapes of all kinds, but they differed from Vermeer in their tonality and irregularity of shape. Digressions like these, one supposes, are instances of what Clark calls art-historical nips of information that give the senses a chance to regroup. But attention soon returns to the picture itself, in this case, to the studio and its peculiar quality of space. The very deliberate placement of the objects in the room suggests a concern for a certain kind of order and arrangement, that was perhaps influenced by Vermeer's profession as an art dealer, an occupation that requires the careful presentation of artworks.

Clark goes on to observe Vermeer's preference in his painting for single figures and his interest in the ways a scene from everyday life can take on allegorical significance. Customarily, allegorical meaning is conveyed by specific objects and figures in a work, but in the case of the *Studio* painting, the subject itself is the creation of an allegory: the model is accoutered to represent Fame, and her figure will fill the painter's canvas shown in the picture. But what an image of Fame! She is restrained and withdrawn and, says Clark, in perfect concordance with Vermeer's own personality. Indeed, Clark remarks that Vermeer was quintessentially the artist who withdraws from the world. He painted primarily for his own pleasure, and there is no evidence that his works ever left the studio, except for this very *Studio* painting, which was on deposit at a baker's against unpaid bills.

Continuing to respond to the work, Clark shifts his attention to the "obsessive character" of the painter shown with his back toward us who is wearing a flamboyant costume and looks, says Clark, "like a gigantic cockroach." It is not certain whether the painter is Vermeer himself or a model, but Clark thinks the painting does invite speculation about Vermeer's character. We are told that Vermeer had a remarkable capacity for recording visual appearances, "an eye which felt no need to confirm its sensations by touch," as had been the usual way during the Renaissance. The special effects Vermeer creates through, for example, "the way in which highlights are rendered as small globular dots of paint" bring his distinctive painting technique to our notice. And so Clark's dialectic of criticism proceeds.

On these short excursions into historical comparison, biography, and guesses about the artist's character Clark gathers information that, while it may not be immediately verified in the features of the objects Vermeer painted, is presented with a view to helping us see the work under inspection more fully and more intelligently and to returning perception to the qualities and significance of the work itself. What, then, is the ultimate value of Vermeer's work, what are the qualities for which we continue to esteem it? Among the characteristics we prize in Vermeer is "his flawless sense of interval," the way in which "every shape is interesting in itself, and also perfectly related to its neighbors, both in space and on the picture plane." Vermeer's is a vision that in effect sees pattern and depth simultaneously. In this respect his work resembles the harmonious finality of Mondrian's paintings. Furthermore, "Everything in Vermeer's picture is ultimately known and loved." We may say that in this instance painting reflects an enlightened cherishing of the world, an understanding of objects gained by holding them dear.[6] Finally, color assumes symbolic meaning: in this studio, writes Clark, "the blue dress and yellow book of Fame, quietly established before the silvery grey of the map, are as much as assertion of faith as the blood-red tunic of Christ in El Greco's *Espolio*" (which Clark also discusses in the same volume). The work's magnificent complexity notwithstanding, it is finally the mysterious rendering of daylight that remains Vermeer's signal achievement.

Clark's account of the *Studio* painting by Vermeer illustrates how description, analysis, characterization, and interpretation interact in aesthetic criticism and shows what a critic would have to do if his estimate of a work's value were questioned or challenged: he would point to the artwork's qualities in support of his judgment and in doing so would be deploying both aesthetic object and critical activity concepts. If we think of Clark as borrowing Beardsley's formula for critical reasoning—*x* is good (is poor) *because* . . .—he might be understood as saying that Vermeer's *Studio* painting (*x*) is remarkable *because* of its light, atmosphere, color, formal harmonies, and aura of mystery, all of which Clark had specified in some detail. Since Clark's critical performance is also noteworthy for the way in which his knowledge and expertise fueled his sustained engagement with a work of art, it provides a clear indication of how art history and art theory (or a sense of the art world) function in aesthetic criticism. Arts educators reflecting on the relevance of the discipline of art criticism to their field would do well to take Clark's writings as a model.

Meyer Schapiro: Cézanne and aesthetic vision

Another instructive example of aesthetic criticism written for the intelligent and interested observer of art is Meyer Schapiro's monograph *Paul Cézanne*.[7] It contains an insightful essay on the life and art of Cézanne plus appreciative descriptions of about fifty of Cézanne's major paintings. The project is similar to Clark's except that Schapiro concentrates on just one artist and his oeuvre.

While in his introductory essay Schapiro does not reflect on his mode of response to works of art, it is apparent that it exhibits a pattern similar to Clark's; it consists of moments of impact, scrutiny, recollection, and renewal. In discussing Cézanne's *Quarry and Mont Sainte-Victoire* (1898-1900, Baltimore Museum of Art),[8] to take merely one representative example from Cézanne's mature period, Schapiro first observes how, unlike earlier versions of the peak in which the view is suspended above the valley, Cézanne in this painting places between the observer and the peak an impressive abyss (or quarry) across which the viewer must look, the effect created being that of a dramatic landscape "filled with striving, titantic energies." Moreover, everything is seemingly staged for our contemplation. Schapiro writes that "like a heroic sculpture" the mountain "is set on a gigantic pedestal of rock enclosed by trees." From there he goes on to describe the character of the mountain peak itself, the ways, we might say, in which the sculpture is rooted to its base and positioned by surrounding foliage and quarry. Cézanne's new way of achieving the illusion of recession into space without recourse to traditional perspective methods is also remarked. As one moves into the background, objects become larger, not smaller, and elements that ostensibly belong to design in depth are subtly interlocked with surface design; for example, the foliage of the tree in the right-hand corner interlocks with the sky, although its trunk reveals its actual position to be in the foreground. Further unification is achieved through color harmonies of slightly modified blues, greens, and oranges. The qualities of the blue sky and orange rocks, however, constitute the strongest contrasting chord of the painting, while a scale of lavender, rose, and purple tones extend across the same depth. Overall, writes Schapiro, "There is a beautiful order in the concept of the objects."

Once again we see the interrelation of description, analysis, characterization, and interpretation in the service of rendering visible the peculiar excellences of a painting. Aspects, qualities, or counters of the objective phenomenal field are perceived and rendered accessible to perception. Many of the features we associate with the conditions and character of aesthetic contemplation, moreover, are present. A complex stratified object is abstracted from an environmental system and framed for detached perceptual scrutiny that requires long concentrated vision in order to ensure the appreciation of the beauty of the work's overall construction and order.

Elsewhere I have remarked how we can read Schapiro's descriptions of Cézanne's interpretations of Mont Sainte-Victoire as both exploratory criticism and evaluative criticism.[9] It is as if Schapiro has himself explored the paintings for their several excellences, rendered a judgment of their qualities, and now invites others into these remarkable fields of aesthetic value. The same description, however, could also be regarded as evaluative criticism in the sense that having declared Cézanne's works excellent, Schapiro proceeds to argue in defense of such a judgment by pointing to the reasons that ground it. It is as if Schapiro too was fitting his judgment into the schema suggested by Beardsley: "*x* is good (or poor) *because*. . . ." Indeed, one might almost think Cézanne created his work to illustrate Beardsley's claim that, when carefully examined, most critical statements about a work of art's aesthetic value can be grouped into statements about its degree of unity (for example, "*x* is well organized, formally perfect, and has an inner logic and structure and style"), its complexity (for example, "*x* is stable, imaginative, and rich in contrasts"), and its intensity (for example, "*x* is vivid, forceful, and full of vitality" or "*x* is tender, delicate, and ironic"). In Schapiro's description of Cézanne's *Quarry* painting, we find all three critical standards—unity, complexity, and intensity—appealed to. Schapiro speaks, for example, of the painting's "titanic energies" (appeal to intensity as a standard), "complex, dynamic form" (appeal to complexity and intensity), "a beautiful order" (appeal to intensity and unity), and so forth. Again, Schapiro is literally saying that Cézanne's *Quarry* painting

Figure 4.2.   Paul Cézanne, *Mont Sainte-Victoire Seen from the Bibemus Quarry*, 1898–1900. Oil on canvas; 25⅛" × 31½". The Baltimore Museum of Art: The Cone Collection, formed by Dr. Claribel Cone and Miss Etta Cone of Baltimore, Maryland, BMA 1950. 19b.

is good *because* of its titanic energies, complex interplay of form and order, and marvelously controlled structure. There is a great deal of support, in other words, for Beardsley's claim that critics in making value judgments of a work's aesthetic value often rely on such canons of judgment as unity, complexity, and intensity. So far as Schapiro's interpretation of Cézanne's mature accomplishments is concerned, Schapiro reiterates the point several times that Cézanne's conception of his objects requires of the spectator the same kind of intense perception that Cézanne exercised in recording his own vision. Cézanne's "is the art of a man who dwells with his perceptions, steeping himself serenely in this world of the eye, though he is often stirred." Indeed, says Schapiro, "because this art demands of us a long concentrated vision, it is like music as a mode of experience—not as an art of time, however, but as an art of grave attention, an attitude called out only by certain works of the great composers."[10]

Regarding Schapiro's critical mode, it only remains to be said that, as in the case of Clark, knowledge of art history, aesthetic theory, and Cézanne's life and circumstances are never discussed for their intrinsic interest alone but for their use in understanding and appreciating Cézanne's distinctive artistic accomplishment—the perfection of his aesthetic way of seeing. "His tendency," writes Schapiro, "coincides with what philosophers have defined as the aesthetic attitude in general: the experience of the qualities of things without regard to their use or cause or consequence."[11]

We are once more treated to intimations of possibility for the teaching of aesthetic criticism in the schools. Schapiro too provides a model of analysis that reveals the special qualities and accomplishment of works of art. He provides an example of what Henry Aiken in the next chapter calls recreative admiring appreciation.

Leo Steinberg: Art and existential encounter

Other Criteria: Confrontations with Twentieth-Century Art[12] by Leo Steinberg contains a number of intriguing insights by an art historian and art critic whose scholarly special interest is Renaissance and Baroque art. In his opening essay, "Contemporary Art and the Plight of Its Public," Steinberg defines a member of a public functionally, that is, as a role played by someone into which he is thrust or in which he finds himself as the result of a given experience. Signac rejecting Matisse's *Joy of Life,* Matisse disliking Picasso's *Les Demoiselles d'Avignon,* and the Cubists denouncing Duchamp's *Nude Descending a Staircase* illustrate Steinberg's notion of persons playing the role of member of a public. "Plight," on the other hand, refers to "the shock of discomfort, or the bewilderment or the anger or the boredom which some people always feel, and all people sometimes feel, when confronted with an unfamiliar new style."[13] The art of the last hundred years has made this condition an endemic reaction to artistic creation. Habits of expectation and response have been constantly disturbed, and change has become the norm.

Steinberg himself is not immune to the discomfort caused by unfamiliarity, as the recounting of his effort to come to grips with an exhibition of paintings by Jasper Johns, and in particular with a work titled *Target with Four Faces* (1955, The Museum of Modern Art, New York), indicates. What was the character of Steinberg's plight as a member of Johns's public?

Steinberg writes that Johns's paintings were frankly puzzling. Painted in either oil or encaustic, they consisted of variations on four themes: numbers, letters, the American flag, and targets. There were also pictures consisting of a wire coat hanger, a canvas to which another canvas was stuck, and yet another with a wooden drawer extending from it, all painted either gray or black. The reaction of the public to such works ranged from enthusiastic acceptance to outright ridicule, but even those who could accommodate such ostensible waywardness could not provide an adequate explanation of what value these works had.

Steinberg's responses are interesting for the quality of introspection they reveal in his own critical disposition. Initially the paintings bored and depressed him; he resented being given tow and paraffin instead of

Figure 4.3.   Jasper Johns, *Target with Four Faces,* 1955. Encaustic on newspaper over canvas, 26″ × 26″, surmounted by four tinted plaster faces in wood box with hinged front. Overall dimensions with box open, 33⅜″ × 26″ × 3″. Collection, The Museum of Modern Art, New York. Gift of Mr. and Mrs. Robert C. Scull.

the usual aesthetic nourishment. But in his response he recognized the typical Philistine's attitude toward anything radically different, and so he reflected on the causes of his negative reaction, especially to the *Target* work. After detailing its contents, Steinberg reports that the sense of deprivation the work induced in him was accompanied by a sense of the potential of such art for adversely affecting the creation and appreciation of all other art. Suddenly, he said, modern painters like DeKooning and Kline no longer seemed daring or radical; they became one with Rembrandt and Giotto in being mere painters of illusion. For in the *Target* work there was no illusion, no metamorphosis of subject, no magic of medium. Everything was just what it was, point blank as it were, and nothing else. Yet artistic status had been conferred on it by virtue of its being exhibited in an artistic context. Still, where was the presence of what we call artistic imagination?

Consistent with Clark's pattern of response, Steinberg kept returning to the work until he thought he began to get the hang of it. It impressed him as being an uncanny inversion of values that conveyed a feeling of solitude more intense than anything he had ever seen in any depiction of desolation. Not only were the organic and inorganic reduced to the same level with mindless inhumanity or indifference, so were all the subjective markers of space, of thereness and hereness. The target is "here" and not where it normally is, "there," while the faces are "there" and thus prevented from performing their usual function in human consciousness. This positioning in effect obliterates normal human relations. All of this, says Steinberg, gives rise to a feeling of desolate waiting; nothing will ever happen to the things in the work; the target will not be shot at, and the human faces will not commune. Nor will drawers ever open, clothes ever hang on hangers, etc. The work suggests a poignant absence from a humanly made environment, a landscape as it were of discarded objects no longer having any function, or a city lacking all life. Perhaps we may say that the world of Johns's pictures is reminiscent of Giorgio de Chirico's metaphysical paintings, but minus the techniques, illusion, space, and minimal signs of human life. Or perhaps we may say, recalling some of Beardsley's remarks, that the pictures reveal a world devoid of those human aesthetic qualities that make the earth appear a more welcoming place and give artistic creation one of its principal justifications. In the world pictured by Johns the human account is closed and bankrupt; the human imprint is absent. (But conjectures along these lines are, I suppose, subject to as much doubt as that Steinberg experienced.) Steinberg's plight, in other words, becomes ours as well. At this point, Steinberg deserves quoting at some length:

What I have said—was it *found* in the pictures or read into them? Does it accord with the painter's intention? Does it tally with other people's experience, to reassure me that my feelings are sound? I don't know. I can see that these pictures don't necessarily look like art, which has been known to solve far more difficult problems. I don't know whether they are art at all, whether they are great, or good, or likely to go up in price. And whatever experience of painting I've had in the past seems as likely to hinder me as to help. I am challenged to estimate the aesthetic value of, say, a drawer stuck into a canvas. But nothing I've ever seen can teach me how this is to be done. I am alone with this thing, and it is up to me to evaluate it in the absence of available standards. The value which I shall put on this painting tests my personal courage. Here I can discover whether I am prepared to sustain the collision with a novel experience. Am I escaping it by being overly analytical? Have I been eavesdropping on conversations? Trying to formulate certain meanings seen in this art—are they designed to demonstrate something about myself or are they authentic experience?

They are without end, these questions, and their answers are nowhere in storage. It is a kind of self-analysis that a new image can throw you into and for which I am grateful. I am left in a state of anxious uncertainty by the painting, about painting, about myself. And I suspect that this is all right. In fact, I have little confidence in people who habitually, when exposed to new works of art, know what is great and what will last.[14]

From an educational theorist's standpoint, there are a number of things that can be said about Steinberg's reflections. But let us first conclude his account. Though he didn't like Johns's pictures or relish their potential effect on the rest of art, he was nonetheless grateful for having discovered what a new work can do for one willing to risk the anxiety that an authentic engagement with it might produce, to chance a genuine existential encounter. Such an encounter can result in the benefit of self-discovery, and in this regard the experience of Johns's work parallels many situations in real life.

With Steinberg, however, we may ask whether it is really art that Johns created or something else, perhaps, as some writers have suggested, statements *about* art but not art in any intelligible sense. Accordingly, was Steinberg's description and assessment really an instance of *aesthetic* criticism? In short, Johns's work, and other comparable pieces, seems to question the conventional wisdom we take for granted in experiencing and talking and writing about works of art. Certainly, as I said, Johns's work casts doubt on the master concepts of this essay: the work of art, aesthetic experience, and aesthetic criticism. By inhibiting aesthetic response, Johns's paintings appear to nullify aesthetic experience and to render aesthetic criticism void. But only, I think, until we take a closer look.

For example, Steinberg does refer to the "commanding presence" of Johns's work (which suggests a degree of intensity) and its workmanlike construction (always a source of aesthetic interest). Steinberg's struggle to make sense of Johns's productions was carried forward by a feeling of detached involvement and ended in a sense of active discovery, both of which are features of aesthetic experience. And Steinberg would not have been able to write as much and as eloquently about Johns as he did if his work were not sufficiently complex. Unity is provided for by a number of integrating elements, for example, choice of subject, technique of painting or construction, and color preference. Organized complexity? Unity in variety? Perhaps not so much as we are accustomed to. This leaves intensity of expression or dramatic character, and it is precisely this category of features that Steinberg found so disturbingly compelling about Johns's work: the feeling of the absence of the human, of desolate waiting, of intense isolation. What then of enjoyment, gratification, consummatory value, the positive affective aspects of aesthetic experience? The moral of Steinberg's existential encounter is precisely that initial dislike and resentment can be converted into admiration and appreciation. So we conclude that Johns's *Target with Four Faces* is an aesthetic object after all, capable of affording aesthetic experience. Its peculiar excellences do not force the abandonment of the master concepts of this essay. Moreover, Steinberg's piece contains all the acts and phases we associate with aesthetic criticism: description, analysis, characterization, interpretation, and evaluation.

We might pause for a moment longer over the import Steinberg eventually assigned to Johns's work. It will be recalled that Steinberg asked himself whether "a sense of desolate waiting" counts as the meaning of the work. Even if we accept it as such, is this an objective interpretation? The issue need not be settled here, if indeed it could be done to everyone's satisfaction, for it is one of the problems that continue to animate contemporary aesthetic theorizing. All we have to recognize is that Steinberg meets the conditions for responsible criticism suggested by Leavis and Trilling—the acceptance of the intellectual obligation to try to set aside personal bias or ideological predisposition in an effort to understand the object as it really is. In this respect Steinberg's dialectical encounter with Johns is exemplary of the critical stance proposed in this essay. He brings a highly developed understanding of art (of art's theory and history) to the task of making aesthetic sense of a puzzling artwork and reports on the humanistic value—the sharpened perception and enlarged understanding—that can arise from the collision of diametrically opposed conceptions of art. Steinberg's claim that his knowledge of art was more a hindrance than a help turns out to have been hyperbolic, for without such a background he would not have been able to recognize what the Johns work was *not;* with it, he could (to use Heath's statement about concepts from the previous chapter) recognize a noninstance of x and proceed to explore alternative possibilities.

Is Johns's painting, we might also ask, artistically excellent? Since Steinberg's experience of it exhibited, as I indicated, most of the characteristics attributed to aesthetic experience and was thus worthwhile and rewarding, the work can obviously be presumed to possess some merit. Whether Johns's art will continue to sustain interest remains to be seen. In future histories of art it may be a mere footnote to a time when art diverged momentarily from its time-honored path, a path that in many ways it is currently retreading. Theorists of aesthetic education are not required to settle matters of this kind, but they should issue a warning against the assumption that somehow work of the sort Johns produces displaces or supersedes art created in a more traditional fashion.

Steinberg's recounting of his difficulties with the Johns painting is contained within a larger discussion of the plight faced by the modern art public when it tries to come to grips with novelties in the art world. But the art public's perplexity is easily generalized to all learners who are compelled to comprehend the new, the difficult, the unfamiliar. We have thus arrived at a basic educational question: How do learners assimilate the new and unfamiliar and gradually reorganize their conceptual frameworks for understanding? It is a problem that confounds all areas of education, has been a special preoccupation of science educators,[15] and is particularly acute, for example, in multicultural education where students are expected to learn to appreciate the arts of different cultures. The conceptual change that we must presume to occur—and as teachers must know how to facilitate—is so important a matter that Stephen Toulmin has made it central to a definition of rationality. In *Human Understanding* he writes that "a man demonstrates his rationality, not by a commitment to fixed ideas, stereotyped procedures, or immutable concepts, but by the manner in which, and the occasions on which, he changes those ideas, procedures, and concepts."[16] This necessity is as apparent in aesthetic education as in other fields, perhaps more so in some respects because of the misconceptions about art the child brings to school and which therefore must be systematically corrected.

Walter Kauffmann: Film and self-awareness

Elsewhere in a discussion of excellence in art,[17] I referred to film critic Stanley Kauffmann's criteria for assessing quality in film, the unquestionably new and distinctive art form of the twentieth century. Kauffmann acknowledges that the conditions and dynamics of filmmaking restrict the capacity of film to achieve the degree of excellence found in other art forms, and he thinks that we should therefore hedge our use of the term "classic" in connection with this art. These reservations notwithstanding, the art of film, no less than other art forms, is in principle capable of high accomplishment and can display imaginative energy, dramatic content, technical finesse, and psychological and spiritual power.

Primarily because films appear as photographed human reality, moral criteria loom large in Kauffmann's criticism, particularly when he judges a film's contribution, or failure to contribute, to self-understanding. In this respect Kauffmann recalls Trilling's belief about the function of literature: to provide knowledge of the self and of the right relation of the self to others and to culture. But just as film is more than its medium, so it is more than its message. The manner in which a film's concern is expressed is vitally important, and it is the film's aesthetic form and dynamics which impress that concern on the viewer's imagination. I now extend the few introductory remarks I previously made about Kauffmann into an examination of his critical review of Michelangelo Antonioni's *Red Desert*.[18]

Before doing this, however, it may be worth recalling what Harold Rosenberg[19] thought quality amounted to in twentieth-century avant-garde art: a certain freshness achieved primarily by repudiating traditional subject matter and the kinds of composition that contained it. Impressionism, for example, literally traded indoor for outdoor painting and hence favored contemporary subjects and a technique and palette that attempted to capture the vibrancy of atmosphere at a particular moment in time. Surrealism, Dada, and Futurism, on the other hand, ransacked the past, the present, psychoanalysis, radical politics, and science itself for their forms and images. In all this, Rosenberg points out, timing was of the essence, for the effect of aesthetic revitalization lasted only as long as discoveries were perceived as genuinely innovative. There were then limits to aesthetic freshening, and when they were reached vangardism soon succumbed to a process of fashionabilizing that increasingly synchronized artistic creation with the rhythms of the marketplace. But in its best moments, says Rosenberg, the avant-garde invigorated an art grown stale and lifeless from the repetitive use of worn-out formulas.

Now freshness can certainly be an aesthetic quality; it attests to vitality and tends to induce a corresponding effect in human consciousness. And it is precisely such a quality that Kauffmann praises in Antonioni's *Red Desert,* a film that addresses the prospect for life in the new industrial settings of the twentieth century. But let us back up and follow Kauffmann's lead.

After stating that *Red Desert* advances the art of film and enlarges our vision of what film can do, Kauffmann briefly recounts the story line. The film is basically about a woman's attempt to conquer her neurosis in the ambience of a new industrial environment resplendent with beautiful forms, shapes, lines, and especially colors. The particular incidents of the story need not detain us here except to say that in Kauffmann's opinion they all contribute to and reinforce the film's principal message: that life is possible in the new world, that the best of the past can be preserved, and that new values will be born. This import is neither explicitly stated nor expressed with false optimism; rather, it is conveyed through the agonized efforts of Giuliana (played by Monica Vitti) to overcome her neurosis. Since her psychological ailment is too deep-seated to give way to easy adjustment, the drama of her struggle becomes the drama of the film. Yet the film manages to convince us that she has sufficient inner resources to make the necessary adaptation.

Artistically, or cinematically, says Kauffmann, the interplay between Giuliana and the industrial environment has the effect of illuminating both. Just as the tension of swirling social change contributes to her condition, so the setting with its ambience suggests the possible resolution of her turmoil in her eventual adjustment. Although, according to Kauffmann, the events and incidents of the film are both implicative and revealing and speak their own symbolic language, it is the film's color that is most impressive.

Figure 4.4.   Michelangelo Antonioni, Still from *Red Desert,* 1964. Rizzoli Film Distributor. The Museum of Modern Art/Film Stills Archives, W. 53rd St., New York City.

Any element or part of a work of art has a contribution to make to its overall effort or character. In *Red Desert* Kauffmann assigns five functions to color. The color is first of all exquisite and lovely to behold and becomes even lovelier on subsequent viewings. Part of our pleasure in perceiving it derives from the recognition that a history of modern painting, from the Impressionists through Andrew Wyeth, lies beneath it. The simple sensuous pleasure we take in this film's color is once again reminiscent of what Aaron Copland called the sensuous plane of musical listening, a plane on which we delight solely in sounds or, in the case of this film, in sheer looks. But color also underlines a fact of the new world: as visitors to many a modern factory can attest, the monochromatic grays of yesteryear no longer dominate the industrial scene. In *Red Desert* color further functions symbolically and expressively to convey the moods of the characters in a variety of settings. For example, in one scene Antonioni had everything painted gray to reflect the protagonists' state of mind. In another instance, red walls create a different effect. Lastly, through color the environment itself is cast as a character in the film; it has become something that the protagonists must reckon with as they move through and engage it. Kauffmann quotes Antonioni regarding his conception of the industrial landscape:

My intention . . . was to express the beauty of this world where even the factories can be very beautiful. . . . The line, the curves of the factories and their chimneys are perhaps more beautiful than a line of trees, of which the eye has already seen too much. It is a rich world, lively, useful. For me, I try to say that the sort of neuroticism which one sees in *Red Desert* is entirely a question of adaptability. There are some people who adapt themselves and others who have not yet been able to do so, for they are too tied to structures or rhythms of life which are now bypassed. This is the case with Giuliana. . . . If I had chosen a normally adapted woman, there would not have been any drama.[20]

Kauffmann states that what keeps the film from being sentimental or a visual cliché is not only the originality of Antonioni's vision (even when it relies on conventional symbolism such as we see in the story about a young girl at a deserted pink beach) but also a realistic understanding of the difficulties persons are likely to experience when they try to deal with social change. Although the film suggests prospects for adaptation, it also makes clear that adjustment is not inevitable and will come only as a hard-won victory. What *Red Desert* presents, then, is an image of hope unadorned, but hope nonetheless.

The film's new and refreshing quality thus does not depend on such things as bright skies or the roofs of quaint farmsteads (which delighted Dr. Watson as he and Holmes traveled by train across the English countryside in "The Adventure of the Copper Beeches," see Appendix I) or on the pointless sort of perfection that Martin Dworkin saw as a defect of *An American in Paris*. Rather, the experience of freshness emerges from a recognition of *Red Desert's* having realized new filmic potentialities through Antonioni's cinematic virtuosity, sense of artistry, invention, and mastery. Skill like this not only keeps the art of film alive and advances it, but in the case of *Red Desert* is placed in the service of articulating a universal human concern: How shall persons cope with the particular situations into which they are thrust?

Regarding the film's overall merit, Kauffmann's praise is almost unqualified (he questions only a detail or two): "In these days of chance music, action painting and pop art [the piece was written in 1965] aesthetic idiocy in prose and poem, monolithic monomania in architecture, in these days when good artists question by act and statement the necessity for art, Antonioni continues to keep the film fresh and relevant: fresh without inane novelty, relevant without facile nostalgic reference. . . . There are few living directors who can be compared with him in level of achievement; there is none who is his peer in shaping the film form itself to the needs of contemporary men." [21] With only slight modification, the words still ring true twenty-five years later; indeed if anything, the cultural condition has worsened.

In the context of this essay, Kauffmann's critical review of Antonioni's *Red Desert* is noteworthy for several reasons. First, it satisfies the principal requirement of aesthetic criticism—it illuminates a work of art *as* art. Certainly it was not Kauffmann's intention to "deconstruct" the film or fit it into Marxist or any other ideological categories. Moreover, while the vision of the film is moral and some of Kauffmann's criteria of judgment are likewise, the moral message is embedded in a filmic form that draws attention to itself and thus creates an arresting tension among subject, theme, and form that has long been considered the hallmark of a successful work of art. Kauffmann's account of the particulars of the film, moreover, gives credence to Sparshott's remark that if a critic attends to the facts of the case, values will tend to take care of themselves. The point is that aesthetic criticism does not exclude all reference to semantic or representational aspects of artworks or totally rule out consideration of a work's moral dimensions. Rather, aesthetic criticism as the term is used here insists on the primacy of aesthetic value and accomplishment and hence stands in opposition to those types of criticism that tend to dismiss them.

Keeping to the distinctions noted earlier, how shall we classify Kauffmann's critique—aesthetic exploratory or aesthetic evaluative criticism? I think it is clear that in this instance Kauffmann has made it his task to pass judgment on the film and that his remarks can be construed as a normative explanation that grounds the judgment. He characteristically resorts to the techniques of exploratory criticism (pointing, comparing and contrasting, characterizing, interpreting, etc.). In effect Kauffmann draws attention to the reasons why *Red Desert* is worthwhile, and he is quite explicit in singling out the good-making features of the film.

Once again, *Red Desert* deserves our attention because in addition to artistically exploiting the known potentialities of film, it realizes new ones, notably through the multiple uses of color and the subtle interacting of the protagonists with their environment, all while it maintains an effective forward movement in a non-Aristotelian manner. That is, the film possesses a unity that is not attained conventionally through the construction of a beginning, a middle, and an end; instead the loosely connected incidents achieve integration by the way they bear on the film's central theme. As mentioned, color is the one cinematic effect that *Red Desert* raises to unprecedented prominence by featuring it as sensuous, symbolic, expressive, and representational. By drawing attention to these uses of color, as well as to skilled technique, dramatic unity, complexity, expressive intensity, and so forth, Kauffmann has supplied aesthetic reasons for the work's value. But the film is also worth seeing for what it says and for its potentially beneficial effects on human attitudes and conduct; in other words, it has merit on cognitive and moral grounds as well. We are told certain facts about life in a modern society undergoing change and are given to understand that this life has certain values and that persons, even those under stress of some kind, have the reserves of inner strength and resourcefulness to cope with the situation. (This is the cognitive aspect of the film.) In the struggle with reality, moreover, we need not, should not, discard those things most precious from the past but should conceive of ways to transmute traditional values for the new age. In *Red Desert* this is accomplished not only by means of the self-awareness that dawns on the major protagonists but also through the film's links with its own brief tradition and the longer tradition of other art forms. In all this the film exhibits a sympathetic but essentially tough-minded moralness. Still, its message has been heard before, and so the film is not radically novel in what it says. *Red Desert* therefore impressed Kauffmann primarily as an instance of an art form realizing itself in ever new and fascinating ways; his judgment of the work's excellence or worthwhileness is as much about its purely aesthetic achievement as about anything else, if not more so.

Kauffmann's method of film criticism is not, of course, inferable from a single sample of his writing. Yet I think this particular piece is representative. And we are not surprised by now to detect evidence of Clark's phases of impact, scrutiny, recollection, and renewal in Kauffmann's approach as well, for they are generic to good criticism. A word might be added about the reference Kauffmann makes to Antonioni's intention in creating this film, because it raises the question of the relevance of knowledge of artistic intention to the assessment of a work of art. Antonioni states that he meant to express the beauty of a certain world and to show that it is possible to adapt to it; does this assertion provide an evaluative standard for judging the film? I think it is clear that Kauffmann's critique would be valid even if he had known nothing of Antonioni's intention, for in the case of this film the meaning or message emerges when we attend to the business of the film itself. The Antonioni quote lends *support* to Kauffmann's interpretation but does not validate it. Indeed, it is difficult to see how knowledge of intentions can in most instances provide a criterion of merit. Certainly when this information is not available, we cannot refer to it. Knowledge of the artist's intention may help us see things we may have missed or understand a message we may have misconstrued and thus may be an aid to appreciating an artwork. But once we have rendered the work's meaning as best we can, we may still have the task of making an independent judgment of its import. It depends on the context whether knowledge of artistic intention can be relevant to exploratory or evaluative criticism.

But back to Kauffmann. He, too, like Clark, Schapiro, and Steinberg, provides a model of aesthetic criticism, as I understand it. Indeed, Kauffmann's criticism recalls some remarks by Francis Sparshott in his essay "Basic Film Aesthetics." A judicious critic, says Sparshott, should be as knowledgeable as possible about a film's merits. "Beyond that," he writes, "the moral and cultural side of a critique must depend on the maturity and sensitivity of the critic's social and moral awareness."[22]

Hilton Kramer: Art and aesthetic value

I have said that "aesthetic criticism" as I am using the term is to be distinguished from ideological, political, or cultural criticism and does not imply a lack of interest in a work's cognitive or moral aspects. Aesthetic criticism, that is, does not require a purely formalist aesthetic; and perhaps I can't emphasize this enough. This point needs reiterating because it is central to the work of yet another "aesthetic critic," Hilton Kramer, whose review of a retrospective exhibition of paintings by the German artist Anselm Kiefer presses further the question of the centrality of the aesthetic in our experience of art.

What is it that for Kramer makes something worthwhile as art? His answer, evident not only in the review to be discussed but in other of his statements as well, is quite clear: it is the quality of aesthetic experience that a work of art provides. A work with little aesthetic value or evidence of aesthetic accomplishment may command our attention but not as the realization of artistic potentialities, in the instance at hand, those of painting. What is interesting about Kramer's critique of Kiefer's work is his suggestion that the vision Kiefer strives to attain is *beyond* the capability of painting to embody and that Kiefer is most successful when he remains within painting's limitations. Imbedded in such a judgment is a notion of art that will surface as we examine Kramer's critique more carefully.

Like Steinberg, Kramer surveys a group of works by one artist, that is, an exhibition consisting entirely of Kiefer's works, but he does not accord as detailed an analysis to any one work as Steinberg did for Jasper Johns's *Target with Four Faces*. Nonetheless, Kramer's discussion of different paintings is adequate for my purposes. The basis for his judgment, moreover, is clearly stated.

After setting the event of Kiefer's exhibition[23] in its context in the contemporary art world and mentioning the unusual solemnity that attended the press review, Kramer proceeds to describe works containing landscapes, images of architecture, and didactic diagrams or charts. On registering the initial impact of the works (the first, it will be recalled, of Clark's four phases of response to art), Kramer said he felt moved by the collection's ambition, scale, technical achievement, and gravitas, qualities that stand out in comparison with the poverty of most vanguard art of the past two decades. Kramer was particularly impressed with Kiefer's attempt to come to terms with Germany's immediate past and its meaning for European civilization. It was as if Kiefer, in directly confronting the horrors of the Nazi era and other aspects of German mythology, folklore, and history, were responding to the challenge issued to European writers and artists to come to grips with the problem of European identity in the modern world. Indeed, says Kramer, the appetite that Kiefer strives to satisfy is for an art that transcends the

Figure 4.5. Anselm Kiefer, *Midgard*, 1980–85. Carnegie Museum of Art, Pittsburgh.

aesthetic and speaks forcefully to the moral imagination. All this, along with Kiefer's talent and giftedness, Kramer found exhilarating. Still, the question for the critic is to estimate what has been accomplished with such extraordinary gifts.

At this point, Kramer sets aside Kiefer's paintings of architectural images and didactic diagrams and concentrates on the symbolic landscapes. The architectural images are too heavily dependent on iconographic programs, and the diagrams are a dead end and in fact no longer interest the artist. The landscapes, on the other hand, though also provided with catalogue descriptions of their symbolism, possess a poignancy, a spiritual yearning, and expressive freedom that render them forceful and arresting as paintings (though materials other than pigments were used to make them). What seems to make the landscapes compelling to Kramer is their ability to transcend specific symbolism and rely for their appeal on their poetic and pictorial power. More specifically, the landscapes are notable for their allegorical character, for the ways in which peculiarly German attitudes toward nature transmute the material aspects of nature into metaphysical conundrums, or better, for the ways in which the landscapes encompass both of these aspects of nature. (In discussing such matters, Kramer recalls Clark's third phase of recollection.)

With so much apparent symbolism, what, we might ask, do these landscape paintings mean? Although they have no highly specific meaning, they do have a subject. Kramer writes that "Kiefer is an artist who imparts to every picture a characteristic emotion—an emotion that is relentlessly dour and obsessed with death. . . . Every painting sounds the requiem note, and the landscape paintings sound that note more effectively than any others." They are, he says, wasteland and scorched-earth images, "images of an earth and a world that is rotting and returning to the primordial mud . . . images of a sublime that has 'fallen' into decay. Their real subject is death, and the death that haunts them is as much the death of art as it is the death of the earth."

But as Kramer scrutinized Kiefer's project (the second phase of Clark's pattern of response), he sensed that the work had something of a Sisyphean character; their effort to contain great regions of human history is fated to fail because, Kramer thinks, it is beyond the capacity of painting, or at least beyond Kiefer's capacity, to accommodate them. Kramer acknowledges that his admiration for Kiefer's paintings is undiminished but says that in estimating and praising the value of this work we should remain aware of the central place the death motif occupies in it.

In what way then is Kramer's a form of aesthetic criticism as understood in this essay? It is first of all committed to illuminating Kiefer's paintings as art and not only as an expression of moral concern. At a time when many writers use "aesthetic" as a throwaway word or deny its usefulness, Kramer records his belief in the importance of aesthetic value, aesthetic accomplishment, and aesthetic experience.

I now turn to Kramer's aesthetic view of art. His discussion of Kiefer's landscapes provides a clue: art most effectively realizes its potentialities and serves us well in its fashion when a significant tension exists between subject, medium, and form; or, as in the case of Kiefer, when pictorial form transcends dependence on hermetic symbolism and achieves spiritual or archetypal expression. "Subject" here does not necessarily imply definable representational aspects of works but may include an obsession with death, just as Johns's concern was with a nonhuman presence. In more pedantic terms, art serves us well when artworks possess intense and significant regional qualities, or, if you will, when artworks exemplify them. Such qualities, in turn, have the capacity to induce aesthetic experience along the lines discussed in Chapter 2. We may say that Kramer has reservations about Kiefer's architectural images and didactic diagrams because of their limited ability to induce aesthetic response. In a word they are too programmatic. And so we are brought back once again to Virgil Aldrich's belief that great art is that which features the interanimation of medium, form, and content. Kramer is in effect saying that in his landscapes Kiefer has composed the special qualities of his materials and subject into a form whose content reveals a pervasive concern with death, the compellingness of which is attributable to the tension maintained between the works' medium, form, and content.

It is interesting to compare Kramer's estimate of the significance of Kiefer's paintings and Kauffmann's assessment of Antonioni's mature films. Both Antonioni and Kiefer are judged to have advanced their respective art forms, Antonioni in the ways previously discussed and Kiefer by his ambitious pressing against the limits of painting. What is more, not only are both artists unquestionably masters of their art, their works also have moral as well as aesthetic significance and generate an intense aesthetic experience. But whereas Kauffmann discovered little to object to in *Red Desert,* Kramer, though exhilarated by Kiefer's work, thought the artist unequal to the task undertaken and limited by his obsession with death. In the *Red Desert* Kauffmann saw hope, the possibility of life, and a faith that the best from the past can be preserved in the process of adapting it to new conditions; there is no such hope in Kiefer's paintings where things are "rotting and returning to the primordial mud."

These contrasting evaluations give rise to some speculation. Could there be a latent judgment that a relentless obsession with death and deterioration detracts from the value of a body of work even when such work has unquestioned artistic merit? And is it possible that art has greater value for us when it manages to convey some hope or affirmation of human perseverance and ability to cope, as seems to be the point of Giuliana's striving in *Red Desert?* If so, then perhaps Albert William Levi is correct when he states that "at its best art functions as an adjunct of humanism—as a reflection of that attitude which is hospitable to the happy, natural, and wholesome enjoyment of the goods of human life in a refined civilization with the accompanying wisdom, temperance, sanity, and balance which that rightfully entails."[24] Unfortunately, contemporary life is neither particularly wholesome nor refined, and many artists believe that its enormities must be impressed on our consciousness through art. So perhaps it comes down to the question of which art form is best suited to that task, and here we may suggest that literature and the dramatic arts are better vehicles than the plastic arts for conveying certain kinds of meaning (or, to put it differently, for incorporating strongly cognitive reasons among those that count toward the good-making criteria of aesthetic judgment). Hence the reason that, on the whole, *Red Desert* can be said to yield a more satisfactory aesthetic experience than do many of Kiefer's paintings may be that the film, though innovative, produces its effects within the medium's proper limits, while Kiefer's paintings distract us from aesthetic contemplation by drawing our attention to the pressure they exert against the medium's confines. But so much for speculation.

As I have said several times, aesthetic criticism as I think of it is limited to attempts which try to illuminate works of art as art, by which I mean descriptions and interpretations of a work's manifold of qualities in such ways as to freshen perception and reward experience. Different kinds of aesthetic criticism can accomplish this task: for example, formalist criticism that stays largely within the boundaries of the work itself; historical criticism that in addition to explaining the factors and forces influencing the creation, reception, and appreciation of works of art also describes their aesthetic qualities; moral criticism that is not indifferent to aesthetic form; and psychoanalytical or psychological criticism that describes the conceptual and expressive content of artworks by yet another route. Once again, I accept a broad notion of aesthetic criticism that excludes only those approaches that do not value aesthetic considerations or accomplishment, for example, certain varieties of Marxist and other ideological criticism and deconstructionism generally.

Richard Wollheim: Painting as an art

Not surprisingly, different interpretive perspectives have different notions of what is objective and acceptable in criticism, as will be seen in the work of Richard Wollheim, the last of the critics to be considered here. His explanation of Poussin's *The Ashes of Phocion Collected by His Widow* (1648, Walker Art Gallery, Merseyside, Liverpool)[25] is a psychological one. He believes that his is the correct interpretation of this painting and that all other art-historical accounts of it are false. How does Wollheim proceed, and in which respects may his criticism be said to be aesthetic as well as psychological?

First of all, Wollheim is a philosopher with a connoisseur's taste of fine art and a bent for psychological explanation. In his book *Painting as an Art* he does not use the data of works of art simply to psychoanalyze Poussin; rather, he employs the insights of psychoanalysis to reveal the pictorial meaning of the works he examines. What for Wollheim are the conditions for pictorial meaning? In a review of Wollheim's book, Michael Podro succinctly states that they are, first,

> that we have the innate capacity to see the look of one thing in something else, say a landscape or a figure in the clouds or in ice crystals on the window; second, that we can make objects in which such "seeing in" is intended, so that when we see one thing in another we can see it as represented and not simply projected there; and third, by virtue of the way the subject—which may be highly indeterminate—is shown and the way the medium is deployed in showing it, the painting may carry both conceptual and expressive meaning. What, for Wollheim, is opposed to meaning is mere association, that is, historical and psychological facts which are related to the work but do not enter into its content.[26]

To understand how Wollheim interprets Poussin's *Phocion* painting we must realize that he does not approach it without first having formulated an idea about the significance of Poussin's work in general. His analysis of the *Phocion* painting thus helps to confirm his sense of Poussin's overall importance; and that importance in turn owes much to Poussin's experience of Stoicism and his conception of human instinct. According to Wollheim, Poussin believed "that there is within human nature an autonomous force of instinct which in its beneficial operation retains its link with birth, with propagation, with self-renewal, a link which, in turn, involves an acceptance of death . . . both of the fact of death, and of our own deathly or destructive side."[27] Wollheim thinks that this conception of instinct permeates all of Poussin's work and that it requires us to modify our view of him as a stern portraitist of rationalistic man. In particular, it forces us to assume a perspective on the *Phocion* painting that is quite different from conventional accounts, for example, Anthony Blunt's perception of it in terms of the painting's geometry and architectural order. This is not what Wollheim sees.

First of all, Wollheim thinks that the painting is best described as exhibiting three distinct zones and that an understanding of the relations among these is crucial for an understanding of the picture. Description hence proceeds in light of an overall interpretation of the sense of the whole. However, even the descriptions of the three zones and their relations, including the activities going on in each of them, contain statements that themselves may be regarded as either interpretive or descriptive. For example, when Wollheim says of the mountain in the third zone of the painting that "an air of untamed mystery attaches to the mountain, and this is intensified by its irrational shape, which its silhouette does not reveal,"[28] is this description or interpretation, or perhaps both, say, interpretive description? I ask this only to underline once again the ambiguity of critical talk about art, although I take it that while the characterization of the mountain may be descriptive, interpretive, or interpretively descriptive, it is not evaluative.

Description, however, is merely the first stage of Wollheim's marshalling of evidence in support of his interpretation. With an impressive display of erudition he goes on to explain that Stoicism does not really require, as the standard view has it, that a painter render landscape geometrically. Poussin was thus at liberty to use landscape expressively in the *Phocion* painting without being presumed to have departed from his Stoic orientation. Wollheim then indicates in some detail the interlocking of the work's surface and depth design, explaining how the bent-over figure gathering Phocion's ashes in the foreground area is associated compositionally not with the middle ground that represents a rationally ordered environment, but with the more ominous and mysterious background and foreground surroundings. He also draws attention to the way the background echoes the foreground foliage:

> In the foreground, by the side of a rustic fountain, the great moral act unfolds, and the look of apprehension with which the attendant figure regards the life of Megara serves to disjoin the foreground from the middle ground. A veil of suspicion falls between them. But the foreground, disjected from the middle distance, now associates itself with the background. Poussin has made the near trees, as they part to reveal the city, rhyme with the distant shape of the mountain: their silhouettes repeat one another. But the strongest link between the two bands of landscape is the elemental force that animates both. Rising in the deserted mountain-top, circumventing the protected, placid life of the city, it rustles the enormous trees that stand above the woman's improvised shrine. The leaves as they sway above her turn and catch the downward rays of the sun.
>
> In her stubborn act of piety the woman has placed herself beyond the world of custom and civic obligation: complacent *sittlichkeit* has nothing to offer her. But she is not alone or unaided. The wind, the little stream that oozes its way into, or out of (we cannot tell which), the darkness of the wood, and the ominous trees that shelter her—these are her accomplices. The energy for such transcendent acts of probity, this picture shows us, comes not from conventional morality, it comes from the natural stirrings of instinct.[29]

Wollheim thinks that such an interpretation might be less persuasive were it not confirmed by a later landscape by Poussin, the *Landscape with Diogenes* (1658, Louvre, Paris). For example, the device that Poussin used in the *Phocion* painting—the entrapment of the distant landscape in the main body of the picture—takes on even greater expressiveness in the *Diogenes* landscape, the uncanny effect, says Wollheim,

Figure 4.6. Nicholas Poussin, *The Ashes of Phocion Collected by His Widow*, 1648. Canvas. Walker Art Gallery, National Museum and Galleries on Merseyside, Liverpool.

resembling that of "a fly caught in a spider's web." (The silhouette of Vermeer's painter, we recall, was said to look like a "giant cockroach"— such is critical talk!) Poussin also uses color expressively by preferring an overall tone that irradiates the picture "with a sense of threat or encroachment." These observations and many more that I have not recorded help to support Wollheim's interpretation of the *Phocion* painting; and while Wollheim asserts that the *Diogenes* painting "confirms" that interpretation, he admits that such confirmation is not actually required. The primary evidence remains the *Phocion* painting itself.

The pictorial meaning of the *Phocion* painting then does not turn solely on the subject matter that its title suggests; rather, we may say that its meaning is a function of the interanimation of subject, form, and medium that expressively conveys Poussin's attitude toward Stoicism, nature, and human nature, and, most of all, his attitudes toward human instinct. It is unlikely that anyone not knowledgeable about either Stoicism, Poussin's attitude toward it, and comparable and different ways of painting landscape could see the picture in quite the way that Wollheim does. But now with his detailed formulation of the work's meaning (having followed his persuasive argument, to us Crittenden's term), we too can share his vision. We can experience the painting not only in terms of its theme and thesis but also notice the ways theme and thesis are compositionally embodied and expressively communicated. We may further ask about the kind of interpretation and judgment that Wollheim gives us, apart, that is, from its being a psychological one. Certainly, it is partly a cognitive judgment, for the work is an excellent example of how a painting can express philosophical ideas. Yet the painting would not merit our attention were it not for its rich aesthetic qualities, so that his interpretation contains a strong aesthetic judgment as well. And since it addresses the important question of the way human life should be conducted, the interpretation additionally has a moral dimension. We are reminded, in other words, that we tend to value masterpieces for their plenitude of values—cognitive, moral, and aesthetic. Perhaps we can also now appreciate why Paul Ziff in discussing a clear-cut case of a work of art selected another of Poussin's works, *The Rape of the Sabine Women* (c. 1636, Metropolitan, New York).[30] What he says in a general way about the *Sabine* painting also applies to the *Phocion* work.

I should add that what interests me about Wollheim's interpretation is not its correctness or incorrectness, although it strikes me as highly plausible (I can see what he describes, and it makes sense), but the *way* he came to terms with Poussin's painting. His account, which is pertinent in light of the discussion of Chapter 3, is an excellent example of what was there called the critical redescription of a work of art. It should also be apparent that Wollheim's aesthetic criticism is of a sort that draws on more than a work's formal and expressive qualities and does not attempt to infer all of a work's meaning directly from the artwork itself. Wollheim's critique involves references to Poussin's artistic intention, his way of working in a medium, and to other sorts of antecedent information. Perception is further aided by comparisons, as Wollheim's numerous references to Poussin's predecessors, contemporaries, and the artist's own later work attest. Finally, although Wollheim does not quite claim infallibility for his judgment, he is firm in his belief that a correct experience of the *Phocion* painting would have to take his treatment of it into consideration and that conventional interpretations of Poussin's landscapes are false. Wollheim does not, that is, doubt the validity of the reasons he adduces in support of his interpretation. Such certitude might impress us as doctrinaire were it not backed up with strong confirming evidence. As it is, Wollheim's firmness of conviction is refreshing; it stands in contrast to the genuine self-doubt that Steinberg felt in his attempt to make sense of Johns's work. But then, Steinberg's challenge was rather different.

A concluding observation: The usual criticism of psychological interpretations of art and appeals to artistic intention in assessing its merit (what Beardsley called intentionalistic criticism) is that they deflect attention from the artwork and its qualities to antecedent or genetic considerations. Objections of this kind are usually justified, for it is often hard to see what a psychological account of an artwork adds to our appreciation of that work's aesthetic value. This is not true of Wollheim's critique; his love and knowledge of painting save him from aesthetic irrelevancy.

CHAPTER 5

Teaching aesthetic skills

> Sensitivity to words is part of pedagogy at large. . . . But words—correct words—are also indispensable to the teaching of art. Critical judgment, appreciation, stylistic analysis, disputations about taste, historical comparisons, and efficient instruction itself depend on the appropriate use of words. Indeed . . . the benefits of teaching art to the young will consist mainly in the pleasure that comes of being able to see and hear works of art more sharply and subtly, more consciously, to register that pleasure in words, and compare notes with other people similarly inclined.
>
> *Jacques Barzun*[1]

The previous chapter extended the discussion of aesthetic criticism by presenting six samples of critical writing. These were chosen to provide acquaintance not only with instances of criticism in action but also with some of the kinds of subsidiary interests—cognitive, moral, psychological—that critics often marshal toward their primary task: elucidating the work of art *as* art. I pointed to the secondary emphases found in much of criticism not as a suggestion that aesthetic educators try to emulate such sophistication and learnedness in their own teaching but to indicate what can be discovered in the critical literature when it is perused for examples and inspiration.

Yet it is one thing to recommend a model for teaching, another to show that its adoption is feasible. This chapter therefore addresses several problems and questions that can be expected to arise when aesthetic criticism is instantiated in teaching practice. To that end, Henry Aiken's "Learning and Teaching in the Arts"[2] will be discussed first. Since Aiken provides an insightful exploration of a major artwork from a distinctly educational standpoint, that is, with the art teacher in mind, his essay effects a good transition from the last chapter.

Henry Aiken: The conditions for knowing, appreciating, and teaching art

Aiken's writing about learning and teaching in the arts is part of his more encompassing concern to see the humanities reinstated in a position of parity with the exact sciences. Contrary to C. P. Snow, who held that it is largely the ideas and sentiments of literary intellectuals that shape the attitudes of the majority toward the world of learning, Aiken believes that in today's academy the scientific ethos and the ideal of abstract generalization and mathematical exactitude constitute the accepted paradigmatic form of knowledge.

Aiken argues that while we are justified in talking about "knowledge," "teaching," and "learning" when we explain our various dealings with artworks, we must realize that in humanistic contexts these terms acquire accents and connotations different from the ones they have in scientific contexts. Yet art and science are not completely divorced or disanalogous. Although scientific inquiry cannot by itself elucidate the art object as art, it does make available much information about art (that is, it provides the material for Clark's third phase of response) that can play a role in elucidation. Conversely, although aesthetic experience has none of the precision of scientific inquiry, the illumination of an artwork depends on powers of anticipation, discrimination, and recognition that, claims Aiken, parallel those required for scientific inquiry.

What, then, are the conditions of our knowledge of art, and how and by what stages is that knowledge reached? In what sense and to what extent can it be the product of teaching and learning? Answers to these questions are suggested in the body of Aiken's essay.

Illuminating the art object as art

Aiken reminds us that not all experiences are cognitive and that of those which are, not all amount to cognitive achievements. Knowledge of art, however, clearly is such an achievement, for although art undeniably affords gratifications, these usually depend on modes of perception that call on the rigorous activity of the human mind. What are these modes of perception or, more particularly, what do we have to know in order to appreciate works of art? Aiken organizes his task of sorting out the ingredients of knowledge of art around the discussion of a concrete example, Giorgione's painting *The Tempest* (c. 1505, Galleria dell' Accademia, Venice).

The first thing we must do when confronting *The Tempest* is to experience it as a perceptual unity distinct from its surrounding field. We must further realize that we are looking at a human artifact and not a gift from the gods or a product of some lucky happenstance. This recognition of human agency changes our approach to the painting. I will add here that for Aiken the several items we need to learn about art do not merely function additively; many of the cognitive accretions effect psychological shifts such that the person with more knowledge does not only see more—that is, has a richer, more detailed, more prolonged encounter with the work—but experiences the work differently, with an altered mindset (another version of Crittenden's assertion that increases in knowledge change "seeing as").

In addition to being aware of the important categorical distinctions between treating something as an object and treating it as an artifact, the

Figure 5.1.   Giorgione, *The Tempest,* c. 1505. Oil on canvas, 31¼″ × 28¾″.
Galleria dell' Accademia, Venice. Marburg/Art Resource, N.Y.

percipient of a work like *The Tempest* must also know how to differentiate between the purposeful and the purposive (here Aiken adopts Kant's
concepts), that is, between an artifact that serves an ulterior end or
purpose and one that has no end beyond itself. In these terms, the work
of art is purposive because it is "something whose artistic virtue is
understood in the successive acts we perform in contemplating its own
internal design"[3] and not something whose excellence lies in serving
well as a means toward some external objective (which is reminiscent
of Sparshott's observation, quoted at the beginning of Chapter 2, that
works of art provide worthwhile experiences merely in being looked at,
listened to, and read). In other words, says Aiken, when we contemplate
an artwork, we should realize that it "is to be treated by us as something
to be appreciated, not necessarily without regard to, but at least without
concern for, whatever ends it may serve for the artist, his patron, the
society in which he lived, and above all ourselves."[4] This is in effect to
subscribe to Panofsky's definition of the work of art as a man-made
object that *demands* to be experienced aesthetically.[5]

Since *The Tempest* is a representational work containing human figures and a number of natural and architectural elements, we make rudimentary sense of it by drawing on past knowledge and experience: we may do this first of all by recognizing likenesses of familiar things. But if we have assumed the proper aesthetic stance, we will not take these likenesses primarily as vehicles of possible information about, for instance, the landscape of Northern Italy and the mode of dress of its inhabitants during Giorgione's time. Rather, we concentrate our attention on the interrelations of these forms within the painting.

Having registered a first impression of this work (Clark's phase of initial impact) and realized that we ought to treat it as a visual composition, what else must we know to do so? Simply, whatever it takes to analyze it (Clark's second phase). That is to say, we now make an effort to notice the relationships not only of the figurative elements but also those among the qualities of line and color, light and shade, as well as the points of stress or emphasis that bring the other recessive and subordinate visual properties of the painting into proper focus. Yet we must avoid attending to representational forms and sensory qualities in isolation or side-by-side, because in any painting of artistic merit the other visual elements continually interact with and qualify the representational ones. As Aiken says, the painting "forcibly demands that we perceive how they [the elements] continually mutually inflect one another: light and shadow setting off the natural forms that comprise the landscape, or on the other side, the placement of mother and child in such a way as to reinforce the linear relations and to draw attention to color relationships which otherwise might not be noticed or else would be seen in an altogether different way."[6] This interanimation melds the composition into a cohesive visual-representational design that is apprehended in an act of what Osborne calls synoptic vision.

However, we might perceive all this and still not grasp levels of significance that lend the work so much of its distinction and power; we might, that is, miss its expressiveness. Aiken explains how various representational and sensory elements combine to articulate a range of emotions, feelings, and moods. For example, the stormy sky with its dark clouds and lightning introduces intimations of threat and foreboding. But these are instantly mitigated by the stability of the sheltering dwellings and other architectural forms and, even more so, by the character of the figures. The young man, although his relationship to the mother and child remains enigmatic, appears friendly and protective, and the young woman with her suckling infant strikes us as serenely at ease, gazing into the distance contemplatively with no hint of apprehension. The overall mood therefore is one of tranquility, composure, and mystery.

Still another kind of knowledge needed for an educated appreciation of a work of art is an awareness of genre. Genre is a consideration that sets a painting within a tradition whose conventions provide a rationale for much of what we notice and how we take it. Genre knowledge, that is, imposes mental sets which can save one from misinterpretation. But we can be equally misled if we remain imprisoned in these mental sets. This is particularly true in the case of *The Tempest,* a painting Aiken chose not only because of his high regard for it and because it has the status of an undisputed masterpiece, but also because it is a transitional work that does not fit comfortably into any niche into which we might be inclined to place it. The ambivalence concerning genre adds to the unusual bafflement this picture arouses.

For example, since the painting depicts tranquil figures in a peaceful landscape setting, we could perhaps call it a pastoral, and some of the characteristics of this genre are indeed present. But Aiken interprets the natural scene not as a semirural retreat, but as a park or garden owned perhaps by someone in a nearby town; it may be an extension of the woman's own home or the property of someone who has made her feel secure. In any event, she is not at the mercy of untamed nature, for if the storm were to break, an easy escape route into town, via path and bridge, is clearly available. The figures are thus perceived in relation to both nature and the city, and this circumstance, according to Aiken, reinforces "a deep sense, not simply of natural affection and compassion and peace, but of a profoundly urban civility."[7] It is as if Giorgione sought to convey a poetic expression of what Albert William Levi calls "civic humanism."[8] Thus *The Tempest,* while reminiscent of the pastoral, also bears the hallmark of much of Venetian art: expressive reminders of the transforming virtues of the city.

Yet we also view *The Tempest* with a vestigial awareness of the Madonna and Child genre of religious painting, specifically, the subgenre that takes the Rest on the Flight to Egypt as its subject. Clearly, however, this is a secular, not a religious, work—except in the extended or metaphorical sense of "religious" that pertains to much great art. For there are embodied in *The Tempest* "feelings of wonder, mystery, and exaltation, which are the benchmarks of that dimension of being known among religious writers as transcendence."[9] In Aiken's interpretation, then, *The Tempest* carries traces of the pastoral and the civic, the religious and the secular, and to intuit the tensions and ambiguities this creates we have to know the normal fields of application of these labels. Finally, this complex work can also be said to exhibit one of the major distinguishing features Kenneth Clark ascribed to masterpieces: it retains a significant relation to the past while simultaneously managing to be expressive of its own time and of the painter's temperament.[10]

This condensation of Aiken's remarks on the subject of knowledge in art—which, in turn, represents but a small part of what Aiken knows and could say about *The Tempest*—gives us some indication of the kind of knowledge we ought to possess in order to appreciate artworks properly. We should know how to (1) view the work as a separate visual entity; (2) take account of its artifactuality; (3) experience it as a purposive artifact, that is, one intended to be appreciated aesthetically; (4) recognize likenesses represented without treating them information-ally; (5) perform the difficult task of maintaining or achieving a synoptic vision of the work while analyzing its representational and sensory components, their relations, and their emergent qualities; (6) interpret the work's mood, human expressive qualities, and meaning or signifi-cance; and (7) accommodate our perceptions (when relevant) to genre expectations and the requirements of the tradition of which the work is a part.

Learning and teaching in the arts

If an art teacher were to discuss a work like *The Tempest,* how, asks Aiken, would he introduce it and where would he start?

Teachers can, of course, count on students' already having absorbed some knowledge of art informally. Even young children understand the difference between play and serious business; make-believe and reality; tales, stories, fables, and reports of actual events. Some students may have had previous experiences with artworks and their peculiar (playlike) mode of existence. Systematic instruction, however, is another matter altogether. It amounts to the complex yet indispensable preparations for appreciating works of art and, especially in its more advanced stages, relies on a great deal of prior integrated learning and teaching, much of it quite deliberate.

Deliberate teaching begins after a superficial pictorial inventory has been taken, for although students may recognize likenesses of trees, houses, and human figures, the specifics of these representational aspects of the work will probably have to be explained to them. Without a teacher's guidance, for example, students may not realize that the figure in the left-hand corner of the painting is a friendly observer-protector, that the mother is sitting quietly and at peace, that shelter is easily accessible. But beyond this simple kind of noticing, an understanding of *why* the work's figurative elements are rendered the way they are, for example, with just this degree of sharpness or blurring, will be much more difficult to attain. We have thus reached the point when it has become necessary to begin teaching students how to recognize the dis-tinctive quality of the treatment of representational forms associated with particular artists, and this can be done only against a background of some knowledge of traditions, genres, and stylistic periods. This kind of learning "is gradually acquired and its relevance established only with the help of a skilled teacher's explanations, descriptions, demonstrations, and gesturings, with the all important aid of slides and recurring visits to galleries of art."[11] In the following example, Aiken shows how a teacher might use paired contrast and comparison of artworks—the time-honored, sometimes derided, but still potent method of art-historical teaching and standard appreciation courses—to help students perceive the special properties of Giorgione's style as they are reflected in *The Tempest*.

> From one point of view, Giorgione, like Bellini before him, is a greater realist than say Giotto, whose linear landscapes are unconcerned with the purely visual values of perspective, and whose figures, themselves often highly abstract, are represented without regard to their natural relations of size. The interest and power of Giotto's landscapes, whose colors have a primarily symbolic and decorative significance, are directed especially to the stimulation of our sense of the tactile values, as Berenson calls them, of the objects in his paintings. Giotto seems scarcely to care how things simply look, but only how they might feel to a hand that caressed them. Like most Venetians, Giorgione is less a draftsman than a painter. He wants, among other things, to open our eyes to make us see more vividly how things look at a certain distance in their characteristic lights and shadows and colors in relation to other objects in the pictorial space. And to this end, his treatment of distant objects is perforce vaguer than that of someone like Giotto or even Bellini. Where Giotto's abstract trees seem almost to be iconographic emblems, Giorgione's, although less sharply outlined, appear immutably as trees in fact look at a certain distance. Moreover, whereas Giotto paints all his objects in his pictures in much the same degree of detail and clarity of outline, Giorgione sets in powerful contrast to the impressionistic background the more sharply focused figures of the mother and child, with her garments, her bodily position, and above all, the visual-tactile quality of her lovely flesh. In his own way Giorgione, too, gives us a powerful sense of tactile values; but because they are not dispersed evenly throughout the picture, they are stressed all the more dramatically as felt qualities of the human figures in the foreground.[12]

In Aiken's view, full or deep aesthetic appreciation presupposes a lengthy and possibly lifelong endeavor, but he does not say how much of it we could hope to accomplish during the years of formal schooling or at what ages students should be inducted into the different levels of artistic knowledge (a few observations on this latter problem will follow shortly). Happily, *The Tempest* is not merely a learned and sophisticated arrangement of representational matter. Its forms are also "wondrously invested in all the qualities and dimensions of distinctively visual perception,"[13] thus providing the teacher excellent opportunities for expanding, sharpening, and refining the perceptual powers (or percipience) of even fairly young students. All other knowledge aside, then, it should be possible to bring home to students that Giorgione is a superb colorist, a painter in love with space as much as color and, above all, a master of illumination. So that they may learn to appreciate these aspects of Giorgione's work, students should be encouraged to attend to visual qualities and their relations and complexes in their own right, and this means that students have to learn to suspend their habit of seeing through sensory qualities to the object. While instructing students in this unaccustomed manner of seeing, teachers should avoid giving the impression that the work is a collection of miscellaneous sense data to be noted separately; rather, teachers should present these qualities in their inter-animation, as they "pull and haul, press forward and recede, glance and glitter, divide and return, tense and relax, threaten and recompose within a moving and expressive composition."[14]

But how are art teachers to accomplish this? By deploying the resources of language, the "correct words" that Barzun says are so indispensable to the teaching of art. Aiken goes even further and is tempted to say that in learning to appreciate art, language itself is the primary teacher. As a teacher, language instructs informally as well as formally. We learn unaidedly how to use aesthetic concepts like "graceful," "elegant," "lovely," or "garish" and also know that these words convey an invitation to look at a thing in a certain way. But aesthetic characterizations like these typically appear only in fairly general and superficial descriptions. More precise linguistic approximations of aesthetic qualities are achieved by making commonplace adjectives—"cold," "flat," "hard," "dry"—do service in an aesthetic context where they do not belong literally. Aiken thinks that figurative language is used to even better effect through verbs of action and their participial and other adjectival derivations. Thus teachers may call attention to the "energy," "efforts," and "powers" displayed in a painter's "thrusting" line, his "shifting" colors, his "broken" forms and "pressing" masses.[15] By such verbal means the teacher attempts to ensure the students' enhanced perception of the work's qualities, elements, and complexes. But "all these wonderful visions will be lost upon us unless the teacher disposes us ever and again to see them together as so many interacting perceptual and imaginal movements of an inimitable artistic concert."[16] (We recall that Schapiro also likened the art of Cézanne to that of a great composer.)

We are left with feeling or mood, meaning or import, which are dimensions of most great art, and Aiken is convinced that teachers can aid students in the appreciation of these expressive values as well. How? At this juncture, Aiken resorts to the ploy I used in the previous chapter: he cites extensively from the writings of critics whose command of language is matched by their capacities for imaginative identification and feeling.

Once again the art critic is held up as an exemplar for the art teacher, but with some qualifications. Aiken believes that a great critic is unlikely to be a great teacher because the critic tends to be preoccupied with judgment and with reasons that will support his verdict. Now, aesthetic judgment is indispensable to aesthetic appreciation and therefore to aesthetic education, but in teaching, judgment can be no more than a means to helping students toward an appreciation of the artwork. Comparing critic and teacher, Aiken says:

> The teacher's discipline and art are stricter, more austere. For his concern is exclusively to bring his students closer to the distinctive being of works of art. His stern and self-effacing task is not like that of the great critic [or art historian, sociologist, or psychologist], simply to call attention to individual strokes of genius. . . . Making continent use of all these resources of understanding . . . his whole vocation is to bring his students to fuller awareness of the continuous evidences in works of art of the creative life which comprises one primary level of every man's own subjective being or actuality.[17]

Art teachers who do their job well also serve students as an exemplar, as "a continuous presence who by his talk and gestures, as well as his reticences, conveys an awareness of what it is to look for true possibilities in a work of art, what it is to find a significant artistic form, and what it is to develop an authentic taste."[18] Inspiring words and a good note on which to leave Aiken, except to add an expression of regret that his essay, which says so much so well in such brief compass, is not more widely known and read.

Harold Osborne: Appreciation as a skill

We have now reached a point when the process of coming to terms with a work of art aesthetically has been described as sufficiently challenging and complicated to be called a skill of quite a high order. The idea of a skill, which in Chapter 3 had already been tentatively linked to concepts and their acquisition, will now be associated more closely with aesthetic appreciation as such. In this connection, it is appropriate to refer once more to Osborne, who defines aesthetic appreciation, which for him is nearly synonymous with aesthetic experience and percipience, as a skill.[19] It is therefore apposite to comment further on the notion of a skill, especially with a view to sharpening the focus on teaching and learning.

When we think of a truly skilled performer, we usually picture someone who acts dexterously, swiftly, fluently, and seemingly from habit. But this appearance is deceiving. Although skills may make use of habits, skills are not identical with them. Habits are instilled by drill in order to produce automatic behaviors that are virtually identical in instance after instance. Though blind and repetitive, habits are not, however, to be denigrated; we could not perform the tasks of our jobs nor get through a single day without good and reliable habits. Yet they can also be inhibiting. In aesthetic experience, for example, the habits of practical activities or those learned in scientific inquiry must be consciously suppressed so that attention may remain fixed on sensuous surfaces.

In contrast to mindless habits, skills are intelligent capacities acquired through training. As Gilbert Ryle marks the difference, "Drill dispenses with intelligence, training develops it."[20] The presence of mind and intelligence in skills poses no hindrance to the subsumption of aesthetic appreciation under the skills category, for it was after all the major objective of the preceding section to show that aesthetic appreciation or criticism itself relies on and accommodates different sorts of knowledge. Still, skills differ from other areas in the ways they use knowledge. In many fields of scholarship the structure of knowledge is encapsulated in a number of basic concepts and principles that can be taught effectively without the cultivation of the practitioner's skills. One can, for example, learn the conclusions and findings of science and understand how they are arrived at without engaging in scientific inquiry itself. One can also learn to master a significant body of art-historical information without being able to exercise the skills of iconographic or iconological analysis. Similarly, a teacher may discourse brilliantly on art and supply many admirable examples of aesthetic criticism without having taught all that is necessary for students to be able to appreciate art. In short, if students are to acquire the skill of aesthetic appreciation, they need to practice it; they need to take the first steps toward performing those perceptual/ mental/verbal operations on artworks that the teacher has demonstrated for them. This is why "training" (once the concept has been purged of any connotations of habituation and mindless rote learning) is better suited than "education" to talk about inculcating skills, for training always suggests trial and error, practice, and, eventually, "getting it right." Osborne amplifies these ideas by saying that "a skill is a trained or cultivated ability to perform in a certain way and the term frequently carries an implication that a person can so perform with more than average dexterity. Thus skill is a potentiality concept. A skill is a dispositional quality or constellation of qualities. It is an ability which a person has continuously whether or not he is manifesting it in present performance at any particular time."[21] To which we add the qualification that a skill possessed continuously is not a skill possessed indefinitely if it is not used; desuetude causes skills to atrophy.

Since skill involves practice and performance, another sort of knowledge (in addition to the kinds listed in the previous section) becomes relevant: procedural knowledge, an awareness of the rules governing performance or at least of the more promising ways of setting about the task. This, too must be taught, but taught mainly to be forgotten in the sense that it is no longer drawn on deliberately but begins to function under the surface or "tacitly," to use Michael Polanyi's term. Hence Osborne understands a skill also as "a cultivated capacity for performance of a sort which involves following a set of rules not all of which are consciously known or can be completely specified by the performer."[22] This means that we know more than we can tell, that training manuals and handbooks describing a skill seldom if ever explain completely what is required for its exercise. Yet "forgotten" is not the same as "lost," for it is the magnitude of a person's apperceptive mass or the richness of the tacit knowledge that comes into play but does not rise into awareness which is primarily responsible for the different degrees of skill we observe. As an example, person **A** may be able to recite all the rules of the game of chess, while person **B** is a remarkably good player who does not know all the fine points of the rules by heart. **A** has learned what he knows in a very obvious way, but not **B**, whose playing depends on certain knacks and senses of the situation that are largely tacit. It is the difference, we may say, between the merely knowledgeable and the truly skillful chess players in Stefan Zweig's short story "The Royal Game."[23] In teaching the skills of appreciation, says Osborne, precepts, maxims, demonstrations, and examples are all indispensable, but the ultimate aim is to help students attain "the latent knowledge and unspecifiable know-how which are the essence of any skill at all."[24]

The "latent and unspecifiable know-how" that students are expected to appropriate through aesthetic education and to build on in their adult careers poses a severe challenge to the teacher that the critic, for example, does not have to face. The critic has achieved success when, through a persuasive argument, he has guided his readers or audience to more enlightened and informed experience of a work of art. This of course is also one of the teacher's goals; he wants his students to see an artwork as he does. But just as important as this result, and perhaps more so, is the process that has led to it, the aesthetic argument or demonstration of aesthetic criticism and all that it entails, for it is this critical performance that defines the aesthetic skills in which students are being trained. It follows that the teacher has to be quite analytical and self-critical about what he is doing; he must make an effort to dredge up as much material as possible from the otherwise latent knowledge that funds his critical performance in order to make sure it gets transmitted to his students. Hence Aiken appears to have been right when he claimed that in some respects the teacher's task is more austere and difficult than the critic's.

Osborne also accepts "connoisseurship" as a designation for the cultivated ability to appreciate works of fine art and the beauties of nature, although he realizes that the term has limitations when used in the context of the arts (where it is associated with the acute powers required for authenticating artworks). This skill of appreciation, however, is not merely of a generally noticing kind; rather, it is "an ability to apprehend complex organizations of visual and auditory wholes and the recondite qualities of such wholes."[25] I now reemphasize that these skills and abilities of aesthetic connoisseurship are cognitive in order to contrast them with practical skills and, more to the point, creative and performance skills and the corresponding connoisseurship of the artist. This latter is to be thought of as the artist's intimate familiarity with his materials, his ability to make fine discriminations among them, and, of course, his skill in employing them. We have thus arrived at a juncture when something might usefully be said about creative and performing activities in arts education curriculums.

I have so far neglected to mention these facets of arts education not because I think them unimportant but simply because the subject of this essay is education for aesthetic appreciation. Creative arts programs have objectives and justifications of their own, developmental considerations and the identification and fostering of artistic talent among them; but I will discuss them here only as they relate to aesthetic appreciation. It is beyond doubt that students who have had some firsthand experience in working with arts materials and trying out different techniques—especially in the earlier years of schooling before aesthetic education proper is begun—approach their training in aesthetic skills with a decided advantage. Although it is perfectly possible for someone to become an art critic or a connoisseur of painting without ever having touched brush to canvas, the person who has manipulated the materials of an art form will have augmented his appreciative skills with an awareness of some of the difficulties and possibilities of the medium. As Osborne asserts, "Some tincture of the artist's connoisseurship of whatever sort can be an invaluable aid to those who appreciate the products of art. For a work is not always—perhaps seldom is—most successfully apprehended as a completely self-sufficient thing, entirely divorced from the processes by which it came into being and the materials from which it was fashioned."[26] Creative-arts teachers often complain of a disappointing long-range "payoff" of their work with students. Young children are usually full of creative enthusiasm, but by adolescence all but the gifted ones will have abandoned artistic pursuits. Aesthetic education could provide compensating value for these arts teachers, because aesthetic education can promise an "afterlife" for the early artistic efforts of children. For when they are considered as preparatory or ancillary to aesthetic education (and a very modest investment of curricular time would, I think, suffice for this purpose), creative activities can be valued in their capacity of adding practically acquired knowledge to the stock that is to inform individuals' transactions with artworks throughout their adult lives.

I conclude this section on aesthetic skills with some observations on the educational respectability of the concept of a skill. (1) Skills are not dependent on special talents possessed by the few but are trained capacities present in varying degrees in everyone, a circumstance we may appeal to when trying to secure aesthetic education in the general curriculum. (2) Objectivity and verifiability should, as I have already mentioned, be preferred and emphasized wherever possible in education, and they are in the case of aesthetic skills. As Osborne tells us, aesthetic appreciation involves a cognitive skill "purporting to apprehend and discriminate qualities residing in the object of attention, qualities which can be recognized and tested by others who have the skill."[27] (3) Skill is a potentiality concept referring to a cultivated capacity for performance—a capacity that students may elect to actualize (and we hope, of course, that they will) but are perfectly free to let lie fallow. In training students for aesthetic skills, therefore, we have not imposed our wills or conditioned or indoctrinated them. We have simply given them the ability to experience aesthetic value. (4) Values describe the human benefit for the sake of which education is undertaken and which, in turn, justifies such education. The benefits of aesthetic experience have already been enumerated. To them we can now add the satisfaction that flows from the exercise of a skill. When we have learned to do something, especially something rather difficult (like the aesthetic appreciation of a complex work of art) and do it well, we are pleased with ourselves, and have reason to be.

Joseph D. Novak: Aesthetic learning—a cognitive approach

A discussion of aesthetic education is incomplete without mention of a learning theory that is congruent with its principal emphasis and direction. The idea of aesthetic education presented in this study stresses the development of a sense of art that in turn presupposes the skills needed for aesthetic appreciation. Since the acquisition of these critical/aesthetic skills involves learning the fundamental concepts and principles of art and the traditions in which they are embedded, a theory of concept learning would seem appropriate. Such a theory has been developed by Joseph D. Novak around the idea of learning through assimilation.

The notion of assimilation learning has roots in cognitive theories of human understanding that can be conveniently traced in the fifth edition of R. L. W. Travers's *Essentials of Learning*,[28] written especially for students of education. For my purposes, however, I follow the lead of Novak's *A Theory of Education*,[29] first published in 1977 and reissued, with a new preface, in 1987. Novak's book draws heavily on the work of David Ausubel, Thomas Kuhn, and Stephen Toulmin and describes an assimilation theory of learning influenced by Ausubel's conception of meaningful verbal learning; Kuhn's discussion of paradigms, paradigm shifts, and revolution in science; and Toulmin's evolutionary model of the historical growth of concepts. What interested Novak in the work of Kuhn and Toulmin was their suggestion that paradigms of intellectual inquiry tend to control intellectual activity for a time and then suddenly or gradually (more likely the latter, Toulmin thinks) get replaced by new paradigms. Novak perceived an analogy between scientific paradigms which guide scientific inquiry and the evolution of conceptual frameworks as described in Ausubel's theory of meaningful learning. I shall briefly outline here Ausubel's theory as explained by Novak. (With some slight changes in emphasis and language, the theory is developed further in the second edition of Ausubel's *Educational Psychology,*[30] coauthored with Novak and Helen Hanesian.)

Following Ausubel, Novak relies on a theoretical construct variously called a conceptual framework, cognitive structure, or conceptual hierarchy. Such a structure is a heuristic device that helps us to imagine the nature of concept acquisition and possession. As it makes assumptions about interior mental processes, Novak's theory differs pointedly from behavioristic accounts of learning. Again, an individual is thought to possess a *cognitive structure* of hierarchically ordered concepts which constitute that person's representations of sensory experience. Since we can be certain that children already possess some of the elements of such a conceptual framework when they enter school, the question for the educator is how additional concepts are acquired and how conceptual frameworks develop.

In the theory under discussion, a person's cognitive structure expands through the process of meaningful learning, during which new information is related to a relevant concept already present in the structure. Or better, new information is *assimilated*. Hence in the second edition of Ausubel's *Educational Psychology,* the expression *assimilation theory of learning* is preferred to "meaningful learning." Because assimilation occurs when a new item is subsumed under a relevant concept within a person's cognitive structure, that concept is termed a subsuming concept or *subsumer*. Subsumers, then, are those concepts in a person's mental framework that have the capacity to assimilate new items. A person's mental framework is thus conceived as possessing potential for evolutionary growth, a feature that makes it a particularly attractive construct for the educational theorist.

Evolution, however, is not merely a matter of accumulating concepts. Assimilation is an *interactive* process during which mental modification of the old and the new occurs. When a new concept is assimilated by a subsumer, the subsumer itself undergoes some change; for example, it may become more *differentiated* in terms of detail and specificity. This means that the subsumer improves its capacity for still further assimilation of information. Simultaneous with the acquisition of new knowledge, adjustments and realignments occur within information already possessed. This continual refinement of conceptual structure has two noteworthy effects. First, because of the subtle modifications of the old by the new, items learned meaningfully are seldom retrieved precisely in the form in which they had been learned. Second, with progressive differentiation new linkages are frequently established between the subsumers themselves. A previously learned concept may be recognized as an element of a larger, more inclusive concept and thus acquire a new potency. This sort of learning, which does not depend so much on the assimilation of new information as it does on recognizing new connections between items already known, is termed *superordinate learning*.

Important in the analysis of assimilation theory thus far is the supposition that persons not only acquire more information, but, due to the concurrent development of their conceptual frameworks, also increase their capacity for further learning. Assimilation learning thus differs from rote learning, in which information is stored within the cognitive structure in an arbitrary, unrelated fashion. Items learned by rote do not contribute much to the conceptual framework's evolution and, lacking firm anchorage, tend to be forgotten quickly. Although memorization is vital for understanding some things, Novak does not believe it contributes significantly to the kind of learning that strengthens the capacity for assimilating additional knowledge.

Novak's theory of assimilation learning—which is also known as *reception learning* and might just as well be called cogent learning—also throws new light on a source of puzzlement and vexation to many people: their inability to remember things once learned in school even though they thought they had overlearned them so well that their possession would be permanent. Although it is true that even items once learned meaningfully will not remain available indefinitely, assimilation learning, which emphasizes the understanding of basic ideas and promotes the capacity for further learning, is still a good hedge against total forgetting. Here it should be recalled that an item learned meaningfully not only modifies a subsumer by expanding its potential for further assimilation but also changes slightly the information already held in the conceptual framework. These modifications, says Novak, appear to be retained. Thus when a concept drops out at the lower end of the structure, the differentiations and the enlarged capacity for learning it had helped to bring about tend to persist even after that particular item is forgotten. Moreover, what can no longer be readily recalled is often quite easily reinstated with a minimum of cues and reminders. Therefore, the person who had once learned, say, aesthetic object and critical activity concepts in a meaningful manner but can no longer name them on demand is still in a better position than someone who never learned them productively at all.

Despite one connotation of the term "reception," reception learning is not passive. The mind is neither an inert receptacle that accepts new ideas indifferently nor a kind of flypaper to which new information simply adheres. Both students and teachers are intensively engaged, and students participate actively in their learning. But it is the teacher's work that is particularly demanding, and it involves at least three separate tasks.

First, since reception learning takes place when new material connects with relevant subsumers already present in a person's cognitive structure, teachers are obligated to ascertain, as far as they can, the nature and extent of the subsumers the students bring with them. Novak thus provides a theoretical basis for something we know intuitively, namely, that we should find out how much people already know about a subject before we try to teach them something new. Second, because new information has less chance of being learned meaningfully when it is offered haphazardly, teachers should arrange instructional materials and sequences in such a way as to make learning more likely to occur. This too sounds commonsensical, yet as one often hears that a teacher's commitment and concern are more conducive to learning than carefully organized instruction, the point merits mentioning. The theory of concept learning, in any case, urges teachers to rely on *advance organizers* as the principal means for building bridges from new to old information. Advance organizers are the more general and inclusive concepts of a discipline or subject. Being more abstract than the learning material they introduce and for which they serve as a bridge, they possess greater explanatory power and integrative capacity. Teachers must therefore identify concepts that promise to be effective organizers. (The notion of advance organizers is one of the differences between productive learning of the sort advocated by Novak and inquiry or discovery methods.) A third task for teachers consists in aiding superordinate learning. That is, teachers should help students become aware of new connections and relations among items already familiar to them. This means that from time to time students should be given opportunities for estimating the progress they think they have made in what Novak and D. Bob Gowin in their *Learning How to Learn* call concept mapping.[31]

It should be clear from even this short sketch that concept learning can proceed only with the help of knowledgeable and skilled teachers dedicated to advancing the understanding and growth of their students. Equally evident is one of the merits of assimilation theory: the fact that it does justice to both the basic concepts and principles of a subject or area of study (namely, its advance organizers and hierarchy of general to lower order concepts) and the cognitive structure of students (namely, their evolving cognitive frameworks). These features satisfy an important requirement of curriculum design, that is, sensitivity to the demands of the subject as well as those of the learner.

The use of a theory like Novak's to shed light on the nature of teaching and learning in the arts may be criticized on several grounds. To many, the image of mind and its workings that Novak projects is simply not credible. To such an objection I can only reply that theoretical representations of mental structures are heuristic devices which attain whatever plausibility they have through practical application, that is, by how well they seem to explain what happens. Others might question the appropriateness to arts teaching of a theory that evolved from a science background and was framed without particular thought about art. Is not such a model excessively cognitive and verbal; does it not leave out of account the important affective component of aesthetic transactions? Here the answer is quite clear, for although knowledge about art and the teaching and learning of aesthetic concepts have been accorded much space in this study, no doubt had been left that these cognitive and conceptual elements would function instrumentally, would be used as means toward enlightened aesthetic experience. Since aesthetic experience is highly gratifying, the affective dimension is amply provided for and would not be encroached on by a theory of concept learning. Furthermore, learning of any kind in any field is accompanied by affect. Goodman even goes so far as to say that one knows with the emotions.

Still others would claim that because the visual arts and music are largely nonverbal, a view of arts teaching that relies as much on discourse as the one recommended here does is improper, if not damaging. But just as there is no conflict between the cognitive and the aesthetic, there is none between the verbal and the aesthetic. Discourse is simply the only way the teacher (and the critic) has for bringing an artwork closer to the percipient. (And it is a fact, as Barzun implied, that people do like to talk about art, to demonstrate their understanding of a work, and to share, as Steiner put it, its extraordinary qualities and richness.) Yet verbal pyrotechnics and convincing aesthetic argument aside, teachers will not succeed in their teaching task until and unless students *discover for themselves,* in their own experiences of art, the properties of an artwork that teachers attempt to capture linguistically. The finding reported in Chapter 3 that persuasive aesthetic arguments are logically distinct, that is, neither inductive nor deductive, implicitly left a space for discoveries to be made by those to whom such arguments are directed.

The mention of "discovery" conveniently leads to a few comments about method, as educators readily associate the term with "discovery learning" or the "discovery method" of teaching. The discovery thesis claims that students learn meaningfully only those things they have hit on by themselves, unaided and unprompted. Novak's theory proposes a different sense for "meaningful learning," one that refers to the attachment of new material to the existing conceptual framework and thus sets itself against loosely structured discovery approaches. Yet an approving account of concept learning can stop short of saying that the teaching method consistent with it is the only one suitable for aesthetic education; far from it. A role can be assigned to discovery. Furthermore, since aesthetic appreciation, as pointed out in the preceding section, is here also defined as a skill that requires to be practiced, other teaching methods—especially those used in training—obviously become helpful as well. The teacher, for example, often demonstrates aesthetic criticism through open-ended dialogue, and this involves coaching students' responses as they tackle artworks on their own, guiding them through puzzles, encouraging them to reflect on their judgments, and prodding them to leaps of understanding. And in probing works of art students deploy a variety of inquiry learning techniques. Finally, to the extent that creative activities contribute to the fund of knowledge needed for aesthetic appreciation, the different methods and techniques involved in teaching these activities also become relevant.

This said, I reaffirm assimilation learning theory as a powerful tool for teaching the basic principles and ideas of important areas of study. A special merit of the theory is that it goes straight to the heart of the problem of teaching students how to learn—of particular importance for aesthetic education, which is meant to fit students for lifelong citizenship in the art world. An approach like Novak's may even be more effective in the preparation of arts teachers as it would force them to think rigorously about their field and its underlying assumptions, about organizing ideas as well as entire hierarchies of concepts, and about structuring these for assimilation by students. This kind of training might give us art teachers who would become impatient with the conditions John Goodlad described in his report on schooling. (It will be recalled that he believed too much time was spent in art classes on playing and performing and not enough on more serious involvement with artworks.)

Finally, the theory of assimilation learning also suggests an agenda of conceptual and empirical research in arts education. When grounded in an appropriate learning theory, research can focus on key problems, and this enhances the prospect that results will have relevance to practice. Assimilation theory can also aid in interpreting the results of research that was conducted with other aims in mind. Developmental accounts of aesthetic development (like Michael Parsons's, to be discussed next) could, I think, be fruitfully analyzed in terms of assimilation theory. From the ways respondents of different age groups and from different social backgrounds talk about an artwork it would be possible to make inferences about their conceptual frameworks for understanding art. Research could then attempt to test the assumptions of assimilation theory by conducting experiments to discover if learning can be improved along the lines suggested. How, for example, do cognitive structures expand and organize and reorganize themselves progressively from the earlier to the later stages of aesthetic development? What are the most effective organizers for building bridges between new information and a person's cognitive structure? What techniques are resorted to to build these bridges? To speculate, an effort could be made to analyze Leo Steinberg's difficulty, discussed in Chapter 2, in light of Novak's assimilation theory. Steinberg in effect stated that his mental framework was insufficient to the task of assessing the value of Johns's work. In this head-on clash of two senses of art, Steinberg's cognitive stock seemed deficient. But eventually Steinberg did come to terms with the work. How? What "subsumers" did he discover in his conceptual structure? How did he fashion interpretive bridges of comprehension? Of course, Steinberg's case is simply an instance of a more general problem with which teachers and researchers constantly have to grapple: How people come to understand and appreciate novel aspects of art and how we can account for their doing so.

Michael Parsons: How we understand art

The illuminating character of Novak's assimilation theory notwith-standing, it remains true that it was framed for learning generally. To advance the argument of the present study, however, the theory should be supplemented with an account of the growth of specifically aesthetic understanding. Such is available in Michael Parsons's cognitive developmental description of aesthetic experience, a groundbreaking work titled *How We Understand Art*.[32]

In discussing Parsons's account, I am less concerned to assess the strength of his hypothesis that aesthetic development passes through five identifiable stages than to examine how the conceptual schemes of the persons he interviewed were determined and how the degree of adequacy for understanding art displayed by these frameworks was established. I am also interested in his investigations into the changing character of aesthetic judgment and what his findings suggest for teaching and learning aesthetic skills. Does Parsons's study, for example, lend credence to Novak's idea that concepts once acquired are not lost but become transfigured into new cognitive patterns and structures? And at what point in aesthetic development might teaching suitably intervene to facilitate aesthetic learning? In particular, given Parsons's familiarity with the problems of aesthetic experience and judgment, how does his writing illuminate some of the central issues dealt with in this book?

How We Understand Art contains a theory that presents aesthetic development in terms of progressively more successful efforts to make sense of a number of artworks, namely paintings. Parsons takes for granted that works of art must be taken seriously in their own right and that their meanings are sui generis. To discover what a particular painting meant to individuals, he analyzed both their reactions to it and the reasons they gave for saying what they did. With its careful attention to verbal statements, Parsons's approach stands in contrast to, and is critical of, cognitive studies of the arts that stress behaviors instead of under-standings. In short, Parsons aimed to accomplish for aesthetic develop-ment what Jean Piaget and Lawrence Kohlberg did for cognitive and moral development, respectively. He declares himself especially in-debted to Kohlberg's study of moral thinking and finds parallels between Kohlberg's stages and his own. While Kohlberg identified six stages of moral development, Parsons differentiated five for aesthetic develop-ment, conflating for his purposes Kohlberg's fifth and sixth stages. But Parsons also progressed beyond Kohlberg in one important respect. Where Kohlberg interpreted the later stages of moral reflection as involving the monologic application of principles privately known, Parsons postulates the emergence of a social factor for the more mature phases of aesthetic growth; that is, his theory provides for an awareness of the views of others and a consequent sense of responsibility for one's own.

Parsons acknowledges a long-standing interest in discourse about art and states that he is particularly interested in understanding why people say different things about the same work of art. He conjectured that this variability is due to the different expectations people bring to artworks. Accordingly, Parsons set himself the objective of rendering explicit the implicit assumptions underlying aesthetic responses.

But Parsons realized that without a solid philosophical foundation, the study of persons' reactions to art risks irrelevancy; he was therefore careful to undergird his hypothesis with insights culled from general philosophy and aesthetics. He draws, for instance, on Kant's differentiation among the empirical, the moral, and the aesthetic and on Jurgen Habermas's theory which holds that these three modes of thought refer to the external world of objects, the social world of norms, and the inner world of the self, each sphere being unique in respect of its peculiar data and meanings. From distinctions like these Parsons infers that there should be three streams of cognitive development, with the aesthetic corresponding to the third realm. This association with the "world of the self" is evident in Parsons's remark "that a response to art is an implicit exploration of self and human nature," to which he adds that "it is so at every stage of development."[33] For Parsons, then, works of art make available avenues to self-understanding, a view of the nature and function of art that he derived mainly from his readings of Collingwood, Dewey, Langer, and Danto. Beside theoretical soundness, Parsons also wants to claim practical usefulness for his work, especially through the guidance it may offer to teachers and parents under whose care and supervision young children undergo the earliest phases of aesthetic growth.

Parsons's research extended over a period of ten years, during which he and his associates elicited responses to reproductions of eight paintings[34] from individuals that included young children as well as college professors. The topics broached in each interview were the same and ranged from subject matter, expressiveness, and medium to form and style. He also requested evaluations of each artwork and asked for the reasons persons gave in support of their judgments. His data led Parsons to conclude that our understanding of art develops sequentially through stages and that it progressively restructures itself as we grow older and have more experience with art. "Each step is an advance on the previous one because it makes possible a more adequate understanding of art."[35] By a stage, Parsons understands "clusters of ideas, and not properties of persons. A cluster is a pattern, or structure, of internally related assumptions that tend to go together in people's minds just because they are internally, or logically, related. To describe a stage is not to describe a person but a set of ideas. People use these ideas to make sense of paintings."[36] Putting it differently, a stage is "a loosely knit structure in which a number of ideas are shaped by a dominant insight about art."[37] Parsons subdivides his five stages into two preconventional and two conventional ones and one postconventional one. He makes it clear, however, that stages are mainly analytic devices that help us to gauge a person's capacity to deal with art and are not, except for the earliest phases, strongly related to biological age. Thus we may find otherwise very competent adults who display arrested aesthetic development in their dealings with art. Before moving to a synopsis of Parsons's five stages, it should be pointed out that each stage describes a developmental phase with respect not only to aesthetic but also to psychological adequacy, that is, a plateau in an improving capacity to understand paintings as well as in the ability to take the perspective of others.

Since in general the pattern of aesthetic development follows that of human development from biological dependency to autonomy, it is not surprising that its first stage (favoritism) is characterized by self-centeredness. Young children do not grasp the complexity of a painting but respond arbitrarily to only selected aspects of a work, particularly to color, which they seem to enjoy. In fact, for young children the degree of pleasure a painting affords forms the only standard of judgment, and the rest of their discussion of the work is marked by free-wheeling association.

Respondents in the second phase of aesthetic growth (beauty and realism) evince a pronounced interest in subject matter and the faithfulness and skill of its depiction; these as well as "beauty" are cited as reasons for favorable assessments of paintings. During both the first and second stages, what is seen in a painting is taken as self-evident; judgments are usually positive and are rendered in an unmediated, unreflective way.

In the third stage expressiveness comes to the fore. Beauty, skill, and realism, which absorbed the greatest share of respondents' interest earlier, are not abandoned but are no longer insisted on, as feeling and emotion have become governing concerns. These affective qualities are remarked on chiefly as they make themselves felt in the percipient's experience of the painting; they are believed to be genuine and are rated most favorably when they are intense and riveting. But expressiveness is not circumscribed by its effect on the percipient's own self since it is now also explored in relation to the artist's inner life. By this stage, then, a quite discernible distance has been traveled from the egocenteredness of the earliest phases. Judgments are made on the basis of a work's originality and the depth of its feeling. Yet a growing skepticism concerning the value of verbal description and the possibility of an objective evaluation are also typical of the third phase of aesthetic development.

Respondents in stage four (style and form) begin to approximate the critical skills and attitudes of experienced observers of art (though they are still not capable of the sophisticated and introspective aesthetic reactions characteristic of the fifth stage). They make increasingly discerning discriminations among the work's medium, form, and content, concentration on which has taken the place of the earlier fascination with expressiveness; furthermore, percipients are now able to distinguish between description and interpretation. Aesthetic experience, in short, has become notably richer and more complex. More importantly, works of art are no longer viewed merely as singular individual achievements existing in a vacuum but are treated as artifacts set in a context and against a historical background. Starting with stage three and certainly by stage four, the framework for understanding art has become significantly expanded by an awareness of traditions and communities of interpretation and judgment. The individual's encounters with art thus begin to take the viewpoints of others into consideration. As for aesthetic judgment and criticism, these are now deemed both necessary and objectively possible. Moreover, in stage four persons engage in interpretation and criticism deliberately and self-consciously, thereby compounding their aesthetic transactions with the dimension of self-awareness. They do not, however, tend to question the norms by which they judge art.

Questioning of this sort is reserved for stage five, the postconventional level of autonomy. Persons who have reached this phase infuse their aesthetic encounters with all the knowledge and experience accumulated up to that point. At this level, writes Parsons, we have become capable of "the self-conscious articulation of the meanings we find in the painting and of our sense of their value. It is a cyclical process, a going back and forth between description, interpretation, and judgment, sometimes the two or three of them all at once, much as the hermeneutic circle cycles around and around. It follows that our judgments will be as varied as our descriptions and interpretations."[38] Along then with the assurance and finesse they have developed in their dealings with artworks and the consciousness of the variability of judgment and interpretation, individuals also begin to express some ambivalence and hesitancy. Judgments are now recognized as separate from interpretations; they are responsibly supported by reasons believed to be plausible and are submitted on the Kantian assumption that others who share the same culture, interests, and conception of human rationality will agree with them. Yet the person who has attained the stage of autonomy realizes that universal agreement in an aesthetic assessment is only an abstract supposition needed to make such judgments possible in the first place. There is no guarantee that the evaluation will be accepted, indeed every likelihood that it will be disputed by some. In fact, the individual is as ready to have his understanding of an artwork challenged as he is to question standards and criteria of judgment. "The result," says Parsons, "is an alert awareness of the character of one's own experience, a questioning of the influences upon it, a wondering whether one really sees what one thinks one sees."[39] This sort of existential self-doubt makes people eager to test and clarify their impressions, and stage five is therefore as notable for its lively and informed dialogue as for its introspection. Parsons found all the stage five characteristics exemplified by Henry, a college professor of art; we have in effect met him before in Steinberg's account of his effort to wrest meaning from Jasper Johns's *Target with Four Faces*. Finally, in the most advanced stage of aesthetic development individuals are also able to actualize to the fullest what, as mentioned before, Parsons takes to be the essential function of art and aesthetic experience: the clarification and understanding of the self. He writes:

> As we clarify our response to a painting, we also clarify our self—our own feelings, meanings, ideals. As we decide on an interpretation, we decide what some of these feelings, meanings, ideals are. We become aware of them as different elements of our response; and we examine them in an effort to get them clearer. And as we judge a painting, we judge the elements of our experience and hold their character and value in question. If we adjust them in light of our sense of their value, we adjust, we could say, our self.[40]

Such a brief survey of Parsons's account of aesthetic development does not do justice to the wealth of knowledge that informs his explanations. The observations I now add, however, will use some of Parsons's ideas to pursue certain lines of thought I've been developing in this essay. The first comment concerns method. It will be recalled that the discussion of Novak's learning theory mentioned that teachers, if they are to organize material for effective assimilation of the new to the old, must first try to ascertain what concepts are present in a student's cognitive structure, as well as their range, elasticity, and suitability as subsumers, and how much progress the student has made in superordinate learning. This is a difficult task, but I submit that the interviews described by Parsons suggest a perfect method for accomplishing it. For this is exactly what Parsons did: to find out what people of different ages and backgrounds already knew about art.

The second point should be obvious but does require emphasis in light of the temper of the times: Parsons views the progression through the stages of aesthetic development as a gradual improvement. This flies in the face of the pervasive relativism in educational thinking that recognizes differences in kind but not in quality or degree of adequacy. Students of education are often unshakable in their conviction that the arts experiences of young children are merely different from, but in no way inferior to, those of aesthetically well-educated adults; to think otherwise is to be guilty of elitism. (Yet surely, if all stages are different but equal, there would be no good reason for teaching to intervene in order to move people from one to another.) Parsons also realizes that his account may be misunderstood as disparaging the aesthetic abilities evidenced in the earlier stages. He is, however, nothing if not sympathetic to the reactions of persons he interviewed and genuinely appreciative of young people's capacity for aesthetic response. His sensitivity and empathy are apparent on every page. But he stops short of sentimentality and the romanticizing of the young; they are not the equals of adult critics and artists. "There is a whole series of insights about paintings that they [young people] do not have and that are of great importance. For this reason many significant aesthetic qualities are inaccessible to them and their experience of art lacks the richness available to adults. Aesthetic development consists precisely in the gradual acquisition of these insights. We reach the later stages only with an education in which we encounter works of art often and think about them seriously."[41] (These remarks call to mind Osborne's about the time and effort required for the cultivation of aesthetic skills.)

It is quite easy to see how Parsons's empirical account of aesthetic development could accommodate Novak's learning theory. We can, I think, interpret Parsons's explanation as postulating an aesthetic conceptual framework (cognitive structure, conceptual hierarchy) composed of groups of subsuming concepts that are dominant at different stages of development and as assuming evolutionary paradigms of understanding that succeed but do not obliterate one another. Each paradigm constitutes a person's representations of the sensory experience of a painting appropriate to that person's level of development. Gradually, new information and ideas interact with the individual's cognitive structure in such a way that both the already present subsumers and the new material undergo change while retaining or increasing their capacity to assimilate still further concepts. For example, in stage three the dominance of the idea of expressiveness suppressed and altered the previously prominent conceptions of subject matter and realistic depiction. During the next higher phase, expressiveness in turn became incorporated into a new configuration dominated by yet another constellation of concepts.

These few hints may be sufficient to indicate how the cognitive growth presupposed by Parsons's hypothesis could be accounted for with the help of a theory of concept learning, but this really does not take us quite far enough. For neither concept learning nor even aesthetic development is, strictly speaking, an end in itself. As we have seen, in Parsons's scheme the ultimate reason for which aesthetic experiences are sought and refined through education is increased awareness and knowledge of self. This we may now add to the list, developed in Chapter 2, of values realized and benefits gained through aesthetic experience: aesthetic gratification (Beardsley), expanded powers of percipience (Osborne), insight and understanding (Goodman), and the ability to function efficaciously within the institutions of the artworld (Kaelin). But self-knowledge should be recognized as also being among the most important professed objectives of liberal or humanistic education. By stipulating it as one of the outcomes of full aesthetic development aided by aesthetic education, we have prepared the ground for a portion of the next chapter: the argument that art should be taught as a humanity and aesthetic education properly considered a part of humanities programs.

CHAPTER 6

Toward an art world curriculum

> If from the widest purview the task of
> the educator is to help and guide others
> in the lifelong business of equipping
> themselves to live in the world of men,
> refining their sensibilities and improving
> the delicacy and range of their apprehen-
> sions, then in the narrower field of aes-
> thetic education the goal may not ab-
> surdly be represented as the provision
> of guidance and help to those who are
> interested in equipping themselves to
> live and move in the world of art, min-
> gling with its inhabitants as persons of
> sensitivity and tact. *Harold Osborne*[1]

Curriculum as itinerary

"To live and move in the world of art, mingling with its inhabitants
as persons of sensitivity and tact"—an appropriate goal for a program
in aesthetic education and one that suggests an image of curriculum as
itinerary, where "itinerary" implies not only a plan for a journey but also
routes to be taken and guides and guidebooks to be consulted. Seen
under the aspect of itinerary, an art world curriculum is a plan of studies
designed to develop dispositions that will enable persons to move through
the art world with a degree of adroitness and expertise. By "inhabitants"
of the art world, moreover, we may take Osborne to mean not only
works of art but also persons who occupy themselves with artworks in
different ways, for example, as artists, art historians, art critics, and
aesthetic auxiliaries of several kinds (see Appendix II).

But what shall be the nature of an itinerary designed to acquaint the
young with the inhabitants of the art world? How extensive is the art
world, and what are its major points of interest? What are the principal
and secondary roads by which it is to be traversed? Some observations
have, of course, already been made that partly answer these questions,
and it may be useful to recall them here.

The examination of art in cultural context in Chapter 1, for example,
accented the temporal dimension of the art world. Kenneth Clark scanned
the history of Western visual art for generalizations about the relations
of art and society, while Jacques Barzun, in describing the evolution of
attitudes toward art and art's role in society, narrowed the purview to the
last 150 years. From another vantage point, Harold Rosenberg and Clifton
Fadiman described what happens when the art world and the media system
of mass communication impinge on each other; the imperatives of the latter
transform the artwork into a package designed, produced, and marketed
for a global audience, with consequent effects on quality (indeed, quantity

becomes a substitute for quality). The system of mass communication, however, is just one social force that tends to annex art. As Monroe Beardsley points out in his analysis, art is also in danger of being assimilated by political ideology and social science, hence special efforts must be made to safeguard art's autonomy.

Fortunately, the art world has not been completely absorbed by society and continues to be an identifiable cultural sector, a loosely structured institution with discernible boundaries and policies. This fact enabled Kaelin to delineate the art world and assign to it a characteristic mission—to provide for the creation, preservation, and appreciation of aesthetic value understood as the capacity of an artwork to effect the kind of meaningful communication that enriches human experience.

If we are to initiate the young into the art world, we must draw attention to its past, present, and continuing evolution toward the future; Chapter 1, as mentioned, allowed a quick look at the relevant terrain, the lay of the land, as it were. The art of travel, however, involves not only knowing where to go and how to get there, but also how to make the most of what is discovered upon arrival; that is, travelers should know how to actualize values of different sorts. The problems of teaching what is required to realize aesthetic values constitute a principal concern of this study. Accordingly, in Chapter 3 Henry Aiken, adopting an educator's stance, described the conditions for knowing, understanding, and appreciating works of art; the discussions of the work of Osborne, Beardsley, Goodman, and Kaelin in Chapter 2 delivered theoretical accounts of the form and dynamics of aesthetic understanding; Chapter 4, via the perceptions of Clark, Schapiro, Steinberg, Kauffmann, Kramer, and Wollheim, illustrated the quality of percipience at issue in experiencing art as art (while Appendix I, through the eyes of yet another set of sensitive observers, will glance at the beauties of nature and of the humanly made environment). The ideal aesthetic percipient, we may say, combines the aesthetic eye of the naturalist Charles Darwin, the literary impressionistic sensibility of a Henry James, the visual percipience of a Kenneth Clark or Meyer Schapiro, and the intensity of vision of a Kandinsky or Van Gogh. All these observers provide clues to what it means to realize aesthetic value, wherever it is found, even when (as in the case of Steinberg's encounter with the works of Johns) one is initially taken aback by what one sees. In short, the preceding chapter gives substance to Osborne's notion of "mingling with the inhabitants of the art world" and how such encounters can secure a peculiar kind of gratification, heightened percipience, understanding, and improvement in the effectiveness of cultural institutions.

What is more, travelers through the art world receive wise counsel when they entrust themselves to the guidance of aesthetic critics. Yet aesthetic criticism is not easily defined, hence Chapter 3 undertook to describe criticism's various modes with the aid of insights provided by

Eaton, Crittenden, and Beardsley. A parallel was established between the professional art critic, who pilots mature individuals through the art world and points out what is and is not worth spending time with, and the teacher-as-critic, who acts similarly in initiating students into the domain of culture. But one has to keep in mind that there are also striking differences between the task of the scholar or art critic and that of the teacher, the special difficulty of the latter having been remarked on by Aiken. I should mention that the idea of the teacher-as-critic is not original, and I merely join several others who have stressed the relevance of art criticism to the teaching of art.[2] But my reasons for endorsing this image of the teacher and learner should by now be apparent. In addition to underscoring the importance to the individual of acquiring aesthetic critical skills needed to understand and appreciate art, the teacher-as-critic image also satisfies the demand that the schools play a part in reconstituting serious and genuine aesthetic judgment in the population and in restoring the advantages of a general appreciation of aesthetic value and accomplishment to society. And, finally, the critic as model for the teacher helps to order and systematize thinking about aesthetic instruction in the schools. As this book understands it, the responsibility of educational institutions is nothing less than that of enabling persons to become critics in their own right and hence less dependent on the opinions and value judgments of others.

Educating persons to critical percipience in matters of art, however, is neither lightly undertaken nor quickly achieved. The sense of art with which the individual encounters and engages artworks can be developed only over a considerable period of time, with different accents and emphases at different stages, depending on a student's phase of aesthetic learning and the particular objectives appropriate to it. It should go without saying that such a protracted educational endeavor requires special curricular provisions. If art is as serious and important a human activity as writers from antiquity to the present have said it is, then its study demands its own curriculum space and time. There should be periods devoted not only to informal familiarization and perceptual training, but also to creative probing and the developing of historical and critical awareness, all of which are prerequisite to acquiring an educated and refined sense of art. The last portion of this chapter will describe an art world curriculum for kindergarten through twelfth grade, one that will include what I have elsewhere called an excellence curriculum for secondary education.

To recommend an art world curriculum at this time is to respond to what might be called the second wave of the excellence-in-education movement of the 1980s, a wave that is dramatizing the lack of elementary knowledge about their cultural heritage evidenced by today's young people.[3] While a mixed bag, the publications of this second wave testify to the major deficiencies that the schools are currently trying to remedy through a number of reform efforts, such as new state requirements for periodical testing in basic skills and knowledge and serious ventures into restructuring teacher education. One can also detect a more pronounced concern for substance in the theoretical literature of arts education, where greater emphasis than previously is being placed on the historical and critical study of the arts.[4] Programs initiated by the public and private sectors further reflect these trends.

One conclusion of my *Excellence in Art Education* was that the growing interest in the relevance of several academic disciplines to arts education—for example, art history, aesthetics, and art criticism— argues for a more humanities-like conception of arts education and of the preparation of arts teachers. Although this seemed to me a logical next step to take, and I will trace its implications presently, it does not seem to have occurred to policy analysts who also call for more rigor and substance in arts education.[5] Yet, theories that could furnish the impetus for a humanities approach to arts education are conveniently at hand, for example, in the writings of Albert William Levi, who interprets art as a humanity in a way that is quite compatible with the theory advanced in this volume.

Albert William Levi: Teaching art as a humanity

First of all I offer the idea of a humanities-like conception of aesthetic education as an *ideal,* yet one that even in being striven for lends amplitude and dignity to the enterprise by associating it with a time-honored tradition.

To the present argument in favor of aesthetic education, Levi lends the point of view of a philosopher of the humanities and culture. Yet he does not confine himself to the lofty heights of abstract thought. As a charter member of the National Council of the Humanities, Levi is sensitive to public policy issues affecting the humanities. It is therefore with the aim of promoting the humanities in an age in many ways hostile to them and of securing their position against contemporary social and educational realities that he worked toward a redefinition of the human-ities in terms appropriate to our time. His philosophical writings on the subject are therefore meant to have practical, that is, educational and pedagogical, consequences. In a number of books and essays,[6] Levi examines the status of the humanities in light of the problems besetting contemporary society; the difficulties posed to humanistic scholarship and teaching by the expansion of course offerings beyond the bounds of Western civilization; the attempt of the democratic ethos to come to terms with an aristocratic tradition of learning and culture; the demand that the humanities demonstrate a causal connection between their sup-posed stewardship of civilized values and the actual conduct of persons; and the preservation of the distinctive claims of the humanities against those of their vigorous new rival, the social sciences. A formidable agenda!

In addressing this agenda, Levi first provides a history of the evolution of the idea of humanities from antiquity to the present (which need not detain us here) as well as a glimpse of his own philosophical presuppositions. It is not necessary, however, to subscribe to the full scope of Levi's metaphysics in order to appreciate the practical significance of his conception of the humanistic domain. To apprehend the distinctiveness of the humanities, I think one only has to assume the existence of two divergent tendencies of mind: the disposition of the understanding and that of the imagination.

The understanding and the imagination express themselves, respectively, in the sciences, or the scientific chain of meaning, as Levi calls it, and in the humanities or the humanistic complex. The two areas differ along three lines: the faculties of the mind they engage, the objects they study, and the language in which they report results (Levi discovers or constructs several triads). Following are a few of the concepts Levi associates with the understanding and the imagination. The language of the understanding animates the scientific chain of meaning and is concerned with true and false propositions, the problem of error, causality, scientific law, prediction and chance, facts, and the stasis or equilibrium of systems, among others. The language of the imagination, on the other hand, is essentially dramatic and opposes appearance and illusion to reality; it is concerned with destiny, human purpose, fate, fortune, tragedy, and the like.[7]

In other words, the most remarkable aspect of the humanistic complex is its central preoccupation with the dramatic dimension and valuational aspects of human experience. The emphasis on value exploration is what makes teaching in the humanities so different from teaching in the natural and social sciences. True, the sciences also have a value component and may be explored from a humanistic point of view, as they are in the history and philosophy of science. Still, says Levi, "the humanities embrace them [values] with an earnestness that is to be found nowhere in the spectrum of knowledge and education," and thus "what the humanities contribute is a unique gift to the valuational consciousness of man."[8] For Levi, values are essentially *"affective-volitional meanings."*[9] By this he understands values to be, in the first instance, concepts or ideas; in the second, loci of approval and disapproval; and in the third, imperatives in the claims they make upon choice and avoidance. This tripartite conception of value is quite easily related to the account of aesthetic education presented in this book: aesthetic *concepts* and skills are taught because they are needed for an educated capacity to perform aesthetic criticism and make judgments *(approval* and *disapproval),* and this form of education is intended to lead students to prefer excellence in art (that is, it will make claims on their *choices* and *avoidances.)*

Saying that the humanities embrace values, however, is merely preparatory to Levi's reformulation of the standard conception of the humanities. His redefinition occurs in the course of his explanation of how, and under what rubrics, values are studied and actualized in the humanities. But after describing Levi's reconception, it should be noted that he sets the humanities apart not only from science, but also from the fine arts. This segregation of the fine arts, however, applies only to their productive functions and is based on a long-standing distinction between knowledge and creativity. In this limited and specialized view, then, the fine arts are taken notice of only as the originators of things that become objects of study for the humanities. But of course the fine arts are much more than that; hence, with suitable qualifications, we may reinstate them in the humanities at a later point.

To return to Levi's redefinition of the humanities: he discusses two ways of understanding them, each with a long tradition, and he characteristically effects a synthesis between them in a third option. One of the two perceptions of the humanities dates from the Renaissance, when, for the first time, a noticeable sense of "looking back" developed, a longing for rediscovery and recovery. Since the objectives of these humanistic searches and researches were ancient texts, tradition came to be understood as the transmission of *literary artifacts*. The effects of this Renaissance accident, claims Levi, persist today, for we too tend to view the humanities as content, for example as great books or masterpieces of art—in brief, as subject matter for courses and curricula. Yet when content is treated as a component part of an educational program, new components—such as the artistic, literary, historical, and philosophical products of India, Africa, and the Far East—get constantly added, so that course offerings become swollen and unmanageable.

But in addition to this *substantive* definition of the humanities as content and areas of study, there is also a *functional* one, which has its origins in the Middle Ages and was in effect adopted by Cassirer (whose view of art as a functional form of human culture was alluded to in Chapter 1). In describing human nature, Cassirer writes:

> The philosophy of symbolic forms starts from the presupposition that, if there is any definition of the nature or "essence" of man, this definition can only be understood as a functional one, not a substantial one. . . . Man's outstanding characteristic, his distinguishing mark, is not his metaphysical or physical nature—but *his work*. It is this work, it is the system of human activities, which defines and determines the circle of "humanity." Language, myth, religion, art, science, history are the constituents, the various sectors of this circle. A "philosophy of man" would therefore be a philosophy which would give us insight into the fundamental structure of each of these human activities, and which at the same time would enable us to understand them as an organic whole.[10]

Functionally conceived, the humanities are arts, skills, or ways of organizing experience and are therefore more properly called the "liberal arts." Levi writes:

> Originating in the ancient world, but coming to flower in the Middle Ages, the idea of the liberal arts rested not upon a content to be mastered, but a technique to be acquired. Grammar, rhetoric, dialectic . . . meant skill in reading, skill in speaking, skill in understanding and in rational argument and, therefore, not knowledge to be added to an intellectual storehouse, but habits to be learned so as to constitute elements of character and perhaps even qualities of personality. This transformed the center of learning from the substantive to the procedural![11]

From the older functional conception of the humanities, Levi takes the idea of arts understood as skills and techniques and hence defines the humanities as *arts* of communication, continuity, and criticism; from the more recent substantive conception of the humanities he takes certain subject areas in which each of the "arts" is most fruitfully and appropriately studied. Thus the arts of communication are supplemented by languages and literatures (and masterpieces of music and the visual arts as well), the arts of continuity by history, and the arts of criticism by philosophy. Briefly stated, the end of humanistic education is the cultivation of three abilities: to think critically, to communicate successfully, and to appreciate one's cultural heritage. "The first," writes Levi, "to think critically, is the aim of philosophy. The second, to communicate successfully, is the meaning of languages and literatures. The third, to walk proudly with one's tradition, is the most formidable task of history."[12]

It should be remembered, however, that the humanities are preeminently about values, that is, benefits that accrue to the individual through the satisfaction of certain basic aspirations. Consequently, for each of his three categories Levi stipulates a separate way of enriching human life. The arts of communication are deeply founded on the quest for expression and response, on "our determination *to be* and our passion *to share experience*." The arts of continuity are founded "upon our perception of the reality of 'time' and *our search for roots*." They answer our need to find a well-defined place in the ongoing stream of time which gave us ancestors and will leave us descendants. "The arts of criticism (philosophy) are founded upon the *human search for reasonableness*. Reflection, thought, criticism are the activities through which we are able to clarify our meanings, identify our values, and so modify . . . the conditions of our existence." Although each branch of philosophy contributes to this quest, aesthetics specifically "attempts to provide the critical standards for how we ought to appreciate and enjoy."[13]

Levi is not content to recite the ways in which persons would be better off for having had a humanities education of the sort he recommends. Like other writers mentioned in these pages, he also believes that society as a whole stands to gain when its members are so educated.

> In the case of the arts of communication this has meant the presentation of languages as forms of life enlarging a limited imagination and producing that mutual sympathy Kant took to be the defining property of social man. In the case of the arts of continuity, comprehending both history proper and the use of the classics of literature and philosophy, presented as elements in a continuous human tradition, this has meant the presentation of a common past in the service of social cohesiveness and enlarged social sensitivity. And finally, in the case of the arts of criticism, this has meant the enlargement of the faculty of criticism, philosophically conceived as intelligent inquiry into the nature and maximization of values. A humane imagination, the forging of a universal social bond based upon sympathy, and the inculcation of a technique for the realization of values then become the ultimate goals of the liberal arts.[14]

Levi illustrates his argument with the language arts and, using some of Shakespeare's plays, shows how literature can be a proper object of study in each of the "arts" (communication, continuity, criticism) that compose the humanities and how it is suited to the realization of the values appropriate to each category.[15] But Levi clearly intends his scheme to accommodate masterpieces in all forms of art—and it does, provided we extrapolate from it in ways that do not compromise the approach to aesthetic education taken in this book.

The call for caution applies principally to the arts of communication. For example, we might be tempted to say that all the arts communicate because each in its own way is a "language." Although this is a popular stance, it raises certain questions. Communicate what, and how? For even when artworks are taken as signs, they perform their symbolizing functions in ways distinct from those of discursive language. It was also pointed out that not all works of art communicate in the sense of conveying messages. Many works are notable simply for a pervasive quality or overall mood. We must therefore make clear what we mean when we claim that the essence of art is communication;[16] for that reason I propose a slight modification. Since most artworks demand to be experienced aesthetically, we may say that by arresting our attention they in effect address us, and when we give them their due, they *disclose* their aesthetic properties, expressive qualities, and human import. Hence I suggest accepting disclosure as a form of communication. Furthermore, the percipient's desire to communicate, to share impressions and judgments with others, has been recognized as a part of the most memorable aesthetic experiences.

The arts of continuity pose no problems for the present scheme, for they were already accounted for in the earlier discussion of the learning that must occur before artworks can be interpreted adequately. Special mention was made of the requirement to understand a work's history, the context of its origination, and the artistic tradition it exemplifies. When we bring knowledge of this sort to bear on a masterpiece of art we may gain humanistic insight into the past that can help us gauge our own location in the flux of time. The values of the arts of continuity are therefore realizable in all the arts.

The values Levi has assigned to criticism generally (that is, philosophy) are also provided for by aesthetic criticism as described in this book. Students are certain to enlarge their capacity for criticism in the process of learning to evaluate works of art. The need for reasonableness is met by the responsibly rational (that is, reason-giving) nature of the aesthetic critical argument described in Chapter 3. Finally, the maximization of (aesthetic) value is, of course, the main objective of aesthetic criticism employed as a teaching method and, indeed, of aesthetic education itself.

To Levi's arts of communication, continuity, and criticism I now add a fourth "c"—creativity, or better, the arts of creation and performance. However, these are admitted to the humanistic complex only as supplementary activities. Their mission is to help expand the student's cognitive framework through aesthetic concepts generalized from practical experience with arts materials and in expressive performance. Levi in fact acknowledges the essential unity of the artistic act (from creation through enjoyment to judgment), and he remarks that persons wanting to appreciate art can deepen their intuitive awareness by engaging in creative endeavors.

Levi formulates no pedagogical prescriptions or principles of curriculum selection, but he does leave teachers a set of questions. Such questions figure in Levi's discussion of Shakespeare's plays, but they can also be used to interrogate the works of the artists discussed in Chapters 4 and 5, namely, Vermeer, Poussin, Cézanne, and Giorgione as well as, say, twentieth-century works of music, film, and dance by Bartók, Bergman, and Balanchine. The questions are: (1) What is its language? (To which I would add, What qualities does it disclose?) (2) What is its structure? (3) What is its style? (4) When was it created? (5) For whom was it intended, its audience? (6) What attitudes does it express? (7) What values does it assert or deny? (8) What message (if any) does it convey?[17]

This concludes the case for locating arts education within the humanities. It can now be asserted that the development of a sense of art in the young through formal schooling involves offering aesthetic education as a humanity interpreted as bringing to bear the arts of communication, continuity, criticism, and creation.

An art world curriculum

Any discussion of curriculum must address not only the question of aims but also the questions of content and teaching method and sequence of instruction. Thought must also be given to the assessment of learning and to ways of implementing ideas within an existing school structure. Some points already made can be taken to apply to various aspects of curriculum planning, design, and evaluation: (1) that the general aim of aesthetic education should be the induction of the young into the art world for the sake of the worthwhile experiences works of art at their best are capable of providing; (2) that the basic content for such a curriculum should be the concepts and skills requisite for understanding and appreciating art as art; (3) that teaching method should take the form of aesthetic criticism and should also be shaped by the decision to teach art as a humanity; (4) that the assessment of learning should consequently concentrate on the progress students make in fashioning conceptual maps suitable for traversing the art world and engaging its inhabitants with sensitivity and tact. Little, however, has yet been said about the problem of the order of learning—what should be studied when and for how long. The question of sequence essentially concerns the kinds of specialization and division of labor that are appropriate to a given subject and set of educational objectives.

Accordingly, I describe four phases of aesthetic learning designed to develop the degree of aesthetic sophistication that this study has taken to be achievable in the years of formal schooling. The four phases are predicated on the belief that the development of the capacity to appreciate excellence in art requires, first of all, guidance toward a preparatory awareness of aesthetic qualities in the natural environment and human artifacts, followed by more formal perceptual training and acquaintance with the institution of art, or the art world. After these two phases, instruction will center on the acquisition of historical knowledge, which in turn will be followed by study in depth of selected major works and the training of the capacity for critical judgment. This may seem an ambitious agenda, but it becomes manageable when it is realized that its objectives are to be reached in stages throughout the entire course of elementary and secondary education. To assume that the development of aesthetic dispositions requires anything less than a full commitment from the schools is to diminish Cassirer's circle of humanity and deny art its position as a fundamental form of human culture. Theorists of arts education, I think, are often too timid in arguing the claims of their field and are content to settle for far less than what is actually needed.

Four phases of aesthetic learning

In speaking of "phases" of aesthetic learning I do not have in mind the kinds of "stages" of aesthetic development described by Michael

Parsons, whose account is based on an empirical investigation of persons' responses to a selection of paintings. While Parsons's study and other empirical research on response to art support the credibility of the phases I describe, my phases are not directly derived from these investigations. My intention is prescriptive, stresses intervention in the learning process, and follows as much from the aims and purposes of an art world curriculum as from research studies. Indeed, I know of no studies which bear on some of my suggestions. An art world curriculum postulates four phases of aesthetic learning, which I associate with grade levels: (1) K–3; (2) 4–6; (3) 7–9; and (4) 10–12.

Phase one of aesthetic learning
(kindergarten and grades 1, 2, 3)

During the first phase of aesthetic learning (K–3), the efforts of teachers to develop an elementary sense of art and the art world exploit the children's innate aesthetic propensities and the delight they tend to express in the sensory and dramatic qualities of things, a capacity often remarked and envied by mature artists. I speak here of the young person's readiness to respond to the sheer qualitative immediacy of life, to its looks, feels, sounds, odors, and so forth. To be sure, works of art are the principal loci of aesthetic value, and in due course children will come to realize why this is so; but in the early years it is the qualities of the world, not just those of artworks, that form the focus of teaching and learning. It is a time, to anticipate some observations in Appendix I, to draw attention to the visual qualities of a summer or autumn day, the character of spring foliage or falling leaves, the beauty of rainbows and sunsets, the occasionally odd appearance of utensils and artifacts, the moods of a cityscape with its diverse sounds, colors, and façades, and the graceful and fluid movements of human beings and animals. Beauty, of course, is not everywhere; it is especially lacking in the impoverished inner cities of our large metropolitan centers. But in school young children can learn about those aspects of the world that reward their attention with enjoyment.

Yet much of the child's natural capacity for aesthetic delight will remain dormant unless measures are taken to draw it out. This can be done not only by guiding the children's awareness in a certain direction but also by encouraging them to register their perceptions through song, drawing, craft, dance, and gesture. In doing all this, in learning that there are things worth looking at and listening for—aspects of things they had not previously noticed—children will be acquiring, informally for the most part, a rudimentary concept of art. When they discover that there are places set aside for just this sort of looking and listening, they will also begin to form an elementary sense of the art world, of a special sort of social institution. Much of this informal kind of aesthetic learning occurs before the child enters school (one recalls Aiken's remarks on this topic). The school builds on this learning and develops a foundation for later, more formal learning. To return to the image of curriculum as itinerary, K–3 aesthetic learning constitutes a period of preparation for the more self-conscious explorations of the art world and encounters with some of its denizens.

A wealth of texts, films, tapes, etc., is available for helping to accomplish the aims of this phase of learning, and many of the suggestions and exercises found in these materials are relevant and can be appropriately used toward these ends. But since many of these exercises were designed for different objectives, they may need to be adapted to suit the requirements of an excellence curriculum. Accordingly, teachers who accept the point of view of this study may well teach some of the exercises with different aims in mind, or more likely, do some things slightly differently. To see the young learner as a potential reflective percipient of art and effective participant in the cultural institution known as the art world could prompt teachers to set tasks and initiate activities that slowly but surely prepare the child for this role. I should add that during this phase of aesthetic learning it is more important for the teacher to have a clear sense of purpose and direction than to organize highly systematic sequential learning tasks. Not all children, for example, need to be working on the same assignment at the same time in order for this phase to accomplish its objectives. What counts is that young children become alert to the world of aesthetic qualities and begin to perceive them in the works of others and in the things they make and perform themselves. If there is a progression in this learning, it is from a heightened awareness of the qualities of natural phenomena to increased perceptiveness of the qualities of works of art, including the children's own products.

It should be emphasized that in an art world curriculum, through which young people are prepared for the realization of a significant part of their humanity, even the earliest phase should be given its own time in the curriculum. This contradicts all those recommendations for arts education for young children that conceive the arts as adjuncts of other activities. But if we are to convince young children of the importance of the aesthetic domain, specialized instruction in a special time period must be set aside for just that purpose. Given the emphasis on excellence in an art world curriculum, it goes without saying that the works and performances to which the children are exposed should be of high aesthetic quality. The aim is to generate an atmosphere in which concern for aesthetic quality becomes deeply engrained. K–3 learning, in Novak's terms, would be a time when the conceptual frameworks learners bring to school undergo expansion through the assimilation of new ideas and experiences. Aesthetic dispositions begin to be formed, aesthetic maps charted. As perhaps their most significant accomplishment in this phase, young children learn to pay closer attention to the qualities of their environment, developing as it were a rudimentary version of object directedness, to recall one of the features of aesthetic experience that Beardsley regarded indispensable.

Phase two of aesthetic learning (grades 4, 5, 6)

During the second phase of aesthetic learning in an art world or excellence curriculum (either label will do), aesthetic instruction becomes more formal and systematic, though not inordinately so, and the disciplines of teaching art as a humanity can be brought to bear more explicitly. Attention is now directed toward different ways of considering works of art, with special emphasis, I would suggest, on understanding artworks in terms of their characteristic structure, expressiveness, and style. In this respect instruction would distinguish some of the differences between the visual, literary, and performing arts and concentrate on the different ways artworks are organized.

All of this is to say that phase two is essentially a time for perceptual training, for learning what to look for, to hear, and to read. It is a time when the young come to discover in greater detail just what there is in artworks to be enjoyed and to be emotionally responded to. What comes naturally to the younger child—intrinsic delight in the sheer qualities of things—is supplemented by greater emphasis on formal analysis of the ways elements or components of artworks form webs of relations. Expressive qualities, which are a function of certain sorts of formal relations, should also be pointed out in examples that the youngsters can grasp. The cultivation of such perceptual habits can be aided through the students' creation of their own expressive designs and compositions. The important pedagogical consideration to keep in mind is that tasks and exercises designed for this phase of aesthetic learning should draw out the young person's capabilities and stretch them as much as possible in order to promote an increasingly complex and comprehensive response to art. Another way of describing the purpose of phase two of aesthetic learning is to say that it strives to further enrich the apperceptive mass or store of tacit knowledge of young people. Since phase two extends over three years (grades 4, 5, 6), courses can be designed in which perceptual tasks become more demanding. This can be done either by gradually presenting more complex works of art to describe, analyze, and interpret, or by studying the same works in greater depth. Likewise, more challenging creative and performing assignments can be undertaken or familiar tasks returned to with difficult expectations.

Phase two will also be the time when young persons, in addition to cultivating their percipience in matters of art, also become more conscious of the art world through trips to museums, galleries, and art exhibitions and the discovery that there are books and television programs devoted exclusively to art. Hence the idea of the art world as a sector of society begins to take shape. In brief, to recall Aiken's terminology from Chapter 3, the young person begins to internalize the conditions for knowing, appreciating, and judging works of art and for understanding that works of art demand to be appreciated in a certain way. Students will also become increasingly aware of the geographic distribution of works of art and begin to form something of an imaginative itinerary for exploring the world of art, a notion of a schedule and timetable, as it were, some of which may later be realized in actual travel. But I anticipate the central emphasis of phase three of aesthetic learning.

The most important achievement of the second phase of aesthetic learning is the acquisition of an elementary concept of art that will enable students to encounter additional artworks with some knowledge of what to do with them; basic perceptual skills having been fashioned, they will be brought to bear. If in the description of phase one of aesthetic learning the key terms are exposure, familiarization, and exploration, the key terms characterizing phase two are work of art, form or structure, and expressive character. The young come to realize that artworks are independent and autonomous artifacts toward which one takes up a special point of view or attitude. The sense of object directedness that was stressed in phase one as an important disposition to develop is now augmented by skills and related concepts which enable percipients to sustain commerce with a work of art. The students' efforts now are characterized by a sense of active discovery as well.

During this stage, it is appropriate to ask young persons not only to perform perceptual and creative tasks but also to give an account of their current understanding of art so that teachers may discover which concepts and relations among concepts they believe are important. It should not be too much to expect, for example, that by the end of phase two of aesthetic learning, that is at the conclusion of the sixth grade, young persons will have command of an aesthetic perceptual map that includes the concepts and skills of "aesthetic scanning,"[18] to use the name of a method that has been proven fruitful for training aesthetic perception in several aesthetic education projects (so long as we disregard those connotations of "scanning" that suggest a quick and perfunctory survey and would thus fail to comport with the careful and sustained analysis of artworks which phase two introduces). With the additions to their cognitive stock supplied by phase two, young people are now ready to explore the art world's historical dimension. Phase three of aesthetic learning in fact constitutes a vicarious time travel through the art world, from the art of the caves to the present.

Phase three of aesthetic learning (grades 7, 8, 9)

Adjusting the four phases of aesthetic learning to Levi's notion of teaching art as a humanity, that is, as taking account of the arts of continuity, communication, and criticism (and also creation), we may now say that phase two of aesthetic learning corresponds in essence to an elementary grasp of the arts of communication, what with the emphasis on perceiving not only the structure and style of artworks but also their expressive character. But an artwork does not materialize in a vacuum, and in addition to being an artist's unique creation it is also a product of a particular moment in the history of a particular culture. Students must therefore be brought to the realization that the understanding and appreciation of a work of art are not complete until the arts of continuity (history) have been brought to bear on it. What is more, knowledge of art history, or at least of art's general outlines and major monuments, is crucial to the experience not only of traditional but of modern works as well. Having previously developed a sense of what a work of art is and how one deals with it, the learner in phase three is poised for assimilating art-historical information that conveys a sense of art's context and its diverse uses. Although the study of the historical dimension of any subject aids in the human quest for identity and meaning generally, familiarity with the history of art additionally plays a vital role in aesthetic understanding itself, as was argued in Chapter 4.

Phase three of aesthetic learning incorporates and builds on the accomplishments of phases one and two, the phases of exposure, familiarization, and perceptual training, but it progresses to even stronger emphasis on formal and systematic learning. History, after all, minimally implies a chronology of events which must be studied sequentially if the values of both continuity and change are to be appreciated. But the humanistic aim of art-historical teaching is to develop in students the ability to see art in the stream of time, as a human concern that has a long past and is still evolving. Another objective is to lead students past some of the mansions ennobling the cultural landscape in which, during phase four, they will spend more of their time. When they are ready to do so, the young will gain an awareness of the enormous wealth of their heritage that should enable them to take pride in their cultural tradition. Needless to say, the study of the art of past ages also helps young people to transcend the provincialism and tyranny of the merely contemporary; they will discover that art is broader than their immediate world of television, the movies, and popular music.

Another parochialism to be overcome is blindness to the aesthetic values found in non-Western civilizations. Much current effort is directed toward correcting this particular deficiency, and it is often carried to the point of overcompensation. Indeed, students are sometimes encouraged to feel guilt and embarrassment over Western cultural values and to accept non-Western traditions uncritically as superior to or at least more benign than their own. We are thus in special need of reasonableness in such matters. Fortunately, there are principles and ideas that can guide us.

First, students should be made to realize that the impulse to art is universal, that it has manifested itself not only throughout human history but in all parts of the globe. It is therefore appropriate that young persons should become acquainted with some of the finest artistic products from different societies.[19] But equality of coverage is hardly possible since that could involve, staying with the visual arts alone, the mastery of the numerous volumes of the McGraw-Hill *History of World Art*. Second, the aim of teaching art as a humanity is to have students communicate effectively and to think historically and critically, while aesthetic education was said to pursue the objective of equipping students with aesthetic critical skills; encyclopedic knowledge is sought under neither definition. Third, Beardsley was earlier quoted to the effect that one important function of art is to make us feel at home in the world; it seems reasonable to assume that students should become comfortable with their own culture before they attempt aesthetic cosmopolitanism. Fourth, to those who object that to increasing numbers of students in our schools Western artistic values are alien, we can reply that regardless of origin, all students are citizens of a country whose major cultural and political institutions, values, and attitudes have been significantly shaped by Western thought; therefore, being introduced to the finest monuments of the Western heritage through common formal schooling is simply part of becoming a knowledgeable and effective citizen. Part, but not all, for there is no denying that the cultural fabric is enriched when the home, the extended family, and the neighborhood preserve and revitalize a host of other traditions as well.

I do not prescribe too rigidly how the history of art should be taught but am inclined to think that the study of prehistory through the Middle Ages would be reasonable for grade seven; Renaissance through the eighteenth century for grade eight; and the nineteenth century to the present for grade nine. I am not suggesting, of course, that much more than a general sense of chronology and of the changing face, sound, and sense of art can be conveyed at this level, but without at least this much acquaintance later appreciative and critical work would be more difficult to undertake. Just as important as art-historical familiarization is the acquisition of a vocabulary—terms like "classical," "medieval," "Renaissance," "mosaic," "fresco," "perspective," "Impressionism," etc.— that will facilitate subsequent study and, incidentally, make a sizable contribution to the stock of words that are indicators of what Hirsch calls cultural literacy.

Undertaken with intelligence and enthusiasm, the historical study of the arts should be a chore neither for the teacher nor for the students. For many artworks, in addition to being cultural monuments and exemplars of period style, feature subject matter that, because of its strangeness and remoteness from their lives, young persons find intrinsically fascinating. Thus a skillful teacher should have little difficulty in gaining and holding students' attention and loosening the grip of the "dead hand of the past."[20] Furthermore, instruction may occasionally be enlivened by activities that take students outside the classroom. They may be asked to explore the immediate environment in search of remnants, echoes, or imitations of architectural styles, perhaps capturing their discoveries on sketchpads or with cameras. Or, having had their eyes opened to the differences between the visual arts of the sixteenth and seventeenth centuries through Heinrich Woelfflin's categories (linear vs. painterly, planar vs. recessional, etc.),[21] students may be encouraged to use these categories to sort other images in their world as well.

Phase four of aesthetic learning (grades 10, 11, 12)

Having explored the world of aesthetic qualities, acquired perceptual habits for experiencing works of art, and gained a sense of art's history, students are now prepared to penetrate to the essence of an excellence curriculum in grades ten through twelve—the study in depth of selected major works with a view to developing critical judgment and establishing a foundation for a personal philosophy of art. In one of its aspects, phase four of aesthetic learning incorporates the third of the set of arts that compose Levi's notion of teaching art as a humanity—the arts of criticism, or philosophy in its ordinary sense of critical analysis. To be sure, in phase four works of art will continue to be understood under the rubrics of communication and continuity, but the emphasis now shifts to criticism, and that in two steps.

During grades ten and eleven, students will be introduced to selected works from the visual, literary, and performing arts that are rich and complex enough to sustain the prolonged, detailed scrutiny typically to be engaged in at this stage. However, care and patience must be exercised by both teachers and students during the deep probing of a work's unique aesthetic qualities and significance, for students are now haltingly beginning to exercise the sophisticated appreciative skills that will stand them in good stead during the forays into the art world they will undertake as adults.

Much of the success of this stage will depend on the teachers' knowledge and discretion in selecting works for study. There are a good many books they can turn to. For the visual arts there is H. W. Janson's *History of Art*[22] and Hugh Honour and John Fleming's *The Visual Arts: A History;*[23] both works feature the major monuments of art. Also helpful are volumes organized around themes, such as Albert Elsen's *Purposes of Art,*[24] and F. David Martin and Lee Jacobus's *The Humanities through the Arts*[25] can be recommended for discussing the major arts from a perceptual vantage point that is compatible with this study. Music and literature specialists will know of comparable books in their areas. In music, Bennett Reimer's *Developing the Experience of Music*[26] comes to mind; it combines scholarly and professional knowledge of music with an educational perspective. One work that attempts to survey the history of both art and music is H. W. Janson and Joseph Kerman's *A History of Art and Music.*[27] (Additional works are mentioned in Appendix 3.)

Instead of a single work, teachers may prefer to discuss artistic and architectural complexes such as the Acropolis in Athens or a Gothic cathedral, both of which combine several art forms. The series of Giotto's frescoes in the Scrovegni Chapel at Padua, Michelangelo's wall and ceiling paintings in the Sistine Chapel, or his group of sculptures from the tomb of Lorenzo and Giuliano de Medici might also be studied, but it is important not to disperse attention too widely. Once again, given the students' stage of aesthetic development, the objective is to gain the most intimate acquaintance possible with a work's unique properties. This distinctiveness is often grasped most easily in side-by-side comparisons. An artwork's excellence is also readily perceived in comparisons with similar works of lesser quality, and its essence in contrast with works—possibly on a related theme—from another culture. It is at this point, I think, that works of art from non-Western civilizations are introduced to best effect. Teachers can take their lead, say, from Benjamin Rowland's *Art in East and West,*[28] which compares a Greek Kouros and a Jain saint, a portrait of Giuliano de Medici and the head of an Indian prince, a Caspar David Friedrich landscape with one by Ma Yuan, or Jacques Maquet's *The Aesthetic Experience,*[29] a work rich in comparisons between Western, Asian, and African art. The works used in these comparisons should be few and wisely selected for, again, the urge toward maximum coverage should be resisted, particularly during this phase of avid and searching engagement with individual masterpieces.

The second stage of phase four of aesthetic learning, in which critical judgments and problems in aesthetics become focal polnts, should have the seminar as the pedagogically most appropriate setting. Students will now be shown how to engage seriously in aesthetic arguments leading to aesthetic judgments or evaluations. In the process they must grasp the all-important distinction between personal preferences, that is, liking an artwork, and informed critical judgment, that is, knowing a work to be good on the basis of defensible reasons. Students will be made acquainted with critical standards and criteria and learn to make and defend aesthetic critiques—but also to yield to the judgments of others if these present a better account of the artwork's aesthetic givens. In other words, students should be made aware of the ethical responsibility they bear toward the work of art, which means that it is less important that they "win" a critical argument than that they achieve the best, most complete realization of the work possible.

Toward the end of phase four, students should possess enough intellectual maturity and aesthetic know-how to begin discussing some of the problems and puzzles surrounding the arts, that is, they may enter the antechambers of formal aesthetics to form an impression of the mental furniture they will need for framing a personal philosophy of art. In dialogic manner, teachers may engage students in discussions of such issues as the relations of art and morality, censorship, the effects of the media of mass communication on the life of culture, the commissioning of public art, and so forth. Many of these problems have a long history and are perennially debated. Other topics are more recent. At the time of this writing, for example, controversy rages over the colorization of black-and-white films. Certain large sculptures erected at public expense are being loudly objected to, not only by those who do not recognize them as "art" but also by persons who are annoyed by works which obstruct views as well as the flow of pedestrian traffic. Just what are the rights of artists when they venture into the public arena? Is the public utterly without recourse? When entertaining questions like these, students not only test their own opinions but come to comprehend some of the ramifications of art and the art world and their relations to other value domains and social institutions.

To summarize, an art world or excellence curriculum has been discussed metaphorically in terms of an itinerary and prescriptively in terms of teaching art as a humanity. It has the following phases:

Phase One of Aesthetic Learning (K–3)
   Informal exploration of the world of aesthetic qualities and familiarization with works of art and the art world.

Phase Two of Aesthetic Learning (Grades 4–6)
   Development of perceptual skills for engaging works of art and continuing introduction to the art world.

Phase Three of Aesthetic Learning (Grades 7–9)
   Development of historical awareness and thinking within the context of Western culture and civilization (with reference to non-Western cultures)

Phase Four of Aesthetic Learning (Grades 10–12)
   Development of critical appreciation of selected major works and of criteria of critical judgment; discussion of some issues in aesthetics.

The curriculum sketched here is one which makes art a required subject from kindergarten through the twelfth grade and is again an ideal. It can be dismissed as hopelessly utopian, however, only by those who do not take art seriously. But if we agree that all persons have a right to the aesthetic gratification, expanded perceptual powers, and enriched understanding that can be attained through fine works of art and that a culture enjoys robust artistic health only when citizens move about the art world with intelligent discernment, then only an educational effort of the kind and scope indicated will, I think, suffice.

Reforming teacher education

It must be conceded, however, that the majority of those currently teaching the arts are not qualified to implement such an aesthetic education program. They need supplemental training and refresher courses in skills they might once have mastered but do not use in the present configuration of arts education. For the future, nothing less than drastic (I shrink from the overused term "radical") reforms in the preparation of teachers, especially those for the secondary years (grades 7–12, or what I called phases three and four of aesthetic learning) will do.

Such reforms could involve transferring the responsibility for training arts teachers for the secondary grades to the humanities departments of colleges of liberal arts, where teaching art as a humanity would find a more congenial and supportive environment than it does in colleges of education or schools of art and design. The preparation of teachers for kindergarten through the sixth grade (for the first and second phases of aesthetic learning) can continue to take place where it now does. The major difference would be one of outlook and orientation; that is, a spirit shaped by the anticipations of an art world curriculum would animate teacher education courses and a different interpretation would be placed on many activities, doubtlessly affecting the way they are conducted.

Transferring the responsibility for educating teachers for the secondary grades of an art world or excellence curriculum to colleges of liberal arts might also redress a condition that demoralizes many student teachers. I refer to the generally deprecating attitude that faculties in the arts and academic disciplines assume toward arts educators and their professional mission. Harry Judge, an Oxford don and observer of American education, has taken note of this snobbish condescension toward educators who, he says, are "constantly sniffed at and spat upon by their academic colleagues."[30] There is no denying the justness of criticism directed at colleges of education when their standards are low and performance poor, but the situation is not likely to be improved if academics wash their hands of education. Some of the stigma could be lifted from arts educators if discipline specialists were held more accountable for these teachers' training. As they already do for prospective teachers of English, mathematics, history, and foreign languages, liberal arts faculties might then prepare humanities teachers for the arts. These rearrangements might even attract academically better qualified young people than those who typically apply for admission to teacher education programs in the arts. Current efforts to reform teacher education, such as those of the Holmes Group,[31] which stress the importance of an undergraduate academic major, may help bring about changes of the kind I have suggested.

Reorganization is also called for in the assignment of curriculum time for implementing an art world or excellence curriculum. Ideally, the visual, literary, and performing arts as taught on the secondary level

General Goal: Building a Disposition to Appreciate Excellence
in Art by Teaching the Concepts and Skills of Art as a Humanity

Arts of Communication	*Arts of Continuity*	*Arts of Criticism*	*Arts of Creation and Performance*
"Language"	Date	Attitudes	Expression
Structure and Qualities	Situation	Values	Technique
Style	Audience	Messages	Interpretation in Performance

Exposure and   Historical Awareness   Exemplar Appreciation
Perceptual Training ────▶   ────────▶   and Critical Analysis

(Phases 1 and 2, K–6)   (Phase 3, Grades 7–9)   (Phase 4, Grades 10–12)

Teaching and learning proceed along a continuum from exposure, familiarization, and perceptual training to historical awareness, critical appreciation, and aesthetic judgment, stressing reception and discovery learning, didactic coaching, and dialogic teaching methods. Evaluation centers on progress in aesthetic mapping and conditions conducive to it. Levi's scheme is amended to include the arts of creation and performance. Smith's is expanded to include teaching from kindergarten through the twelfth grade.

Figure 6.1.   An Art World Curriculum (K–12)

should, as Theodore Sizer recommends in *Horace's Compromise*[32] (the best of the volumes associated with the excellence-in-education movement), be organized into one department of the arts in order that the insights and experiences of different specialists may inform the teaching of art as a humanity. This does not necessarily imply team teaching, although in some instances a group of dedicated art, music, and literature teachers might well want to explore cooperatively how instruction during phases three and four (grades 7–12) can be systematically organized in ways that would develop historical awareness, cultivate the appreciation of major works, and refine critical thinking and judgment in matters of art.

The reforms required, then, are not minimal, nor could they be enacted in a short period of time. The program envisioned is one that requires at least a decade of planning, experimentation, and advocacy. An excellence or art world curriculum, in short, is for the year 2000 and beyond, a plan for the future. Moreover, once arts education is conceived as one of the humanities or, better, taught as a humanity in Levi's sense; once the preparation of art teachers is accorded the seriousness it deserves; and once the public recognizes that the study of art is truly substantive and demands rigorous perceptual and mental activity, school requirements for the arts should receive greater support than they now do. Finally, the articulation of ideals, visions of the future, and scenarios is never useless as it promotes thinking about alternatives. Just as works of art present images of human possibility, so do theories of education. Given the point of view expressed in this study, the arts, as a basic form of human culture, are far too important to command anything but our best efforts.

CHAPTER 7

Issues: the two cultures and policy

In discussing the four issues in this chapter and the next, I adopt a different analytical approach to each. The analysis of the two cultures debate presents a survey of the controversy stimulated by C. P. Snow's essay *The Two Cultures and the Scientific Revolution*. I first summarize the substance of the essay's ideas and indicate how the debate they generated evolved and underwent change through a variety of critical populations. I then suggest some ways in which art radically differs from science. The discussion of policy proceeds from a conceptual analysis performed by Donna Kerr, which I adapt for my own purposes. To understand the meaning of ideology I identify different meanings of the term and recommend how it might be used in discussions of aesthetic education. My remarks about postmodernism consists of a configurational understanding of one of its progeny, deconstruction; that is, a picture or pattern of beliefs and tendencies is developed from the efforts of a number of writers who have tried to understand it.

The two cultures: The continuing debate

Despite its plural meanings which have encouraged some to doubt its usefulness, the term "culture" continues to animate contemporary intellectual and educational discussion. Albert William Levi's search for the meaning of culture and his attempt to solve its riddle[1] and E. D. Hirsch, Jr.'s interest in cultural literacy[2] are but two cases in point. Nelson Goodman's writings have also raised in novel terms the question whether the two cultures of the arts and sciences are essentially similar or dissimilar in respect of their aims and function. Perhaps, however, what is needed as much as such efforts is an examination of the form and dynamics of the debates the term culture generates. Accordingly, I will discuss the advent and evolution of the two cultures debate, one of the major intellectual controversies of the mid-twentieth century.

In a suggestive discussion of the ecology of ideas, Bertrand de Jouvenal[3] asks what would be involved in taking a census of ideas which could be classified by order, kind, species, and variety. Such a census would involve not only counting heads but also inspecting minds with a view to discovering how many of them contained a particular idea or some semblance of it. As a result, an idea could be said to have a population of a certain number. The entire human population could then be regarded as an environment inhabited by differently sized populations of ideas. A census of this kind, says de Jouvenal, would enable us to discern whether certain ideas are gaining or losing ground or are being set aside for the moment. We could also learn something about the dependence and competition among ideas; the ways, for example, in which some ideas are propelled into partly hostile and partly propitious environments and move through the human population, where they are affected by the various environments they encounter and by the activities of individual minds. If it were actually possible, says de Jouvenal, to gain an understanding of the ecosystem of ideas, then we might be in a better position to detect which ideas in the current population will be embraced in the future and what their fate might be. After all, if ideas are a moving force in human affairs, then it is in our interest to try to comprehend their origins, careers, and possible futures.

As de Jouvenal's proposed classification implies, ideas come in various guises and are accorded different kinds of reception. Scientific ideas are treated more harshly than social and moral ideas; contrary to popular belief, scientific ideas do not simply drop from the sky onto fertile soil. It may be some time before the standing body of scientific knowledge accommodates them. Things tend to be different with moral or normative ideas; they are more subject to immediate diffusion, and in a relatively short time may come to exercise what de Jouvenal calls a ruling in contrast to a merely reigning function.

What has all this to do with the two cultures debate? I think de Jouvenal's ecological image prompts us to take a new look at it. His analysis also helps μs to appreciate the fact that society is a collection of interdependent systems of ideas and events undergoing uneven rates of change, and this is a promising way to think about things.

We may begin by noting that the influence of Charles Darwin's *The Origin of Species* did much to create the climate in which science finally came to be accepted in the modern world. By 1959 when the *The Two Cultures* essay appeared, just 100 years after the publication of Darwin's great work, many had come to believe that the culture had in effect become a scientific one, an awareness that prompted Jacques Barzun to reply to Snow, "One culture, not two," the scientific one.[4] At about the same time Solon Kimball and James McClellan,[5] two educational theorists, were saying that science had in fact become the operative religion of Americans, and they argued for the centrality of scientific rationality in formal education. One might have thought that Snow had also accepted the fact of a scientific culture, except for his curious statement that "it is the traditional culture, to an extent remarkably little diminished by the emergence of the scientific one, which manages the western world."[6] On the face of it, the observation lacked credibility, for it seemed to imply that government bureaucracies were run by literary intellectuals, by natural Luddites.[7] However, as Snow explained later, what he meant was that by virtue of being pervasive in education the antimodern attitudes of literary intellectuals had seeped into the minds of the educated population at large, including government officials who make policy decisions. The literary intellectuals, who constituted one of Snow's two cultures, posed a problem because their attitude toward the human condition generally was counterproductive of improvement; it held back and impeded the crucial work which science and technology had to do. On the other hand, the most urgent problems of the modern world were the gap between the rich and the poor and the obligation of rich countries to help poor ones head off massive starvation. Left to itself this situation had potentially grave and disastrous consequences; and, while it is a challenge to all advanced societies, it was clear to Snow that Western nations bear an especially heavy responsibility. Snow believed that as a group, scientists (and mainly physical scientists), who constituted Snow's second culture, have the capability and will to attack this problem. The conditions of their work make it natural for them to hope and look ahead; they have, Snow said, the future in their bones. Conversely, literary intellectuals tend to look back, to agonize over man's position in the universe, to hold antisocial ideas, and to hope that the future will not arrive. Snow therefore believed scientists and science education should be given more attention to educational and governmental decision-making.

Of interest about the two cultures debate here is not so much whether Snow's analysis was on the whole accurate or whether he chose the right way to dramatize his major concern, but how the analysis was received. What ideas were seized upon and discussed, disputed, applied, and extended? How did these ideas move through the population? What other ideas did they come into conflict with? What, to follow de Jouvenal, were the *general* ideas of Snow's analysis and their *particular* propositions? Still further, what portions of the analysis were rejected? What, looking back, seems to be the debate's discernible residue?

At present, the two cultures debate can be described as a continuing drama in which three acts have thus far unfolded. Act one opened with Snow's essay in 1959 and consisted of a period of intense discussion, analysis, and criticism, including the highly critical response by the Cambridge humanist F. R. Leavis.[8] Act two dates from 1964 when Snow took a second look at the original analysis in light of the critical discussion of the intervening years.[9] Act three opened in 1971 when Snow published *Public Affairs*,[10] a volume that reprints the original essay, the second look, and other essays on related topics and wherein Snow's perspective on the whole debate can now be conveniently examined. In effect, *Public Affairs*, especially Snow's introductory and closing remarks and his lectures "The State of Siege" and "The Case of Leavis and the Serious Case," was Snow's third look at the two cultures controversy. A fourth act is perhaps opening as efforts are made to regard the debate from different vantage points; for example, by Roger Scruton[11] who recalls Leavis's concept of culture and uses it to question the lack of attention given to aesthetics and aesthetic experience in modern philosophy, and by critical theorists who are casting a reductionist eye over the issues.[12]

We may now describe the advent and evolution of the two cultures debate, that is, the appearance of Snow's essay, its general and particular ideas, their movement through the population, and their social acceptance and rejection.[13]

The first curious thing to notice is that Snow's 58-page essay, written in a simple, direct style, should have stimulated so much reaction and been so variously interpreted. In his second look, Snow suggests that such a reaction indicates that the ideas were not original and that there was something to them. In short, the time was right, and the atmosphere was receptive.

What were the *general* ideas of the original two cultures essay? It is clear that Snow wanted to arouse concern over what he perceived to be the most pressing problem of the modern world: the dangerously widening gap between rich and poor countries and the moral obligation of wealthier societies to help underdeveloped ones. For Snow the only hope for doing this lay in the acceptance of the scientific revolution and the application of science and technology to problems of food production, overpopulation, and the improvement of living conditions. But the use of science and technology was being impeded by a condition in society that Snow characterized as the problem of the two cultures: the gulf between physical scientists on one side and literary intellectuals on the other. Each culture tended to think and feel in distinctive ways and each lacked an adequate understanding and appreciation of the other. Snow made it clear that while he generally deplored this situation, he found the attitudes of literary intellectuals especially troublesome because as a group they lacked optimism and a sense of the future. Since in Snow's view the sentiments of the literary culture, or what he also called the traditional or humanist culture, were pervasive in the society and had even infiltrated the minds of politicians and decision makers, a frontal attack on such attitudes was called for. It was time that society accepted the scientific revolution and used it to solve pressing world problems. Snow thus decried a situation, particularly evident in his own country, that did not pay sufficient attention to science in education and decision-making. One corrective was to be the reform of education in order to provide persons with a common culture that included scientific literacy as an essential component. His fear, however, was that educational forms had crystallized and were impervious to change.

These then were the general ideas of the two cultures analysis: the moral obligation of rich countries to help poor ones; and the need to reform education so as to provide persons with a common culture that included scientific literacy. These two general ideas, which we may call the moral and the practical ideas, were buttressed with secondary themes and a few suggestions for action. How were these ideas received?

First of all, they were not received in the order just stated. The practical idea of educational reform was seized on first. Because the society into which the two cultures analysis was injected was already ill at ease with the increasing compartmentalization and specialization of life, the notion that science and literature had become too alienated from each other and should be on better speaking terms was generally accepted, or at least it was not perceived as highly controversial. It was thought that excessive specialization was undesirable and that efforts should therefore be made to close the communications gap between the two cultures. Snow's essay thus became required reading in numerous schools, the pedagogical issues became the topic of many articles and books, and Snow reported that he had achieved some influence on Swedish education.

Contributing to the acceptance of the notion of excessive specialization were Snow's elementary tests for scientific literacy, which need not be rehearsed here. It might be said that they had something of the impact of genuine culture shock, although it is more properly termed the shock of ignorance. Scientific ignorance in a scientific culture is an embarrassment, and, again, it seemed as if something could be done about it. Indeed, so generally uncontroversial was Snow's complaint about scientific illiteracy that he did not have to spell out educational details. Others were willing to do it for him. But this activity was hampered by Snow's remarks about the moral qualities of scientists and humanists which gave scientists a better bill of moral health. Not surprisingly, humanists, that is, teachers of literature, literary critics, philosophers, historians, etc., tended to close ranks in response to Snow's characterization. Snow remarked they reacted along disciplinary lines, as a culture, with varying degrees of patience or exasperation or qualified acceptance, but in large disagreeing with him. At least this seemed to be the case with the first and second waves of response from humanists, the principal theme of which was that Snow had unjustly criticized them and the traditional culture.[14] Today, the attitude of some humanists toward their own literary culture is more complicated. It is safe to assume, however, that Snow would have had little patience with contemporary literary intellectuals who propound deconstruction.

Snow's tactics had the effect of bringing the battle between the two cultures into the open for all to see, but this does not seem to have served his purpose of trying to prod human conscience. The spectacle of scientists and humanists skirmishing in public was not always exemplary of intellectual debate. And if it is characteristic of the processes involved in the acceptance of social ideas that a certain amount of distortion and deformation of issues occurs, the two cultures debate was no exception.

But, more importantly, a number of contributions were made to the controversy which centered attention not on the morality of the protagonists but rather on the epistemology of the sciences and the humanities, on their distinctive ways of knowing and forms of knowledge.

My earlier comment on the debate,[15] for example, which characteristically sidestepped the moral issue, introduced Crane Brinton's distinction between cumulative and noncumulative knowledge[16] as a basis for distinguishing between the two cultures, a distinction that recurred in the later stages of the debate and which Snow referred to in his third look.[17] As Brinton had put it, the point of the distinction is that cumulative fields of understanding, for example those of natural sciences, offer a greater possibility of achieving a consensus of belief and exhibit a distinctive relation of contemporary to past opinion. That which science no longer regards as true does not figure in the work of present-day scientists and exists only as an object of historical interest; it has no contemporary scientific value. This, Brinton said, is the way science typically advances; it discards ideas no longer considered useful in understanding or solving problems. In noncumulative fields of knowledge, however, for example those of the humanities, the situation is different in regard both to the kind of consensus it is possible to achieve and the relation of present to past thinking. In the arts and humanities it is more problematical to speak of advance and progress. We can still learn from Plato and Aristotle, can still appreciate the vitality of Renaissance art, can, in short, still receive inspiration from yesteryear's classics. For scientists, however, much of yesteryear is in effect a closed book which they feel they have no need to consult. We might say that the humanist views tradition as a deep vista, extending far back into time. It is a space in which humanists freely travel back and forth. Tradition for the scientists, however, is quite different. Its relation to his work is more like the background to a shallow relief than a deep vista.

This is not the whole story, of course, but it does suggest a genuine difference in the attitudes and ways of knowing of scientists and humanists, one, moreover, that has important educational consequences. Indeed, this epistemological focus is one of the major consequences of the discussion of what I have called the practical idea in Snow's original essay. Many of the curriculum proposals since 1959, although not always taking their lead from Snow or the two cultures debate, emphasize distinctive ways of knowing, meaning, and understanding. It is also quite possible that by stressing the communication problems of scientists and humanists the two cultures debate helped to create the conditions for what the late Walter Kaufmann called the new interdisciplinary age.[18] The practical idea of the two cultures debate thus may have had two contradictory offshoots: one in the direction of separate instruction in each of several different ways of knowing; the other in the direction of interdisciplinary studies. What about the general moral idea—the claim that rich countries have the obligation to help poor ones?

The moral problem was always the most pressing one for Snow, but unlike the practical problem of repairing communications between the two cultures, which was perceived as uncontroversial and worth doing something about, the moral idea was largely rejected. The reason was not that the idea was repugnant (which is how many regarded Darwin's idea of natural selection); heading off starvation and improving the living conditions of the poor could hardly be so construed. Why then did the moral appeal fail? Snow acknowledged that his strategy was in part to blame, but he thought that the values and conditions of life in the West also have something to do with it.

The two cultures discussion got off track first because of the Luddite reference and the response by Leavis and then in part because of Snow's self-confessed failure to distinguish carefully in the original essay between the moral and the educational issue. Some have conjectured that in order to concentrate concern on the moral issue Snow had to get peoples' attention, and this he did by dramatizing the problem of the two cultures. It seems more likely however, as Snow himself later admitted, that he simply used poor judgment. It was not, for example, until the end of the original 1959 essay that "the three menaces" which stand in our way—the H-bomb, overpopulation, and the gap between the rich and the poor—were specifically brought into the discussion. In retrospect, Snow said that he wished he had called the original essay "The Rich and the Poor," and in the prologue to *Public Affairs,* published eleven years after the original essay and with the benefit of hindsight, he sets out the issues unambiguously in their order of importance: thermonuclear war, the gap between rich and poor countries, overpopulation, the nature and rational uses of technology, and the need for widespread scientific literacy.

De Jouvenal would, I think, suggest that the moral idea was also rejected because its dormant propositions were not sufficiently spelled out. Little space was devoted to them, and they were not sufficiently dramatized. This did not happen until Snow's "The State of Siege" lecture,[19] but by then interest in the debate was cooling.

Deficiencies in description and dramatization, however, explain the rejection only in part. In "The State of Siege," Snow remarks that the tensions of the modern world encourage enclave-making. Persons form groups for the purpose of protecting themselves from the harsh realities of the external world. Secure within such enclaves, they shut out the rest of the world. The pursuit of self and personal gratification within enclaves, moreover, contributes to the contemporary cult of authenticity, which has been described as largely adversarial in character.[20] The division and fragmentation of societies into enclaves—linguistic, racial, sexual, national, etc.—is, Snow believed, as dangerous as the ossification of social and educational institutions, the forms of which must be broken if any progress toward solving world problems is to be made. But Snow thought the prospects for doing so were not good.

Recalling de Jouvenal's discussion of the acceptance and rejection of normative ideas, it may be said in summary that since the particular propositions entailed by the moral obligation to help poor countries were not adequately formulated and dramatized in the original two cultures essay, no sense of urgency attached to the moral obligation. Nor does it seem likely that much would have happened even if the implications of the moral idea had been spelled out and dramatized. For most persons local or national interests take precedence over concern for international welfare. It is thus not surprising that the moral appeal of Snow's analysis was largely ignored.

This ends a brief foray into the ecology of social ideas. The two cultures debate exhibits all of the characteristics associated with the processes of acceptance and rejection. The moral and practical ideas were immediately received into a partly friendly, partly hostile environment where they made their way through the population while becoming compounded with some ideas and engaging others in debate. The ideas were analyzed, discussed, criticized, extended, applied, rejected, and then reexamined once again in new contexts. Along the way, and toward the end more with respect to the moral idea, the practical propositions entailed by the general ideas were increasingly articulated. Such articulation, says de Jouvenal, is a precondition for forecasting the extension of ideas into the future and for thinking about the kinds of action we might take.

Where do we stand on the two cultures debate today? The feeding of starving populations is technologically possible, and the moral will to tackle the problem is not lacking. Only pockets of political resistance stand in the way. Disarmament has become an important topic of discussion among the most powerful nations, and some modest progress toward it has been made. The gap between the rich and poor still exists, although it is evident that some nations are making strides in reducing it. But overall the three menaces that Snow identified—thermonuclear war, overpopulation, and the gap between the rich and poor—are still with us and will be for some time.

Educationally, the problems attending the two cultures controversy continue to be debated. University administrators periodically call for greater communication between scientists and humanists, but the tendency is to acknowledge the need for more understanding and cooperation while maintaining distinct organizational arrangements and career paths. The question of the cumulativeness or noncumulativeness of scientific and humanistic knowledge has been subjected to intensive analysis, the result of which has been to weaken what to Brinton seemed an obvious and useful distinction. I will not summarize this literature here[21] and will say only that the radical skepticism of some types of literary theory, particularly thinking along deconstructionist lines (to be discussed in the next chapter), seems to deny the possibility of progress in our understanding of literature. Accordingly, this has prompted defenders of literary meaning to point out what is in fact genuine advance in our interpretation and understanding of literary works. Then there is the more technical or objective dimension that humanistic scholarship has assumed generally. Compilations of systematic bibliographies and the cataloguing of an artist's oeuvre can be considered as much a part of the scientific chain of meaning as they are of the humanistic complex.[22]

But it is not necessary to retain Brinton's terminology in order to say something important about the differences between science and art, between the scientific chain of meaning and the humanistic complex. Nor need making this distinction controvert Nelson Goodman's reasons for stressing the commonalities between scientific inquiry and artistic creativity. We may agree that the general aim of both science and art is enlightenment and understanding and that scientific and aesthetic inquiry both presuppose curiosity, imagination, and creativeness. Both also provide satisfaction. Yet the fact remains, and Goodman does not deny this, that the criteria of judgment in each domain are different. I doubt, for example, that any piece of scientific work will ever be judged true or fruitful because it projected, say, an "image of a pure contemplativeness without pathos," which is the way Schapiro describes Cézanne's *The Card Players,* or because it reveals "the drama of the self, the antagonism of the passions and the contemplative mind, of activity and the isolated self," which is the way he interprets Cézanne's *The Bather.*[23] In brief, it will be a much different science than the one we now have when scientists describe works of science with the kind of expressive language critics use to talk about works of art. We do not, that is, look to the warranted assertions of science for sensuous lyrical qualities or expressive subtleties of light, color, and space, to say nothing of innumerable human moods dramatically projected by works of art. And while, to be sure, an astronomer may enjoy a star's twinkle, it is not mainly for the sake of aesthetic delight that he studies the constellations of the heavens. He is principally concerned to determine their size, location, composition, magnitude, and distance from the earth and other stars. This is what he uses his research funds for. If what he observes has color and dramatic character, so much the better. But in reporting his observations in a scientific journal his aim is not expressive but descriptive portrayal.[24] And his account had better be free of paradox and ambiguity, acceptable, says D. N. Perkins,[25] as qualities of literature but not of scientific explanations. True, we hear of the beauty, elegance, and economy of scientific theories and mathematical proofs, but these are special abstract qualities and not the bearers of the kind of sensuous and human import that we find in works of art.

In truth, we get to the heart of the distinction between scientific enterprise and other, more practical, kinds when we articulate more carefully the special aims of science. As Israel Scheffler[26] has explained, in their drive to get truthful representations of the phenomena studied, scientists attempt to formulate systems of lawlike statements in the terminology of a given discipline that are judged by the criteria of logical coherence, explanatory power, and heuristic efficacy. In the search for more general understanding, theories become increasingly systematic, abstract, and autonomous and thus more and more remote from the terms of ordinary language and practical experience. By no stretch of the imagination can similar aims, methods, and criteria be said to characterize the efforts of artists. The works of artists do not contain lawlike statements nor are they subject to judgment by logical criteria. Moreover, artistic creation, at least historically, is not remote from the concerns of ordinary human experience; more often than not it attempts to illuminate them. Neither are artworks, even when they happen to promote humanistic insight, judged for the contribution they make to systematic understanding. Works of art stand their own aesthetic ground, which is what we usually mean by saying they are autonomous. There is, in other words, no artistic chain of meaning, only, as Aiken pointed out, individual works that must be appreciated in a certain way.

Finally, we may distinguish the sciences and the arts in regard to the status of their products (theories and works of art, for our purposes) as either messages, museum pieces, or classics, to borrow still more terminology from Albert William Levi, who in turn borrows from Merleau-Ponty.[27] Consider, for example, a classic in the sciences and one in the arts, say an esteemed scientific theory and a recognized masterpiece. Perhaps we can say of each that it is a thing of beauty and a joy forever: of the scientific theory because it is an enduring testament to man's disposition to discover abstract relationships among natural phenomena that order understanding of the physical universe, even if in time the theory is falsified; of art, because artworks are permanent repositories of fresh experience and creative possibility.[28] Yet there is a sense in which over time the no longer useful or falsified scientific insight becomes something of a museum piece, that is, something of purely antiquarian interest, while the masterpiece of art, though it may be in a museum, does not. The masterpiece is kept fresh through the magic of its medium and its capacity to transcend both the doctrine and the period that gave rise to it.[29] Not so with the invalidated or neglected scientific discovery. Though we may still admire the human ingenuity that made it possible and appreciate the insight that it once contributed, it no longer engages us in the way that the masterpiece does. Few make pilgrimages to historical scientific shrines, while the throngs that crowd museums must be carefully monitored and controlled. True, some artworks are, or will become, neglected museum pieces relegated to the overflowing warehouse of some museum, to be exhibited only occasionally, if at all. But such works may be resurrected during one of the artistic revivals that have become a common phenomenon; that is, styles once held in low esteem and qualities long unappreciated will once more be perceived as interesting and compelling. Nor is it necessary for rediscovered styles to have any relevance to the work of contemporary artists. The situation in science, however, is quite the opposite. Here museum-piece status is quite irrevocable, and the traditional insights of science will be resorted to only on those rare occasions when they happen to be of some interest to ongoing inquiry. The head of a major medical research center once said that student interest in the history of science is acceptable so long as it doesn't impede work on solving important problems, the nature of which students discover from reading textbooks that are revised every two or three years.[30] But this in effect insures that there will be no time for historical studies.

The above conditions and others account for the fact that there is a greater scope for art than for science appreciation. This may be unfortunate, but the overriding reason is the character of scientific inquiry and the abstractness and remoteness of its products from ordinary life. Works of art are more immediately relevant and appeal directly to fundamental human instincts. Without then in any way denigrating the great accomplishments of science and while acknowledging Goodman's efforts to explain the common functions of art and science, a theory of aesthetic education will concentrate on the uniqueness of art and the special roles it can play in human life.

Policy

It is a commonplace that policy should be formulated only with clear reference to a state of affairs to be realized through the policy's implementation. This book has described one such state of affairs; it assumes that as a result of having received instruction in the concepts and principles of aesthetic criticism, persons will be disposed to admire excellence in art for the sake of the worthwhile experience that works of art at their best are capable of affording. Policy for aesthetic education thus should provide direction in bringing about such a state of affairs. But policy for arts education has not always been conceived in this domain-specific manner, nor has it always stressed distinctively aesthetic objectives. And there are a number of policy issues that are still not understood. I accordingly discuss the nature of policy generally and educational policy specifically and indicate some ways policies can avoid being sidetracked by extra-educational, and, in the case of arts education, extra-aesthetic considerations. In doing so I draw heavily on Donna H. Kerr's *Educational Policy* and her article "Aesthetic Policy."[31]

As Kerr points out, the term "policy" is often used loosely in such maxims as "Honesty is the best policy" and "The best policy is no policy," but a policy also suggests something that has been carefully reasoned through and adopted only after considerable deliberation about a number of important questions. Such deliberations have a special character because they center on decisions about what courses of action to take in certain situations. Policies, therefore, are designed to systematize and regulate activities in order to bring about a desired state of affairs. This might suggest that policy-making, implementation, and evaluation are essentially pragmatic enterprises which receive direction and support from simple know-how and empirical knowledge. To a considerable extent this is true, but ideas and theory also enter into the formulating of the purposes of a policy, and ethical considerations are relevant to a policy's enforcement. With this in mind we may turn to a number of questions that will keep aesthetic policies on track, some that are more or less obvious and others that deserve more attention than they have received. In the following I condense Kerr's discussion of the purposes, contexts, implementation, effectiveness, and justification of policies, extrapolating along the way for thinking about policy for aesthetic education.

The first point to be made about a policy may seem like a relatively trivial one: a policy requires a context for its enactment and assessment. So far as a theory of aesthetic education is concerned, this context is provided by the schools since no other institution is capable of educating the large majority of the young to aesthetic vision. The only reason for mentioning this is that occasionally policymakers advocate a nonconventional system of delivering educational services that would minimize the role of the schools. Born of weariness with educational institutions and despair over their alleged futility and possible harmfulness, these interests seek alternative ways of effecting aesthetic learning. Yet there can be no substitute for the day-to-day, long-term systematic learning that schools can provide.

The context for enacting policies for aesthetic learning having been decided, the next point to address is the nature of the proper authority for policy formation and implementation. Even the most finely wrought policy is useless unless its authors are policy-authorizing agents with acknowledged *de jure* powers. Policy-making authority derives from either laws and regulations or customs and traditions and may be reflected in organizational tables, chains of command, supervisory relationships, and the like. What complicates matters so far as education is concerned, and this is particularly true in the case of aesthetic education, is the fact that in addition to *de jure* authorizing agents there are individuals and interest groups with considerable *de facto* power over policy. The primary interests of these groups may be more social, cultural, and political than educational in nature, and this sometimes leads to the adulteration of educational objectives. The response of educators to such outside influences has taken different forms—from enthusiastic approval and cooperation to dismay and resignation to critical analysis and countermoves. But it seems reasonable to advise that because the intentions of these external agencies are antithetical to genuine pedagogical objectives, teachers should resist encroachment by such groups and insist on the primacy of educational considerations.

Policy language differentiates between agents authorized to formulate policy and those who implement its provisions and assess its effectiveness, although in practice these groups of agents may overlap. The relationship between authorizing and implementing agents would appear to be nonproblematical, yet in the case of arts education especially, it can be complicated by the choice of the implementing agency. Talk about alliances between schools and other cultural institutions may result in a disproportionate amount of aesthetic instruction being shifted to external organizations which lack both the resources to carry out a policy's objectives and employees sufficiently knowledgeable about educational theory. Indeed, personnel in these agencies often harbor animosity toward the schools and disrespect for teachers. In the language of policy, the use of community resources (arts councils, museums, and so forth) implies enlisting as implementing agents of the schools' educational policies organizations that lie outside the administrative authority of educational institutions. During the 1960s and 1970s, this tendency, a manifestation of "de-schooling" sentiments, was exemplified in an extreme form in what was then called "alternative education." Curiously, educators prepared and certified to teach art in the schools often looked with favor on developments of this kind, apparently oblivious of the fact that, if widely adopted, they would have challenged traditional forms of authority and eroded the teachers' own power and status.[32] School administrators generally regarded alternative schemes of arts education from a purely pragmatic point of view and tended to welcome them for reducing school expenditures. What should have been learned from this is that a policy ought to give assurance that sufficient control and supervision can be maintained over its implementing agents. If a policy fails to fulfill this provision, its effectiveness will be difficult to judge.

Questions of a policy's effectiveness turn, on the one hand, on the adequacy of the suggested means for accomplishing policy tasks and, on the other, on indicators of actual accomplishment of tasks. Policy analysis and evaluation thus tend to center on (1) the availability and proper use of resources; (2) ethically acceptable methods of teaching; (3) institutional arrangements called for by (1) and (2); and (4) the clientele to be reached, or the distribution-of-learning question.

Different views can be maintained about policy effectiveness, here understood as the adequacy of means to ends. At one pole of the spectrum we find the kind of policy that recommends learning should progress toward its designated purpose through precisely defined incremental steps; this is the method associated with advanced forms of competency-based and performance-based conceptions of learning modeled on government policies for management by objectives.[33] The other extreme is characterized by overstated claims for the efficacy of free, creative self-expression and the type of flexible, nonstructured curriculum usually associated with it.[34] Intuition rejects both extremes; some order is indispensable to learning, but opportunities for personal choice should also be provided.

There is another sense, apart from task accomplishment or goal achievement, in which effectiveness is a criterion for policy assessment. A policy is after all a set of statements and thus subject to the usual standards of coherence, consistency, and comprehensiveness. An incoherent, contradictory, and shortsighted policy is not likely to be very effective; yet it is not uncommon for policies with just these defects to make it from the drawing board into implementing channels. A policy statement, in short, should be a cogently argued document and not an outpouring of unrestrained rhetoric. Policies guilty of the latter offense can usually be attributed to either a lack of necessary knowledge on the part of the formulators of the policy or mere thoughtlessness. Policy thinking may also be derailed by a number of procedural and substantive mistakes, among them overemphasis on sheer activity and organization for their own sakes at the expense of work toward goal achievement; ill-conceived ideas about the uses and usefulness of the arts which result in a misguided instrumentalism; and images of learning that fail to distinguish between training appropriate for professionals and general education for nonspecialists.[35]

The question of effectiveness also involves the justifiability of the goals and methods of arts education. For example, it would be difficult to justify an *educational* policy that did not attempt to further primarily educational ends or that left too much to the imagination in the area of implementation. Nor is a policy justified solely because there is reason to believe that the tasks and activities it undertakes to systematize and regulate are likely to produce the state of affairs described in the policy's purpose. For it is precisely that purpose or set of objectives which stands in need of justification in order for the policy as a whole to be acceptable. Policymakers must therefore be prepared to defend the worthwhileness of their policy objectives. And such a defense, once again, should be mounted on strictly educational grounds.

But what are the grounds of defensibility? It is not enough that the policy issues from a legitimate educational authority. Nor do probability of effectiveness, general approval, or endorsements by prestigious groups and organizations add up to a justification. Polls may ascertain a preference for a policy, but not its justifiability, for a thing's being desired does not necessarily count as evidence for that thing's worthwhileness. Popularity cannot prove that the purpose of a policy is such that any thoughtful person ought to approve it.

The justification of a policy for aesthetic education requires a judgment not only of what is desirable but of what is educationally right and what this implies for schooling. To reflect about these matters one needs to have conceptions of human nature, ethical and social ideas, and ideas about the good life. Questions of effectiveness and justification, in other words, lead in the direction of theory, educational as well as aesthetic, the two philosophical foundations of policy-making in arts education. But theoretical discussion can take place at different levels of abstraction and generality: at the level of the purposes of education generally and at the level of specific subjects. Subject- or domain-specific policy purposes—though they would derive their ultimate sanction from higher-order educational goals and objectives—should be defended in terms that reflect the unique contribution expected of the domain in question, in the instance at hand, the domain of aesthetic education. Policies, say, for science education would not take one very far if all that was stipulated as an educational outcome were an enlightened appreciation of the world of science. Something like the acquisition of the key concepts and procedures of the sciences would be a more sensible objective. And so it is with arts education. Domain-specific purposes, concepts, and skills must be articulated and defined in a way that makes their relationships to the arts readily apparent.[36] Appendix II provides a model for setting out such concepts and skills for teaching the concept of aesthetic criticism.

Domain-specific purposes, concepts, and skills in aesthetic education should, of course, be based primarily on *aesthetic* considerations, or what is involved in illuminating art as art. Yet acceptance of such a commonsensical assumption would seem to be the exception rather than the rule when one considers some of the goals set for arts education. Among recent and current objectives for arts education, for example, are the following: (1) strengthening the skills of basic literacy (basic education); (2) helping the handicapped (special education); (3) developing interests, attitudes, and values of all kinds (affective education); (4) cultivating interpersonal relations (psychological-humanistic education); (5) acquiring occupational skills (career education); (6) synthesizing cognitive and affective learning (confluent education); (7) developing flexible and tolerant dispositions (creativity education); (8) building personal pride and identity (ethnic education); (9) developing an appreciation of non-Western societies (multicultural education); and (10) reforming both schools and society (political education). And this is not an exhaustive list.

That educational policy generally can be deflected from its proper course rather easily by a variety of external interests and pressures—by prevailing federal winds, funding patterns of the private sector, and philanthropic caprice—is obvious. That this should happen so easily with arts and arts education policies, that is, that they should derive their legitimacy from principally extra-aesthetic values, is disappointing to say the least, for the arts are, comparatively speaking, relatively nonutilitarian in character and function. We expect them, as Sparshott and Aiken put it, to provide worthwhile experiences merely in being looked at, listened to, or read. Dewey, too, the instrumentalist *par excellence,* came to realize that the essence of the aesthetic consists principally in its consummatory value.

But to return to matters of policy. Why should aesthetic education so often be construed as a handmaiden to extra-aesthetic objectives? A lack of understanding of both the domain in question and principles of policy-making is one reason. Here the prescription is proper education in both. Only persons uninformed about art as well as policy, for example, would assume that the principal values of aesthetic education can be secured incidentally to, or as a by-product of, the teaching of other school subjects. Yet it has been claimed that aesthetic education occurs whenever reproductions of art are used to illustrate social or political history, when dance performers contort themselves to illustrate geometric shapes in math classes, when some drama is injected into teaching to make it more interesting, or when the teaching environment is given a more attractive appearance. We know confusion reigns when a multimedia reenactment of Theodore Roosevelt's last campaign speech by a group of junior high school students is offered as an exemplary instance of arts education.[37]

All of these instances of what may be called the decorative dimensions of teaching and learning may have a place, and within ethical limits teachers are obviously justified in doing whatever they think will bring about desired outcomes. But the decorative or dramatic *dimensions* of schooling should not be confused with *subject-specific* instruction or be considered an adequate substitute for it. The arts have their own history, values, and puzzles and deserve separate curriculum time and space. To believe anything else is to imply that the arts have no particular value apart from their instrumental uses. Instances of outright bad faith are provided by educational reformers who in fact do understand the true complexity of art and the demands it makes on teaching and learning but who nonetheless exploit art's popularity and appeal in order to effect general school reforms that may have little to do with the serious study of art. It is irresponsible, for example, to regard the arts as a "potent catalyst" for just about any educational change one wants.[38] Ultimately, those who equate the aesthetic dimensions of schooling with arts education itself and those who attempt to cast the arts in the role of educational reformer or revolutionary deny students opportunities to cultivate aesthetic dispositions through sustained involvement with art. In other words, crude instrumental conceptions of aesthetic or arts education are inherently anti-art and anti-arts education.

The matter thus comes down to the question of conduct becoming the legitimate policymaker who formulates policies intended to influence teaching and learning art in the schools. Mindlessness and intellectual carelessness are of course to be avoided in every phase of the policy-making process. And keeping the following questions in mind can help to keep policy thinking on target. (1) Is the policy in question actually a policy; that is, is it clear enough about what should be done and toward what end? Is the context for the enactment and assessment of the policy clearly indicated? (2) Is the policy a truly educational policy, or does it subserve essentially noneducational aims and interests? (3) Did the policy originate from a legitimate source? (4) Is the policy justifiable with respect to defensible educational theory, on the one hand, and subject-specific objectives, on the other? (5) Is there some provision for sufficient regulation or control over the policy's implementing agents? (6) Is there reason to believe that the proposed assignments, tasks, and activities are adequate to securing policy objectives? (7) Have adequate decisions been made about resource allocation? (8) Have alternatives been seriously entertained?[3]

CHAPTER 8

Issues: ideology and postmodernism

Ideology

The preceding examination of policy suggested that policy-making for aesthetic education can occasionally be guilty of bad faith and special pleading. As these notions are commonly associated with ideological thinking, it has now become appropriate to ask about the meaning of ideology and how ideological attitudes affect our deliberations about art and aesthetic education. The topic of ideology was briefly alluded to in Chapter 1 with a reference to the reduction of art to nonaesthetic values implicit in certain strands of Marxism. I now want to approach the subject more directly by looking at different senses of "ideology" in the literature of aesthetic education. First, however, a few observations on the meaning of the term and its use in discussions of the relations between art and society.

Raymond Williams has pointed out that since its introduction into the French language in the late eighteenth century, the term ideology has implied the science of ideas, conscious but diffuse social thought, revolutionary thought, the masking of reality, abstract thought, and false consciousness, ·ideas derived from material conditions, class interests, and any kind of belief system whatsoever. In these meanings we discern both the pejorative and nonpejorative senses of the word, and, as Williams points out about Marx, both senses can sometimes be found in the writings of the same person. Williams thinks that the pejorative sense of ideology tends to prevail today: "Sensible people," he writes, "rely on *experience*, or have a *philosophy*; silly people reply on *ideology*. In this sense *ideology* . . . is mainly a term of abuse."[1]

Williams may be correct, but it is also the case that a writer's age and interests may influence which sense of ideology is favored. Older writers who recall the ideological controversies of the earlier part of this century—the controversies that swirled about the nature of Stalinism, for example—are apt to think of the negative connotations of the term, while younger writers are less prone to do so. The point, however, is that since the term has so many different meanings and connotations, anyone addressing the topic has an obligation to define which meaning is intended.

Art and ideology

The problems with the concept of ideology—its vagueness, the propensity of writers in opposing ideological camps to give it conflicting meanings, and the fact that even writers of the same ideological persuasion interpret it differently—are multiplied when the concept is explored in juxtaposition with the equally vague concept of art. Consider the following examples.

Ernst Fischer, a Marxist writer, attaches importance to the relations of art and ideology when he writes that "historical development . . . is not merely a matter of ideological struggle reflecting the struggle between classes, nations of systems, but at the same time . . . the struggle of the *practice and recognition of truth* against the dominant ideology."[2] Fischer characterizes this latter struggle as "the revolt of reality against false consciousness"[3] and believes that it can be waged by means of scientific, philosophic, and *artistic* thought. As it is something that is false and must be exposed and corrected, "ideology," in Fischer's use, clearly has a pejorative connotation. What is more, art, along with science and philosophy, becomes a potent weapon in the arsenal of truth.

Another Marxist writer, Herbert Marcuse,[4] echoes these beliefs but with a different emphasis. For Marcuse, art is not merely one of a number of combatants in the war against ideology; by its nature art is preeminently qualified for such a role because of its inherent opposition to ordinary consciousness and prevailing social relations. Art is always radical and necessarily protests, subverts, and transcends conventional thinking and social relations. Not only that; because art inevitably opposes ordinary consciousness, it is ideological, in, however, a nonpejorative sense. Marcuse thus preserves the basic Marxist principle that art cannot be politically neutral, but he goes beyond conventional Marxism in his belief that art performs its ideological function primarily through its aesthetic form and not its explicit revolutionary content.

What can be made of these and similar points of view? We may first dispense with the belief that significant artistic expression must reflect unambiguously and directly the ideas of a guiding religion, myth, or social ideal. Cézanne's art is a significant counterexample: Schapiro remarks that "if there is an ideology in his work, it is hidden within unconscious attitudes and is never directly asserted. . . ."[5]

Second, the belief that art necessarily opposes ordinary consciousness and the dominant forces in society has been refuted by Albert William Levi,[6] who himself appreciates the social origins of cultural phenomena. Citing seventeenth-century Dutch genre painting as a case in point, Levi observes that the history of art provides impressive examples of works that celebrate the status quo and existing social values. In other words, art neither necessarily advocates change nor inevitably contains oppositional and transformational elements. The idea that it does is a quite modern one, and preoccupation with it has resulted in an overemphasis on the adversarial function of art.

Third, the idea that art is a staunch ally of truth is rendered problematical by the career of Lionel Trilling. In *The Liberal Imagination*,[7] Trilling expressed the belief that ideological abstraction, distortion, and rigidity could be effectively countered by the variousness, complexity, and difficulty of literature and the senses of possibility it presents; that is to say, ideology could be countered by art. This was Trilling's response to the Stalinist ideology of the 1930s. However, two decades later he was no longer certain. Perhaps because of his having resolved his ambivalence about the import of modern literature, Trilling came to believe that art does not always tell the truth or the best kind of truth and that it can even habituate us to falsehoods.[8] This skepticism was expressed toward the highest forms of literature and not toward the products of popular culture against which the charge is commonly leveled. In short, Trilling seriously undercuts Fischer's claim about the effectiveness of art as a weapon against the falsehoods and distortions of ideology.

And so the critical literature on art and ideology goes: point-counter-point, example-counterexample. This state of affairs guarantees that confusion will be further compounded when a third element—education—is added to the formula. As a way of providing some perspective on the relations of art, ideology, and aesthetic education, I limit myself to a discussion of three possible viewpoints.

Ideology and aesthetic education: Three views

In "The Aesthetic Attitude and the Hidden Curriculum,"[9] David Gordon presents a view of the curriculum that enjoys some currency. Though Gordon does not use the term ideology explicitly, it is clear that the power to affect learning that he attributes to the hidden curriculum is what others refer to as the tacit ideology of schooling. It is important to understand how Gordon defines his key terms.

By "aesthetic education" Gordon means a program of studies intended to instill in pupils the aesthetic attitude, an attitude that is characterized by a disposition to cherish things noninstrumentally, that is, for their intrinsic rather than their extrinsic values. By the "hidden curriculum" Gordon (following Jane Roland Martin) means those potential learning outcomes of schooling that may be intended, are often unintended, but are certainly not openly acknowledged. Schooling as understood by Gordon includes both physical arrangements and formal and informal human relationships. Although the messages of the hidden curriculum are absorbed unconsciously, their redundancy, persistence, and consistency make them more powerful and influential than those of the manifest curriculum. What does the hidden curriculum teach?

According to Gordon, the hidden curriculum is anti-aesthetic since it teaches that human activities are *not* intrinsically worthwhile. Human activities are valued mainly as means to ends, even though the ends may occasionally be remote. In this respect, the messages of the hidden curriculum coincide with those of the manifest curriculum, for it too is largely means-oriented, particularly in its vocationalism. The only exception to this pervasive instrumentalism in the acknowledged visible curriculum is the small segment of time devoted to aesthetic activities, where intrinsic values are supposed to come into their own. But aesthetic education is destined to fail for it is overwhelmed by the combined thrust of the overt and the hidden curriculum. Gordon's pessimistic verdict is that aesthetic education is defeated by a pervasive ideology of instrumentalism.

Some questions can be raised. It can be argued that the primary purpose of aesthetic education is to help learners realize aesthetic value and not appreciate intrinsic values per se.[10] We prize things, strictly speaking, not for themselves but for what they contribute to the fulfillment of our wants and desires. If it is aesthetic value and enjoyment we want from works of art and works of art are preeminently capable of providing them through aesthetic experience, then works of art are instrumental to this kind of value experience. We may thus speak, as Beardsley does, of an instrumental theory of aesthetic value. Aesthetic education is further instrumental in the way all schooling is because it equips learners with skills to experience works of art (and other aesthetically valuable objects) that they will use upon leaving school. It will be recalled that Kaelin believes aesthetic education can be instrumental to the efficacy of cultural institutions.

The more we think about it, the notion of a hidden curriculum presents further difficulties. How, it may be asked, can something so obscure and inaccessible to observation be the source of such a clear and powerful ideological message that has the same adverse effects on everyone while leaving them unaware that they are being so affected? In truth, the thing "hidden" is often the political agenda of proponents of the hidden curriculum idea. The belief is that the whole environment of schooling—human, physical, ideational—combines to such potent results that before improvement is possible in any area of education the entire structure must first be brought down. Gordon thus concludes gloomily that there can be no aesthetic education so long as the ideology of instrumentalism pervades the hidden curriculum; only the most drastic educational change can make schooling safe for aesthetic education.[11] I have discussed Gordon's views mainly because the attitude they reflect—pessimism about gradual reform and powerlessness in the face of ideology—is quite evident in current educational theory.

In "Ideology and Aesthetic Education,"[12] David Swanger understands "ideology" nonpejoratively as a generic term properly applied to belief systems held in conjunction with practical precepts. Ideology implies both belief and action and is especially concerned to explain the moral basis of action so it can justify certain activities over others. Three features can be extrapolated from Swanger's account of ideology.

Ideologies involve both belief and action, and since actions and activities are designed to accomplish different things, ideologies may be associated with different spheres of action, including schooling. Ideologies need not therefore be interpreted as expressions of false consciousness that distort the thinking of an entire age, society, or social class; they may simply be more or less rational and encompassing. Since it is a function of ideologies to explain and justify practice, it is possible to discuss and assess them objectively. There is no need then to think of ideologies in connection with covert forces or a hidden curriculum. However, since once established ideologies have a strong tendency to stay established, they become resistant to change.

Swanger writes about ideology in a straightforward, matter-of-fact way. He deplores the tendency of ideologies toward stagnation, and although he has no illusions about the difficulty of modifying entrenched ideologies, he is not without hope. Ideologies can accommodate themselves to change provided pressure is applied. What is to supply this pressure? For Swanger, the animus is art. Apparently in agreement with Marcuse he thinks that art is inherently radical and destabilizing. Art pits innovation against the status quo and is antithetical to entrenched ideology. The purpose of aesthetic education thus becomes the introducing of students to a domain of instruction best suited to forestall the hardening of ideological arteries. Aesthetic studies alert pupils to the values of freshness, creativity, and innovation with the expectation that they will come to want such values in other areas of human experience. This is similar to what the early Trilling believed when he thought that art could counter the abstractness of ideological thinking.

Aesthetic education has a second mission that, according to Swanger, involves a venture into the realm of ideology writ large. He would have the ideology of material consumption give ground to a way of life based on *pro*sumption, essentially an ethic of conservation. An emphasis on prosumption would foster positive attitudes toward activities that would be sparing in their use of nonrenewable resources. Since aesthetic activities are exemplary in this respect, aesthetic education would be congruent with the demands of the future.

Swanger's analysis has much to recommend it. He writes clearly, criticizes in a constructive manner, and places the problem in historical context (discussing, for instance, Plato's distrust of the potentially harmful effects of certain kinds of art and his insistence that art should reflect the ideals of the republic). Still, some questions can be asked. The first regards Swanger's belief that teachers in aesthetic education programs should be practicing artists. But the callings of art and teaching do not always mesh well and the recommendation may merely be one more instance of what Barzun calls the professional's fallacy: that knowledge of the craft of a thing is necessary in order to understand it.[13] Moreover, as Hildred B. Redfern has observed, a large part of aesthetic education should be devoted to the cultivation of critical reflection about art which presupposes skill and finesse on the part of teachers in conducting classroom dialogue. "It is precisely his concern for . . . this aspect of arts education that will make an educator pause before handing over his job to professional artists, no matter how skilled they are in their sphere. . . ."[14] A second question turns on Swanger's characterization of art as inherently radical. As I've said, this is a relatively modern idea refuted by numerous historical examples. As for the ideal of prosumption as a future way of life, it is an attractive notion (though perhaps less so for those developing nations that are rushing toward consumption as fast as opportunities permit). This aspect of Swanger's thought, however, does give it a forward-looking character that in its moderate utopianism contrasts markedly with Gordon's pessimism. One should caution, however, that in using aesthetic studies to advance a new attitude— prosumption or any other—aesthetic education would be pressed into serving nonaesthetic ideas and that this could jeopardize the autonomy of art. It would be more to the point to say that aesthetic education, by diligently pursuing its strictly aesthetic objectives, has a good chance of affecting attitudes.

A third option about the relations of ideology and aesthetic education also understands ideology unpejoratively as simply a set of beliefs. In "Aesthetic Education as a New Ideology"[15] Diederik Schönau asks whether the idea of aesthetic education implies an ideology within education, that is, the ideology of a particular curriculum area or subject, or whether it implies a new ideology of education itself, that is, the idea that all of education should be seen under the aspect of the aesthetic. In truth, Schönau is less interested in the relations of ideology and aesthetic education than in the forces and developments which gave rise to present-day thinking about aesthetic education. In this connection he mentions modern alienation, psychoanalysis with its interest in creativity, the humanistic reaction against behaviorism, the need of a scientific and technological society to assuage its feelings of guilt over sacrificing aesthetic values, and not least the opportunistic astuteness of aesthetic educators themselves whose penchant for organization he observes. He hopes that this penchant will not result in the uncritical transmission of a new ideology.

In concluding this section, it may be reiterated that Gordon, Swanger, and Schönau represent three possible relations of ideology and aesthetic education: aesthetic education defeated by ideology, aesthetic education opposed to recalcitrant ideology, and aesthetic education simply as an ideology, as a set of beliefs.

A fourth view

A fourth view of the relations of ideology and aesthetic education that contains no surprises or radically new departures is possible. It simply attempts to reconcile elements from the perspectives just discussed.

From Schönau may be taken the idea of an ideology of aesthetic education as a set of beliefs (although I prefer to think in terms of a philosophy or theory of aesthetic education). Such a theory or ideology should be responsible to two major considerations: the autonomy of art and theoretical adequacy. Preserving the autonomy of art implies the safeguarding of its aesthetic function. This function has been described in terms of the worthwhile experiences that art at its best can provide.

The second consideration to which an ideology of aesthetic education should be kept responsive is theoretical adequacy. How well does it satisfy the criteria of coherence, consistency, and comprehensiveness? Are connections between beliefs and practices plausible and defensible? Have certain activities been justified or merely rationalized? Does the ideology provide a moral basis for action? Educational theorists have studied questions like these and have formulated standards for the evaluation of educational theories which should be helpful to aesthetic educators.[16]

Keeping these two considerations in mind—the autonomy of art and the theoretical adequacy of a set of beliefs about aesthetic education— the problem of social change can now be addressed. The study of the distinctive values of art, which is the proper subject for aesthetic education, may well produce those changed attitudes and values that social reformers want to achieve by more direct methods. It is reasonable to suppose that by honoring the autonomy of art, aesthetic education can contribute indirectly to an enhanced quality of life. For it is quite possible that students who have acquired the capacity to appreciate good art will become impatient with inferior art and discourage its production, just as those most sensitized to aesthetic qualities in general will demand a more attractive habitat.

Postmodernism

Postmodernism in one of its several meanings expresses characteristic millenial anxiety and a feeling that a turning point in modern life has been reached that requires new categories of thought and different modes of artistic expression.[17] Many of our traditional assumptions about the nature of knowledge, truth, and reality are no longer felt to be adequate.

Further doubt is cast on the purported civilizing power Matthew Arnold and F. R. Leavis attributed to the touchstones of the great tradition.

Millenial anxiety, existential despair, and cultural disenchantment, however, are not the whole story. Other meanings of postmodernism derive from the inveterate tendency of intellectuals to explore ideas for the intrinsic interest of doing so, a pursuit that may ultimately lead to major revisions in the ways we think about a good many things. Such revisionism is less an expression of angst than of a desire to move around the mental furniture of the mind. The motives of some philosophical revisionists, however, may also be more specifically reformist, in which case the explicit aim is to bring about new political states of affairs.

The numerous meanings of postmodernism must be recognized before it is possible to address its significance for reflecting on contemporary problems. In what follows I discuss a strand of postmodernist thought, deconstruction, that has nihilistic implications for thinking about the arts and aesthetic education. Though originating in developments in the philosophy of language and having application mainly in theorizing about literary criticism, its thesis is now being generalized to other contexts, including aesthetic and educational theory. Its conception of "text" is now held to have near universal application; it is as if all the world has become an endless series of texts of which, as deconstructionist belief would have it, only misreadings are possible. One consequence for arts education is that teachers of art are being subjected to some unorthodox performances at their conferences and in their journals, the point of which is seldom understood. But what is deconstruction and what are its consequences for a theory of aesthetic education? Better, why should it be rejected by theorists of aesthetic education? In setting out the meaning of deconstruction, I follow the lead of those who have attempted to explain its basic premises. My interpretation of deconstruction stands or falls on the strengths of the critical literature that has developed in response to its fundamental theses.

In an insightful analysis of the radical skepticism of deconstruction, M. J. Wilsmore[18] perceives deconstruction as a threat to the traditional status of literature and the ways we have tended to study and teach it. Deconstruction challenges the conventional view that literature consists of identifiable poems, short stories, novels, plays, etc., the meaning, intelligibility, and value of which can be revealed through rational, objective criticism. Deconstruction is in effect an assault on Western notions of meaning, objectivity, truth, intention, rationality, and reason as they influence thinking generally, including thinking about the history, criticism, and teaching of literature. Deconstruction, says Wilsmore, also radically challenges those who place value on transmitting the cultural heritage. Although deconstruction is a philosophy of language associated principally with the writings of the French philosopher Jacques Derrida, it has caught hold largely in departments of English where Derrida's followers have put his ideas to various uses, and it is these uses that interest Wilsmore. We might say that Wilsmore reports on the ways deconstruction has been received and further interpreted, somewhat in the way I had observed the ways the two cultures debate unfolded.

At one point Wilsmore states that the skepticism of the deconstructionists cannot be understood apart from their social and political beliefs. These beliefs assert that embedded in the language of traditional literary criticism are bourgeois attitudes that falsely assume the possibility of the objective determination of a text's meaning. Such objective determination, claim deconstructionists, is impossible, owing to the purportedly value-laden character of all language and the unavailability of a neutral stance outside of language by which to determine the truth about anything. What is more, unmasking the apparatus of objective criticism reveals the true underlying purpose of traditional criticism—the attempt, through the control of language, to wield power over literary and pedagogical institutions and to enjoy the economic and political rewards offered by this power. But since traditional critical theory and belief can claim no universal validity, such criticism is in effect just another form of creative writing that expresses a personal, subjective point of view.

What all this means is that interpretive criticism, insofar as it attempts to explain the meaning of a work of art, is meaningless, for all interpretive statements stem from misreadings and thus are false. All critical commentary can do is to graft its own text onto other texts in a continuously expanding mass of text, one consequence of which is the blurring of distinctions between text and commentary and writer and critic. Another consequence is that the ensuing mass of texts denies any special place or status to the touchstones or classics of the cultural heritage. The implications for curriculum and teaching are obvious: one is free to pick and choose according to the heart's desire since a text's aesthetic value, meaning, or significance are of no importance compared to the opportunity the text provides for the creation of additional texts. In different terms, deconstruction undermines the authority of the cultural tradition and releases the hold it has on teaching and learning. The value of cultural continuity and communication goes by the boards, as does the traditional idea of liberal education which claims that a human career is best shaped through the disciplined testing of a self against the best that has been thought and created. An image (mine not Wilsmore's) is brought to mind of mighty buildings caving in on themselves as strategically placed explosives are detonated. More will be said about the general social and political posture of deconstructionists. Meanwhile, what is involved in deconstructing a text?

Deconstructionist criticism is inherently negative in that it consists not of revealing a work's plenitude of literary values and meaning but of the unmasking of what are called the logocentric tendencies of language. A logocentric tendency is any tendency that manifests a bias toward such concerns as truth, reason, rationality, logic, etc., and toward the spoken rather than the written word.

In describing deconstructionist critical methods, Wilsmore first mentions the critic's detection of conventional binary opposites—for example, speech/writing, truth/fiction, literal/metaphorical, and so forth—in which the left-hand term, by virtue of being assigned a superior status, disrupts the right-hand term, when in actuality, according to deconstructionists, the right-hand term is a condition of the possibility of the left-hand term. For example, speech cannot be the binary opposite of and have superior status over writing inasmuch as all of the characteristics of writing are a precondition of speech. And when we understand the characteristics of writing—"the free play, or undecidability within every system of communication, the endless displacement of meaning."[19] as Wilsmore puts it—then we are released from the idea that individuals can ever completely understand the meaning of language, or of each other, for that matter. From this deconstructionists derive the assumption "that what we think of as meaningful language is just a free play of 'signifiers'—a never-ending 'grafting' of text onto text."[20] One effect of this view of language is the displacement of logocentric tendencies. For example, "the binary opposite of man/woman is displaced, and it is 'shown'—by the deconstructive criticism—that man is but a variant of woman—a disrupting of the values placed on the primacy of the male in society over the female."[21]

Another deconstructionist critical move is to make central what is usually considered marginal or unimportant. For example, deconstructionists are keen on sifting out key words that reveal the logocentrism of a text under scrutiny, words a writer may have used unself-consciously or merely considered insignificant. They further draw attention to the actual figurative character of language that was formerly considered literal.

One further consequence of a deconstructionist stance toward a text is the blurring of the traditional distinction between philosophy and literature, for the distinction erroneously implies the binary opposites of truth/rhetoric. But since meaning cannot be anchored in any reference in the real world—for signs only signify signs—philosophy too reveals the rhetorical bias of all language. Philosophy as literature is text which is but part of an endless mass of expanding texts. By erasing the lines that formerly separated different forms of thought, including the one between philosophy and literature, deconstructionists assert the impossibility of a set of literary texts functioning as touchstones against which other works of literature are judged. "This is done," says Wilsmore, "by denying that there were ever any members of such a canon and thereby repudiating the existence of what we call our 'literary heritage'."[22]

At this point I find an analysis of deconstruction by Annette Barnes also quite helpful. As she explains it in her *On Interpretation*, [23] texts in the deconstructionist scheme of things are signs that are semiotically independent; that is, texts are independent of authors (individual or collective), context of production, readers (individual or collective), and the objects of significance, or external referents. It is this independent status that enables signs to function as signifiers, but not in connection with any of the above. How does an independent signifier signify?

Barnes writes:

> Literary texts are made up of marks on paper, marks that have already been written. . . . These already written marks function as signifiers in virtue of their ability to retain the past, for these marks are "traces." A trace is a remainder of something that is already absent. Its function of standing for something no longer there is its function of substitution or supplementation. But to stand for something that cannot itself be present is not only to retain the past, it is also to efface it, for to be past is to be effaced. Moreover, although traces are traces of something, they are not traces of some original, rather a trace is a trace of a trace which is, in its turn, a trace of a trace *ad infinitum*. Signs for Derrida signify other signs. . . . "Differance," a neologism which Derrida introduces to cover both differences and deferment, sets the play of signification going. The meaning of any sign lies in the relations of difference, its difference from other signs, and its meaning is perpetually deferred, the referent can never be fully present to the signifier. [24]

I suppose this is a way of saying not that the medium is the message but rather that the traces of the medium, which are inherently ambiguous, signify only other inherently ambiguous traces; we thus have infinite regress, and the concept of meaning becomes highly attenuated, if not meaningless.

What are some of the consequences of deconstruction and deconstructive method? Several have already been mentioned, but it is especially noteworthy for the purposes of this essay that deconstruction would relieve critics and teachers of literature from any obligation to regard a work of art as an autonomous independent entity. Artworks would no longer be approached in a suppliant mood and experiencing them would no longer result in feelings of object-directedness and detached affect, nor even, for that matter, in the enlightenment or understanding they can yield about worlds, to use Goodman's terminology. Certainly, it would be irrelevant to try to improve the cultural institution of art via a program of aesthetic studies that stresses aesthetic experience, to recall Kaelin's line of thinking. Rather it would seem that texts are merely the loci of certain kinds of happenings, random collections of signifiers adding up to nothing, except, of course, to what deconstructionists say they imply about the logocentric tendencies of Western bourgeois thinking. Or perhaps deconstruction should be more properly character-ized as—but, no, the temptation to conjure up images of vacuity, absur-dity, negation, nihilism, nothingness, and meaninglessness must be resisted. Far from advancing the scientific revolution or helping to bridge the gap between the scientific and literary cultures, the premises of deconstruction allow for only one culture—a culture of ambiguous signs.

Critics have castigated deconstruction for its intellectual terrorism and nihilism. Given its radical challenge to traditional notions of language, truth, meaning, and communication, such condemnation is perhaps un-derstandable; yet deconstruction seems susceptible to careful but effec-tive defusing. Both Wilsmore and Barnes prove to be astute critics. Where the deconstructionists err, says Wilsmore, is in presupposing what they purport to deny, namely, that many things are after all capable of being identified as certain kinds of object or discourse having distinc-tive features or qualities. Barnes likewise points out that when decon-structionists address their audiences, they must work with the very logocentric tendencies and concepts they call into question. Barnes thus realizes that, according to deconstructionist precepts, her own (I would say illuminating) account of deconstruction would be futile, for it is just one more text of signifiers grafted onto a giant intertext that consists of nothing but traces of traces, etc. Yet this is just one of the paradoxes spun by deconstruction. Consider also its attitude toward interpretation.

In ordinary parlance, says Wilsmore, interpretation implies rendering something intelligible, if not in terms of a thing's ultimate meaning then at least in terms of what *can* be seen, heard, or understood. An interpretation, that is, is *of* something, and about that something it is possible to make intelligent statements. *Hamlet* is a play, a tragedy, and is about Hamlet's revenge for his father's death. This does not mean that interpretation cannot be controversial or subject to correction, that works cannot be experienced from more than one point of view, or even that they must be value-free. It is simply, says Wilsmore, that "there are practices for identifying works of literature, and they [critics] have the means for both appreciating and describing what they also have the means to identify."[25] Descriptions of literature, moreover, are also "in-tended to mediate a special response from us to the work of art, based on its features, as described. Hence they are intended to be affective, and as such, are likely to have evaluative implications—to be evaluative at one and the same time as they are descriptive."[26] Such remarks recall those of Eaton and Crittenden recorded in Chapter 3. Hence open-textured criticism, that is, criticism that admits a degree of ambiguity and variable interpretation, can be descriptive and amenable to standards of correctness and truth. That words can be used both descriptively and evaluatively does not rule out the possibility of an objective judgment of something. As Wilsmore puts it: "In making the work intelligible for us, the critic 'shows' us the work *by* describing its properties in such a way as to allow us to respond fully to it for what it is."[27]

In conclusion, Wilsmore points out that the issue for objective criticism is not whether there is a neutral stance from which criticism speaks but whether a work is intelligible and objective for a *reader*, and we might add for a viewer or listener. The deconstructionist's unorthodox stipulation of the meaning of interpretation must not deflect us from this awareness. "In its ordinary use," she writes, "it makes perfectly good sense to say of the critic that he has given us something of the meaning of the work if what he has written about it could be said to be 'adequate,' 'fair,' 'perceptive,' 'thoughtful,' 'reasonable,' 'incisive,' etc."[28] All terms, I hasten to add, that fit the descriptions of the writers discussed in Chapter 4. Nor need we think that objective criticism will give us *the* meaning of a work, for that cannot be determined independently of context in which meaning is sought. But it does not follow from the deconstructionist argument, says Wilsmore, that all assessment is biased, that right readings are impossible, or that all criticism is necessarily ideological in the sense that it consists of a thrust for power. And this latter remark returns us to Wilsmore's belief that deconstruction cannot be properly understood apart from its political motives.

Peter Shaw[29] agrees with Wilsmore and states that anyone who attempts to take the measure of deconstruction must realize that it emanates from a considerably Marxified academic environment and coincides in many ways with the revolutionary agenda of Marxism. True, not all deconstructionists are Marxists, and some Marxists are impatient with the obscurity of deconstructionist writing, yet the explicit political intent of books and articles that continue to be written in a deconstructionist vein lends support to Shaw's belief that deconstruction's most significant feature is its political dimension.[30] He believes that radically minded intellectuals have moved beyond the protests and demonstrations of previous decades and are now trying to undermine the structures of language, understanding, and communication that lie at the heart of Western thought.

Other writers outside the deconstructionist camp seem less worried, saying that we are probably better off for having deconstruction, or that at least its politics is nothing to get alarmed about. Joseph Margolis[31] takes this calmer view, for he thinks deconstruction is simply a cautionary tale that humbles us in our quest for certainty of knowledge. Its thesis, he says, "is simply this: that proposals of *any* kind that presume to match language with reality (a reality independent of language and unencumbered linguistically)—so that the structures of the latter are correctly represented in the former, yielding truth—are forms of radical self-delusion."[32] Whether or not one agrees with it, says Margolis, this is a reasonable thesis and suffers only when its use becomes over-elastic or an exaggerated form of intellectual play. If deconstruction has a Nietzschean character, it is simply because it urges a more self-conscious awareness of inevitable failure in our search for truth. Moreover, since we map reality with a number of linguistic or conceptual schemes, no one scheme has priority over the others so long as each minds its conceptual manners. Deconstruction thus yields neither a better philosophy, anthropology, linguistics, nor psychoanalysis. In fact, says Margolis, "*It literally does nothing*. Its best role is to nag us from within, while we do what we do—what we cannot afford to ignore all the while the deep mortality of every possible way of understanding . . . sinks in."[33]

Jerome Bruner[34] seems to share Margolis's sentiments. He is not perturbed by deconstruction and pragmaticism, two varieties of post-structuralism. He thinks their premises are consistent with the modern revolution in philosophy, science, and politics and consonant with his own outlook of constructionism, a doctrine that, like Goodman's, postulates not the discovery but the creation of worlds. Bruner does acknowledge, and distances himself from, a "harebrained perspectivalism that is living out its sunset in Paris and New Haven and in the intellectual suburbs"[35] where it exists "in faddish enclaves with a dwindling clientele, addicted more to slogans than to substance."[36] Like Margolis, however, Bruner appears to be unconcerned about deconstruction's political motives.

Considered strictly in terms of its abstract philosophical premises perhaps deconstruction is not a cause for serious concern, for if Margolis is right it really does not do anything. The cultural effects of deconstruction*ism*, however, of deconstruction flexing its political muscle, cannot be overlooked, for these consequences are potentially devastating; and where Bruner sees a setting sun others see a triumphantly rising one. In a discussion of deconstruction, Roger Kimball[37] claims that far from fading from the scene deconstructionists now dominate intellectual life at our most prestigious institutions of higher learning, a fact which is celebrated periodically in journalistic accounts of the status and high regard deconstructionists enjoy at major universities.

The most alarming aspect of deconstructionism to Frederick Crews, one of the foremost critics of deconstruction, is its abandonment of an empirical ethos in favor of what he calls "theoreticism," or "frank recourse to unsubstantiated theory, not just as a tool of investigation but as anti-empirical knowledge in its own right."[38] This "emancipation" is celebrated as a "freedom from fact" and it encourages the manipulation of data, the substitution of subjective impressions for objective findings, and wholesale invention. As if in support of Crews's claim, David Bromwich[39] remarks that basic errors of literary interpretation that ordinarily would defeat the credibility of a thesis no longer prevent its publication, for motives and interests lie elsewhere. Lies and fabrications are sins no more.

Theoreticism is an encompassing term that captures the disposition and stance of deconstructionism. Theoreticism denies the possibility of objective understanding and indulges a range of strategies that, on the one hand, reject interpretation itself if it is taken to imply the construal of a text's meaning, and, on the other, regard works of art as mere pretexts for the creation of additional texts. These assumptions rule out the idea of cumulative advance in our understanding of works and of what texts tell us about the self and its relations to an external reality and make impossible the knowledge that literature has characteristically been believed to provide. Not only that; since deconstructionists hold that texts are inherently incoherent and contradictory, the next step follows inexorably—a critique of a text becomes just as important as the text itself, or more so. Thus to radical skepticism and dogmatism is added what can only be called arrogance. We should therefore not be surprised when we are told that there are no longer privileged texts whose status rests in their power and capacity to satisfy enlightened aesthetic interest or to perform a distinctive humanistic function. Today privileged texts, classics, touchstones, and masterpieces are derogated in terms traditionally reserved for the condemnation of privileged classes.

To reiterate, behind much of the discrediting of the concepts of logic, rationality, objectivity, communication, meaning, authority, and reality is a Marxist revolutionary agenda that understands such notions as the means by which the elites of a capitalistic middle-class society maintain their power and control its members. According to this doctrine, whoever strikes a blow against logocentric concepts therefore strikes a blow for freedom and against bourgeois hegemony. Shaw does quote a Marxist writer who expresses concern over a "growing reactionary movement in the academy to recover the ideals of logic, reason, and determinate meaning and to repudiate the radicalism of the sixties and seventies,"[40] but he believes that the writer's fears are unfounded as no significant dent has been made in the doctrine's influence. Moreover, says Shaw, the charge of reactionaryism is typically brought against critics of deconstructionism. Indeed, he remarks the commonplace that in many academic departments today nothing less than an avowal of radical political beliefs is tolerated. Indeed.

Deconstructionism and liberal education

I remarked in discussing Wilsmore that deconstructionism poses a major challenge to the tradition of culture and liberal learning inherited from the nineteenth century. That ideal, true to its classical and neoclassical inspiration, rested on the belief that human selfhood is best shaped and realized when it tests itself against the best that has been thought and created. In trying to master the difficult materials that are the great touchstones of culture, individuals discipline their powers of intellect and refine their sensibilities. In the period following the death of Matthew Arnold, this tradition of culture and learning became known as the Arnoldian ideal; its most vigorous exponent in the twentieth century was F. R. Leavis. A few of the better universities, colleges, and schools still honor this tradition, and in such places it continues to be memorable for all who have had the opportunity to experience it. That the Arnoldian ideal is compatible with the democratic ethos is evident from Arnold's imperative that technical and professional knowledge must be translated into terms understandable by the nonspecialist and brought to bear on those matters that most concern us. Those who do this effectively are among the great men and women of culture, the true apostles of equality.[41] This theme was echoed by Dewey in his call for socially responsible artists of mass media communications who could interpret for nonspecialists the meanings of ideas and events.[42]

As Arnold's own career testifies, apostles of culture can take up residence in different places, although today we take it for granted that it is in higher education that the great project of humanizing knowledge should be carried forward. Yet we find that English departments, and increasingly departments of art history, communications, and education, are populated not with Arnold's apostles of culture but with exponents of the new nihilism. When deconstructionists dethrone privileged texts they strike at the heart of liberal education. In "de-meaning" texts (if I may be permitted a typically deconstructionist play on words), deconstructionists assume that texts have no relevance and perform no distinctively human function.

According to its critics, many of whom have impressive credentials, much of deconstructionism consists of sheer dogmatism, pretentious exaggeration, and questionable hypothesis. It is dogmatic, says Tzvetan Todorov,[43] to assume that all readings to date have been misreadings, hyperbolic to claim that texts bear no significant relation to reality, and questionable to lump imaginative literature, theoretical discourse of all kinds, and the empirical reports of the sciences together into one category. The indiscriminate use of buzzwords such as "power" is particularly inexcusable as it leads to failure to distinguish between brutal police-state repression and constraints inherent in the use of reason.

Deconstructionism and aesthetic experience

Literary works are, of course, works of art which on one view of their function can arouse variable degrees of aesthetic interest. What does deconstructionism do to the idea that a work of art is a humanly designed object that demands to be experienced aesthetically? The question is crucial since it implies that a work of art is something that makes demands on respondents and is rendered intelligible not through deconstruction by a critic, but through the avid participation and experience of respondents.

Three features of aesthetic experience are particularly important in this context. The first two are complementary: there is the unquestioned authority of the work of art (*it* makes demands) and the respondent's ready submission to the work's powers. This implies a percipient's willingness temporarily to suspend and suppress ancillary interests and inclinations. "Submission to the work" suggests a careful, disciplined exploration of a work's constellation of elements, or, as Goodman might say, of its functioning as a certain kind of symbol. This kind of interaction with a work amounts to an appreciation of the way writers, artists, and composers transfigure artistic materials into an aesthetic object distinguishable by its peculiar interanimation of elements, in short, an appreciation of artistic process and product. The compellingness of such interanimation is what constitutes the aesthetic demands of the work. In this respect, it is closer to the truth to say that the function of criticism is not to deconstruct texts but to point out how works of art, resplendent in their intense unified complexity, have the capacity to make qualified readers and percipients themselves feel more coherent, complete, and fulfilled. In contrast, deconstructionists systematically invert values and method, a tactic, Jacques Barzun has observed, endemic in much modern and contemporary art but now grown stale.

This leads to the values we have said aesthetic experience bestows: a peculiar gratification, unusual mental stimulation, and a special way of understanding. Such benefits must figure importantly in any justification of aesthetic education. But the realization of these values and the state of personal well-being they ensure are not possible under the deconstructionist prescription; it accepts neither the authority (or again, in Marxist terminology, the hegemony) of the art object nor the respondent's suppliant attitude toward it. It is the critic, newly empowered, who reigns supreme.

The actual and potential losses wrought by deconstructionism are, I think, enormous and constitute far too high a price to pay. Deconstructionism deprives us of all the wisdom and meaning embedded in the great works of the cultural tradition that humans have resorted to time and time again both for a sense of connectedness with the past and for charting new directions for the future. It is also inhibitive of those felt qualities of aesthetic experience which enrich response to art. Wilsmore goes so far as to say that "deconstructionist scepticism, taken to its logical conclusion, would deny the existence of art altogether. It ceases to express itself within the artistic forms of humanism, and ends in nihilism."[44] Given all of the above, we are in a better position to appreciate Allan Bloom's assessment of deconstruction; he says that in its

essentials it appeals to our worst instincts by flattering popular democratic sentiments and preferring mystifying philosophical doctrine to
really serious things.[45]

Back to culture

Although they are still outside today's intellectual mainstream, refuta-
tions of deconstructionist premises are becoming more common. Some
are arguing that works of art are not necessarily incoherent and meaningless, that reading and communication are possible, and that truth, knowledge, and reality, though problematic, are not simply will-o'-the-wisps.

Consider, for example, the reaction of George Steiner, who has also
seriously pondered the uses of language. Forcefully, almost combat-
ively, Steiner reminds us that "the process of textual interpretation [and
by "texts" Steiner means pictures, poems, and musical compositions] is
cumulative. Our readings become better informed, evidence progresses,
substantiation grows. . . . [T]here *is* a best reading, there is a meaning
or constellation of meanings to be perceived, analyzed, and chosen over
others."[46] Further, "across the millenia, a decisive majority of informed
receivers has not only arrived at a manifold but broadly coherent view
of what the *Iliad*, or *King Lear* or *The Marriage of Figaro*, is about (the
meanings of their meaning), but have concurred in judging Homer,
Shakespeare and Mozart [and I would add the giants of the visual arts,
Raphael, Titian, and Michelangelo] to be supreme artists in a hierarchy
of recognition which extends from the classical summits to the trivial
and mendacious."[47] There is then, to recall Brinton's terminology that
was featured in the two cultures debate, an important cumulative aspect
to art criticism. Moreover, Steiner emphasizes, as did Beardsley, that
we must be suppliant before the work; it is primary, the critique that
addresses it is secondary. To believe anything else constitutes a perver-
sion of commonsense and the calling of teaching. (This realization was
doubtless what John Fisher had in mind when he commented on the
implications of deconstructionist and reader-response theory by first
printing and then erasing an editorial, leaving only the blurred lines of
the text and a number of legible references to the pertinent literature.
Librarians requested the replacement of what they thought were defective
copies, but readers got the point: if a text has so little status, substance,
or coherence, then why not print mere traces of it?)[48]

And Steiner goes on. Even though it may require an act of faith, we
must read and perceive *as if* a text or a work has meaning, *as if* its
content matters, *as if* "the text (the piece of music, the work of art)
incarnates . . . a real presence of significant being"[49] that cannot be
dissolved by deconstructive maneuvers. Or, as Barzun has put it: even
though the last word about art must be mystery, this does not entail that
we cannot act as if we know more than we do.[50]

But even if we could nullify the deconstructionist thesis and were successful in recovering the ideals of logic, reason, and meaning, it might be said that all we have done is to have restored the empirical ethos and reconquered the ground for empirical knowledge and the sense of a shared reality that underlies day-to-day transactions. We would not have established a special territory for the arts that distinguishes them from the sciences. Roger Scruton is concerned to mark this distinction, and this is how he goes about it.

In an inaugural lecture at Birbeck College of the University of London, Scruton[51] recalls the two cultures debate and its chief protagonists, C. P. Snow and F. R. Leavis. He mentions Leavis's devastating rebuttal of Snow's principal thesis but observes that the question Leavis raised—whether science can be the locus of culture—was largely ignored by philosophers.

Putting the discussion of Leavis's idea of culture in his own terms, Scruton states that science cannot induct persons into culture because "to possess a culture is not only to possess a body of knowledge or expertise; it is not simply to have accumulated facts, references and theories. It is to possess a sensibility, a response, a way of seeing things, which is in some special way redemptive." He goes on to say that "culture is not a matter of academic knowledge but of participation. And participation changes not merely your thoughts and beliefs but your perceptions and emotions."[52] Can science, Scruton asks, induce this sense of response and participation in persons or does it lead in the opposite direction? Scientists and others will reply, rightly I think, that scientific inquiry also has a participatory subjective dimension and is not impersonal or cold.[53] But Scruton is correct in pointing out, as Scheffler also has done, that the insights of pure science are framed in highly abstract terms and refer less and less to the world of immediacy, appearance, and personal concern that we inhabit every day. Rather, science explains a world of which only a small part can be rendered visible and which only a tiny elite can understand. To be relevant to human concerns, says Scruton, philosophy must recover the world we all live in.

Assuming, controversially I think, that culture now has the redemptive power that religion once possessed, Scruton suggests that it is to culture's sacred book and its great touchstones that we must turn to justify our participation in the world. Since touchstones give meaning and significance to human existence and liberate our moral sense, Scruton assigns a major role to aesthetic education, and it would seem to be precisely the role Schiller described in his *Letters on the Aesthetic Education of Man*.[54] Scruton concludes that what great works of art give us is aesthetic understanding, or what John Ciardi[55] once called aesthetic wisdom: that body of knowledge and experience that enabled Aeschylus, Shakespeare, and other great writers to fashion their unique sense of the world. For

Scruton, then, aesthetic understanding is tied to a justification of human experience and has an important moral aspect.

Scruton believes that great works of art convey what he calls intentional understanding that aims to describe, criticize, and justify the world as it *appears*, not as science often reports it to be. Unlike scientific understanding that distances us from the realities of everyday life, intentional understanding attempts to reconcile us to them. It is through the concepts of intentional understanding that we experience the world as meaningful. Scruton thus presents yet another justification of the humanities, of the humanistic complex described by Levi in Chapter 6 and its distinctive purposes and concepts that stand in contrast to the scientific chain of meaning.

Scruton seems to be saying that the humanities—that is, literary and aesthetic education—must be emphasized not only to counteract modern philosophy's relative indifference to aesthetics and philosophy of art and the low ranking it accords them, but also to combat the new nihilism. The defection of literary critics and theorists, their decision to follow, say, Derrida and deconstructionism rather than Matthew Arnold and the great tradition of culture, constitutes a devastating development in contemporary intellectual life. I take Scruton to be calling for a return to the Arnoldian ideal of culture and offering himself as guide and philosophical successor to Leavis. Like Leavis, Scruton considers response and participation central to the idea of culture. Since both response and participation are distinctive of aesthetic experience and are explained and discussed in aesthetic theory, it is easy to see why Scruton turned to aesthetics as a remedy for the current situation in philosophy and to aesthetic education as a corrective for the condition of culture.

Levi has suggested that during periods of radical devaluation and cultural decline the task of criticism is to restore order in intellectual, moral, and aesthetic realms. This, he thinks, is the true meaning of humanism—humanism as criticism in the service of remoralization. Justifiable pessimism notwithstanding, it may still be possible for higher education to muster the wherewithal to remoralize itself. The failure of certain vanguard artists to proclaim the death of art suggests that what was sundered can be restored. Doubtlessly, postmodernism and its aberrant progeny will also pass from the scene and normalcy will once more prevail in cultural and educational realms. Until then we shall need reminding of what art can be and the important role it can play in the human career. So far as art criticism and the teaching of aesthetic skills are concerned, we do well to assume, as the writers discussed in this volume do, that rationality and objectivity in the aesthetic domain are both possible and desirable. That is, we may believe with Barnes that "texts have meanings which are privileged by the culture or tradition, and thus that a certain kind of communication is possible . . . among those who share the same form of life. To assume, that is, that customs and habits embedded in forms of life are enough to justify particular interpretations."[56] All of which is to say that it is possible "to assume that we have better or worse understandings of texts—correct and incorrect understandings, not merely more or less ingenious or creative or workable ones—including texts of authors, critics, and metacritics"[57] and, we will add, those other "texts" of artists and composers, works of visual and performing art and the critical literature devoted to them. In other words, we have sound reasons for doing what we've always done and what we must do.

Aesthetic experience

> . . . pretty well everyone would accept that mapping the anatomy of aesthetic experience is of central importance as groundwork for the exploration of aesthetic problems.   *Harold Osborne*[1]

> The time is . . . ripe to direct our attention to another important, yet neglected concept—viz., "aesthetic experience"—which occupies a prominent place in the philosophy of art.
> *Michael H. Mitias*[2]

> . . . the idea of aesthetic experience deserves systematic clarification at the hands of philosophy and not rejection as something empty or nonsensical.
> *T. J. Diffey*[3]

These observations, all from Mitias's anthology titled *Possibility of Aesthetic Experience* (1986), reveal that the concept of aesthetic experience is still on the agenda of contemporary philosophical aesthetics. Osborne misrepresents matters when he says "pretty well everyone" will agree that the concept is of central importance, and Mitias misleads when he says the concept has been neglected, for it has in truth been a preoccupation of a number of twentieth-century theorists. It is still customary, for example, for books and anthologies on aesthetics to contain discussions of aesthetic experience. To be sure, vanguard aesthetics, if we may call it that (for example, varieties of postmodernism that go by the names of poststructuralism, deconstruction, Marxism, etc.), sets less store by aesthetic considerations, but Diffey's remarks may, I think, be taken as an indirect comment on such trends. And when we consider the history of interest in what the concept of aesthetic experience implies, it seems unlikely that such a basic concern of the human mind will soon fade away. Before providing some examples of aesthetic response, it will be helpful to recall some of the highlights of the history of such interest, for which I turn to Władysław Tatarkiewicz's brief history of the idea of aesthetic experience.

In his *History of Six Ideas*,[4] Tatarkiewicz locates the roots of the concept of aesthetic experience in the writings of classical antiquity and traces thinking about the concept through later antiquity, the Middle Ages, the Enlightenment, and the last hundred years, culminating in Roman Ingarden's and Tatarkiewicz's own version of the concept. True, says Tatarkiewicz, the term "aesthetics" was not coined until the eighteenth century by Alexander Baumgarten and "beauty" and "taste" were often used to discuss the type of interest implied by the contemporary term aesthetic experience. But a concept, he says, is not equivalent to

a term, and well before the eighteenth and nineteenth centuries there
was interest in understanding the nature of human response to beauty
and art. Tatarkiewicz thinks that the concept of aesthetic experience is
at least as old as Pythagoras, who wrote that "life is like an athletic
contest; some turn up as wrestlers, others as vendors, but the best appear
as spectators."[5] And by "spectators" Tatarkiewicz assumes Pythagoras
meant those and only those who assume an aesthetic attitude. At least
the image of a spectator taking an aesthetic attitude toward something
is the one he holds in view as he reviews the literature on aesthetic
experience.

Central to Tatarkiewicz's account is a recurring dualism distinguished
in Latin by *sensitivus* and *intellectus*, or sensory and intellectual cognition. The former was sometimes called *aestheticus*, though only in
theoretical philosophy and not in discourses on beauty and art and the
experiences associated with these. In the eighteenth century Baumgarten
brought the two terms together in the notion of sensitive cognition
(*cognitio sensitiva*), which he identified with the cognition of beauty
(*cognitio aesthetica*, or *aesthetica* for short). The continuing interest in
aesthetic experience, by whatever term that designated it, ultimately led,
in the work Kant, Herbart, and Hegel, to the acceptance of aesthetics as
one of the principal divisions of philosophy, along with logic and ethics.
The terms "aesthetic" and "aesthetics," then, though they originated in
Latin, are relatively late additions to philosophical terminology. What
is more, it is only in modern aesthetic theory that two of the major
concepts of aesthetics, the aesthetic and the artistic (the other being
beauty) become closely associated. As we have seen, in the thinking of
some theorists the belief that works of art are preeminently suited to
induce aesthetic experience was sufficient to constitute such capacity as
the defining feature of art.

The classical concept of aesthetic experience implied interest in both
the features of what is seen and heard and in the special mental faculty
responsible for perceiving beauty. Descriptions of the former are found
in Aristotle's writings and of the latter in Plato's. Plotinus in late antiquity
followed Plato and contributed the idea that only a sense of beauty
enables one to perceive beauty, along with certain moral and spiritual
qualities of mind, while in an Aristotelian vein Aquinas in the Middle
Ages believed that aesthetic pleasure was distinct from the instinct for
human survival, or what we now call the aesthetic in contrast to the
practical attitude. The few statements on aesthetic experience by Plato,
Aristotle, and Plotinus, says Tatarkiewicz, are of extreme historical
importance. "They contain the earliest description (in its relevance perhaps unsurpassed) of the aesthetic experience and the earliest reflections
on the mental capacities which render this experience possible."[6]

The Platonic tradition in the Middle Ages was perpetuated by Boethius
who also presupposed a special faculty of the mind without which we

could not account for the fact that people enjoy listening to the same sounds. The name for this special faculty varied from "inner sense of the soul" (Erigena) to "spiritual vision" (St. Bonaventure). In time this inner sense came to be known as the sense of beauty. Like Aquinas, Erigena also anticipated modern ideas in his distinguishing of the contemplative from the practical point of view. The former does not covet a beautiful object but is attracted by its beauty, the perception of which is akin to perceiving the glory of God and his works.

In the Renaissance, theorists adopted both the idea of beautiful objects and a special mental faculty appropriate to beauty's perception and described this attitude as either active (Ficino) or passive (Alberti). That is, aesthetic experience implied either an active sense of beauty or mere passive acquiescence in it, and both conceptions of aesthetic experience found acceptance within the circles of the Florentine Quattrocentro. Once the possession of special mental powers to perceive beauty was accepted, however, it became natural to inquire whether such powers were rational or irrational. As evidenced by the vogue of Aristotle's *Poetics* and Vitruvius's theory of the visual arts, the former view held sway. Later, however, in the Baroque period, Gian Vincenzo Gravina expressed a contrary view; he said that the perception of beauty was a function of a mind possessed by irrational emotions that resulted in dreaming with one's eyes open, a state, that is, of delirium (*delerio*), a view that seemed to recall Plato's theory of the divine madness of the artist except that Gravina extended it to the aesthetic experience of the spectator as well.

The questions about aesthetic experience asked by writers in antiquity, the Middle Ages, and the Renaissance then turned mainly on the nature of the requisite faculties and attitudes responsible for the perception of beauty. Yet in reviewing the history of the concept, Tatarkiewicz discerned an additional question: Did aesthetic experience fulfill any kind of need? Plato's response was that aesthetic experience both made sense of and was the end of human existence, whereas much later, in the eighteenth century, J. B. Dubos said that aesthetic experience satisfied a fundamental need to occupy the mind in order to avoid boredom. Boredom could be overcome either through difficult or dangerous activities or through art and aesthetic experience. Dubos's view, however, had few adherents in his day.

As we move into the Age of the Enlightenment, aesthetic questions were less about the nature of beauty and the beautiful than about taste (*goût, gusto*), which implied an interest in why people think certain things are beautiful and worth enjoying. This type of psychological interest was expressed first in England and then in Germany. The major eighteenth-century figures in England were Locke and Shaftesbury whose analysis of mind on the one hand and the nature of emotions and values on the other produced a sober intellectualism and a poetic anti-intellectualism, respectively, with Locke's intellectualism tending to prevail.

Interest in the concept of taste arose over continuing curiosity about the faculty responsible for aesthetic experience, and theories of taste began to complement doctrines emphasizing either perception, reasoning, or intuition. Taste, it was believed, was exercised less for the intense perception of beauty than for the discrimination of beauty from ugliness. Kant termed the faculty of taste *sensus communis aestheticus* and believed its purpose was to determine what everybody likes. In France, Diderot stressed the varieties of taste and its unequal distribution, while in England, Shaftesbury was positing a sense of beauty given to everyone, which he coupled with a sense for recognizing goodness that resulted in a moral sense. Francis Hutcheson then distinguished the two faculties and in so doing described beauty as a passive faculty that was not the object of rational knowledge. As Tatarkiewicz puts it, "knowledge of beauty is not attained by means of comparison, reasoning, application of principles; beauty is immediately perceptible through the specific sense."[7] Though there were efforts to identify a number of senses of beauty, the concept of one sense of beauty remained dominant and is typical of the writings of Hutcheson, Burke, and Hume, and later, Santayana. Hume, however, along with Hartley, no longer assumed a specific sense of beauty and held instead that things are capable of evoking a sensation of aesthetic satisfaction by virtue of association, a belief also held by Hartley and Burke (in a modified version). For example, on the question of the subjectivity or objectivity of aesthetic experience Shaftesbury believed that beauty was an objective quality of objects whereas Hutcheson regarded beauty as a sensible quality of subjective responses. Tatarkiewicz points out that while Hume was extreme in his belief that beauty exists only in the mind of the beholder, he often expressed ideas that were far from being subjective. He also wrote, for example, that it was the order and structure of beauty which were responsible for occasioning the delight and satisfaction gained from it. We also recall in this respect Hume's remarks about the role of argument in realizing the proper relish of a work of art (quoted at the opening of Chapter 3). Beardsley also selected remarks by Hume for the opening of his *Aesthetics*, a work that strives for an objective understanding of how we think about art.

Enlightenment thinking in Germany also expressed an interest in aesthetic experience but used methods that yielded different results. Alexander Baumgarten, once again the originator of the term aesthetics, believed aesthetic experience was cognitive, albeit sensual, and hence an inferior kind of cognition, in large because aesthetic experience itself was so obscure. Baumgarten both followed and rejected tradition in admitting the cognitive status of aesthetic experience and its irrational character. The state of affairs soon became such that it demanded a significant synthesis of diverse views, and it was Kant's special accomplishment to integrate English and German thought on the subject.

Following English thinking, Kant believed that the basis of aesthetic experience is noncognitive and subjective. Yet the claims of aesthetic experience consist in more than the pleasure it affords; aesthetic judgments also make claim to universality. The peculiar character of aesthetic experience lies precisely in the fact that its judgment does not have sufficient justification but is nonetheless irrefutable. Aesthetic experience, however, is not only noncognitive, nonconceptual, and subjective, and its judgments universal, it is also disinterested in that the image, or form, of an object is more important than its material existence. And yet for all its subjectiveness and noncognitiveness the pleasure afforded by aesthetic experience is of the whole mind and not restricted to sensuous pleasure. What is more, though aesthetic experience is subjective, it does contain an imperative, but an imperative for which there is no rule that can determine those things which will please. From this it would seem to follow that each object must be judged separately and that aesthetic experience is individual and subjective. Yet, writes Tatarkiewicz, "as human minds are built similarly, there are grounds for expecting that an object which pleases one man will please others as well; therefore aesthetic judgments are characterized by universality, although it is a very special *universality* since it resists definition by any rules."[8] Special indeed!

And, in truth, although Kant's ideas about aesthetic experience followed logically from his speculation about aesthetic judgment and were acknowledged to be a brilliant attempt at synthesis, they proved, says Tatarkiewicz, to be too complex, and simpler explanations were soon sought. An experience the features of which are disinterestedness, nonconceptuality, formality, fullmindedness, subjective necessity, and ruleless universality was literally too much for many writers to accept.

A simpler conception of aesthetic experience was provided by Schopenhauer who, going beyond Enlightenment thinking, stated that aesthetic experience is essentially contemplation, or the sensation realized when practical attitudes are forsaken and attention is directed solely at a thing beheld. Describing this stance, Tatarkiewicz writes:

A man experiences this sensation when he assumes the beholder's attitude, when—as Schopenhauer wrote—he forsakes the usual, practical attitude toward things, when he ceases thinking of their origin and purpose and concentrates solely on what he has before him. He ceases to think abstractly and bends his powers of mind to the beholding of objects, submerges himself in them, fills his consciousness with what he beholds—with what he has before him. He becomes oblivious of his own personality, curbs his will; the subject becomes a reflection of the object, there is no longer in his consciousness a division into onlooker and what is looked upon; his entire consciousness is filled with a pictorial representation of the world. This state of mind, this passive submission to objects, Schopenhauer termed beholding, *contemplation, aesthetic pleasure* (*aesthetisches Wohlgefallen*) and the "aesthetic attitude" (*aesthetische Betrachtungsweise*).[9]

Typically, Tatarkiewicz mentions numerous antecedents of such notions; they recall, for example, not only Kant but also Pythagoras, Aristotle, and Aquinas. But Tatarkiewicz credits Schopenhauer with in effect formulating a new concept; all the more pity then, he also says, that Schopenhauer then drowned it in an intolerable metaphysics that took contemplation to be the solace of an ever-restless will. Still, this has not prevented theorists from taking what is useful in Schopenhauer's description.

In the last hundred years the attention of theorists has shifted more explicitly from the concept of beauty to that of aesthetic experience, the psychological interest in which after 1860 led to the formulation of aesthetics as an experimental science. Such interest continues today even though aesthetics is now largely regarded as a branch of philosophy. The shift away from the concept of beauty was due to the belief that while it was impossible to discover the common features of beautiful things, it was conceivable that the common features of aesthetic experience could be identified. Yet this belief too proved overly optimistic, and it spawned numerous theories that emphasized different features, chief among which were what Tatarkiewicz calls simple hedonistic and cognitive theories; others stressed illusion and isolation, and still others disinterestedness and euphoria. He also discusses some corollaries of active and passive conceptions of contemplation. Summarizing them rather sweepingly, Tatarkiewicz states that these theories ranged from the belief that aesthetic experience was an irreducible experience incapable of being analyzed (Wundt and Fechner) to rejections of such a view in favor of those stressing either the pleasure of aesthetic experience (Santayana), the enlightenment it provided (Croce and Fiedler), its fictitiousness and disengagement from reality (Lange), the spuriousness of its feelings and judgments (Hartmann and Meinong), and its exemplifications of play, or a gamelike quality (Schiller). Active theories of aesthetic experience tended to feature such notions as empathy (Lipps) while others stressed their converse, passive submission (Bergson and Ducasse).

Corollaries of cognitive theories attempt to clarify the conditions of aesthetic experience, especially in regard to the ways the aesthetic attitude isolates objects through bracketing (Hamann), psychical distancing (Bullough), disinterested attention (Kant), and holistic perception (Arnheim). In reaction to cognitive accounts of aesthetic experience, theories of euphoria (Valéry and Brémond) denied any cognitive description of aesthetic experience, preferring instead to stress their thrilling, enchant-

ing, or mystical qualities; the assumption was that this effected communion with a mysterious sense of reality and induced a repose resembling
prayer. But such an account, Tatarkiewicz points out, fails to account
for the compound character of aesthetic experience, for example, Nietzsche's notions of the Dionysian and Apollonian modes of experience,
or for the fact that in Tatarkiewicz's own view there are different kinds
of aesthetic experience.

Regarding the legacy of efforts to analyze the nature of aesthetic
experience, under whatever term writers used to describe it, Tatarkiewicz
remarks that if accounts differ so widely, it is because different thinkers
had different interests. Some sought to define aesthetic experience while
others attempted to provide a theory of it. Still others looked either to
its conditions, the mental faculties presupposed by it, the features of
objects that induced it, or the feature of the experience itself. The
difficulty facing all these attempts at definition and theorizing is, of
course, the diversity of our experience of things, an awareness that
prompted me to provide at least four accounts of aesthetic experience in
Chapter 2. In brief, concludes Tatarkiewicz, and I agree, the concept of
aesthetic experience is a complex one.

Tatarkiewicz concludes his brief survey with a reference to Roman
Ingarden's account of aesthetic experience. The compound character of
aesthetic experience, Ingarden thinks, is due to its passing through a
series of stages of different character during which it exemplifies both
intellectual and emotional components and active and passive stances.
According to Tatarkiewicz, Ingarden believed that

> the beginning of an aesthetic experience is marked by what he calls an "initial
> emotion" having the character of an excitement. The second stage of the
> experience occurs when, under the influence of that excitement, we turn our
> entire consciousness toward the object that aroused it; the normal course of
> consciousness is arrested, its field is narrowed, interest centres on the per-
> ceived quality. Then the third stage begins a "concentrated beholding" of that
> quality. At this third stage the aesthetic experience may cease, but it may also
> continue. If it does continue, the subject faces the object that he has now
> formed and communes with it, responding emotionally to what he has himself
> produced. Thus in aesthetic experience there occur successively: pure excite-
> ment on the part of the subject, the forming of the object by the subject, and
> the perceptive experiencing of the object. The earlier stages have an emotional
> and dynamic character which in the final stage recedes before contemplation.[10]

This account of the stages of aesthetic experience resembles Clark's
description of his mode of response to works of art—impact, scrutiny,
recollection, and renewal—and Parsons's account of the stages of aesthetic development, especially the fifth stage that accents reflection and
self-questioning. Indeed, Ingarden's account supports Parsons's belief
that stage five aesthetic experiencing is superior to that of previous

stages. Tatarkiewicz's own account of aesthetic experience is likewise a pluralistic or compound one and is consistent with his belief that the concept of aesthetic experience can only be rendered by giving alternative conceptions of it. Whether the concept of aesthetic experience is vitiated when characterized this way is a relevant question, but, once again, it is difficult not to believe that a concept that has interested so many writers from antiquity to the present, including some of our best philosophers, is one that refers to a significant human instinct and is thus of perennial importance.

These scant references to the history of the concept of aesthetic experience permit a few observations about my discussion of aesthetic experience in Chapter 2 and elsewhere. Like their predecessors, Beardsley, Osborne, Goodman, and Kaelin have special interests and ask different questions, and thus their theories and conclusions vary. Beardsley, for example, wanted to ground a theory of aesthetic value in aesthetic experience. This led him to deemphasize the relevance of the cognitive and moral dimensions of works of art in estimating their artistic goodness. In one of his last essays on the topic, however, he admitted to having had only qualified success in doing this.[11] And though Beardsley's concept of aesthetic experience is a complex and compound one, he tended to believe it had a preeminent or characteristic function; aesthetic experience was noteworthy mainly for its peculiar feeling of gratification. In its complexity, we may say, Beardsley's recalls Kant's account of aesthetic judgment, and in its featuring of gratification Schopenhauer's aesthetics which stressed the pleasurable sensation of concentration.

Consisting of approximately seven features, Osborne's theory of aesthetic experience is likewise complex yet singular in its effect; it holds that aesthetic experience is valuable above all for its strengthening of the powers of percipience. Osborne's account draws inspiration from both Kant and eighteenth-century British thinkers, but he corrects Kant who believed that aesthetic judgment is largely of form alone. Goodman, on the other hand, concentrates not on the qualities of the felt experience of art but on the features of artworks which he understands as characters in a symbol system. About all Goodman says about aesthetic experience is that mind in responding to art is active not passive (recall the different opinions about this in historical accounts of aesthetic experience) and that feelings and the emotions are part and parcel of aesthetic knowing. Goodman, then, discusses aesthetic experience in connection with the understanding of aesthetic symbol systems. In respect of his claims for the capacity of works of art to provide enlightenment, Goodman too has many predecessors, but perhaps just as, according to Tatarkiewicz, Schopenhauer's predecessors did not keep him from articulating a new concept, so perhaps Goodman may also be said to have done likewise. It perhaps goes without saying that Kaelin's account of aesthetic experience also has antecedents as well as accents that are his own, for example, his emphasis on the ways in which aesthetic experience exemplifies human freedom and contributes to the efficacious functioning of cultural institutions by helping them to realize their primary function of creating and preserving aesthetic value.

The varieties of aesthetic experience that theorists have articulated as well as a brief account of their antecedent ideas recall the theme of this essay, that is, that a proper understanding of art forces upon us the conclusion that art variously has the capacity to gratify, stimulate mind, and enlighten. And such an idea, Harry S. Broudy points out, goes back at least to Cicero who attributed to rhetoric, and presumably to art, the ability to move, delight, and inform. With Cicero, says Broudy, we continue to believe that works of art "do say something, are expressive, and in some sense communicate even as they please and move."[12]

I now provide some examples of recorded responses to scenes of nature, ordinary objects, and works of art from which I think we may infer the presence of many of the features, values, and consequences of aesthetic experience discussed in the theoretical literature.

Let us begin with Osborne who in his *The Art of Appreciation* begins an account of aesthetic experience by drawing attention to some simple moments of daily awareness.

> We pass our lives, strenuously or languorously, in a never-ending give and take with a partly malleable, partly resistant environment, material and human, adapting it to our ends when we can and accommodating ourselves to it when we must. Occasionally the busy flow of life's intricate involvements is interrupted as there occur sudden pauses in our practical and theoretical preoccupations, moments of calm amidst the turmoil . . . as our attention is caught by . . . the rhythmic rise and fall of susurration on a summer's day, the smoky calligraphies of wheeling birds painted on a transparent grey sky in winter, the grotesque contorted menace of an olive tree's branches, the lissom slenderness of a birch, or the sad sloppiness of a rain-crushed dandelion. Sometimes, if more rarely, we catch a glimpse of familiar things in an unfamiliar light. Commonplace objects suddenly shed their murk and enter the focus of attention. Perhaps for the first time in our memory we *see* a familiar sight.[13]

In other words, the qualitative immediacy of life itself is the primary material of aesthetic experience. Some people, however, find it difficult to respond to even the simple qualities of things. At least this seems to have been the case with a rather well-known fictional character. For example, in "The Adventure of the Copper Beeches," we come across Sherlock Holmes and Dr. Watson traveling by train through the English countryside:

> By eleven o'clock the next day we were well upon our way to the old English capital. Holmes had been buried in the morning papers all the way down, but

after we had passed the Hampshire border he threw them down and began to admire the scenery. [Or so Watson thought.] It was an ideal spring day, a light blue sky, flecked with little fleecy white clouds drifting across from west to east. The sun was shining very brightly, and yet there was an exhilarating nip in the air, which set an edge to a man's energy. All over the countryside, away to the rolling hills around Aldershot, the little red and gray roofs of the farm-steadings peeped out from amid the light green of the new foliage.

"Are they not fresh and beautiful?" [exclaimed Watson] . . . with all the enthusiasm of a man fresh from the fogs of Baker Street.

But Holmes shook his head gravely.

"Do you know Watson, . . . that it is one of the curses of a mind with a turn like mine that I must look at everything with a reference to my own special subject. You look at these scattered houses, and you are impressed by their beauty. I look at them, and the only thought which comes to me is a feeling of their isolation and of the impunity with which crime may be committed there."

"Good heavens!" [cried Watson] . . . "Who would associate crime with these dear old homesteads?"

[To which Holmes said] "They always fill me with a certain horror. It is my belief, Watson, founded upon my experience, that the lowest and vilest alleys in London do not present a more dreadful record of sin than does the smiling and beautiful countryside."

"You horrify me!" [said Watson].

"But the reason [replied Holmes] is very obvious."[14]

Holmes went on to explain why the beautiful and smiling countryside is so vile (a view, we may take it, not shared by many of his nonfictional countrymen). The point, of course, is not the beauty or vileness of the English countryside but the potentially inhibiting nature of professional preoccupation. Thoughts about crime were too much with Holmes for the aesthetic instinct to surface and break through.

Indeed, the reactions of Holmes and Watson are reminiscent of another famous pair of companions who met and decided to take a walk outside the city walls of Athens. The meeting is described in Plato's dialogue *Phaedrus* and is recalled by Albert William Levi.

Socrates and Phaedrus meet by chance, and when Socrates asks: "Where do you come from, Phaedrus my friend, and where are you going?" Phaedrus replies: "I take my walks on the open roads for it is more invigorating than walking in the colonnades in the city." Socrates is at last persuaded to accompany Phaedrus for a walk outside the walls, and as they turn off the road to rest beside the Ilissus, a quiet country stream, Socrates in spite of himself exclaims over the beauty of the place. "Upon my word, a delightful resting place, with this tall, spreading tree, and a lovely shade from the high branches. Now that it's in full flower, it will make the place ever so fragrant. And what a lovely stream under the plane tree, and how cool to the feet! . . . And then too isn't the freshness of the air most welcome and pleasant, and the shrill summery music of the cicada choir! And as crowning delight the grass, thick enough on a gentle slope to rest your head on most comfortably. In fact, my dear Phaedrus, you have been the stranger's perfect guide." "You, my excellent friend," replies Phaedrus, "strike me as the oddest of men. Anyone would take you, as you say, for a stranger being shown the country by a guide instead of a native—never leaving town to cross the frontier, nor even, I believe, so much as setting foot outside the walls." And Socrates answers: "You must forgive me, dear friend, I'm a lover of learning, and trees and open country won't teach me anything, whereas men in the town do. . . ."[15]

Had not civic and moral concerns been so pressing, however, perhaps Socrates would have had a greater disposition to delight in the qualities of simple things, for example a falling leaf, which is Pepita Haezrahi's model for aesthetic experience. In her *The Contemplative Activity* she writes:

Our leaf falls. It detaches itself with a little plopping sound from its place high up in the tree. It is red and golden. It plunges straight down through the tree and then hesitates and hovers for a while just below the lowest branches. The sun catches it and it glitters with mist and dew. It now descends in a leisurely arc and lingers for another moment before it finally settles on the ground.

And she goes on:

You witness the whole occurrence. Something about it makes you catch your breath. The town, the village, the garden around you sink into oblivion. There is a pause in time. The chain of your thoughts is severed. The red and golden tints of the leaf, the graceful form of the arc described by its descent fill the whole of your consciousness, fill your soul to the brim. It is as though you existed in order to gaze at this leaf falling, and if you had other preoccupations and other purposes you have forgotten them. You do not know how long this lasts, it may be only an instant, but there is a quality of timelessness, a quality of eternity about it. You have had an aesthetic experience.[16]

Upon the need to rake up fallen leaves, we may assume that aesthetic interest quickly subsides, but the immediate impression of nature's beauties, which Socrates remarked and of which Haezrahi speaks, deserves some comment. In his *A New Theory of Beauty*, which represents something of a renewal of interest in the concept in contemporary aesthetics, Guy Sircello remarks the characteristically exclamatory character of our responses to beauty of different kinds.

We don't, generally speaking, simply see, hear, feel, taste, or otherwise apprehend beauty. Beauty is typically an attention-getter; we suddenly notice it; it breaks into our consciousness. Moreover, it does so gratuitously; it does so despite the fact that we may not have been looking for it, despite the fact that we had no inkling it was going to be there. The beauty of the freeway interchange that we have never seen before suddenly dawns on us as we drive through it. The exotic face of a stranger in the crowd "leaps out" at us as we push our way along in our usual everyday daze. But even beauties we have seen many times before can catch our notice. We anticipate the majestic view as we round the bend, and, as always, it grabs our attention as it comes in sight.

In these situations beauty always appears the "aggressor." The metaphors we use to describe the experiences all point to this fact. Beauty "catches" our attention; it "breaks on us"; it "leaps out" at us; it "strikes" us. We seem powerless before its pull. It seems as if it is not we who give our attention to beauty, but beauty that, as it were, forces our attention on it. Thus we often sensibly recoil when we notice beauty; our head draws back, or feels as if it does.

This "impact" that beauty has on us is not merely emotional. It may be true that "my heart leaps up when I behold the rainbow in the sky," but so do my eyes "light up." The element that I want particularly to stress in our reaction to beauty is its effect on our senses, our perceptual faculties, our minds. Specifically, this effect is one of "expansion." Our eyes are "filled" with the beauty of the landscape, our ears with the sweetness of the melody, our mind with the elegance of the argument. It is as though the receptive faculty were growing larger to take in the abundance offered it. Visual beauty, especially, is like a light dawning on us, flowing out from its source and filling the world and us with itself. Medieval philosophers were sufficiently impressed by this phenomenon to insist that beauty is, in part, *claritas*, which has been aptly translated as "radiance."

Finally, beauty has a tremendous holding power for us. When we perceive a beautiful thing, we don't want to let it go, we never want to stop perceiving it. It is as if our eyes wanted to drown in the sight, our ears in the sound. When the beautiful thing has disappeared, or we have gone our way, we sense a loss, we feel·let down.[17]

This sense of beauty is revealed in numerous passages from Darwin's journals. Darwin, who unlike Holmes did not let his professional interests inhibit his capacity for aesthetic experience, records the following response to a vista in the Andes Mountains:

When we reached the crest and looked backwards, a glorious view was presented. The atmosphere resplendently clear; the sky an intense blue; the profound valleys; the wild broken forms; the heaps of ruins, piled up during the lapse of ages; the bright-colored rocks, contrasted with the quiet mountains of snow; all these together produced a scene no one could have imagined. Neither plant nor bird, excepting a few condors wheeling around the higher pinnacles, distracted my attention from the inanimate mass. I felt glad that I was alone: it was like watching a thunderstorm, or hearing in full orchestra a chorus of the *Messiah*.[18]

Neither Sircello's remarks about our responses to beauty nor Darwin's reaction were exclusively to nature, and so we may consider examples of aesthetic response to humanly made artifacts as well, both large and small. Here is the Russian painter Wassily Kandinsky looking at Moscow an hour before sunset.

> Pink, lavender, yellow, white, blue, pistachio green, flame-red houses, churches—each an independent song—the raving green grass, the deep murmuring trees, or the snow, singing with a thousand voices, or the allegretto of the bare branches, the red, stiff, silent ring of the Kremlin walls and above, towering overall like a cry of triumph, like a Hallelujah forgetful of itself, the long, white, delicately earnest line of the Uvan Veliky Bell Tower. And upon its neck, stretched high and taut in eternal longing to the heavens, the golden head of the cupola, which is the Moscow sun amid the golden and coloured stars of the other cupolas.[19]

In contrast, Henry James, the novelist and inveterate traveler, provides, a more muted response to another great city. When he thought of Venice he said that it was not so much its grand vistas that came to mind as

> a narrow canal in the heart of the city—a patch of green water and a surface of pink wall. The gondola moves slowly; it gives a great smooth swerve, passes under a bridge, and the gondolier's cry, carried over the quiet water, makes a kind of splash in the stillness. A girl crosses the little bridge, which has an arch like a camel's back, with an old shawl on her head, which makes her characteristic and charming; you see her against the sky as you float beneath. The pink of the old wall seems to fill the whole place; it sinks even into the opaque water. Behind the wall is a garden, out of which the long arm of a white June rose—the roses of Venice are splendid—has flung itself by way of spontaneous ornament. [And for a dash of dramatic contrast.] On the other side of this small waterway is a great shabby façade of Gothic windows and balconies—balconies on which dirty clothes are hung and under which a cavernous-looking doorway opens from a low flight of slimy watersteps. It is very hot and still, the canal has a queer smell, and the whole place is enchanting.[20]

But artifacts come in all shapes, sizes, and qualities. Here, for example, is L. A. Reid on something as modest as a shallow-bowled spoon. He writes that

> the lines are smooth, easy, liquid, flowing; the handle is deliciously curved, like the tail of a leopard. And strangely, without contradiction, the leopard's tail is finished with little raised nodules like small grapes. It is a queer mixture of a leaf and a leopard. The texture is grey and dull like river mist, and it is lit with soft lights shining out of it like the moon out of a misty sky. The sheen is white-grey satin: the bowl is delicately shaped with overturning fastidiously pointed fronds; it is restrained and shallow, yet large enough to be generous. The lines are fine and sharp, with clear edges. Thus described, such a concatenation of qualities may sound absurd and incongruous. But if

you hold the spoon in your hand, you feel it as a kind of poem, which in a strange way unites all these, and many other, values into a single whole. You feel as you see it that you are living in a gracious world, full of loveliness and delight.[21]

"If you hold the spoon in your hand, you feel it as a kind of poem"— that is, when you use the spoon its different aspects are unified in the way that a poem is often said to harmonize disparate things. A spoon has probably never been so affectionately described, and Reid's description reminds us that appreciable visual value can be found in objects of ordinary use. Indeed, it was Reid's special sensitivity to visual values that prompted Lionel Trilling in his review of Reid's *A Study of Aesthetics* to quote Reid's description.

But just what, we may ask, actually happens when the mind shifts from one point of view to another—from a professional, practical, civic, or moral point of view to an aesthetic one? In an essay devoted to mapping the structure of knowledge in the arts, which includes an account of cognition in the aesthetic experience, Harry S. Broudy conjured up the following situation (which reminds one of numerous scenes from Hollywood musicals):

Suppose we observe our neighbor walking briskly down the street on a weekday morning. The walk has a certain rhythm and pace, but our perception of it is likely to be no more than a registration of clues for inferences about what our neighbor is up to. . . . Suppose now that our neighbor suddenly breaks into a little hop, skip and jump routine. Our interest perks up immediately, forcing strange hypotheses into our minds as to what might be the cause of this unusual behavior. The walking has become expressive of something; joy, excitement, or nervousness. In any event, we now watch the scene more intently. As we do, suppose our neighbor wheels about to face us and begins a fairly simple tap dance. At this juncture we either call the police, or we become absorbed in the dance itself. The practical and intellectual attitudes will then have begun to turn into the aesthetic attitude. Our interest is in perceiving the field and the motions within it.

If, however, the neighbor continues the tapping indefinitely our interest flags. The field has been explored; there is no further surprise to be anticipated, no further excitement. But suppose he varies the routine; suppose the rhythms become more complicated; suppose out of nowhere music sounds with a rhythm synchronized to the dancing; suppose a female dancer appears and joins our neighbor in his act. Suppose now instead of the drab ordinary street clothing, the dancers acquire brilliant costumes and that the simple music swells to a multi-instrumented orchestra. By this time our practical concerns with our neighbor will probably have been completely submerged in our aesthetic interest. Instead of one sense many of our senses are functioning at a high rate of intensity; instead of monotony there is variation of a pattern, there is contrast of pace, male and female, light and heavy, tension and release, a building up of climax and resolution. Before our eyes, so to speak, an ordinary piece of pedestrianism has been turned into a work of art, that is, into a field designed for perceiving and for not much of anything else.[22]

Broudy further remarks that the degree of interest occasioned by works of art will be a function not only of their formal complexity but also of the nerves of life they touch. The experience of blue skies, falling leaves, and tap dancing may be refreshing and moving, but not profoundly so. But if, says Broudy, "the dance is a caricature (a sketch) of war, of death, of love, of tragedy, of triumph, our perceiving becomes serious in the sense that we are beholding an expression that is also trying to be a statement about something so important, so close to the big issues in human life, perhaps so dangerous, so revolting that we have not yet formulated language to state it clearly."[23] Perhaps, says Broudy, such works "portray impulses and instincts that man would just as soon forget he had."[24] Such impulses, we may say, are expressed in Picasso's famous mural the *Guernica*, described by E. F. Kaelin:

> When we respond to a shape as a representation of a bull or horse, our experience deepens: more of the world is now includable within our brackets. If we look more closely, we can identify other objects: a broken warrior, frozen in rigor mortis, his severed arm still clutching a broken sword; a mother in agony over the death of her child; a woman falling through the shattered timbers of a burning building; a flickering light; a wounded dove, its peace gone astray. . . . Let the mind play over these images and an idea grips the understanding: the wages of war, as it is currently conducted, are death and destruction. . . . So interpreted, our experience of *Guernica* deepens and comes to closure in a single act of expressive response in which we perceive the fittingness of this surface—all broken planes and jagged edges in the stark contrast of black and white [that is, the way the picture looks]—to represent this depth [that is, the work's import], the equally stark contrast of the living and the dead.[25]

Broudy and Kaelin remind us of the human capacity to delight in artworks that express the darker side of human existence, a fact which deserves remarking. For example, when one speaks of delight as a characteristic or essential feature of our aesthetic experience of works of art, a quick rebuttal is that so many works of art are either horrifying, dreadful, or unsettling that it is nothing less than irresponsible to insist on the primacy of the hedonic aspect of our commerce with artworks. Yet this response is too quick and unreflective, and the reason is that what pleasure and delight mean in an aesthetic context is not properly understood. For example, in Beardsley's "Aesthetic Experience Regained," which John Fisher has called a model of philosophical analysis, Beardsley responds to criticisms that pleasure or satisfaction cannot be an essential feature of aesthetic experience. Commenting on Marshall Cohen's purported counterexample—that the muzzles of the guns

pointed at us in Eisenstein's film *Potemkin* "are positively menacing"—
Beardsley points out that "it is not the battleship *Potemkin* that confronts
us when we go to a motion picture theater to see the Eisenstein film, but
merely a picture of it. And this picture does not in any way menace us,
but instead offers us the *quality* of menace—a quality that we deeply
enjoy in its dramatic context."[26] Similarly, Diané Collinson, in a philosophical essay titled "Aesthetic Education," emphasizes that we must
understand how "aesthetic delight" is properly applied to our experiences
of artworks if it is to encompass, say, the fearfulness of a Francis Bacon
painting, the horrific tension of *Waiting for Godot*, or the anguish of
Marlowe's Faustus. "It is not," says Collinson, "that it describes the
character of every appropriate experience in the presence of works of
art, but that it is characteristic of ultimate aesthetic approval. It is a
delight that clarity has been achieved, that something matchless, intelligible and illuminating has been present to us."[27]

But to continue; in contrast to the landscape of destruction and suffering that Picasso presents in the *Guernica*, Cézanne features in his works
what Meyer Schapiro in Chapter 4 called the qualities of pure aesthetic
vision. I have already referred to Schapiro's characterization of Cézanne's *Card Players* and his *Quarry and Mont Saint-Victoire*; here is
Schapiro on yet another landscape containing the mountain in southern
France that Cézanne immortalized, his *Mont Sainte-Victoire* (1885–
1887, London, Courtauld Institute). It might be said that Schapiro finds
in Cézanne's landscape many of the same remarkable qualities, finesse,
and synthesizing of opposites that L. A. Reid found in his spoon,
though, of course, in a work of much greater magnitude, subtlety, and
significance. Schapiro writes:

> It is marvelous how all seems to flicker in changing colors from point to point,
> while out of this vast restless motion emerges a solid world of endless expanse,
> rising and settling. The great depth is built up in broad layers intricately fitted
> and interlocked, without an apparent constructive scheme. Towards us these
> layers become more and more diagonal; the diverging lines in the foreground
> seem a vague reflection of the mountain's form. These diagonals are not
> perspective lines leading to the peak . . . [rather they] conduct us far to the
> side where the mountain slope begins; they are prolonged in a limb hanging
> from the tree.
> It is this contrast of movements, of the marginal and centered, of symmetry
> and unbalance, that gives the immense aspect of drama to the scene. Yet the
> painting is a deep harmony, built with a wonderful finesse. It is astounding
> how far Cézanne has controlled this complex whole.[28]

Much of the writing that passes for art criticism today pays little attention
to the kinds of formal and aesthetic qualities favored by artists like
Cézanne and more to content that features social and political relevance.
Yet lovers of art will always delight in the kinds of qualities that Cé-

zanne's works feature, and one may conjecture that his aesthetic vision will ultimately have more staying power than works which strive to make explicit social judgments. Formal qualities are, after all, the redeeming values of works whose subjects have lost their interest for us. Again no lover of art has to be argued into appreciating formal and aesthetic qualities; it is only the current moment in criticism that seeks other values in art that makes it necessary to point out what otherwise should go without saying.

With descriptions of works by Picasso and Cézanne we return full circle to the discussions of aesthetic criticism in Chapter 4, where the emphasis was not on nature's beauties or more practical human artifacts but on works of fine art and, in the case of Steinberg on Johns, borderline cases of such. If the discussion of aesthetic experience and aesthetic criticism in Chapters 2 through 5 was tipped too heavily toward works of art, perhaps this appendix helps to balance accounts. Yet there should be little reason to doubt that works of fine arts created by mature and serious artists have by and large a far greater capacity to invite and sustain aesthetic experience than do most other things. We need not assume that aesthetic experience is the generic term for our experience of art, for we have seen that any number of things can be viewed aesthetically. Neither must the concept of aesthetic experience be sharp in order to be useful; and while theoretical analysis may cast doubt on the coherence of the concept and question whether anyone has really pinned it down sufficiently, I don't think that we can seriously doubt that what the writers I have quoted are reports of aesthetic experiences of nature, ordinary objects, and works of art. What is more, while John Hospers understands the problems involved in trying to isolate strands of human experience and giving them names, such as aesthetic experience, he also believes "that to throw out the term 'aesthetic' entirely because of difficulties in its application, at least in certain instances, is surely the counsel of despair. The term 'aesthetic' has arisen in our language for a reason, and . . . it seems to mark off . . . some territory occupied by nothing else—hence the need for the term."[29] We might say that the term "aesthetic education" has also come into the language for a reason. Given the political and ideological atmosphere in which so much educational theorizing takes place today, aesthetic education has an important new role to play.

In concluding, it will be helpful to recall some of the polarities and paradoxes of aesthetic experience. The first duality is that even though the mind is actively engaged in discovering new things during aesthetic experience, aesthetic experience also has moments of reverie. Aesthetic experience is both euphoric and exhilarating, serene and contemplative. There is the further apparent paradox that though in certain senses works of art are fictional and of the imagination, which is to say works of art are not actual slices of life, they also manage to convey an understanding of life. Aesthetic experience thus stimulates the senses and provides insight, which is to say that it is both affective and cognitive. It can further be a tonic for the human soul; we often stand taller and feel a sense of expansion after an intense aesthetic experience. This is what in Dewey's terms constitutes its consummatory value. But inherent in the aesthetic freshening of experience is what Sircello called the experience of melancholy that often follows, so that a work of art construed as an artifact that can induce a high level of aesthetic experience may result in psychological letdown as well.

But overall I think the examples I've recorded reinforce the values ascribed to aesthetic experience in Chapter 2: variously, depending on the work itself and a person's capacity for responding to it, the aesthetic experience of works of art tends to yield a high degree of gratification, stimulates the powers of the mind, produces understanding, and contributes to the efficacy of an important institutional practice. Perhaps so broad a conception of art's function in regard to aesthetic experience is not elegant enough for theorists for whom precision of analysis and the search for defeating counterexamples are ideals; but educational theory can tolerate a degree of inelegance so long as it recognizes that things are complex and does not unduly distort or misrepresent them. Whatever the difficulties with the concept of the aesthetic, those who have tried to understand the aesthetic strand of human experience have, I think, made important contributions to our understanding of the various habits of the human mind. In following analyses and arguments, pro and con, of aesthetic experience, much can be learned about the nature of human experience. In particular, writings about aesthetic experience have much to say about the ways we make sense of works of art. Accordingly, accounts of aesthetic experience contribute to a better understanding of what is involved in developing a sense of art in the young.

The art world and aesthetic skills: a context for research and development

> To analyze an aesthetic object is precisely to get acquainted with its finer details and subtler qualities, to discover, in short, what is there to *be* enjoyed— to be responded to emotionally. The alternative to analysis is a half-cocked, crude emotional reaction to the gross, obvious features of the object.
> *Monroe C. Beardsley*[1]

The purpose of this appendix is to recall some of the points made about cultural institutions, artistic merit, and the teaching of critical skills in the major body of the essay. The discussion telescopes some important considerations relevant to formulating a policy for aesthetic education and suggests an appropriate program of research. The initial occasion for the remarks was a conference the work of which consisted of setting an agenda of research for aesthetic education.[2]

Any effort to set an agenda for research in aesthetic education must, of course, rest on a conception of the enterprise in question. In this essay I have set out one such conception; I take the purpose of aesthetic education to be the development of the ability to appreciate excellence in art for the sake of the worthwhile experiences that art at its best is capable of providing. Appreciative ability, it has been argued, is best fostered through the acquisition of aesthetic critical skills. What I will do in this appendix is to recall once more the larger social and cultural context in which aesthetic education takes place and provide some direction for research in the teaching of aesthetic skills.

The art world and policy

As Kaelin implied in his remarks about the institutional significance of art and aesthetic education,[3] the art world may be considered under two aspects, one abstract and the other concrete. Abstractly, the art world is a domain of value, principally aesthetic value, and is significant for the quality of experience provided by its characteristic objects, namely works of art. But this is to say that the art world is not only a domain of value but also a concrete, distinguishable sector of society with a number of components. These constituent parts may be identified as artists, artworks, audiences, and auxiliaries, the latter consisting of all those who provide a range of services in a variety of cultural organizations, for example, museums, galleries, art councils, state and government agencies, foundations, etc. It is clear that such a congeries is not directed by an overall policy but by innumerable policies which critics say are often ill-conceived individually, at cross purposes collectively, and generally devoid of theory from any perspective. It is conceivable, however, that a minimal consensus might be achieved by those shaping policy in these diverse contexts that could at least provide a conceptual handle on the art world.

If such a consensus accepted Beardsley's analysis in his "Aesthetic Welfare, Aesthetic Justice, and Educational Policy,"[4] it might consist of assent to the following. In their many different ways all members of the art world ultimately contribute to the creation, preservation, and enhancement of aesthetic value and hence to the promotion of the aesthetic well-being of individuals and the aesthetic welfare of society. Though the concept of aesthetic welfare cannot be sharply defined, it refers to a desirable state of affairs that is conceivable, progress toward which should be notable, and the absence of which would be painfully evident. The notion of aesthetic welfare as formulated by Beardsley rests on one unargued assumption: "That it can be not only enjoyable but also desirable for experience to have a high aesthetic level."[5] Furthermore, "when a rise in the aesthetic level of experience occurs without loss of other desirable qualities, experience always becomes more desirable."[6] An individual enjoying a high aesthetic level in his experience is at that moment in a state of aesthetic well-being. If this is shared by many members of a society, aesthetic welfare can be said to exist. Hence, "the *aesthetic welfare* of a society at a given time consists of all the aesthetic levels of experience of members of the society at a given time."[7]

Experiences with high aesthetic levels, however, depend on objects having the capacity to induce and sustain them. As this book has claimed several times, the capacity of objects to raise the level of experience constitutes their *aesthetic value*. Although objects of practically all kinds have traces of aesthetic value understood as a capacity to afford a quality of experience, works of art tend to possess it in greater concentration and hence to have a greater capacity to raise the aesthetic levels of individuals' experience than do other aesthetic objects. Works of art, therefore, hold potential for contributing most to aesthetic welfare. The totality of aesthetically valuable objects may be called the *aesthetic wealth* of a society.

Aesthetic wealth, however, is mere potentiality. Though necessary for bringing about aesthetic welfare, aesthetic wealth cannot by itself assure it (as is easily realized by imagining a society blessed with vast aesthetic riches that are all locked away in vaults). Beardsley therefore introduces *aesthetic justice* as another precondition for aesthetic welfare. It refers to equity, or fair distribution, and requires some geographical dispersal of aesthetically valuable objects and performances. Generally speaking, though, aesthetic justice would be served by equalizing access either through sharing the aesthetic wealth or by bringing people to it. One thing aesthetic justice calls for, then, is a fairer distribution of *aesthetic opportunities.*

But more nearly equal aesthetic opportunities understood merely as access are not enough for aesthetic justice to prevail. Even if large numbers of people were to be transported into the presence of objects of great aesthetic value, the aesthetic levels of their experiences, and hence the aesthetic welfare, would not increase appreciably unless such persons also possessed the critical and appreciative skills to engage aesthetic value objects appropriately. To aesthetic welfare, aesthetic wealth, aesthetic justice, and aesthetic opportunity must be added *aesthetic capability.* It, too, ought to be more equitably distributed among the population. Aesthetic welfare thus depends not only on sufficient aesthetic wealth being made widely accessible but also on people's ability and, it must be emphasized, inclination to make the most of their aesthetic opportunities. This preliminary definitional task is schematized below:

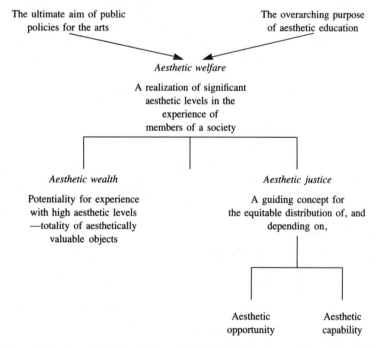

Figure II.1. Reproduced from R. A. and C. M. Smith, "The Government and Aesthetic Education: Opportunity in Adversity?" *Journal of Aesthetic Education* 14, no. 4 (October 1980), 7.

Such a conception of aesthetic value can do several things. In theoretical terms, aesthetic value can figure prominently in a definition of art as a humanly made artifact intended to give a marked aesthetic character to experience. In practical terms, it can help decide how best to manage aesthetic wealth. In societal terms, a concept of aesthetic value both explains and justifies aesthetic well-being and welfare as worthy policy objectives. For example: Society can have no more legitimate aim for its policies than the raising of the quality of the experience of its members; aesthetic value (that is, benefit to the individual) is actualized in each instance in the experience of a percipient; when members of society have numerous occasions for experiencing high levels of aesthetic value, a general state of aesthetic welfare prevails; consequently, the cultivation of aesthetic well-being and welfare are defensible objectives for both public policy and school instruction.

We may now elaborate further on the relationships to aesthetic value maintained by the various constituents of the art world. While artists create the conditions for aesthetic well-being and welfare, they must rely on the auxiliaries of the cultural service field to provide opportunities for aesthetic experiences. We may say that the provision of such opportunities confers a vestigial dignity on all the frenzied marketing, collecting, managing, and exhibiting activities that lend to the art world its appearance of a thriving, booming enterprise. Yet we have been reminded by Kenneth Clark that we are far from knowing what we are doing in providing greater access to art. A theory of aesthetic well-being and welfare could provide some guidance. It could also be a response to Jacques Barzun's observation that at the present time no coherent theory guides the happenings of the vast institution of art.

So much for artists, artworks, and auxiliaries; what remains for audiences? In formal terms, audiences engaging works of art are actualizing aesthetic value in experience. But despite the rising attendance figures museums and other cultural organizations report, it is questionable that such actualizing is happening at a very high level. Interest in art is also accompanied by bewilderment, puzzlement, and indifference. Indeed, the public is so rarely critical of anything done in the name of art that it is news when it does express an opinion.[8] This situation, which many judge to be a symptom of cultural malaise, bespeaks an inability to cope with aesthetic phenomena, an incapacity for aesthetic judgment, and an overall lack of concern for the aesthetic quality of life. That a public for art exists is plain enough, but it is not on the whole a discerning public. How could it be, one might ask, with so little serious effort expended in the society on substantive aesthetic education? Yet a discerning public is required for a satisfactory level of aesthetic well-being and welfare. In short, the aesthetic value capacity of an object must be matched by a percipient's ability to actualize it, and the responsibility for cultivating aesthetic percipience must fall largely to the schools; no other institution is capable of accomplishing the task. The public schools are strategic because of the percentage of its students that do not go on to college. Aesthetic justice thus requires that the schools provide the principal opportunities for persons to become aesthetically educated. The art world and its member institutions receive their ultimate social justification from the role they can play in bringing about a satisfactory degree of aesthetic well-being and welfare. Since, however, the contributions of such institutions depend on a discerning public, they too have a vested interest in aesthetic education. A strong societal case thus exists for aesthetic education.

A societal demand, however, has to be translated into an educational policy. In the case of aesthetic education, policy-making presupposes an awareness that one of the basic purposes of schooling is to induct the young into various domains of human value, of which aesthetic value is one. The way the young learn to realize aesthetic value in their lives is by acquiring requisite critical skills of perception and judgment, the character of which has been discussed in previous chapters of this volume.

At this point it has once more become apposite to counter some possible objections to the emphasis I place on critical skills. The usual complaint is that critical analysis dampens enjoyment. Yet intense aesthetic experience of some magnitude *presupposes* the possession and exercise of skills carefully and assiduously acquired over a long period of time. As Beardsley's remarks at the opening of this appendix indicate, a full measure of aesthetic gratification is simply unavailable to the untutored. True, during the practice of aesthetic skills response may be less spontaneous, but the promise is that skilled practice rendered habitual purchases deeper, more enriching response and the prospect for greater gratification. The intelligent exercise of a skill, moreover, involves more than rote drill and repetition of a set of pat procedures; rather it is a complex mental activity that cannot be entirely learned. We recall Michael Polanyi's point that there is an unspecified aspect of skillful practice that remains latent and cannot be taught. No one, for example, can be taught to criticize with the insight and finesse of the critics discussed in Chapter 4. All this duly considered, Chapter 3 nonetheless showed that it is possible not only to classify types of reasons and judgments and to explain some of the principles at work in them, but also to identify teachable types of skills and concepts (which are schematized in this appendix). In brief, criticism in certain respects lends itself to teaching by rules and methods. But it is important to understand that by rules I mean nothing more than pragmatic tips on how to engage a work of art if one is to realize the peculiar gratification, mental stimulation, and understanding it is capable of providing. Perhaps such rules are best understood in terms of "if . . . then" statements. For example: *If* you would perceive and appreciate the character, subtlety, and significance of a work of art, *then* pay close attention to its manifold of characteristic features and do not be sidetracked by irrelevant thoughts and associations; *if* you would appreciate the function or significance of an element in a composition, *then* be prepared to understand it in a context of other elements which may give it a special import; *if* you would appreciate the peculiar qualities of certain kinds of traditional painting, *then* know how artists tend to draw upon and to modify traditional conventions (as Giorgione did on pastoral genre conventions in *The Tempest*); *if* you would understand and appreciate the qualities of certain kinds of abstract or nonobjective paintings, *then* know something about the ways in which the properties of pigment and form themselves can express vibrant qualities of natural landscape and overtones of human tragedy and suffering (as they do in the paintings of Richard Diebenkorn and Robert Motherwell, respectively);[9] *if* you would attribute certain conceptual and expressive meaning to a work, *then* be prepared to show how such meaning is validated by the painting's interanimation of elements (as Wollheim did in explaining Poussin's *Phocion* painting and Kauffmann in interpreting Antonioni's *Red Desert*); *if* you would understand many works of art (both representational and nonrepresentational), *then* be prepared to go beyond their titles and ostensible subjects and probe for their underlying levels of significance; etc., etc. Doubtless there are more "rules" than this for the perceiving and appreciating of artworks, but, as Aiken implied in his discussion of the conditions for knowing and appreciating a work of art as art, such rules must be limited. In general, as Kaelin points out, relevance will be a function of how one brackets a work for criticism. What falls outside such brackets is the area of irrelevance. An art historian or anthropologist expands brackets of consideration while an aesthetic critic tends to narrow them. Of course, as previously pointed out, it's not always possible to decide what's in and outside of wherever one decides to place brackets, which was the source of self-doubt expressed by Steinberg in his discussion of the work of Jasper Johns. It is part of a teacher's knowledge and teaching finesse to know when to expand and contract frames of relevance.

In response to those who assert that an overemphasis on the practice of aesthetic critical skill denigrates the role of creative activities and performance, two things may be said. First, giving a detailed account of a work of art of some complexity is a kind of performance, a critical performance,[10] several examples of which are provided in Chapter 4; and, second, I do not deny the usefulness of creative and performing activities in cultivating the capacity to appreciate excellence in art. I simply put them in the service of developing aesthetic percipience and deemphasize them at the secondary level in favor of teaching critical appreciative skills. I believe the prospects for developing aesthetic percipience in the young are greater than the prospects for developing creative or performing skills. A state of diminishing returns is quickly reached in creative and performing activities, while progress is likely to be more cumulative in the training of appreciative capacities. And this is important, for progress in learning fosters confidence in both the learner and the teacher. Not that the schools in general make the most of the creative and performing activities they do provide (if, that is, we would believe John Goodlad's observations in his study of schooling). One can only speculate how much knowledge and critical appreciation are sacrificed and opportunities for genuine aesthetic learning lost when schools permit marching bands to spend inordinate amounts of time preparing for sports events, and parades and competitions of all kinds, in all of which a quite limited repertoire of music is performed over and over. The story of the "band triumphant"[11] and its educational consequences is a scandalous one that, were it more fully exposed, should incite indignation.

Finally, a skills approach to aesthetic education is likely to assure a greater measure of transfer of learning to adult lives and thus make formal schooling more effective for a greater number of individuals; while few have artistic talent or join the art world as creators or performers, appreciable numbers have the capacity to join the art public. In doing so, they help render, in Kaelin's terms, cultural institutions more efficacious, and, in Beardsley's, raise the level of the aesthetic welfare. To round out the range of possible benefits afforded by aesthetic experience, we may say that persons will derive not only a high degree of gratification (Beardsley's primary consequence) but also strengthen their powers of percipience (Osborne's theme) and reshape their worlds (Goodman's leitmotif).

So we return to the matter of teaching aesthetic skills in a way that is demonstrably related to projected outcomes, pedagogically circumspect, and professionally dignified. All of this can be accomplished by concentrating on the aesthetic value situation and its imperatives, a situation that consists of an object with aesthetic value capacity and an individual with the potential to realize it. Realizing that potential means developing the capacity for critical awareness which involves learning how to approach a work of art, learning what kind of interest to take in it, what properties to explore and ignore, and in what sequence to do all this. First impressions precede scrutiny, scrutiny spawns interpretation and judgment, and judgment yields critical description, or redescription as the case might be. Persons who experience works of art need not judge their excellence, but it is good practice for students to learn how to do so. Learning requires evidence that students have attended to certain tasks properly, and verbal accounts are a convenient, if not the only, means for determining this. In the aesthetic situation then we may say that individuals, though in a dispassionate and contemplative frame of mind, are perceptually and mentally engaged in acts of appreciation which include both active apprehending and valuing. During appreciation individuals perform certain perceptual and critical operations which constitute the exercise of aesthetic skills. The task of teaching thus becomes the teaching of the basic skills of aesthetic appreciation. To be sure, the term "appreciation" does not enjoy a very good press, but I hope that the treatment accorded it in this book helps to restore some of its credibility. Perhaps we might even speak of a new appreciation of art.[12] Finally, an account of aesthetic education that is rooted in a capacity to appreciate the excellence of art for the sake of the worthwhile experience that art at its best is capable of providing throws light on certain attitudes toward excellence and judgment in matters aesthetic, especially on a tendency that we might call nonjudgmentalism, which deserves a few words.

First of all, it should be pointed out that teaching for excellence and judgment is currently under attack from a number of perspectives. Operating at one level is an anti-intellectual populism that assumes all distinctions of value are undemocratic. This view can be dismissed as inconsistent with the true values of democracy. At quite another level we find Goodman who believes that an excessive concern with excellence has been responsible for a certain constriction of aesthetic theory. "To say that a work of art is good or even to say how good it is does not after all provide much information, does not tell us whether the work is evocative, robust, vibrant, or exquisitely designed, and still less what are its salient specific qualities of color, shape, or sound. Moreover, works of art are not racehorses, and picking a winner is not the primary goal."[13] Well, yes and no. In Beardsley's view, to say that one work of art is better than another is to say that it has a greater capacity to occasion aesthetic experience and that this capacity inheres in precisely the kinds of qualities Goodman mentions. True, the verdict "this is good" in itself contains little information, but it is just the beginning of a critical judgment. A good critic goes on to give reasons which ground his judgment and such reasons feature a work's special properties, qualities, and meanings. And while works of art are not racehorses, outstanding works are in a sense "winners," having been set apart as worthy of our special attention. If Goodman says less about artistic merit than other aspects of art it is because, once again, his interest lies mainly in the cognitive functioning of artworks and in what makes art the symbolic system it is.

Yet I think it neither possible nor wise to ignore the question of excellence in art. It is not just the societal demand that requires us to address it; there is also the educational consideration that only outstanding works of art exemplify the full range of aesthetic possibility and thus bring out the full range of skills necessary to encompass such possibility. And if the aesthetic is one of the important domains of human value, it is incumbent on educators that they familiarize students with outstanding examples of objects which enshrine it. I therefore reaffirm the importance of acknowledging excellence in art and think that it stands badly in need of recognition and appreciation. So far as the anti-intellectualism of doctrinaire populism is concerned, I judge it to be detrimental to the development of aesthetic human potential. It is moreover arguable whether populists speak on behalf of the large majority. Richard Hoggart[14] and Sir Roy Shaw,[15] for example, both of whom are sensitive to British working-class attitudes and aspirations, think that populists (or communitarians) misinterpret the values and aspirations of working-class people.

A few words now about critical skills and research. The skills of aesthetic appreciation are both perceptual and critical; discerning must precede describing, analyzing, interpreting, and evaluating. The reason for exercising critical skills is to apprehend correctly a work's elements, relations, qualities, and meanings (when there are such). Once more, while the critical discourse of students is not the only means, it is the principal means by which it is possible to detect the character of their aesthetic responses. Aesthetic instruction therefore pays careful attention to what students say about artworks, to the ways in which they map their aesthetic understanding, to recall Novak and Gowin's terminology in their *Learning How to Learn.* The character of students' discourse reflects the degrees to which relevant concepts and skills are being learned. The two charts that follow thus stress relevant types of concepts, skills, and judgments; the first lists the general skills and concepts of critical description, analysis, interpretation, and evaluation; and the second, the types of critical reasons and judgments which are grouped into categories and illustrated with sample critical statements. The second chart is in effect an elaboration of the last skill listed in the first chart, evaluation. The first chart has encouraged dance[16] and music education[17] specialists to devise similar ones for understanding better the nature of aesthetic criticism in these two art forms, and two film theorists[18] have found Beardsley's categories of analysis and his theory generally helpful in formulating a countertheory to current critical methods. English educators, of course, have been mapping for some time the categories of response to literature, if not necessarily along the lines Beardsley suggests.[19] The schemes in question are not intended for use with young children, although teachers of art at any level would do well to make their content part of their own conceptual frameworks. The anticipated difficulties are more or less educated guesses at this time, although I'm certain that some additional and perhaps more appropriate ones could be hypothesized from Michael Parsons's study of aesthetic development discussed in Chapter 5.

As was the case with the scheme of critical judgments and reasons discussed in Chapter 3, the schemes of aesthetic skills, though based on Beardsley's *Aesthetics,* are not found in diagrammatic form there. And though derived from Beardsley, I don't see that the concepts and skills in question conflict with the theories of Osborne, Goodman, or Kaelin. The principal differences among these writers turn on the ways artworks are isolated or bracketed for aesthetic attention, on the ways in which an artwork's features, characters, or counters function, and on what works of art are preeminently good for. I don't see that these interests rule out the necessity for cultivating relevant aesthetic concepts and skills. I am not saying, incidentally, and this should be abundantly clear from the topics discussed in this volume, that the purpose of aesthetic education is simply to provide instruction in the use of critical skills. I have long believed, and now E. D. Hirsch, Jr.,[20] has dramatized the matter, that the separation of skills and substantive content is unproductive of cogent learning. If the aesthetic is an important domain of human value, if it constitutes a major form of thought and action, if it is a realm of human concern that produces exemplary instances of its distinctive objects, if it has a live tradition that continues to influence thinking and creation, then the kinds of objects skills are honed on cannot be a matter of indifference. The demonstration of a high level of aesthetic skill demands objects which bring the entire range and complexity of that skill into play.

Categories of analysis and judgment

A few words are in order as a preface to the charts to follow. In setting out Beardsley's scheme of critical analysis and judgment, I have, of course, favored a certain terminology over others that could have been chosen. It is important in talking about art to distinguish the general categories in which we may discuss it and the more specific concepts associated with or subsumed by the general categories. So far as the general categories are concerned, we have a choice among the following: (1) Virgil C. Aldrich's[21] medium, form, and content, where content is interpreted subject matter (when there is such) that is embedded in a form (or pattern or composition) that features not only the content but also the medium (or the special qualities of materials, for example, tonalities, etc.); John Hospers's[22] mediumistic and transmediumistic aspects, the former of which imply sensuous and formal elements and the latter representational, expressive, and ideational aspects of artworks; Harold Osborne's[23] semantic, syntactic, and expressive information, which refers to the representational, formal or structural, and the dramatic character of objects; H. Gene Blocker's[24] preference for representation, form, and expression; Francis Sparshott's[25] reference to presence as well as structural and expressive aspects; David Martin and Lee Jacobus's[26] form, content, and subject matter; and Harry S. Broudy's[27] sensory, formal, technical, and expressive aspects; etc.

Adequately defined and qualified, any of these sets of general categories is useful, although it must be realized that the terms in question are quite general and are connected with many others; consider, for example, that Beardsley associates with the category of relations among the components of a visual aesthetic object the concepts of form, structure, texture, balance/imbalance, etc. I tend to use Beardsley's terminology because it reflects an effort to devise a language for talking about art that misleads as little as possible, aesthetic terms being notorious for their inherent ambiguity. Hence the term "expression" is not found in Beardsley's vocabulary because of its numerous and conflicting senses, referring at once, as Hospers[28] has pointed out, to the process by which a work was brought into being, the properties of which a work is expressive, the meaning (conceptual or emotional) conveyed by a work, and the emotions and feelings aroused by it. Beardsley prefers "human regional quality" to "expression" because the former term refers unambiguously to a property of the object itself. Thus instead of the conventional triad of sensory, formal, and expressive aspects of works, or form, content, and subject matter, etc., Beardsley offers the language of elements, relations, complexes, regional qualities, fused complexes, and wholes, all of which can be discussed in connection with the general notion of part-whole relationships.

Briefly, an element, the most basic property of a work, is a partless part; a complex is a group of parts; relations refer to the ways parts and complexes fuse into webs or patterns; qualities imply the emergent properties of complexes, some of which are human qualities; and a whole means the configuration yielded by all the rest. All of the works discussed in this book can be analyzed in such terms. And while elements (partless parts) are included in this list, it is complexes and fused complexes and their regional (configurational, gestalt, emergent) qualities which preoccupy critics.

Beardsley does not include meanings, or the semantic aspects of artworks, in his scheme because it is not clear to him that all artworks mean something, at least in the conventional sense of "mean." Thus it is not as basic a category as the others. But I don't think much harm will be done if we add "meanings" to the list of basic categories of analysis and qualify it by adding "when present." This enables us to count meanings as one aspect of a complex that can fuse with other meanings which give rise to the overall meaning, import, or significance of the whole. This has the additional advantage, as Chapter 3 suggested, of incorporating cognitive reasons as relevant ones in judging artistic merit. So we can, I think, usefully speak of elements, relations, complexes, meanings (when present), and wholes as our basic categories of analysis. This terminology, moreover, helps to underline the object directedness of aesthetic response; it helps keep attention riveted on the artwork. Application of such categories comes after the initial impact a work has made and during what Clark calls the period of close scrutiny.

The sensory mode of the elements, relations, and complexes will, of course, depend on the art form in question—painting, poem, music, film, dance, architecture, and so forth. Yet aesthetic quality concepts seem to have broad applicability. It is common, for example, to use the same characterizing terms when talking about all the arts. As Barzun has remarked, analogy, or the recognition of similarity in difference, is the great rule to follow in both perceiving and criticizing. Accordingly, reliance on analogy should perhaps be added to the "rules" mentioned earlier. Indeed, says Barzun,

> the subject matter of all the arts is a unity, even though the expressive means and the relative powers of the several arts differ. Music cannot paint, nor literature yield colors, nor architecture have a beginning, a middle, and an end. Yet as time goes on and techniques keep pace with desires, the legitimate analogies multiply. There is "tone color" in music . . . "rhythm" in painting, "dissonance" in architecture . . . word-music in poetry and prose . . . sculpture marked with pictorial effects, and painting full of plastic sensations. All of these arts, moreover, may be associated with one another's nominal "subjects" and may be rightly characterized as dramatic, serene, gay, sinister—as well as by a thousand other qualities.[29]

For more detailed explanations of the categories of analysis and the elements of music and literature as well as the visual arts, Beardsley's writings should be carefully read in their entirety.[30] Because the visual arts are what I know best, I have illustrated his concepts of critical analysis with examples from painting. But I trust it can be seen how this general approach applies to all the arts. To repeat, the scheme to follow is derived from Beardsley's *Aesthetics* and is continuous with the discussions of aesthetic criticism in Chapters 3 through 5 of this volume.

It should be noted that while Beardsley subsumes genetic and affective statements under aesthetic judgment, he believed that such statements were less relevant to assessing a work's artistic value than aesthetic objective statements, where by "objective" he means remarks directed toward features of the object itself rather than to antecedents or effects. That is why he pays more attention to this kind of judgment. But, again, Beardsley's systematic discussion of critical evaluation must be read in its entirety for an appreciation of its richness and insights.

It is appropriate in a volume that has placed so much emphasis on judgment and criticism as capacities by which an artwork's value is rendered accessible to recall the important role that judgment and criticism play in art and human life. First Beardsley; he believed that when a critic exerts judgment upon the work of another "he subjects himself

Aesthetic Skills and Concepts

1. Skills	2. Concepts	3. Anticipated difficulties inherent in concepts. Students may have problems in:	4. Anticipated difficulties based on misconceptions. Students may reflect (though they need not articulate) the belief:
1.1 discerning and describing the components of a visual aesthetic object.	2.1 the visual field (or picture plane) 2.11 shape 2.112 size 2.113 position 2.114 color quality 2.1141 hue 2.1142 lightness/darkness 2.1143 saturation 2.12 complexes (clusters of elements) 2.13 line 2.131 line-area 2.132 boundary line 2.133 broken line 2.14 figure and mass 2.15 depth 2.16 movement	3.1 3.11 coping with the inadequacy of discursive language to the task of describing perceptual qualities. 3.12 realizing that so-called dependent qualities of elements (a *cool* color, an *assertive* line) are as phenomenally objective, i.e., part of the visual field, as basic qualities (e.g., a blue color, a thick line). 3.13 learning to accept the fact that although tertiary qualities (those belonging to complexes) cannot be located in the elements and are unpredictable in their emergence from them, they are *not* subjective, emotional, affective—in short, are not contributed by the percipient.	4.1 4.11 that analysis and detailed description of a visual aesthetic object is misguided because, as the whole is more than its parts, analysis can reveal nothing significant about the aesthetic object and may even be destructive. 4.12 that visual designs are exemplars of a nondiscursive language that speaks directly to our feelings and can be dealt with only on their own (affective, nondiscursive) terms.
1.2 discerning and describing relations among com-	2.2 form (the total web of relations) 2.21 structure 2.22 texture	3.2 3.21 continuing to overcome the problems identified in 3.11 and 3.12 above, since the task is still one of isolating compo-	4.2 4.21 that a genuine dichotomy exists between form (here taken to mean the abstract elements of

ponents of a visual aesthetic object.

2.23 types of relations
2.231 dual relations
2.2311 similar
2.2312 contrasting
2.2313 indifferently different
2.2321 balance/imbalance (resulting from distribution of elements)
2.2322 equilibrium/disequilibrium (created by implied movement)
2.2323 harmony

nents (relations) and describing them in terms of dependent as well as emergent properties (an *uneasy* balance, a *bold* structure).

3.22 achieving a uniform understanding of, and perhaps stipulating a definition for, some of the concepts that have become fuzzy in usage—"form" is sometimes taken to mean shape or geometric pattern or the work seen abstractly; "texture" may refer to tactile or surface properties; "style" has many different meanings; etc.

a work) and subject, meaning that

4.211 only the formal properties are the truly important ones (as borne out by the development of contemporary art toward abstractness and a concomitant sloughing off of subject matter, i.e., of that which appeals to the unsophisticated) and

4.212 subject matter, where it does occur, should be disregarded.

4.3
4.31 that the interpretation of a work of art constitutes an invitation to being "creative" or "imaginative," inventing stories and calling forth associated ideas (notions often implanted in the elementary grades).

4.32 that the task of interpretation always involves discovery of what the work "has to say to us," i.e., some message couched in propositional form.

continued next page

1.3 interpreting a visual work of art.

2.3
2.31 characterization of overall quality (mood, attitude, tone)
2.32 representation
2.321 depiction object
2.322 portrayal object
2.323 subject (action or scene portrayed or depicted)
2.324 abstraction and distortion
2.325 symbolism
2.33 content (relation of design to subject)

3.3
3.31 understanding that even non-representational works of art usually have a definite overall quality (e.g., eeriness, joyousness)
3.311 that is not to be confused with the percipient's reaction to the work and is not properly called its "meaning."
3.312 gaining access to a work with unfamiliar subject or symbolism.
3.32 perceiving the subtle relationships between subject and design—their congruence or incongruence—from which content emerges.
3.33

Aesthetic Skills and Concepts (continued)

1. Skills	2.	Concepts	3. Anticipated difficulties inherent in concepts. Students may have problems in:	4. Anticipated difficulties based on misconceptions. Students may reflect (though they need not articulate) the belief:
1.4 assessing the aesthetic worth of a visual work of art	2.4		3.4	4.4
	2.41	valuing (prizing, liking)	3.41 coming to recognize the difference between liking (prizing, valuing) a work of art and assessing (judging, estimating) its aesthetic value.	4.41 that since "nonjudgmentalism" is the only defensible attitude to take toward works of art, attempts at evaluation are invidious.
	2.42	evaluating		
	2.421	critical reasons		
	2.4211	genetic reasons		
	2.4212	affective reasons	3.42 accepting the requirement to support aesthetic judgments with relevant reasons.	
	2.4213	objective reasons		4.42 that pervasive relativism proves the impossibility of any standards in art; attempts at evaluation are therefore futile.
	2.422	criteria (standards, canons)		
	2.4221	unity	3.43 differentiating between acceptable and unacceptable reasons.	
	2.4222	complexity	3.44 appreciating the peculiar logic of the criteria or standards on which aesthetic judgments may be based.	4.43 that aesthetic judgments (especially when made by teachers) amount to an effort to impose personal subjective, indefensible values on others.
	2.4223	intensity of quality		
	2.423	evaluative reasoning		
	2.4231	merits		
	2,4232	defects		
	2.424	judgments		

Table 1. Aesthetic Skills and Concepts Derived from Beardsley's *Aesthetics*.

to some rather exacting standards by which the better judgment can be discriminated from the worse. This is not a realm where anything goes. And if a critic cannot claim to possess the power of invention that would have made him a poet [or a painter or a filmmaker, etc.], he may lay claim to possess something very precious—the ability to lead others to what is good. This is what gives him not merely the name of a critic but the substance."[31] So far as the place of criticism in human life is concerned, we may agree with Sparshott when he observes that a life without criticism is not worth living, for serious criticism by definition addresses the complex values of human experience. "Critical activity seeks and finds, if it does not create, experience that is worth dwelling on. The old fear that criticism might dissolve enjoyment has no ground. Only a mindless enjoyment could be thus melted, and a mindless enjoyment is never enough for people with minds."[32] And since our students have minds, neither is mindless enjoyment sufficient for them. Aesthetic education, therefore, leads the young to what is good and excellent in art.

The Language of Critical Evaluation

(1) Cognitive: Praise the work for making a contribution to our knowledge.
it is profound.
it has something important to say.
it conveys a significant view of life.
it gives insight into a universal human problem.

(2) Moral: Moral value is ascribed or denied to the work.
it is uplifting and inspiring.
it is effective social criticism.
it promotes desirable social and political ends.
it is subversive.

(3) Aesthetic: This category is divided into (4), (5), and (6), below.

(4) Genetic: These judgments refer to something existing before the work itself,
to the manner in which it was produced, or its connection with
antecedent objects and psychological states.
it fulfills (or fails to fulfill) the artist's intention.
it is an example of successful (or unsuccessful) expression.
it is new and original (or trite).
it is sincere (or insincere).

(5) Affective: Judgments referring to the psychological effects of the aesthetic
object upon the percipient.
it gives pleasure (or gives no pleasure).
it is interesting (or dull and monotonous).
it is exciting, moving, stirring, rousing.
it has a powerful emotional impact.

(6) Objective: This category is divided into (7), (8), and (9), below.

(7) Unity: it is well-organized (or disorganized).
it is formally perfect (or imperfect).
it has (or lacks) an inner logic or structure or style.

(8) Complexity: it is developed on a large scale.
it is rich in contrasts (or lacks variety and is repetitious).
it is subtle and imaginative (or crude).

(9) Intensity: (of human regional qualities in the work.)
it is full of vitality (or insipid).
it is forceful and vivid (or weak and pale).
it is beautiful (or ugly).
it is tender, ironic, tragic, graceful, delicate, richly comic.

Table 2. Types of Reasons and Judgments Derived from Beardsley's *Aesthetics*.

A unit on teaching aesthetic criticism

This unit is predicated on the belief that the visual arts can contribute significantly to humanistic education understood as the enrichment and extension of an individual's potentialities. The contribution to self-cultivation which instruction in the proper appreciation of visual aesthetic objects can make occurs under the three identifiable yet interrelated rubrics set forth below as objectives. The art of painting has been singled out for this unit, though with suitable modifications the material can be adapted to the literary and performing arts.[1]

Objectives

1. To acquire a distinctive mode of interacting with the visual aspects of the environment (the aim being to enlarge awareness through a unique set of responses to the world).
2. To learn a method for actualizing visual aesthetic values in their most highly developed and thus most satisfying manifestations (the aim being to extend awareness of works of fine art through a new set of skills).
3. To understand the humanistic import of works of art (the aim being to enrich awareness through an understanding of some of the unique characteristics as well as abiding concerns of mankind).

Assignment

The principal reading assignment for this unit is the handout "The Elements of the Visual Arts" which is to be reproduced and distributed to students the first hour for use throughout the unit.

Contents

A. Introduction
B. Elements of the Visual Arts: Painting
C. Suggestions for Teaching
D. Reading Suggestions

Introduction

As it addresses itself to the realization of individual human potential, humanistic or liberal education is necessarily a form of value education. This value orientation should, of course, also be dominant in that portion of the humanities program devoted to the visual arts, which is the reason why the objectives stated above were couched in terms of benefits to individual awareness. A design for humanistic or value education, however, must go beyond the formulation of objectives to some indication of suitable value objects—that is, objects through which students may realize the projected values—and of instructional emphases and procedures intended to guide students in their value quest. To this end the objectives for this unit have been supplemented by two sets of additional considerations. It is hoped that the resultant scheme will articulate for instructors only important and central considerations and help them to avoid overwhelming students with superfluous facts.

Objectives. 1. A distinctive manner of confronting visual reality; 2. A method for actualizing aesthetic values of the highest order; 3. An awareness of humanistic import.

Value Objects. a. Objects, man-made or natural, that elicit and sustain aesthetic experience, i.e., a "special mode" of confronting the world; b. Masterpieces of the visual arts having the capacity to yield high-order aesthetic value; c. Those works in the visual arts that exemplify, illustrate, or make vivid human concerns and values.

Instructional Emphases. i. The student's contribution to aesthetic experience, i.e., the attitude and disposition to be cultivated; ii. The skills of aesthetic criticism, i.e., description or analysis, interpretation, and evaluation; iii. Knowledge with which to approach works of art so as to achieve insight and understanding.

The above scheme lends itself to further adumbrations that might be of interest to the instructor using this unit. First of all, there is a top-to-bottom movement from the very broad and general to the more specific (1, 2, 3, to a, b, c, to i, ii, iii). By subdividing this sequence into three columns one arrives at a rough indication of the objectives and of suitable content for each of the three hours of instruction (that is, 1, a, i; 2, b, ii; 3, c, iii).

Second, there is a horizontal organization from the simple and basic to the more complex and inclusive. For example, students should have acquired some sense of what it means to experience something aesthetically before they engage in more critical analysis. And they ought to have had some practice in describing a work of art and characterizing its overall effect before undertaking more complicated forms of interpretation in terms of humanistic understanding. This simple-to-complex sequencing is also reflected in the nature of the suggested value objects to be presented in each of the three class hours: first to be introduced are ordinary objects which serve very basic human needs; these same objects will then be displayed as the subject matter of a series of paintings; next come paintings depicting these same sorts of objects in some human context, with the latter gradually gaining predominance; finally, objects and human figures will be part of rather complex paintings that invite interpretation of humanistic import. It is believed that the strategy of starting with ordinary subject matter will help beginning students to center their attention on aesthetic qualities of visual aesthetic objects. If students were first introduced to a richly figurative work, their curiosity about its subject matter might impede their aesthetic perceptiveness.[2]

The elements of the visual arts: Painting (student handout)

However casually persons respond to their general visual environment,[3] where paintings are concerned one should insist that they be looked at closely and with discernment. But, what precisely, does one look for?

In one respect paintings are not different from other complex entities that we learn to respond to—we want to know what they are, how they are put together, what makes them "work," that is, how they produce the effect they do. This means that we take stock of parts or elements, clusters of elements or complexes, relationships that obtain between complexes, and the emergent qualities of such relationships. It is the mark of aesthetically educated persons that they are able to examine paintings in this manner, that they can analyze and describe them appropriately. This, however, requires conversance with a number of terms and concepts that may be called aesthetic object concepts, some of the most fundamental of which will now be discussed.

The surface of a painting is frequently referred to as the *picture plane*. On any such picture plane one can discern a number of items or elements (we are speaking abstractly now and not in terms of an inventory of objects represented) called *areas*. Areas can differ from each other in a number of ways: *shapes* (circular or triangular or rectangular or irregular), *position* (in relation to the picture plane, as for instance "in the upper right corner" as well as in relation to each other such as "to the right of" or "immediately below"), and *color quality* (hue, lightness, and saturation).

Another important concept is that of *line*. This would be any identifiable link between two positions on the picture plane that establishes a perceptual path between them. It should be realized that such a "path" need not always be in the form of an actual connecting line drawn on the surface. Very important to the analysis of visual designs are so-called "invisible lines" that flow through the composition between certain of its areas.

Visible, unbroken lines can be independent elements on the picture surface or boundary lines between areas. However, a line that turns on itself so that its ends are fused circumscribes a *figure*—a bottle, a flower, a human form, or some nonrepresentational item. (It should be mentioned that it is seldom proper, especially when dealing with contemporary non-objective paintings, to go to great lengths trying to "figure out" what some shape or element is meant to be, since it is not necessarily meant to be anything in particular. However, when describing such a picture we usually use the expedient of referring to its areas in terms of what they roughly resemble: a starlike figure, a funnel-shaped object, and so forth.)

We have considered a picture plane with several areas on it. But, of course, they are not just dispersed indiscriminately; they are grouped, arranged in some way. Clustering of elements in a particular sector of the picture plane produces *visual density*. Furthermore, areas or figures or elements are not created equal; there is *visual dominance* and *visual subordination*. This is partly dependent on size (obviously a larger figure will subordinate others), partly on position (for example, elements at the center of the picture plane tend to be more prominent), and partly also on color (certain colors more than others attract attention and help certain areas to stand out).

Although the picture plane is, objectively speaking, two-dimensional, it will almost never appear so to the eye. As soon as some visual elements are placed on it, a degree of *depth* is created even when space is not pictorially represented (as it would be in a landscape painting, for example). Certain colors have the property of seeming to advance or recede; overlapping shapes are usually read in terms of spatial relationships of being "behind" or "in front of." Through these and other devices, then, the painting acquires an impression of three-dimensionality. This illusion makes it possible for the picture to have *visual volume* or *mass*, the magnitude of which depends on how much of the space is partly filled and how much is void.

However, the concepts of mass and volume apply not only to the picture space as a whole but also to the figures placed within it. They, too, can have the property of three-dimensionality, of being more or less weighty and solid. There are different ways in which painting lends weight and solidity to its shape, but one of the most effective is the use of *light*. It emanates from some source, often located within the represented space, and by playing over, shading, and highlighting the forms arranged within that space, light helps to give them the appearance of fullness and volume.

Just as it would be next to impossible to compose a visual design that is perfectly flat or two-dimensional, so it is hard to imagine one that would be without some implicit *movement*. It may run along the visual paths already mentioned and guide the eye on its exploration of the composition. This would be essentially a surface movement. However, there is also spatial movement, such as that of diagonal lines seemingly thrusting into the picture space. And then there is the subtler movement of tension, of attraction and repulsion, as that between elements which seem to be pushing forward from the picture plane and others that appear to be receding away from it.

A most important term is that of *form*. It is also a very problematic one since different and conflicting meanings have been attached to it. For instance, some say that form means the total web of relations among a work's parts. Taken in this sense, there would be nothing in a painting that would not also be a formal element. Form can also be taken to refer to only the more prominent, large-scale relationships in a painting. But then form becomes synonymous with what is usually meant by *structure* which, in turn, is very close in meaning to *composition*. It is not necessary to insist on a precise nomenclature. Thus when it is said of a painting that it has a triangular form (or structure or composition), this indicates that the visual paths connecting the most prominent areas form a triangle. The thing to bear in mind about form or structure, then, is that it refers to relationships, how the work is put together, what makes it cohere (or fall apart if there is a weakness of form).

Texture is yet another vague concept. Many understand it to denote the tactile surface of the painting, that is, whether the paint is applied smoothly, thickly, with regular or irregular brush strokes, and so forth. Others contrast textures to structure and take it to mean small-scale relationships in the work—transitions between neighboring parts, color gradations, and the like.

Finally, there is *style,* another confused and much abused term. To simplify matters, it is perhaps best to remember that style has to do with recurrences of certain features. The term style is also used to classify artworks produced in given historic periods. The characteristics associated with period styles are simply those features that tend to recur in the paintings from that time. In the case of Italian Renaissance style, for example, recurrent properties would be, among others, clarity of outline, a certain stability of structure (achieved through a preference for horizontals, verticals, and a compositional arrangement that is complete within and reinforces the picture frame), and an overall quality of dignity, serenity, and repose. Paintings identified as Baroque, on the other hand, would evidence recurrence of another set of features: drama, excitement bordering on the theatrical and hysterical, a blurring of outlines to emphasize movement, a preference for diagonal lines and for compositions that seem to spill out over the picture frame. When one speaks of the style of a particular artist, one also has recurrences in mind—they are simply what an artist's works seem to have in common, the artist's handwriting, as it were.

Up to this point we have developed a modest catalogue of things one should look for in a painting. We now turn to *aesthetic qualities,* which are the perceptual properties that belong to the elements and complexes of a visual design, and, of course, the properties possessed by the work as a whole. Once one has assumed a sufficiently receptive attitude toward an aesthetic object, one should have no problem becoming aware of a whole array of its aesthetic qualities; they quite insist on being noticed. But difficulties do develop when we attempt to describe these qualities; our vocabulary is no match for their variety and subtlety. One makes do with what the language has to offer and often describes aesthetic qualities in terms of primary and dependent attributes: a warm red, a cool blue, a refreshing green. Warm, cool, and refreshing, the dependent attributes, are qualities a painting cannot possess literally; they are ascribed to it metaphorically. To take two other examples, lines have direction (horizontal, diagonal, vertical), configuration (waving, zigzag), and thickness; but they may also be—metaphorically but undeniably just the same—meandering, irresolute, or nervous. Shapes, in addition to being square, smooth, or irregular, can also be commanding, shrinking, or aggressive. Misunderstanding occurs when it is assumed that the adjectives used metaphorically to describe dependent properties of elements such as lines, colors, shapes or to characterize the overall quality of larger complexes are somehow subjective contributions by the percipient. Fortunately we do not have to resolve the aesthetic controversy regarding the status of aesthetic qualities. For pedagogical purposes, we may emphasize that aesthetic qualities, primary or dependent, literal or metaphorical, are objective, that is, they belong to the object and are noted, not supplied, by the observer. Hence when one speaks of an "uneasy balance" one does not mean that one is made to feel uneasy, or that the painting feels uneasy; what one does mean is that this is the sort of balance the work has.

Suggestions for teaching

First class hour

The first hour, while being preparatory to the kind of critical awareness required by paintings, also pursues an objective of its own: to persuade students that a special sort of attention must be exercised in order to extract from the visual environment in general and from works in the visual arts in particular whatever aesthetic value they have to offer. As will be explained shortly, this mode of interacting with visual objects will require of students a measure of effort and self-discipline. This notion, however, might meet with disbelief due to certain deeply entrenched popular opinions. One is that since paintings are visual objects, the untrained eye should be adequate to perceiving them. Another is that since aesthetic experiences are reputedly enjoyable, they should be completely effortless and spontaneous.

The instructor wanting to disabuse students of these prejudices might launch a brief discussion of the different kinds of experience individuals are in fact capable of having. The inventory, to which students should be invited to contribute, should include practical, emotional, cognitive, moral, political, and others. Aesthetic experience would certainly be an item on any such list. Yet it is obviously different from many others in that it involves looking at some external object; it belongs, in other words, to the class of perceptual or visual experiences. But that class contains other experiences beside the aesthetic, for there are various ways of "looking at" or "seeing" objects.

Students might now be confronted with a collection of objects from which one of the possible themes for the unit will be evolved. The theme is that of different human interests surrounding a basic necessity of life—food. The objects selected then would be a selection of comestibles, perhaps some fruit and vegetables. Students can be asked not only to look at the objects, but to try to think of different ways of looking at them. Specifically, they should come to understand that what one sees depends largely on the aims and purposes one brings to a situation. The following should be noted and discussed.

First of all, there is a sort of casual visual experience in which the object is rarely taken note of but is instead instantly transformed into a stimulus to flights of fancy, reminiscences, and the like. For example, one person noticing some apples might simply lapse into memories involving apples. This is *not* an aesthetic form of seeing and attending, though at one time it was believed—and to some extent still is today—that it is the function of the visual arts to entice the imagination to wander where it will. But clearly, flights of fancy abandon the object of perception in favor of private and subjective reveries. The undesirability of this underscores a first noteworthy feature of aesthetic experience: *strictest attention to the perceptual object.*

This attention to the perceptual object is also neglected in a second kind of inappropriate reaction, and that is a purely emotional response. To be sure, it may not be easy to illustrate this point by use of the objects now before the students; cabbages and cucumbers are unlikely to incite strong passions one way or another. Still, it is important to emphasize that aesthetic experience is not primarily emotional. This idea may arouse disbelief and even resentment; it must therefore be clarified. One should grant that aesthetic experiences can provide enjoyment; successful commerce with aesthetically rich objects can in fact be quite exhilarating and gratifying. However, these feelings are the concomitants or results of a properly focused aesthetic experience; they are not themselves at the focus of that experience. That focal point must at all times be occupied by the visual aesthetic object itself. Students' responses in the form of

"It makes me feel . . ." or "I feel that . . ." should in this sense be discouraged. They are not so much descriptions of the object as they are reports on the inner state of the percipient. Such reactions can, however, usually be converted into statements about the perceptual object with little difficulty. For example, "I really feel calm, relaxed, and at ease with this work" could be translated into "This work has a calm, serene, quiet quality."

Yet minute attention to certain features of the perceived object combined with a relative emotional detachment still does not uniquely define aesthetic experience. People will look closely at an object for a variety of reasons and will tend to notice primarily those of its visual properties that answer their purpose. Apples, for example, may be regarded from a number of *practical* points of view: the shopper will examine the fruit carefully for defects; the person who prefers a certain flavor will note the properties that differentiate a Jonathan from a Red Delicious or a Rome; the retail merchant might watch for size, and so forth. An apple would probably be scrutinized most closely by a pomologist, yet the pomologist's interest would be primarily *theoretical* or *scientific* rather than practical or aesthetic.

Evidently aesthetic perception cannot be distinguished from other types of seeing merely by the intensity of one's concentration on the object. Rather, what makes it different is a percipient's absorption in *visual appearance for its own sake*. Individuals having an aesthetic experience of an object, then, attend closely to its surface properties largely to the exclusion of other considerations—such as how the object makes them feel, what they might learn about it, how they could use it, how its appearance affects cash value, and so forth. In short, persons hold in temporary abeyance other and more customary modes of experience. One might say that aesthetic experience involves a kind of unselfishness, a willingness to set aside other interests in order to allow the object to display what may now be called its aesthetic qualities. This way of interacting with external reality also yields a distinctive value—awareness of the aesthetic aspect of the world which reveals objects in their perceptual richness, completeness, and uniqueness. It should not be difficult to concede that persons who never learn to experience aesthetically remain stunted in their personal development.

Students should by now have some sense of what aesthetic experience involves—a detached and fairly unemotional yet thorough absorption in an object's perceptual properties or aesthetic qualities—and how aesthetic experience differs from other types. They should be asked next to attempt to experience each of the displayed objects aesthetically, concentrating on shapes, colors, textures. Students should also be encouraged to talk about what they notice, though they might find this unexpectedly difficult to do owing to the rather underdeveloped state of the repertory of words that can be matched to perceptions.

Aesthetic attention encompasses not only particular objects but also relationships between them. Various arrangements and groupings of the objects should now be pointed to in order to make students realize that some are more satisfactory than others. The purpose of these short exercises, though it need not be articulated, is to prepare students for the concepts of elements, relations, complexes, and qualities discussed in the Student Handout.

The time has come for a transition from ordinary objects to works of art. Below is a list of paintings, still lifes for the most part, suitable for the present context. Slides of the paintings could be shown fairly rapidly, though student comment should not be discouraged. Some of the dates of these works should be mentioned to demonstrate that artistic representations of so mundane a subject as victuals have had wide appeal throughout the ages.

List of paintings

Composition with Fruit and Game, 1st century B.C., wall painting from Pompeii, National Museum, Naples.

Peaches and Glass Jar, c. A.D. 50, Herculaneum, National Museum, Naples.

Mu-ch'i, *Six Persimmons,* 13th century, Daitokuji, Tokyo, Japan.

Pieter Aertsen, *The Meat Stall,* 1551, Uppsala University Museum of Art.

C. Arcimboldi, *Bowl of Vegetables,* c. 1565, seen as a head when inverted, Museo Ala Ponzone, Cremola, Italy.

L. Susi, *Still Life,* 1619, St. Louis City Art Museum.

Juan Sanchez Cotàn, *Quince, Cabbage, Melon, and Cucumbers,* 1630, The Fine Arts Society of San Diego, California.

Jan Darldz de Heem, *Still Life,* 1640, Louvre, Paris.

Willem Kalf, *Still Life,* c. 1650–1690, Rijksmuseum, Amsterdam.

Jean-Baptiste Siméon Chardin, *Still Life: Bowl of Plums,* 1759, Phillips Collection, Washington, D. C.

Luis Meléndez, *Still Life,* 1772, Prado, Madrid.

Raphael Peale, *Still Life,* 1818, Detroit Institute of Arts.

Edouard Manet, *Still Life with Carp,* 1864, Chicago Art Institute.

Henri Fantin-Latour, *Still Life,* 1866, National Gallery of Art, Washington, D. C.

Vincent Van Gogh, *Still Life with Apples and Two Pumpkins,* 1885, Rijksmuseum Kröller-Müller, Otterlo, The Netherlands.

Paul Cézanne, *Still Life with Basket of Apples,* 1890–1894, Chicago Art Institute.

Juan Gris, *Breakfast,* 1914, Museum of Modern Art, New York.

Henri Matisse, *Variation on a Still Life by de Heem,* 1915–1917, private collection.

Pierre Bonnard, *Le Compotier Blanc*, 1921, private collection, New York.

Henri Matisse, *Still Life with Studio, Interior of Nice*, 1923, Collection Mrs. Albert D. Lasker, New York.

Pierre Bonnard, *Dining Room on the Garden*, 1934–1935, Solomon R. Guggenheim Museum, New York.

René Magritte, *The Listening Chamber*, 1955, Collection William N. Copley, New York.

Tom Wesselmann, *Great American Still Life No. 19*, 1962, Collection Mr. and Mrs. Burton G. Tremaine, Meriden, Connecticut.

Claes Oldenburg, *Giant Hamburger*, 1962, Art Gallery of Ontario, Canada.

Robert Indiana, *Eat/Die*, 1962, two paintings, collection of the artist.

Andy Warhol, *Campbell's Soup*, 1965, Leo Castelli Gallery, New York.

William Bailey, *Still Life—Table with Ochre Wall*, 1972, Yale University Art Gallery.

Janet Fish, *#90, Two Apples*, 1978, Robert Miller Gallery, New York.

James Valerio, *Still Life*, 1979, Prudential Insurance Company of America.

Carolyn Brady, *Blueberry Jam*, 1979, Nancy Hoffmann Gallery, New York.

Discussion questions for the first hour

After the slides have been shown, or perhaps at appropriate junctures during the showing, students might be asked questions similar to the following:

1. Do you think it is easier or more difficult to attend aesthetically to real objects or to painted representations of them?
2. How is the percipient aided by the fact that the painting as a visual aesthetic object is delimited, that is, framed?
3. Attention has previously been paid to perceptual relationships between real objects. How does the surface area of a painting become important to relationships between the painted objects?
4. Think of depictions of food items as we are accustomed to seeing them in advertising. Are they different from the paintings just shown? If so, in what ways?
5. Could many, or indeed any, of these paintings be used for advertising? Why? Why not?
6. Which of the works impressed you most, and why?
7. Would you say that realistic, real-to-life depiction was the major concern of most of these artists?
8. It is often said that art expresses great ideas or deep emotions. Do you think any of the works just shown do so? If so, in what way? If not, why not? What other functions do you think the visual arts can serve?

The Student Handout should be distributed for study in preparation for the second class hour. Its material forms a transition between the first two hours. It is hoped that the memory of paintings viewed during the first hour will help make the content of the Handout more concrete to students. Furthermore, having read and understood the Handout will permit students to deal with greater skill and confidence the works to be discussed in the second hour.

Second class hour

The purpose of this hour is twofold. The primary objective is to give students some practice in *aesthetic criticism,* some opportunity to demonstrate their growing critical awareness. During the first part of the hour this will be restricted more or less to analysis and description of a work of art; during the latter part the concepts of subject matter and content and the critical skill of interpretation will be introduced.

A secondary objective is to give some indication of how art can take a simple theme and exfoliate it into something of considerable human interest. More to the point, students will be made aware of the human propensity for elaborating and refining the satisfaction of basic needs into occasions that have intrinsic values of their own: eating to satisfy hunger becomes the family meal, the jovial party or picnic the festive banquet. And students should also begin to note that in many instances a painting is not content to record the multifarious human interactions that accompany meal-taking but supplies something almost amounting to a commentary upon them.

Since the hour will be devoted chiefly to critical discourse about works of art, a matter barely touched on previously might open the discussion: the difference between works of art and ordinary things experienced as aesthetic objects. (Students are, of course, to be asked first what *they* think that difference is.) The main distinction is not the presence or absence of the sorts of items presented in the Handout—a scenic vista may have more of them than a work of modern minimal painting. Rather, the most telling difference lies in the obvious fact that paintings are human artifacts; works of art can in fact be defined as artifacts specifically designed to be experienced aesthetically. It is their having been made for a purpose, among other things, that makes it possible to bring the full gamut of critical skills to bear upon them. With natural objects one is usually content to take in their aesthetic properties and declare oneself more or less delighted; it is unusual to analyze, interpret, and evaluate them. But works of art have a maker who is responsible for their being what they are. Furthermore, whatever other intentions an artist may have had, the completed work always displays an *aesthetic* intention, which is to be interesting to perception because of the nature of its elements, relations, and qualities.

When it is suggested that a work of art may usefully be regarded as a humanly designed artifact that has the capacity to afford a high degree of aesthetic experience, or that it is something intended to give a marked aesthetic character to experience, the point is not that this is all that an artist might have intended—in many instances that would be obviously wrong—but that aesthetic values are properties of all artworks, whatever their other values may be, and it is their overall aesthetic value that ultimately makes them worthwhile to look at. It is therefore reasonable to assume then that in inviting a viewer's aesthetic interest, works of art are doing what they do best. Aesthetic criticism does not ignore the semantic aspects or meanings of a work, but it does take account of the ways in which meaning is a function of a network of relations and qualities which make works of art what they are. This is what it means to illuminate a work of art as art and not only as a social or cultural document. Aesthetic criticism, that is, is a way of doing justice to a work of art.

The instructor will now want to determine whether and how well the Handout has equipped students to take a first step toward critical analysis and description. To this end, one of the still lifes viewed during the preceding hour can be shown, namely, H. Fantin-Latour, *Still Life* (1866, National Gallery, Washington, D. C.).

Discussion

Students should be invited to talk about this work with some of the concepts contained in the Handout. This will also give the instructor an opportunity to clear up lingering misunderstandings. It is expected that students will discover on their own most of the characteristics of this work indicated below. If not, astute questioning and prodding by the instructor will help them notice these features:

1. In the main, the objects represented are of three kinds: vessels or containers (vase, cup, basket); natural objects (flowers, fruit); flat objects (book, tray, tabletop). The basket, being crudely manufactured of natural materials, is intermediary between natural and man-made objects.
2. The smaller objects are principally of two kinds: roughly spherical, self-enclosed, weighty (fruit); delicate, fragile, and open (cup, flowers). The peeled orange on the tray is intermediary between open, hollow and solid, massive objects.
3. The color scheme is divided by an imaginary diagonal line running from the upper left-hand to the lower right-hand corner of the painting. Below and to the left of that line, colors are generally warm, dark, more earthy (fruit, basket, table, tray). Above and to the right of that line, the colors are cooler (book, vase, flowers, background).
4. Despite the roughly bipartite color division described above, there are subtle gradations of color—emergings into prominence and fadings away—that move counterclockwise in an approximately circular pattern. Yellow and orange colors appear and are concentrated in the fruit basket,

Figure III.1.   *Still Life;* Henri FANTIN-LATOUR; National Gallery of Art, Washington; Chester Dale Collection (Date: dated 1866; Canvas; 24⅜″ × 29½″).

are carried through the fruit on the table and tray, and fade out in the trace of gold on the rim of the cup and saucer. White begins to appear on the inside of the orange peel, is stronger in the cup, stronger still on the side of the book, and makes sporadic reappearances in the flowers and the highlights on the vase. Blue has its largest area in the book cover but is at its most striking in the vase; it then disappears in the shadows of the leaves. The latter, of course, introduce green, which is repeated in the one leaf tucked between the fruit and echoed, more faintly, in two of the apples and pears.

5.   The most isolated object is the vase with flowers. It neither overlaps nor is overlapped by any other form. Still, it is integrated with the overall design in a number of ways. There is a triangular relationship in terms of similarity of shape among the most prominent of the flowers, the cup to the right, and the peeled orange to the left. In terms of color, a line extends from the two lightest flowers to the cup, another through the pink and red flowers to the red apple on the right within the basket. Two other color relationships are between the blue of the vase and that of the book, and the green of the leaves and the green in the basket.

6.   Despite an initial appearance of stasis, the design is subtly brought to life through a number of criss-crossing diagonals and the absence of strong horizontals and verticals. How, it might be asked, would the composition change if (a) the tabletop paralleled the picture frame, and (b) the orange on the tray was moved slightly to the right so as to form a vertical axis with the vase?

7.   Though still lifes generally lack drama and tension, a muted note of precariousness and unease is introduced by the tray projecting perilously beyond the table surface.

In the next series of paintings to be shown, the human figure will emerge, at first merely in conjunction with food items and the still life, but soon as the center of interest. Because of this added complexity, the slides should be prefaced by some remarks about the relationship between subject matter—what the picture represents—and the purely aesthetic or formal properties, or the "how" of the presenting. This distinction between the what and the how (which is not as clear-cut as it is here made to appear for the sake of manageability) is sometimes marked as one between form and content or presentation and representation. But it is perhaps easiest to distinguish between subject matter and content. As subject matter one indicates in simple and straightforward (that is, unanalyzed and uninterpreted) terms what the painting shows us: an inventory of figures and objects, or a type of scene and setting. Determination of content, on the other hand, requires the percipient to consider how the aesthetic qualities of the work make the objects appear in a distinctive and often startlingly unexpected light, how the figures are characterized and, in the case of some complex representational paintings, how the work is to be interpreted.

Perhaps the following three categories are helpful here, though they are by no means precise. (1) All paintings, even totally nonobjective ones, have a distinctive overall quality or tone; that is, having noted all the various qualities that belong to all of its component parts, one usually becomes aware of a quality, though perhaps not a definable one, that belongs to the whole but not necessarily to all of any of its parts. (One can easily think of abstract paintings that are, on the whole, gloomy or joyous.) (2) Most figurative or representational paintings also have a content which may be at variance with its subject matter. It is difficult to make this clear in connection with still lifes since they are for the most part formal exercises. In this connection students may recall the painting by Magritte entitled *The Listening Chamber* which manages to make an apple into an oppressive, menacing thing; an apple is the subject matter, menace its content. Another example might be Bonnard's *Le Compotier Blanc*. Here the subject matter of fruit is bland and almost unrecognizable, yet the content could be called "juiciness" because of the fruity, appealing colors used elsewhere in the painting. (3) In the case of some representational paintings, especially those containing human figures, the determination of content may involve a somewhat more sustained effort called an interpretation, and we sometimes call the content which is arrived at via interpretation the "meaning" of the work. The works to be shown presently will give students some indication of what interpretation is and when it is appropriately undertaken.

Slides to be shown

The following works, or a suitable selection from or substitutes for them, should again be presented fairly rapidly with only minimal commentary. The paintings depict examples of several of the different types of human attitudes and concerns connected with eating and drinking for physical survival and, under more prosperous conditions, with the sheer enjoyment of food and drink. The slides have been grouped thematically.

1. The subject matter of these three paintings has to do with the preparation of meals. It should also be noted that the human figure moves from being an adjunct to a still life to a position of prominence.
    a. Pieter Aertsen, *Kitchen Scene with Christ in the House of Martha and Mary*, 1553, Boymans-van Beuiningen Museum, Rotterdam.
    b. Jean-Baptiste-Siméon Chardin, *Home from the Market*, c. 1738, Louvre, Paris.
    c. Diego Velazquez, *Old Women Cooking Eggs*, 1618, National Gallery of Scotland, Edinburgh.
2. Annibale Carraci, *The Bean Eater*, c. 1585, Galleria Colonna, Rome. This is the first painting showing a single figure, a peasant, eating alone simply to satisfy his hunger.
3. The subject of peasants at their meals became a favorite with genre painters. Often it served mainly to present picturesque peasant types, as with:
    a. Louis Le Nain, *Peasants at Supper*, 1641, The Louvre, Paris.
    b. Vincent Van Gogh, *The Potato Eaters*, 1885, Stedelikj Museum, Amsterdam. Here and in the next work, the emphasis is on the solemnity and gratitude of those who do not take their meals for granted.
    c. Charles de Groux, *Grace before the Meal*, 1874, Musée des Beaux-Arts, Ghent.
4. Even more popular was the theme of meals and merrymaking, of people enjoying both food and drink and each other's company.
    a. Jacob Jordaens, *The King Drinks*, 1638, Musées Royaux des Beaux-Arts, Brussels.
    b. Jan Steen, *Merry Company*, c. 1666–1670. Mauritshuis, The Hague, Netherlands.
    c. Jan Steen, *The Garden of the Inn*, n.d., Staatliche Museen, Berlin.
    d. Pierre August Renoir, *The Luncheon of the Boating Party*, 1881, Phillips Collection, Washington, D.C.
5. Mealtime is also an occasion when children receive special attention and instruction.
    a. François Boucher, *Le Déjeuner*, 1739, Louvre, Paris.
    b. Jean-Baptiste-Siméon Chardin, *Benediction*, 1740, Louvre, Paris.
6. So common a subject as eating and feasting lends itself easily to moralizing.
    a. Hieronymous Bosch, (Early Period, 1475–1480) *Gula (Gluttony)*, from *The Seven Deadly Sins*, Prado, Madrid.
    b. Peter Brueghel, *The Land of Cockaigne*, 1567, Alte Pinakothek, Munich. Ostensibly an illustration of a popular fable (subject matter), the content of this work is gluttony and self-indulgence.
    c. Jean Le Clerc, *Memento Mori*, 1615–1620, The Isaac Delgado Museum of Art, New Orleans.

7. Meals can be extended and formalized into banquets—great and often stately events. Painters have left records of such affairs, sometimes complete with portraits of the principal figures.

   a. Limbourg Brothers. January page, *Book of Hours of the Duke of Berry*, 1416, Musée Condé, Chantilly. The warlike scene in the background is a tapestry.

   b. Paolo Veronese, *Marriage at Cana*, 1590, Louvre, Paris, While ostensibly a religious work, it is very much a portrayal of a Venetian gala event.

   c. Frans Hals, *Banquet of the Officers of the Guild of Archers of St. George of Haarlem*, 1639, Frans Hals Museum, Haarlem.

8. Some modern works offer a stark contrast to the scenes viewed thus far.

   a. Edward Hopper, *Nighthawks*, 1942, Art Institute of Chicago. In this cold and aseptic-looking restaurant, consumption is reduced to the minimal cup of coffee.

   b. Edward Kienholz, *The Beanery*, 1965, Stedeljik Museum, Amsterdam. People crowd around this lunch counter, yet there is none of the conviviality and relaxed spirit seen in earlier paintings. The figures are faceless, alienated, anonymous.

9. Biblical episodes that unite the protagonists around a table have challenged many artists.

   a. Hieronymous Bosch, *Marriage at Cana*, Early Period 1475–1480, Boymans-van Beuiningen Museum, Rotterdam.

   b. Leonardo da Vinci, *Last Supper*, 1495–1498, Santa Maria delle Grazie, Milan.

   c. Michelangelo Caravaggio, *Christ at Emmaus*, c. 1598, The National Gallery, London.

An extension of the last theme, that is, biblical scenes, will provide students practice not only in analyzing and comparing paintings but also in interpreting their content. The subject matter in the following three paintings is the same, for example, the Last Supper, but each painting is subject to a different interpretation. The works to be presented are: Leonardo da Vinci, *Last Supper* (previously shown); Andrea del Castagno, *Last Supper*, c. 1445–1450, S. Apollonia, Florence; Tintoretto, *Last Supper*, 1592–1594, San Giorgio Maggiore, Venice.

Discussion

Students should discuss points of similarity and difference of the three above-mentioned works. All three works should be examined in terms of these concepts: (1) scene represented, (2) space, (3) lighting, (4) figures, (5) emphasis, (6) content. The specific objective is to have students realize how items 1 through 5, singly or collectively, influence item 6.

It is suggested that the Castagno and the Leonardo be compared first as they are superficially similar.

Figure III.2.　Andrea del Castagno, *The Last Supper*, c. 1445–50. Fresco. S. Apollonia, Florence. Alinari/Art Resource, N.Y.

1. Both works depict that moment during the Last Supper when Jesus prophesies his betrayal.
2. Both works are murals on the wall of a refectory, that is, a dining hall in a monastery. Both give the illusion of being architectural extensions of those halls. However, in the Castagno painting that extension is a beautiful pavilion of little depth. Vision is arrested by strong elements that parallel the picture plane (especially the table and the vividly patterned marble insets in the wall). In the Leonardo, the dining hall is more austere, but it displays the painter's mastery of the science of spatial organization. Vanishing lines guide the eye toward the figure of Christ on whom they seem to converge. Thus the formal elements of the composition also reinforce the thematic emphasis.
3. In both works the lighting is even and natural, in the Castagno its source being the windows to the right. The light lends volume and plasticity to the figures but avoids strong contrasts.
4. Most interesting are differences in the placement and characterization of figures. In the Castagno, the figures are presented in a severe row of shapes all but one of which depart little from a rigidly upright position. The figures have a hard, sculptural quality which underscores their frieze-like arrangement. In the Leonardo, the figures compose themselves into four groups of three, two to either side of Christ. One discovers more interaction between them and, most importantly, a great diversity of individual response. In fact, the whole is a careful psychological study of how different types would react to the intelligence just received. Though clearly drawn and isolable, these figures are not nearly so detached—both pictorially and psychologically—as those in the Castagno.
5. Emphasis in a painting of this subject would necessarily fall on the figure of Christ. In the Leonardo this is obviously the case. Jesus is

Figure III.3.   Leonardo da Vinci, *The Last Supper*, c. 1495–98. Mural painting, 15'1⅛″ × 28'10½″. Santa Maria della Grazie, Milan. Alinari/Art Resource, N.Y.

at the center, framed by the lighted window area. The figure assumes the shape of a stable, attention-commanding triangle and the gestures of the other figures point to it. The character of secondary interest, Judas (the one upsetting the salt cellar) is not accentuated nearly as much as it is in the Castagno. Here Judas receives almost as much emphasis as Christ. Judas is visibly set apart—on our side of the barrier formed by the table, deprived of a halo, and somewhat larger in scale. The chief device for drawing the eye to the figure of Christ is the lively marble pattern above it.

6.   Because of the solemn relieflike character that the Last Supper scene assumes in the Castagno, the content could be interpreted as the timelessness of the significance of the event, with a subsidiary meaning, due to the prominence of the Judas figure, perhaps being that of the loathesomeness of betrayal. The content of the Leonardo, because of the striking rendering of psychological differences of expression, could be the human significance of the event, that is, the shock and disbelief at the discovery of evil.

Tintoretto's version of the Last Supper is amazingly different on all points.

1.   The picture portrays the moment when Jesus offers the bread and wine as the sacrificial body of redemption.

2.   The setting is more like a rustic inn than a banquet hall; the meal in progress appears less formal. The spatial composition is more open in comparison with the other works. The drastic diagonals of the table and floor lead to an indefinite point beyond the picture. Thus the viewer's

attention is pulled into the picture with a rush but is then brought forward again, attracted by the large figures in the foreground.
3. The illumination is almost melodramatic, emanating from sources both natural (the lamp) and supernatural (the luminosity surrounding the Christ figure). Light falls strongly and unevenly on the figures, creating vivid contrasts.
4. Figures are greater in number and, owing to the deep picture space, of many gradations of size. But even the larger figures are less isolable. This more intricate relationship is due to the tendency of the eye to move swiftly across the figures, led on by the strongly lighted areas and contrasting colors.
5. Emphasis on the principal figure is created solely by light, that is, the radiance issuing from Christ.
6. The main effect of the picture is one of involvement and excitement (created by the qualities of spatial movement, lighting, and strong color contrasts) as well as mystery (due to the dark, shadowy areas but also the presence of the angelic host above, taking shape miraculously in the smoke from the oil lamp). The content of this picture, therefore, could be the mystical rapture appropriate to the religious meaning of this moment.

Further discussion

1. Compare the works just discussed to other interpretations of the Last Supper, for examples,:
   a. Andrea del Sarto, *The Last Supper*, 1526–1527, Convent of S. Salvi, Florence.
   b. Dirk Bouts, *The Last Supper*, 1464–1667, Collegiate Church of St. Pierre, Belgium.
   c. Salvador Dali, *The Sacrament of the Last Supper*, 1955, National Gallery, Washington, D.C.
   d. Emil Nolde, *The Last Supper*, 1909, Stiftung Seebüll Ada and Emil Nolde, Neukirchen (Schleswig), Germany.
2. Further compare interpretations of the Supper at Emmaus, for examples:
   a. Michelangelo Carravaggio, *Supper at Emmaus*, c. 1600–1601, National Gallery, London.
   b. Jacopo Bassano, *Supper at Emmaus*, 16th cen., Cittadella, near Vicenza.
   c. Jacopo Pontormo, *Supper at Emmaus*, 1525, Uffizi, Florence.
   d. Rembrandt, *Christ at Emmaus*, 1618, Louvre, Paris.

Third class hour

The general objective of this hour is to explore whether visual works of art can help students achieve humanistic understanding and insight, and if so, what forms such understanding might take. The underlying

Figure III.4. Tintoretto, *The Last Supper*, 1592–94. 12′ × 18′8″. San Giorgio Maggiore, Venice.

assumption is that humanistic understanding is essential to success in the quest for self-cultivation.

A first task is to detect the students' notion of humanistic understanding and of how it might serve them. Adolescents in particular are concerned about personal identity and the search for self which in a pluralistic society undergoing rapid changes in its basic attitudes, beliefs, and values is difficult, to say the least. Discussion might center on what seems to remain constant about the human condition in the midst of so much change, or whether there is anything stable about human nature over time. In particular, does the past continue to serve persons in important ways? An interest in the past for its relevance to the present has always been essential to the meaning of "humanistic" and "the humanities," and this sense should be retained when we speak of "humanistic understanding." The original question of whether the art of painting could be a potential source of humanistic understanding can now be answered provisionally. Paintings, in addition to being artifacts designed for aesthetic experience, are also historical documents and can be examined as such. What they can document or, if this is too strong a word, suggest and intimate about the lives and values of those who made and those who admired them is the topic to be taken up presently.

But first it is necessary to ensure that the shift in emphasis now about to occur does not confuse students and obscure the achievement of the preceding two hours. It will be recalled that those hours were devoted to developing the attitude proper to the aesthetic experience of perceptual qualities in general and the analytic and interpretive skills needed to apprehend the full aesthetic value of paintings in particular. Stress was placed on the self-sufficiency and the self-enclosedness of aesthetic experience. It was maintained that in aesthetic experience proper, the individual considers only the internal, perceptual evidence supplied by the work of art and largely disregards external relations with reality. Clearly with the introduction of the notion of humanistic understanding, the purely perceptual orientation must be augmented. For whatever humanistic knowledge can be culled from a painting does for the most part depend to a considerable degree on external knowledge—historical, art historical, biographic, and iconographic.

The material to be developed now, however, is not really antithetical to what has gone before. As mentioned in the Introduction, to obtain the maximum benefit from a work of art, one ought to realize its aesthetic value in critical assessment of its aesthetic properties. However, the way these aesthetic qualities are perceived is often greatly influenced by some kinds of external knowledge gained about the work. For example, one may have a perfectly enjoyable aesthetic experience of a painting depicting a number of objects. Yet should one learn that the painting is an allegory and that each object in it has a given symbolic meaning, a qualitative change in subsequent perceptions of the work's aesthetic qualities is sure to occur. To put it differently, although for pedagogic purposes aesthetic experience, critical skills, and humanistic understanding are being treated separately, they should not be construed as having no points of contact in the actual experience of works of art.

The two principal works to be considered continue the theme of feasting and banqueting, though many of the other works to be shown do not. The first portion of the discussion will center on Pieter Brueghel, the Elder, *The Peasant Wedding* (c. 1565, Kunsthistorisches Museum, Vienna).

If the instructor thinks the time well spent, students could be asked briefly to analyze and describe the work along lines with which they should by now be somewhat familiar. They might notice, for example, (1) a similarity in structure to Tintoretto's *Last Supper*; (2) the relative flatness of the figures; (3) the unifying function performed by color, especially red.

Discussion: Works by Brueghel

Students should be asked what they have, quite literally, "learned" merely from looking at this picture and without being given much information about it. The two most obvious items are: (1) what Dutch peasants looked like around the year 1550; (2) that around the middle of the sixteenth century there apparently was a market for this sort of picture.

But what sort of picture is it and what does its presence at that time signify? Here, of course, one must have recourse to outside knowledge. The work is in a tradition called genre painting and is, in fact, an early sample of it. Genre paintings have ordinary objects or common people in everyday activities as their subject matter. Their emergence represents something of a revolution in taste since—and this one also has to know in order to appreciate fully the significance of this work—until about that time respectable subject matter for painting was almost exclusively religious or mythological. The fact that people were now ready to decorate their homes with paintings depicting peasants clearly means that secular concerns received more attention. We should probably resist, however, the temptation to infer an awakening social consciousness from the fact that simple country folk were now thought worth immortalizing in paint.

Brueghel was one of the most innovative artists in history, but not only because he was among the first genre painters. He was also a great deal more independent than artists before him as he very rarely had to rely on commissions. That left him as free in the choice and treatment of his subjects as the modern painter. But such freedom does not necessarily mean that the artist "expressed himself," as we would put it today, in each of his works. Whether the artist had a point of view or attitude that he chose to embody in his work can be established—though perhaps never conclusively—only after examination of the whole body of his work.

Figure III.5.   Pieter Brueghel, The Elder, *The Peasant Wedding*, c. 1565. Panel, 45″ × 64″. Kunsthistorisches Museum, Vienna. Marburg/Art Resource, N.Y.

For example, it is difficult to say whether *The Peasant Wedding* suggests any particular attitude toward its characters. The figures are certainly not idealized or sentimentalized (as they would be centuries later in romantic depictions of stalwart tillers of the soil). One could say that people are set down in a rather matter-of-fact way. But perhaps not quite; connoisseurs of Brueghel's works might detect even in this rather sedate gathering a leaning toward the unflattering, as in the plain, smug bride (in front of the green wall-hanging). This quality is much more pronounced in a painting which is almost a companion piece to this one, *The Peasant Dance*, (c. 1567, Kunsthistorisches Museum, Vienna).

These peasants are certainly a boisterous and not altogether lovely lot. They are not caricatures and are not condescended to, yet there is an undeniable emphasis on uncouthness. Nonetheless, we should not hasten to conclusions about Brueghel's "view of human nature," since "human nature" is an abstract concept and can be depicted only with difficulty. However, when one finds preference for a certain rendering of the human figure throughout an artist's career, one could take it as suggestive of the artist's conception of this type as typical, that is, representative of what he found most prevalent among his contemporaries.

Another noteworthy structural feature of *The Peasant Wedding* is that visual access is gained to the scene across a large tray (a door taken off its hinges, actually) with dinner plates, while the entire left corner is given over to drinking vessels. This stress on food and drink should recall *The Land of Cockaigne* (previously shown), where the pies on the roof closely resemble the plates on the tray. We said of this work that its content was probably gluttony and self-indulgence. We can now go further and claim that *The Land of Cockaigne* ascribes these traits to all mankind—the knight, the peasant, and the scribe being representative types—and that it seems to suggest that these human weaknesses are ineliminable. This interpretation also depends on another design motif frequently used by Brueghel: wheel-like and circular shapes to symbolize repetition, recurrence, lack of change. Here the three figures are disposed as the spokes of a wheel, the table above them is suggestive of a wheel, and circular forms abound. In short, if this work does indeed give us something to understand about human nature, it does so on the formal as well as on the narrative level.

Returning to *The Peasant Wedding,* a third feature this work has in common with several other of Brueghel's paintings is the tendency to obscure the main protagonists. This is a wedding scene; but which of the male figures is the bridegroom? It is difficult to say. Even the bride, though visually more isolable, remains in the background.

Show *The Procession to Calvary* (1564, Kunsthistorisches Museum, Vienna)

Students should be asked which three characteristics of Brueghel's art are exemplified in this work. They are:

1. The main figure, Christ stumbling under the weight of the cross, is nearly lost in the crowd, though it is at the center of the picture.
2. The crowd, depicted as Brueghel's contemporaries (a common practice in religious painting to encourage emotional identification with the subject), teems with crude, jostling, and pummeling types, eagerly anticipating the spectacle of an execution.
3. Again there are wheel-like and circular shapes to indicate that what goes on here is about what one should expect, people being what they are. Notice, for example, the circle formed by the early arrivals, the several torture wheels on their poles (with some fragments of the last victims still attaching); the improbably situated—and therefore symbolical— windmill, going round and round on its circular platform.

Additional remarks: The group in the right foreground, that is, Mary, St. John, and the mourning women, are the only ones showing sorrow, but they are decidedly not part of the unfolding scene. In dress and attitude they closely resemble Flemish paintings of a century earlier. This only further accentuates the behavior of a mindless mob. The painting also makes clear why Brueghel was renowned as a landscape painter. The beautiful vista in the left background contrasts with the blighted patch of ground, littered with reminders of past executions and soon to be overcast by the dark clouds to the right.

Students should now be asked how, considering the elements just pointed out, they would interpret the painting.

One piece of historical information has been deliberately withheld thus far: the soldiers who are along to keep order and see that the crucifixions come off as scheduled wear the red coats of the Spanish occupation forces of Brueghel's day. It would, that is, be easy to read

Figure III.6.   Pieter Brueghel, The Elder, *The Peasant Dance*, c. 1567. Panel, 45″ × 64¼″. Kunsthistorisches Museum, Vienna.

some form of political protest into this work. However, one should keep in mind that since the scene is set in Brueghel's own time, these soldiers can be said simply to belong here.

The case is perhaps somewhat different, however, with *The Massacre of the Innocents* (c. 1566, Kunsthistorisches Museum, Vienna). First of all, we see here another art form Brueghel originated: the winter landscape, for this biblical scene is taking place in a Dutch village in mid-winter. This time the red-coated soldiers are the executors of a particularly cruel and inhuman measure. Those with some knowledge of sixteenth-century European history would find in the painting an obvious analogy between the slaughter of innocent infants and the brutalities visited on the Dutch under the Spanish occupation. Those with more precise historical information would recognize, though, that at the time this work was painted the most feared of the Spaniards, the Duke of Alba, had not yet arrived; the worst was yet to come. So, once more, the evidence is not clear-cut. This was gone into chiefly to underscore one point: we have to be careful about what kinds of external knowledge we accept as relevant to gaining a humanistic perspective on a work of art.

Finally, many of Brueghel's qualities are epitomized in *Magpie on the Gallows* (1568, Landesmuseum, Darmstadt). Once more we see reminders of death (gallows, skull) but also salvation (cross). Human life goes on as usual, and there is nothing edifying about it. The work might be a reference to a proverb then current in Holland and Germany: "The way to the gallows leads through pleasant pastures." But the most striking thing is the great beauty of the landscape. Gustav Glück writes: "It is just the contrast between the folly of man and the beauty of nature which corresponds so well with Brueghel's conception of the world and of mankind."[4]

Figure III.7. Pieter Brueghel, The Elder, *The Procession to Calvary*, 1564. Panel, 49″ × 67″. Kunsthistorisches Museum, Vienna. Marburg/Art Resource, N.Y.

Figure III.8. Pieter Brueghel, The Elder, *The Massacre of the Innocents*, c. 1566. Panel, 43 ¾" × 63". Kunsthistorisches Museum, Vienna.

Figure III.9.   Pieter Brueghel, The Elder, *Magpie on the Gallows*, 1568. Panel, 18″ ×
20″. Landesmuseum, Darmstadt.

Questions

1.   "Humanistic understanding" may at times mean merely learning some-
     thing about people of a past era. Have these paintings provided such
     knowledge?
2.   More often, however, "humanistic understanding" is not so much some
     item of factual knowledge as a new insight, a greater awareness, or a
     deeper appreciation. Have these works helped you gain any of these?
3.   Do you concur with what we can take to be Brueghel's estimate of the
     relative worth of the world of man and the world of nature?
4.   How do you think that the meaning of *The Procession to Calvary* could
     be conveyed in present-day terms, that is, in a modern painting?

Discussion: Two works by Veronese

Project Paolo Veronese, *Marriage at Cana* (previously shown). The
Italian painter Paolo Veronese (c. 1528–1588) was a contemporary of
Brueghel's, yet a greater contrast is hard to imagine. Brueghel, as said,
rarely took commissions; Veronese had all that he and his workshop
could handle. Many of Brueghel's customers were of the prosperous

Dutch middle class. Veronese worked chiefly for the Venetian aristocracy, decorating their villas in close cooperation with the architects. This explains Veronese's virtuosity in painting architectural settings, which contrasts with Brueghel's sensitivity to nature. In Brueghel, according to Charles de Tolnay, "the new valuation of *life,* the new conception of *nature* and the new *consciousness of God* appear in him for the first time fused into a *coherent picture of the world.*"⁵ Veronese is more concerned simply to delight the eye, which he does superbly. In his art the Venetian tradition of sumptuous paintings of pageantry reached its high point.

We intimated as much when this work was first shown briefly. That it is really a celebration of the glories of culture of Venice and indeed of the age is attested to by the number of portraits it contains in the guise of these figures. The group of musicians in the center, for example, gives us, among others, a portrait of Veronese on the left and of the great Titian on the right. There are portraits of royal personages such as Emperor Charles V, King Francis I of France, Queen Mary of England, and the Sultan Suleiman I of Turkey. Veronese was not being irreverent in combining a religious subject with this display of secular power, wealth, and pomp. Quite the contrary. "If I ever have time," he once wrote, "I want to represent a sumptuous banquet in a superb hall, at which will be present the Virgin, the Saviour, and St. Joseph. They will be served by the most brilliant retinue of angels which one can imagine, busied in offering them the daintiest viands and an abundance of splendid fruit in dishes of silver and gold. Other angels will hand them precious wines in transparent crystal glasses and gilded goblets, in order to show with what zeal blessed spirits serve the Lord."⁶

The main reason for touching on this is to guard against certain misapprehensions that can occur when we try to gain an understanding of the spirit of an age from its paintings. When some faith—religious beliefs or a political doctrine—is firmly established and unchallenged, its expression in art often takes on greater freedom, less literalness. This does not have to mean that people were negligent about their faith; it may merely indicate that they were very secure in it. But when that faith comes under attack or begins to waver, greater fervor in artistic expression and doctrinal purity in representation will often be officially insisted on. Veronese was to learn this after he had painted *The Feast in the House of Levi* (1573, Galleria dell' Accademia, Venice).

We must remember that this was the age of the Counter Reformation when the Catholic Church consolidated itself against further inroads by Protestantism and actually regained much territory. At the Council of Trent (1563) certain guidelines for the arts were decided upon. It was decreed, for instance, that images should not be painted and adorned with seductive charm and that no unusual image should be exhibited unless it had been approved by the bishop of the diocese. Veronese had painted this work as a *Last Supper*. It was thought unusual, and Veronese

Figure III.10. Paolo Veronese, *Marriage at Cana*, 1563. Canvas. Louvre, Paris.

Figure III.11. Paolo Veronese, *The Feast in the House of Levi*, 1573. Canvas, 18'3" × 42'. Galleria dell' Accademia, Venice. Alinari/Art Resource, N.U.

was called before the Inquisition. He was questioned particularly about the inclusion of buffoons, a man with a bleeding nose, men dressed as German soldiers (heretics), and the like. Part of his answer was: "We painters take the same license the poets and jesters take. . . . If in a picture there is some space to spare, I enrich it with figures according to the stories. . . . I paint pictures as I see fit and as well as my talent permits."[7] Veronese was given three months to correct the picture. He did not comply but instead changed the title to the present *The Feast in the House of Levi*. He was safe in doing this since the Scriptures provide no details about this incident.

Two points are important here. The most obvious is the fact that this is a historic incident of censorship. Less obvious to us today but more relevant to gaining an understanding of the role of the artist is Veronese's defense of his painting. An artist is demanding the freedom to be guided by aesthetic considerations, filling the picture space with what looks good to him. Veronese's art itself may not hold as much interest for us today as that of Brueghel, but the society in which he moved and which he celebrated, the forces that impinged on his life and tried to alter his art, and the way he stood up to them are still important for forming a proper appreciation of the development of the art of painting.

Questions

1. Are there anywhere in the modern world equivalents to the guidelines for the arts established by the Council of Trent, and are they being enforced?
2. Do you think that when art touches on people's values and beliefs, it should be as direct and literal as possible?
3. Can false pictures subvert true belief? What are contemporary opinions about the potency of visual images to influence people, and how are these opinions expressed?
4. Do we have artists today who, like Veronese, celebrate the accomplishments of our civilization?
5. What do you think is the proper role for the artist in society?

Notes to Appendix III

1 This unit was originally written as one of fifteen prepared for a project titled A Contemporary Course in the Humanities for Community College Students (NEH Grant ED-10555-74-412), James J. Zigerell, Project Director, Ralph A. Smith, Project Coordinator. Additional funds were provided by the Lilly Endowment. The materials were developed by faculty and staff from the City Colleges of Chicago, Coast Community College District of California, and Miami-Dade Community College. The unit discussed here was originally titled "Developing Critical Awareness: Visual Arts" and was developed by C. M. Smith. The unit has been edited and adapted for this volume.

A condensed version of the original unit was published in *Studies in Art Education* 25, no. 4 (Summer 1984), 238–244. Though the unit was prepared for beginning community college students, it can be modified for either secondary school instruction or the college level by simplifying, condensing, or, as the case might be, increasing the degree of complexity. It can also be used in teacher-training programs as an example of how to organize a unit of instruction. Comparable units can, of course, be designed for the literary and performing arts.

2 This point is usually overlooked by those who believe that the only way to involve students is by stressing the social relevance of contemporary works of art. My experience is that students are willing to address any kind of task provided its point is made apparent. And, of course, there is the danger of confusing social or cultural with aesthetic criticism.

3 The Student Handout follows in large the analysis of a visual design in Monroe C. Beardsley's *Aesthetics: Problems in the Philosophy of Criticism*, 2nd ed. (Indianapolis: Hackett, 1981), pp. 88–96, 168–77.

4 Gustav Glück, *Peter Brueghel, The Elder* (New York: George Braziller, 1936), p. 48.

5 As quoted in Glück, p. 10.

6 Quoted in William Fleming, *Arts and Ideas*, 7th ed. (New York: Holt, Rinehart and Winston, 1986), p. 308.

7 George Boas and Harold H. Wrenn, *What Is a Picture?* (Pittsburgh: University of Pittsburgh Press, 1964), p. 136.

Additional reading suggestions

Rudolf Arnheim, *Art and Visual Perception: A Psychology of the Creative Eye* [1954] (Berkeley and Los Angeles: University of California Press, 1974). A standard reference in the literature. This new version was completely rewritten.

George Boas and Harold Holmes Wrenn, *What Is a Picture?* (Pittsburgh: University of Pittsburgh Press, 1964). A lucid introduction to the art of painting. Organized around problems and themes.

Kenneth Clark, *Civilisation* (New York: Harper & Row, 1969). Text to the film series. A well-illustrated, civilized explanation of history and culture from the fall of the Roman Empire to the present day, dealing with a wide range of ideas.

Edmund B. Feldman, *Varieties of Visual Experience*, 3rd ed. (Englewood Cliffs, N.J.: Prentice-Hall, 1987). Contains a discussion of art criticism and is well illustrated.

E. H. Gombrich, *The Story of Art*, 13th ed., revised and enlarged (New York: Dutton, 1978). An excellent introductory text.

H. W. Janson and Joseph Kerman, *A History of Art and Music* (Englewood Cliffs, N.J.: Prentice-Hall, n.d.).

Relates the history of both arts while retaining the autonomy and independent development of each when required.

H. W. Janson and Anthony Janson, *History of Art*, 3rd ed. (Englewood Cliffs, N.J.: Prentice-Hall, 1981).

This volume continues to be the standard history of principally Western art.

F. David Martin and Lee A. Jacobus, *The Humanities through the Arts*, 3rd ed. (New York: McGraw-Hill, 1983).

A systematic attempt to subsume the major arts under the humanities with "Perception Keys" to aid the student.

Harold Osborne. *The Art of Appreciation* (New York: Oxford University Press, 1970).

An excellent interpretation of appreciation written from an aesthetic standpoint. Concentrates on the visual arts.

Erwin Panofsky, *Meaning in the Visual Arts* [1955] (Chicago: University of Chicago Press, 1982).

Of particular interest is the Introduction, "The History of Art as a Humanistic Discipline."

Stephen Pepper, *Principles of Art Appreciation* (New York: Harcourt, Brace & World, 1949).

One of the standard works in the literature.

D. W. Prall, *Aesthetic Analysis* [1936] (New York: Thomas Y. Crowell, 1967).

A classic in aesthetics.

John Richardson, *Art: The Way It Is*, 3rd ed. (Englewood Cliffs, N.J.: Prentice-Hall, 1986).

A highly literate and readable introduction with ample illustrations.

Ralph A. Smith, ed., *Aesthetics and Criticism in Art Education: Problems in Defining, Explaining, and Evaluating Art* (Chicago: Rand McNally, 1966).

Indicates the relevance of aesthetics, art history, and art criticism to the teaching of art in the schools. Contains four appendixes: "A Questionnaire for Picture-Analysis" and "The Criticism of Criticism" by Thomas Munro; "The Categories of Painting" by Monroe C. Beardsley; and "Parts of the Cinema" by Robert Gessner.

Joshua C. Taylor, *Learning to Look: A Handbook for the Visual Arts* (Chicago: University of Chicago Press, 1957).

Still a helpful approach to perceiving the visual arts.

Heinrich Woelfflin, *Principles of Art History* [1915]. Trans. M. D. Hottinger (New York: Dover, n.d.).

Still invaluable for its method of paired comparison of artworks in different styles.

Richard Wollheim, *Painting as an Art* (Princeton: Princeton University Press, 1987).

An example of psychological aesthetic criticism.

Notes

Introduction

1 Lawrence A. Cremin, *The Genius of American Education* (New York: Vintage Books, 1966), p. 108.
2 Jacques Barzun, ed., *Pleasures of Music* (New York: Viking Press, 1960), p. 16.
3 Israel Scheffler, *Of Human Potential* (Boston: Routledge & Kegan Paul, 1985), p. 5.

Chapter 1   Art in cultural context

1 Albert William Levi, "The Poverty of the Avant Garde," *Journal of Aesthetic Education* 8, no. 4 (October 1974), 12.
2 Ernst Cassirer, *An Essay on Man* (New Haven: Yale University Press, 1944).
3 Jacques Barzun, "Art and Educational Inflation," *Journal of Aesthetic Education* 12, no. 4 (October 1978), 16.
4 John Goodlad, *A Place Called School* (New York: McGraw-Hill, 1984), p. 220.
5 Arnold Hauser, *Philosophy of Art History* (New York: Alfred Knopf, 1959), p. 369: "One can hardly make any statement about art without having to admit, in some context or other, the very opposite. The work of art is at once form and content, an affirmation and a deception, play and revelation, natural and artificial, purposeful and purposeless, within history and outside of history, personal and superpersonal."
6 For reproductions of both Caravaggio and Stella, see Frank Stella, *Working Space* (Cambridge: Harvard University Press, 1986).
7 See Leo Steinberg, "Contemporary Art and the Plight of Its Public," in his *Other Criteria: Confrontations with Twentieth-Century Art* (New York: Oxford University Press, 1972), p. 15; and Harold Rosenberg, *The Anxious Object: Art Today and Its Audience* (New York: Horizon Press, 1964). The Steinberg essay was first published in 1962.
8 See Charles Frankel's remarks in "The New Egalitarianism and the Old," *Commentary* 56, no. 3 (September 1973). Cf. R. A. Smith, "The Question

of Elitism," in *Excellence in Art Education*, updated version (Reston: National Art Education Association, 1987), pp. 67–83.

9 Kenneth Clark, "Art and Society," in his *Moments of Vision* (London: John Murray, 1981), pp. 63–81.

10 Quoted by John Canaday in his *Lives of the Painters*, Vol. 1 (New York: W. W. Norton, 1969), p. 16.

11 Henry Adams, *The Education of Henry Adams* (New York: Modern Library, 1931), chap. 25.

12 For extensive references to the literature on environmental aesthetics, see Yrjö Sepänmaa, *The Beauty of Environment* (Helsinki: Svomalainen Tiedeakatemia, 1986).

13 Thomas Crow, "The Return of Frank Herron," in *Endgame: Reference and Simulation in Recent Painting and Sculpture* (Cambridge: MIT Press, 1986), p. 18: "Certain schools, such as Cal Arts, have begun to function as efficient academies for the new scene, equipping students with both expectations and realizable plans for success while still in their twenties."

14 Jack Burnham, *Great Western Salt Works: Essays on the Meaning of Post-Formalist Art* (New York: Braziller, 1974).

15 Joseph Bensman and Arthur J. Vidich, *The New American Society: The Revolution of the Middle Class* (Chicago: Quadrangle Books, 1971).

16 Clark, *Moments of Vision*, p. 79.

17 Ibid.

18 Barzun, *The Use and Abuse of Art* (Princeton: Princeton University Press, 1974).

19 Ibid., p. 17.

20 Rosenberg, *The Anxious Object*, chap. 3; and *The De-definition of Art* (New York: Horizon Press, 1972), chap. 2.

21 Rosenberg, *Artworks and Packages* (New York: Horizon Press, 1969); and *Art and Other Serious Matters* (Chicago: University of Chicago Press, 1985).

22 Rosenberg, *Artworks and Packages*, p. 12.

23 Ibid., p. 13.

24 Mentioned by Francis Sparshott in "Showing and Saying, Looking and Learning: An Outsider's View of Art Museums," *Journal of Aesthetic Education* 19, no. 2 (Summer 1985), 72.

25 Rosenberg, *Art and Other Serious Matters*, p. 51.

26 Rosenberg, *Artworks and Packages*, p. 15.

27 Ibid., p. 16.

28 Rosenberg, "Avant-Garde," in Louis Kronenberger, ed., *Quality: Its Image in the Arts* (New York: Atheneum, 1969), pp. 419–49.

29 See the opening essay in Hilton Kramer's *The Age of the Avant-Garde: An Art Chronicle of 1956–1972* (New York: Farrar, Straus and Giroux, 1973), pp. 3–19.

30 Clifton Fadiman, "Communication and the Arts: A Practitioner's Notes," in Howard E. Kiefer and Milton K. Munitz, eds., *Perspectives in Education,*

Religion, and the Arts (Albany: State University of New York Press, 1970), pp. 312–28.

31 Ibid., p. 318.

32 Raymond Williams, *Television: Technology and Cultural Form* (New York: Schocken, 1975), p. 59: "It is clearly one of the unique characteristics of advanced industrial societies that drama as an experience is now an intrinsic part of everyday life, at a quantitative level which is so very much greater than any precedent as to seem a fundamental qualitative change."

33 Raymond Williams, *The Long Revolution* (New York: Harper & Row, 1966). The long revolution consists of three: a democratic, an industrial, and a cultural revolution, the last being concerned mainly with communications and the extension of literacy.

34 John Dewey, *The Public and Its Problems* (Denver: Alan Swallow, 1927), pp. 183–84. Cf. R. A. Smith, "The Mass Media and John Dewey's Liberalism," *Educational Theory* 25, no. 2 (April 1965), 83–93, 120.

35 Monroe C. Beardsley, "Art and Its Cultural Context," in his *The Aesthetic Point of View*, ed. Michael J. Wreen and Donald M. Callen (Ithaca: Cornell University Press, 1982), pp. 352–70.

36 Ibid., p. 352.

37 John Dewey, *Art as Experience* [1934] (Carbondale and Edwardsville: Southern Illinois University Press, 1987). A volume in the collected works of John Dewey, edited by Jo Ann Boydston. Introduction by Abraham Kaplan.

38 Beardsley, "Art and Its Cultural Context," p. 356.

39 See Beardsley's forward to Stefan Morawski's *Inquiries into the Fundamentals of Aesthetics* (Cambridge: MIT Press, 1974), pp. ix–xvi.

40 Beardsley, "Art and Its Cultural Context," p. 359.

41 See the essay on Freud in Lionel Trilling's *Beyond Culture* (New York: Harcourt Brace Jovanovich, 1978), pp. 77–102.

42 Beardsley, "Art and Its Cultural Context," p. 370.

43 George Steiner, "Humane Literacy," in his *Language and Silence* (New York: Atheneum, 1976), p. 100.

Chapter 2   Art in philosophical context

1 Francis Sparshott, *The Theory of the Arts* (Princeton: Princeton University Press, 1982), p. 3.

2 Monroe C. Beardsley, *Aesthetics: Problems in the Philosophy of Criticism* (1958) 2nd ed. (Indianapolis: Hackett, 1981). Contains a Postscript 1980.

3 Abraham H. Maslow, *The Farther Reaches of Human Nature* (New York: Viking Press, 1972).

4 The distinction, which contrasts the differences between the intuitive and scientific orientations of the mind, is a central theme of the writings of Jacques Barzun. Acknowledging his debt to Blaise Pascal, who gave an account of the orientations in his *Pensées*, Barzun provides a compressed

paraphrase of the distinction in his *Clio and the Doctors: Psycho-History, Quanto-History, and History* (Chicago: University of Chicago Press, 1974), pp. 91–92.

5 Monroe C. Beardsley, *The Aesthetic Point of View: Selected Essays*, ed. Michael J. Wreen and Donald M. Callen (Ithaca: Cornell University Press, 1982), pp. 285–97.

6 Beardsley, "Postscript," in *Aesthetics: Problems in the Philosophy of Criticism*, p. 1xi.

7 The term "gratification" is featured in Beardsley's "The Aesthetic Point of View," in his *The Aesthetic Point of View*, p. 22. For a tracing of Beardsley's efforts to characterize the hedonic character of aesthetic experience, see R. A. Smith, "The Aesthetics of Monroe C. Beardsley: Recent Work," *Studies in Art Education* 25, no. 3 (Spring 1984), 142–45.

8 See, for example, Beardsley's "An Aesthetic Definition of Art," in Hugh Curtler, ed., *What Is Art?* (New York: Haven, 1983), pp. 13–29. The volume is dedicated to Beardsley.

9 Beardsley, "The Aesthetic Point of View," in *The Aesthetic Point of View*, pp. 15–16.

10 Beardsley, "Aesthetic Welfare, Aesthetic Justice, and Educational Policy," ibid., pp. 111–24.

11 Beardsley, "The Aesthetic Point of View," ibid., p. 34.

12 Harold Osborne, *The Art of Appreciation* (New York: Oxford University Press, 1970), chap. 2.

13 Osborne, "The Twofold Significance of 'Aesthetic Value,' " *Philosophica* 36, no. 2 (1985), 5–24; and "Education in an Affluent State," *Journal of Aesthetic Education* 20, no. 4 (Winter 1986), 103–7.

14 Lionel Trilling, *The Liberal Imagination* (New York: Harcourt Brace Jovanovich, 1979), p. xiii.

15 Osborne, "The Twofold Significance of 'Aesthetic View,' " *Philosophica*, 22.

16 Nelson Goodman, *Languages of Art*, 2nd ed. (Indianapolis: Hackett, 1976).

17 Goodman, *Of Mind and Other Matters* (Cambridge: Harvard University Press, 1984), p. 1.

18 Goodman, ibid., pp. 7–8.

19 Ibid., p. 9.

20 Ibid., p. 84.

21 Howard Gardner, David Perkins, and Vernon Howard, "Symbol Systems: A Philosophical, Psychological, and Educational Investigation," in David R. Olson, ed., *Media and Symbols: The Forms of Expression, Communication, and Education* (Chicago: University of Chicago Press, 1974), pp. 27–55.

22 Goodman, *Ways of Worldmaking* (Indianapolis: Hackett, 1978), chap. 4.

23 Ibid., p. 67.

24 Goodman, *Of Mind and Other Matters*, p. 57.

25 Ibid., p. 136.

26 Ibid.
27 Ibid., p. 62.
28 Ibid., pp. 136–37.
29 Ibid., pp. 135–36.
30 Goodman, *Ways of Worldmaking*, p. 65.
31 Goodman, *Of Mind and Other Matters*, p. 59.
32 Ibid., pp. 60–61.
33 Francis Sparshott, *The Theory of the Arts* (Princeton: Princeton University Press, 1982), p. 597.
34 Goodman, *Ways of Worldmaking*, pp. 68–69.
35 Goodman, *Of Mind and Other Matters*, p. 137.
36 Ibid., pp. 82–83.
37 Ibid., p. 138.
38 Ibid., p. 5.
39 Ibid., p. 137.
40 Goodman, *Ways of Worldmaking*, p. 70.
41 Goodman, *Of Mind and Other Matters*, p. 85.
42 See, for example, E. F. Kaelin, *An Existentialist Aesthetic: The Theories of Sartre and Merleau-Ponty* (Madison: University of Wisconsin Press, 1962); *An Existential-Phenomenological Account of Aesthetic Education* (Department of Art Education: The Pennsylvania State University, ca. 1969); *Art and Existence* (Lewisburg: Bucknell University Press, 1970); and "Aesthetic Education: A Role for Aesthetics Proper," in R. A. Smith, ed., *Aesthetics and Problems of Education* (Urbana: University of Illinois Press, 1971), pp. 144–61.
43 Kaelin, "Aesthetic Education: A Role for Aesthetics Proper," in R. Smith, ed., *Aesthetics and Problems of Education*, pp. 151–55.
44 Ibid., p. 154.
45 Ibid., p. 155.
46 Kaelin, "Why Teach Art in the Schools?" *Journal of Aesthetic Education* 26, no. 4 (Winter 1986), 64–71.
47 Ibid., p. 66.
48 Ibid., p. 68.
49 Ibid., pp. 69–70.

Chapter 3   Art in educational context—The concept of aesthetic criticism

1 Israel Scheffler, "Philosophical Models of Teaching," in his *Inquiries: Philosophical Studies of Language, Science, and Learning* (Indianapolis: Hackett, 1986), p. 321.
2 George Steiner, *George Steiner: A Reader* (New York: Oxford University Press, 1984), p. 7.
3 Henry D. Aiken, ed., *Hume's Moral and Political Philosophy* (New York: Hafner, 1948), p. 178.
4 Scheffler, "Philosophical Models of Teaching," p. 320.

5   Ibid., p. 321.
6   H. Gene Blocker, *Philosophy of Art* (New York: Scribner's, 1979), p. 3.
7   Morris Weitz, *The Opening Mind* (Chicago: University of Chicago Press, 1977), p. 25.
8   John Wilson, "Education and Aesthetic Appreciation: A Review," *Oxford Review of Education* 3, no. 2 (1977), 202. Cf. his *Thinking with Concepts* (New York: Cambridge University Press, 1963).
9   P. H. Heath, "Concept," in Paul Edwards, ed., *The Encyclopedia of Philosophy*, vol. 2 (New York: Macmillan and Free Press, 1967), p. 177.
10 Marcia Eaton, *Basic Issues in Aesthetics* (Belmont: Wadsworth, 1988).
11 Ibid., p. 105.
12 Ibid., p. 114.
13 Jakob Rosenberg, *On Quality in Art: Criteria of Excellence, Past and Present* (Princeton: Princeton University Press, 1967).
14 Eaton, *Basic Issues in Aesthetics*, p. 118.
15 Ibid., p. 122.
16 I have discussed the question of elitism in my *Excellence in Art Education: Ideas and Initiatives*, updated version (Reston: National Art Education Association, 1987), chap. 4.
17 Eaton, *Basic Issues in Aesthetics*, p. 121. The implicit reference Eaton makes is to Kant's antinomy of taste. As DeWitt H. Parker puts it in his classic *The Principles of Aesthetics*, 2nd ed. (New York: Appleton-Century-Crofts, 1946), p. 103: " . . . as Kant pointed out, it is characteristic of conversation about art that the participants try to reach agreement in their judgments without acknowledging common principles with reference to which disputes can be decided. And yet, since no man is content to hold an opinion all by himself, but each tries to persuade the others of the validity of his own judgment, it would seem as if there must be some axioms or postulates admitted by all. Hence what Kant called the antinomy of taste: Thesis—the judgment of taste is not based on principles, for otherwise we would determine it by proofs; antithesis—the judgment of taste is based on principles, for otherwise, despite our disagreements, we should not be quarreling about it."
18 Brian S. Crittenden, "Persuasion: Aesthetic Argument and the Language of Teaching," in R. A. Smith, ed., *Aesthetic Concepts and Education* (Urbana: University of Illinois Press, 1970), pp. 227–62.
19 Ibid., p. 231.
20 Ibid., p. 241.
21 Lionel Trilling, "Mind in the Modern World," in his *The Last Decade: Essays and Reviews 1965–1975* (New York: Harcourt Brace Jovanovich, 1977), p. 122.
22 Crittenden, "Persuasion," p. 239.
23 Ibid., p. 242.
24 Ibid.

25 Frank Sibley, "Aesthetic Concepts," in Joseph Margolis, ed., *Philosophy Looks at the Arts*, 3rd ed. (Philadelphia: Temple University Press, 1987), pp. 45–6.
26 Crittenden, "Persuasion," p. 243.
27 Ibid., p. 244.
28 Ibid.
29 Ibid., p. 262.
30 Ibid., p. 229.
31 Ibid., p. 254.
32 Ibid., p. 256.
33 See Monroe C. Beardsley, *Aesthetics: Problems in the Philosophy of Criticism* (1958), 2nd ed. (Indianapolis: Hackett, 1981); *The Possibility of Criticism* (Detroit: Wayne State University Press, 1970); *The Aesthetic Point of View*, ed. Michael J. Wreen and Donald M. Callen (Ithaca: Cornell University Press, 1982); and "The Classification of Critical Reasons," *Journal of Aesthetic Education* 2, no. 3 (July 1968), reprinted in R. A. Smith, ed., *Aesthetics and Problems of Education* (Urbana: University of Illinois Press, 1971), pp. 435–44. All references are to this latter source.
34 Beardsley, "The Classification of Critical Reasons," in R. A. Smith, ed., *Aesthetics and Problems in Education*, p. 443.
35 Ibid.
36 Ibid.
37 Beardsley, *The Possibility of Criticism*, p. 43.
38 Beardsley, "The Classification of Critical Reasons," p. 444.
39 Ibid.
40 Ibid., pp. 437–48.
41 Ibid., p. 440.
42 Peter Kivy, *The Corded Shell: Reflections on Musical Expression* (Princeton: Princeton University Press, 1980), chap. 1.
43 Morris Weitz, *Philosophy in Literature* (Detroit: Wayne State University Press, 1963), especially the epilogue.
44 Beardsley, "Aesthetic Experience," in *The Aesthetic Point of View*, p. 292.
45 In this connection, some seldom remarked words of Beardsley's might be noted, for they clearly indicate the relevance of external knowledge to our understanding of works of art, knowledge which critics of Beardsley have sometimes said he does not sufficiently stress. For example, in his *Aesthetics* (1958, 1981), pp. 52–53, he writes: "We do not come to the object cold, and . . . our capacity to respond richly and fully to aesthetic objects depends on a large apperceptive mass. This may include some previous acquaintance with the general style of the work, or of other works to which it alludes, or of works with it sharply contrasts. All this may be relevant information for the perceiver. . . ."
46 In R. A. Smith, ed., *Aesthetics and Criticism in Art Education* (Chicago: Rand McNally, 1966); *Aesthetic Concepts and Education* (1970) and *Aes-*

thetics and Problems of Education (1971), both published by the University of Illinois Press at Urbana, Illinois: *Excellence in Art Education*, updated version (Reston: National Art Education Association, 1987); and, as editor, to date, of twenty-two volumes of the *Journal of Aesthetic Education*.

47 This is implicit in R. A. and C. M. Smith, "The Artworld and Aesthetic Skills: A Context for Research and Development," in Stanley S. Madeja, ed., *Arts and Aesthetics: An Agenda for the Future* (St. Louis: CEMREL, 1977); reprinted in the *Journal of Aesthetic Education* 11, no. 2 (April 1977), 117–32. Cf. Appendix II.

48 Harry S. Broudy, "On 'Knowing With,' " in H. B. Dunkel, ed., *Philosophy of Education: 1970*, Proceedings of the 26th Annual Meeting of the Philosophy of Education Society (Edwardsville: Philosophy of Education Society, 1970), pp. 89–103.

49 Michael Polanyi, *The Tacit Dimension* (New York: Doubleday, 1966) and Polanyi and Harry Prosch, *Meaning* (Chicago: University of Chicago Press, 1975).

Chapter 4 Examples of aesthetic criticism

1 Monroe C. Beardsley, "Critical Evaluation," in *The Aesthetic Point of View*, ed. Michael J. Wreen and Donald M. Callen (Ithaca: Cornell University Press, 1982), p. 319.

2 Kenneth Clark, *Looking at Pictures* (New York: Holt, Rinehart and Winston, 1960).

3 Ibid., p. 15.

4 Ibid., p. 16.

5 Quoted remarks of Clark are all from his discussion of Vermeer in *Looking at Pictures*, pp. 101–9. Note: In their *Visual Arts: A History*, 2nd ed. (Englewood Cliffs, NJ: Prentice-Hall, 1986), p. 474, Hugh Honour and John Fleming assign to Vermeer's painting the title *The Art of Painting* because of the discovery that this is the title his widow gave it. The model is said to be posed with the attributes of Clio, the Muse of History, and the authors suggest that the painting may have been intended to convey the idea of painting as a liberal art. The allegorical meaning of the painting remains unknown.

6 The reference is to Harry S. Broudy, *Enlightened Cherishing: An Essay on Aesthetic Education* (Urbana: University of Illinois Press, 1972).

7 Meyer Schapiro, *Paul Cézanne* (New York: Harry N. Abrams, 1952).

8 Quoted remarks of Schapiro's description on the *Quarry* painting are found on page 110.

9 R. A. Smith, "Teaching Aesthetic Criticism in the Classroom," *Journal of Aesthetic Education* 7, no. 1 (January 1973), 38–49.

10 Schapiro, *Paul Cézanne*, p. 9.

11 Ibid., p. 16.

12 Leo Steinberg, *Other Criteria: Confrontations with Twentieth-Century Art* (New York: Oxford University Press, 1972).

13 Ibid., p. 5.

14 Ibid., p. 15.

15 See, for example, Hugh Petrie, "Do You See What I See? The Epistemology of Interdisciplinary Inquiry," *Journal of Aesthetic Education* 10, no. 1 (January 1976), 29–43.

16 Stephen Toulmin, *Human Understanding*, vol. 1 (Princeton: Princeton University Press, 1972), p. x.

17 R. A. Smith, *Excellence in Art Education*, updated version (Reston: National Art Education Association, 1987), pp. 35–36.

18 Stanley Kauffmann, "Red Desert," in his *A World on Film* (New York: Dell, 1967), pp. 313–19.

19 Harold Rosenberg, "Avant-Garde," in Louis Kronenberger, ed., *Quality: Its Image in the Arts* (New York: Atheneum, 1969), pp. 419–49.

20 Kauffmann, *A World on Film*, p. 315.

21 Ibid., p. 319.

22 Francis Sparshott, "Basic Film Aesthetics," *Journal of Aesthetic Education* 5, no. 2 (April 1971), 34; reprinted in Gerald Mast and Marshall Cohen, eds., *Film Theory and Criticism*, 2nd ed. (New York: Oxford University Press, 1979), pp. 321–34.

23 Hilton Kramer, "The Anselm Kiefer Retrospective," *The New Criterion* 6, no. 6 (February 1988), 1–4. Quoted remarks of Kramer are from this review.

24 Albert William Levi, "The Poverty of the Avant Garde," *Journal of Aesthetic Education* 8, no. 4 (October 1974), 5.

25 Richard Wollheim, *Painting as an Art* (Princeton: Princeton University Press, 1987).

26 Michael Podro, "Content and Connotation," *Times Literary Supplement*, 8–14 April 1988, 390.

27 Wollheim, *Painting as an Art*, p. 207.

28 Ibid., p. 215.

29 Ibid., pp. 218, 220.

30 Paul Ziff, "The Task of Defining a Work of Art," *The Philosophical Review* 62, no. 1 (January 1953), 58–78.

Chapter 5 Teaching the skills of aesthetic criticism

1 Jacques Barzun, "Art and Educational Inflation," *Journal of Aesthetic Education* 12, no. 4 (October 1978), 20.

2 Henry Aiken, "Learning and Teaching in the Arts," *Journal of Aesthetic Education* 5, no. 4 (October 1971), 39–67, with responses by John Fisher and Monroe C. Beardsley. Originally published as the Lowenfeld Lecture for 1969 by the National Art Education Association; reprinted in Aiken's *Predicament of the University* (Bloomington: Indiana University Press,

1971), pp. 239–71. I follow the version in the *Journal of Aesthetic Education*. Aiken's remarks are directed toward the status of teaching art in higher education, but they are relevant to a teaching of aesthetic understanding at the lower levels as well, especially in the secondary grades.

3 Aiken, "Learning and Teaching in the Arts," p. 49.
4 Ibid., p. 44.
5 Erwin Panofsky, "The History of Art as a Humanistic Discipline," in his *Meaning in the Visual Arts* [1955] (Chicago: University of Chicago Press, 1982), p. 14.
6 Aiken, "Learning and Teaching in the Arts," pp. 45–46.
7 Ibid., p. 47.
8 Levi, "Art and the General Welfare," *Journal of Aesthetic Education* 7, no. 4 (October 1973), 44–48.
9 Aiken, "Learning and Teaching in the Arts," p. 48.
10 Kenneth Clark, *What Is a Masterpiece?* (New York: Thames and Hudson, 1979), pp. 10–11.
11 Aiken, "Learning and Teaching in the Arts," p. 54.
12 Ibid., pp. 52–53.
13 Ibid., p. 54.
14 Ibid.
15 Ibid., p. 56.
16 Ibid., p. 57.
17 Ibid., p. 59.
18 Ibid., p. 63.
19 Harold Osborne, "Appreciation as a Skill," in his *The Art of Appreciation* (New York: Oxford University Press, 1970), pp. 1–15.
20 Gilbert Ryle, *The Concept of Mind* (New York: Barnes & Noble, 1965), p. 43.
21 Osborne, "Appreciation as a Skill," p. 3.
22 Ibid., p. 6.
23 Stephan Zweig, "The Royal Game," in John Hospers, *Understanding the Arts* (Englewood Cliffs: Prentice-Hall, 1982), pp. 1–28. Cf. Walter Clark, Jr., "Some Thoughts on Teaching Creativity," *Journal of Aesthetic Education* 20, no. 4 (Winter 1986), 27–31.
24 Osborne, "Appreciation as a Skill," p. 7.
25 Ibid., p. 8.
26 Ibid., p. 10.
27 Ibid., p. 15.
28 R. L. W. Travers, *Essentials of Learning*, 5th ed. (New York: Macmillan, 1982). For a history of cognitive science, see Howard Gardner, *The Mind's New Science* (New York: Basic Books, 1985; epilogue to paperback edition, 1987).
29 Joseph D. Novak, *A Theory of Education* (Ithaca: Cornell University Press, 1987).

30   David P. Ausubel, Joseph D. Novak, and Helen Hanesian, *Educational Psychology: A Cognitive View*, 2nd ed. (New York: Holt, Rinehart and Winston, 1978).

31   Joseph D. Novak, and D. Bob Gowin, *Learning How to Learn* (New York: Cambridge University Press, 1984). In this book the authors describe a method of concept mapping for meaningful learning that features what Gowin calls a Vee heuristic. See page 182 for a concept map that represents an understanding of art. What I have in effect done in this volume is set out something of a concept map of aesthetic criticism, although I have not visually displayed it in the manner shown in the Novak and Gowin volume.

32   Michael J. Parsons, *How We Understand Art: A Cognitive Developmental Account of Aesthetic Experience* (New York: Cambridge University Press, 1987).

33   Ibid., p. xiii.

34   For example, Jean Renoir, *The Luncheon of the Boating Party*; Ivan Albright, *Into the World Came a Soul Called Ida*; Pablo Picasso, *Guernica* and *Head of a Weeping Woman with Hands*; Paul Klee, *Head of a Man*; George Bellows, *Dempsey and Firpo*; Goya, *Lo Miso*; and Marc Chagall, *La Grande Cirque*.

35   Parsons, *How We Understand Art*, p. 5.

36   Ibid., p. 11.

37   Ibid., p. 20.

38   Ibid., p. 123.

39   Ibid., p. 25.

40   Ibid., p. 124.

41   Ibid., p. 27.

Chapter 6   Toward an art world curriculum

1   Harold Osborne, "Taste and Judgment in the Arts," *Journal of Aesthetic Education* 5, no. 4 (October 1971), 27.

2   Several references to the literature on teaching criticism are contained in R. A. Smith, "The Changing Image of Art Education: Theoretical Antecedents of Discipline-based Art Education," *Journal of Aesthetic Education* 21, no. 2 (Summer 1987), 3–34.

3   See, for example, Diane Ravitch and Chester E. Finn, Jr., *What Do Our 17-Year-Olds Know?* (New York: Harper & Row, 1987); Lynne V. Cheney, Chairman, *American Memory* (Washington, D.C.: National Endowment for the Humanities, 1987); E. D. Hirsch, Jr., *Cultural Literacy* (Boston: Houghton Mifflin, 1987); and Allan Bloom, *The Closing of the American Mind* (New York: Simon and Schuster, 1987).

4   See R. A. Smith, "The Changing Image of Art Education," pp. 3–34.

5   In this connection see Samuel Lipman, "Cultural Policy: Whither America, Whither Government? *The New Criterion* 3, no. 3 (November 1984), 7–

15; and my comment on Lipman's essay in my "Policy for Arts Education: Whither the Schools, Whither the Public and Private Sectors?" *Design for Arts in Education* 89, no. 4 (March/April 1988), 2–11.

6 For examples, Albert William Levi, *Philosophy, Literature, and the Imagination* (Bloomington: Indiana University Press, 1962); *The Humanities Today* (Bloomington: Indiana University Press, 1970); "Literature as a Humanity," *Journal of Aesthetic Education* 10, nos. 3–4 (July-October 1976), 45–60; and "Teaching Literature as a Humanity," *Journal of General Education* 28, no. 4 (Winter 1977), 283–87.

7 Levi, *Philosophy, Literature, and the Imagination*, pp. 44–49.

8 Levi, *The Humanities Today*, p. 46.

9 Ibid., p. 48.

10 Ernst Cassirer, *An Essay on Man* (1944) (New Haven: Yale University Press, 1970), pp. 67–68.

11 Levi, "Literature at a Humanity," *Journal of Aesthetic Education*, 52.

12 Levi, "Teaching Literature as a Humanity," *Journal of Aesthetic Education*, p. 283.

13 Ibid., p. 54.

14 Levi, *The Humanities Today*, p. 85.

15 Levi, "Teaching Literature as a Humanity," *Journal of Aesthetic Education*, pp. 55–59.

16 See, for example, E. H. Gombrich's cautionary remarks in "The Visual Image: Its Place in Communication," in his *The Image and the Eye* (Ithaca: Cornell University Press, 1982), pp. 137–61.

17 Levi, "Literature as a Humanity," p. 60.

18 For a description of aesthetic scanning, see Harry S. Broudy, *The Role of Imagery in Learning* (Los Angeles: J. Paul Getty Trust, 1987), pp. 52–53.

19 For some cautionary observations regarding the study of the arts of different societies, see R. A. Smith, "Forms of Multi-cultural Education in the Arts," *Journal of Multi-cultural and Cross-cultural Research in Art Education* 1, no. 1 (Fall 1983), 23–32. The article draws heavily on Walter Kaufmann's discussion of the art of reading classic texts in his *The Future of the Humanities* (New York: Thomas Crowell, 1977), chap. 2.

20 In my own efforts to involve fourth- and fifth-graders in works remote from their immediate world, I had no difficulty holding their interest. The young can become as absorbed in the spatial ambiguity of abstract works and the attitudes of characters in religious paintings as in dramatic action scenes.

21 Heinrich Woelfflin, *Principles of Art History* [1915], trans. M. D. Hottinger (New York: Dover, n.d.).

22 H. W. Janson and Anthony Janson, *History of Art*, 3rd ed. (Englewood Cliffs, N.J.: Prentice-Hall, 1986).

23 Hugh Honour and John Fleming, *The Visual Arts: A History*, 2nd ed. (Englewood Cliffs, N.J.: Prentice-Hall, 1986).

24 Albert E. Elsen, *Purposes of Art*, 2nd ed. (New York: Holt, Rinehart and Winston, n.d.).

25 F. David Martin and Lee A. Jacobus, *The Humanities through the Arts*, 3rd ed. (New York: McGraw-Hill, 1983).

26 Bennett Reimer, *Developing the Experience of Music*, 2nd ed. (Englewood Cliffs, N.J.: Prentice-Hall, 1985).

27 H. W. Janson and Joseph Kerman, *A History of Art and Music* (Englewood Cliffs, N.J.: Prentice-Hall, n.d.).

28 Benjamin Rowland, *Art in East and West* (Cambridge: Harvard University Press, 1954).

29 Jacques Maquet, *The Aesthetic Experience* (New Haven: Yale University Press, 1986).

30 Harry Judge, *American Graduate Schools of Education* (New York: Ford Foundation, 1982), p. 25.

31 *Tomorrow's Teachers: A Report of the Holmes Group* (East Lansing: Holmes Group, 1986).

32 Theodore Sizer, *Horace's Compromise* (Boston: Houghton Mifflin, 1984), pp. 132–33.

Chapter 7   Issues: The two cultures and policy

1 Albert William Levi, "In Search of Culture," *Journal of Aesthetic Education* 11, no. 4 (October 1977), 9–34; and "Culture: A Guess at the Riddle," *Critical Inquiry* 4, no. 2 (Winter 1977), 299–329.

2 E. D. Hirsch, Jr., *Cultural Literacy: What Every American Needs to Know* (Boston: Houghton Mifflin, 1987).

3 Bertrand de Jouvenal, *The Art of Conjecture*, trans. Nikita Lary (New York: Basic Books, 1967), pp. 251–56.

4 Jacques Barzun, *Science: The Glorious Entertainment* (New York: Harper & Row, 1964), chap. 2.

5 Solon T. Kimball and James E. McClellan, Jr., *Education and the New America* (New York: Random House, 1962), chap. 8.

6 C. P. Snow, *The Two Cultures and the Scientific Revolution* (New York: Cambridge University Press, 1963), p. 12.

7 Snow uses "Luddite" to stand for persons generally opposed to technological change. Ned Ludd was a purported member of a group of early nineteenth-century British workmen who destroyed labor-saving machinery as a protest.

8 F. R. Leavis, *Two Cultures? The Significance of C. P. Snow* (New York: Pantheon, 1963). Also contains an essay by Michael Yudkin titled "Sir Charles Snow's Rede Lecture."

9 C. P. Snow, *The Two Cultures and a Second Look* (New York: Cambridge University Press, 1964). Also contains the original 1959 essay.

10 C. P. Snow, *Public Affairs* (New York: Scribner's, 1971).

11 Roger Scruton, "Modern Philosophy and the Neglect of Aesthetics," *Times Literary Supplement*, 5 June 1987, 604, 616–17.

12 George Levine, ed., *One Culture: Essays in Science and Literature* (Madison: University of Wisconsin Press, 1987).

13 For a more detailed account of such evolution, see R. A. Smith, "The Two Cultures Debate Today," *Oxford Review of Education* 4, no. 3 (1978), 257–65.

14 The most incisive critique was Lionel Trilling's "The Leavis-Snow Controversy," first published in *Commentary* (June 1962) and reprinted in Trilling's *Beyond Culture* (1968) (New York: Harcourt Brace Jovanovich, 1978), pp. 126–54.

15 Ralph A. Smith, "Art Education and the Two Cultures," *Art Education Bulletin* 17 (December 1964), 5–9.

16 Crane Brinton, *Ideas and Men*, 2nd ed. (Englewood Cliffs: Prentice-Hall, 1963), pp. 8–13.

17 C. P. Snow, "The Case of Leavis and the Serious Case," in his *Public Affairs* (New York: Scribner's, 1971), pp. 93–97.

18 Walter Kaufmann, "The Interdisciplinary Age," in his *The Future of the Humanities* (New York: Crowell, 1977), pp. 184–214.

19 C. P. Snow, *The State of Siege* (New York: Scribner's, 1969); reprinted in Snow's *Public Affairs*, pp. 199–221.

20 This point is also made by Lionel Trilling in his *Sincerity and Authenticity* (New York: Harcourt Brace Jovanovich, 1980).

21 For a continuing symposium on knowledge and the humanities, see the *Journal of Aesthetic Education* 18, no. 3 (Fall 1984), 77–94; and 21, no. 4 (Winter 1987), 87–102. The Winter 1984 issue reprints Brinton's discussion of the distinction and has responses by John Wilson and Barbara Cowell, and D. Bob Gowin and Debra A. Dyason; the Winter 1984 issue contains commentaries by Harry S. Broudy and Abraham Edel.

22 To borrow Albert William Levi's distinction in his *Literature, Philosophy and the Imagination* (Bloomington: Indiana University Press, 1962), pp. 45–49.

23 Meyer Schapiro, *Paul Cézanne* (New York: Harry N. Abrams, 1952), pp. 88, 68.

24 To borrow Virgil C. Aldrich's distinction in his *Philosophy of Art* (Englewood Cliffs: Prentice-Hall, 1963), pp. 49–53.

25 D. N. Perkins, "Art as Understanding," *Journal of Aesthetic Education* 22, no. 1 (Spring 1988), 111–31.

26 Israel Scheffler, *Of Human Potential* (Boston: Routledge & Kegan Paul, 1985), p. 5. Scheffler also makes important distinctions between potentiality as a capacity, a propensity, and a capability, which are pertinent to understanding the task of developing a disposition to appreciate excellence in art.

27 Albert William Levi, *Philosophy as Social Expression* (Chicago: University of Chicago Press, 1974), chap. 6.

28 Robert Penn Warren, *Democracy and Poetry* (Cambridge: Harvard University Press, 1975), p. 72.

29 Hannah Arendt, *The Human Condition* (Chicago: University of Chicago Press, 1958), p. 167: "Even if the historical origin of art were of an exclusively religious or mythological character, the fact is that art has survived gloriously its severance from religion, magic, and myth."

30 Remarks by Sol Spiegelman as part of the Fourth Tycokiner Memorial Lecture "The 'I' and 'Me' of Art and Science," presented at the University of Illinois at Urbana-Champaign in the Spring of 1978.

31 Donna H. Kerr, *Educational Policy: Analysis, Structure, and Justification* (New York: David McKay, 1976) and "Aesthetic Policy," *Journal of Aesthetic Education* 12, no. 1 (January 1978), 5–22.

32 On this tendency and others, see R. A. Smith, "Formulating a Defensible Policy for Art Education," *Theory Into Practice* 23, no. 4 (Autumn 1984), 273–79.

33 This approach has been critically examined by a number of writers in R. A. Smith, ed., *Regaining Educational Leadership: Critical Essays on PBTE/ CBTE, Behavioral Objectives, and Accountability* (New York: John Wiley, 1975).

34 For a critical examination of this tendency, see Barbara Leondar, "The Arts in Alternative Schools: Some Observations," *Journal of Aesthetic Education* 5, no. 1 (January 1971), 75–91.

35 For a discussion of these fallacies, see R. A. Smith, "Policy and Art Education: A Review of Some Fallacies," *High School Journal* 63, no. 8 (May 1980), 343–61.

36 For the current tendency of cognitive psychologists to study domain-specific instruction, see David Henry Feldman, "Developmental Psychology and Art Education: Two Fields at the Crossroads," *Journal of Aesthetic Education* 21, no. 2 (Summer 1987), 243–59.

37 Charles Fowler, "Integral and Undiminished: The Arts in General Education," *Music Educators Journal* 64, no. 5 (January 1978), 30–33.

38 The notion of art as a catalyst for achieving educational reform was featured in the rhetoric of the Artists-in-Schools program of the National Endowment for the Arts. See R. A. Smith, "An Analysis and Criticism of the Artists-in-Schools Program of the National Endowment for the Arts," *Art Education* 30, no. 5 (September 1977), 12–19.

39 For a discussion of these questions, see R. A. Smith, "Justifying Policy for Arts Education," *Studies in Art Education* 20, no. 1 (1978), 34–42.

Chapter 8 Issues: Ideology and postmodernism

1 Raymond Williams, "Ideology," in his *Keywords: A Vocabulary of Culture and Society* (New York: Oxford University Press, 1976), p. 130.

2 Ernst Fischer, *Art Against Ideology* (New York: George Braziller, 1969), p. 44.

3 Ibid.

4   Herbert Marcuse, *The Aesthetic Dimension* (Boston: Beacon Press, 1978), p. ix.

5   Meyer Schapiro, *Paul Cézanne* (New York: Harry N. Abrams, 1952), p. 30.

6   Albert William Levi, "The Poverty of the Avant-Garde," *Journal of Aesthetic Education* 8, no. 4 (October 1974), 6.

7   Lionel Trilling, *The Liberal Imagination* [1950] (New York: Harcourt Brace Jovanovich, 1979), preface.

8   Trilling, *Beyond Culture* [1965] (New York: Harcourt Brace Jovanovich, 1978), preface.

9   David Gordon, "The Aesthetic Attitude and the Hidden Curriculum," *Journal of Aesthetic Education* 15, no. 2 (April 1981), 51–63.

10 For a criticism of the concept of intrinsic value, see Monroe C. Beardsley, "Intrinsic Value," *Philosophy and Phenomenological Research* 26, no. 1 (September 1965), 1–17.

11 Barbara Leondar has some interesting things to say, largely critical, about efforts to reform arts education along political and ideological lines in her "The Arts in Alternative Schools: Some Observations," *Journal of Aesthetic Education* 5, no. 1 (January 1971), 75–91.

12 David Swanger, "Ideology and Aesthetic Education," *Journal of Aesthetic Education* 15, no. 2 (April 1981), 33–44.

13 Jacques Barzun, *The House of Intellect* (New York: Harper & Brothers, 1959), p. 12.

14 H. B. Redfern, *Questions in Aesthetic Education* (Boston: Allen & Unwin, 1986), p. 93.

15 Diederik Schönau, "Aesthetic Education as a New Ideology," *Journal of Aesthetic Education* 15, no. 2 (April 1981), 45–63.

16 For example, Richard Pratte, *Ideology and Education* (New York: David McKay, 1977). Also, R. A. Smith, "Ideologies, Art Education, and Philosophical Research," *Studies in Art Education* 24, no. 3 (1983), 164–68.

17 For a volume that traces the numerous meanings of postmodernism, see Ihab Hassan, *The Postmodern Turn* (Columbus: The Ohio State University Press, 1987).

18 M. J. Wilsmore, "Skepticism and Deconstruction," *Man and World* 20 (1987), 437–55.

19 Ibid., p. 442.

20 Ibid., p. 443.

21 Ibid.

22 Ibid., p. 444.

23 Annette Barnes, *On Interpretation* (New York: Basil Blackwell, 1988), esp. pp. 95–105.

24 Ibid., pp. 76–97.

25 Wilsmore, "Skepticism and Deconstruction," p. 449.

26 Ibid.

27 Ibid., p. 450.

28 Ibid., p. 453.
29 Peter Shaw, "The Politics of Deconstruction," *Partisan Review/2* 53, no. 2 (1986), 253–62.
30 See, for example, G. Douglas Atkins and Michael L. Johnson, eds., *Writing and Reading Differently* (Lawrence: University Press of Kansas, 1985), especially the essay by Vincent B. Leitch; and Cary Nelson, ed., *Theory in the Classroom* (Urbana: University of Illinois Press, 1986).
31 Joseph Margolis, "Deconstruction: A Cautionary Tale," *Journal of Aesthetic Education* 20, no. 4 (Winter 1986), 91–94.
32 Ibid., p. 91.
33 Ibid., p. 94.
34 Jerome Bruner, "Afterword," in his *Actual Minds, Possible Worlds* (Cambridge: Harvard University Press, 1986), pp. 151–60.
35 Ibid., p. 155.
36 Ibid., p. 159.
37 Roger Kimball, "The Academy Debates the Canon," *The New Criterion* 6, no. 1 (September 1987), 31–43.
38 Frederick Crews, *Skeptical Engagements* (New York: Oxford University Press, 1986), p. 164.
39 David Bromwich, "Recent Work in Literary Criticism," *Social Research* 53, no. 3 (Autumn 1986), 414–15. Bromwich describes how the imposition of an ideological perspective can attribute qualities to a character that are inconsistent with a text's own internal evidence. The context for his remarks in Gayatri Chakravorti Spivak's "Three Women's Texts and a Critique of Imperialism," *Critical Inquiry* 12, no. 1 (Autumn 1985), 243–61.
40 Shaw, "The Politics of Deconstruction," p. 262.
41 The standard reference is Matthew Arnold, *Culture and Anarchy* (1869) (New York: Cambridge University Press, 1969), p. 70.
42 John Dewey, *The Public and Its Problems* (New York: Henry Holt, 1927), esp. chap. 5.
43 Tzvetan Todorov, "All Against Humanity," *Times Literary Supplement*, 4 October 1985, 1093–4.
44 S. J. Wilsmore, "The New Attack on Humanism in the Arts," *British Journal of Aesthetics* 27, no. 4 (Autumn 1987), 338.
45 Allan Bloom, *The Closing of the American Mind* (New York: Simon and Schuster, 1987), pp. 379–80.
46 George Steiner, "Viewpoint: A New Meaning of Meaning," *Time Literary Supplement*, 8 November 1985, 1262.
47 Ibid.
48 John Fisher, "Editorial," *Journal of Aesthetics and Art Criticism* 40, no. 2 (Winter 1981), 119–20.
49 Steiner, "Viewpoint: A New Meaning of Meaning," p. 1275.
50 Jacques Barzun, *The Use and Abuse of Art* (Princeton: Princeton University Press, 1974), p. 122.

51 Roger Scruton, "Modern Philosophy and the Neglect of Aesthetics," *Times Literary Supplement*, 5 June 1987, 604, 616–17.
52 Ibid., p. 616.
53. See, for example, Israel Scheffler, "In Praise of the Cognitive Emotions," in his *Inquiries: Philosophical Studies of Language, Science, and Learning* (Indianapolis: Hackett, 1986), pp. 347–62.
54 Friedrich Schiller, *On the Aesthetic Education of Man in a Series of Letters* (English and German facing), ed. and trans. Elizabeth M. Wilkinson and L. A. Willoughby (London: Oxford University Press, 1967). Cf. Vernon Howard, "Schiller: A Letter on Aesthetic Education to a Later Age," *Journal of Aesthetic Education* 20, no. 4 (Winter 1986), 8–11.
55 John Ciardi, "Esthetic Wisdom," in R. A. Smith, ed., *Aesthetic Education Today: Problems and Prospects*, with an introduction by Kenneth Marantz (Columbus: The Department of Art Education, The Ohio State University, 1974), p. 76. With responses by Albert William Levi and Harry S. Broudy to which Ciardi responds. Ciardi's remarks were first published in the *Saturday Review*, 8 April 1972, 22.
56 Barnes, *On Interpretation*, p. 105.
57 Ibid.

Appendix I Aesthetic experience

1 Harold Osborne, "What Makes an Experience Aesthetic?" in Michael H. Mitias, ed., *Possibility of the Aesthetic Experience* (Boston: Martinus Nijhoff, 1986), p. 117.
2 Michael H. Mitias, "Preface," p. ix.
3 T. J. Diffey, "The Idea of Aesthetic Experience," in Mitias, ed., *Possibility of Aesthetic Experience,* p. 12.
4 Władysław Tatarkiewicz, "The Aesthetic Experience: History of the Concept," in *History of Six Ideas*, trans. Christopher Kasparek (Boston: Martinus Nijhoff, 1980), pp. 310–38. The other five ideas Tatarkiewicz discusses are art, beauty, form, creativity, and imitation.
5 Quoted by Tatarkiewicz, p. 310.
6 Ibid., p. 315.
7 Ibid., p. 320.
8 Ibid., p. 323.
9 Ibid., p. 324.
10 Ibid., pp. 337–38.
11 Monroe C. Beardsley, *Aesthetics: Problems in the Philosophy of Criticism*, 2nd ed. (Indianapolis: Hackett, 1981), p. 1xi.
12 Harry S. Broudy, "On Cognition and Emotion in the Arts," in Stanley S. Madeja, ed., *The Arts, Cognition, and Basic Skills* (St. Louis: CEMREL, 1978), p. 21.

13 Harold Osborne, *The Art of Appreciation* (New York: Oxford University Press, 1970), pp. 20–21.

14 Arthur Conan Doyle, *The Complete Sherlock Holmes*, vol. 1 (New York: Doubleday, n.d.), pp. 322–23.

15 Albert William Levi, "Nature and Art," *Journal of Aesthetic Education* 18, no. 3 (Fall, 1984), 5–6. Levi continues: "If Phaedrus had been Wordsworth he would have known what to answer. 'Let Nature be your Teacher!' O Socrates, 'One impulse from a vernal wood/May teach you more of man,/of moral evil and of good,/Than all the sages can.' But Socrates probably would not have been impressed. His outlook was thoroughly Athenian, thoroughly city-bred, and if he searched for wisdom in the comfortable conversations which men held with one another, these conversations themselves were centered upon the civic and moral interests of the Greek *polis*: What is justice? What is courage? What is temperance? What are human love and friendship? How can the aristocracy of the noble nature be restored?"

16 Quoted by Osborne in *The Art of Appreciation*, p. 25.

17 Guy Sircello, *A New Theory of Beauty* (Princeton: Princeton University Press, 1975), pp. 19–20.

18 Charles Darwin, *The Voyage of the Beagle*, abridged and edited by Millicent E. Selsam (New York: Harper & Row, 1959), p. 216. I first noticed this passage in a course syllabus titled "Design of Alternative Futures," written by John Dieges, the University of California at Berkeley, 1969.

19 Quoted by Harold Osborne in his *Abstraction and Artifice in Twentieth-Century Art* (New York: Oxford University Press, 1979), p. 103. But for a view of Moscow, say, an hour after sunset, here is the observation of a perceptive contemporary: "To watch dusk descend on Moscow is to watch a city vanish. It is as though it sinks into the sandy soil that limits high-rise construction in this horizontal capital.

   "To see Moscow at night is to be struck by what you do not see, and to long for neon—the electronic exuberance that is freedom's signature in the form of capitalism's crackling energy." George Will, *News-Gazette* (Champaign-Urbana, Illinois), 13 March 86, A-4.

20 Morton D. Zabel, ed., *The Art of Travel: Scenes and Journeys in America, England, France and Italy from the Travel Writings of Henry James* (New York: Doubleday, 1958), pp. 396–97.

21 The quotation is from L. A. Reid, *A Study in Aesthetics* (New York: Macmillan, 1931), pp. 101–2. Quoted by Lionel Trilling in "Criticism and Aesthetics," in his *A Gathering of Fugitives* (1956) (New York: Harcourt Brace Jovanovich, 1978), p. 147.

22 Harry S. Broudy, "The Structure of Knowledge in the Arts," in Stanley Elam, ed., *Education and the Structure of Knowledge* (Chicago: Rand McNally, 1964), pp. 91–92; reprinted in R. A. Smith, ed., *Aesthetics and Criticism in Art Education* (Chicago: Rand McNally, 1966), pp. 34–35.

23 Ibid., p. 92.

24 Ibid.

25 E. F. Kaelin, "Aesthetic Education: A Role for Aesthetics Proper," in R. A. Smith, ed., *Aesthetics and Problems of Education* (Urbana: University of Illinois Press, 1971), p. 154.

26 Beardsley, "Aesthetic Experience Regained," in his *The Aesthetic Point of View: Selected Essays*, ed., Michael J. Wreen and Donald M. Callen (Ithaca: Cornell University Press, 1982), p. 89.

27 Diané Collinson, "Aesthetic Education," in G. Langford and D. J. O'Connor, eds., *New Essays in the Philosophy of Education* (London: Routledge & Kegan Paul, 1973), p. 200.

28 Meyer Schapiro, *Paul Cézanne* (New York: Harry N. Abrams, 1952), p. 74.

29 John Hospers, *Understanding the Arts* (Englewood Cliffs: Prentice-Hall, 1982), p. 380.

**Appendix II   The art world and aesthetic skills:
A context for research and development**

1   Monroe C. Beardsley, *Aesthetics: Problems in the Philosophy of Criticism*, 2nd ed. (Indianapolis: Hackett, 1981), p. 76.

2   R. A. and C. M. Smith, "The Artworld and Aesthetic Skills: A Context for Research and Development," in Stanley S. Madeja, ed., *Arts and Aesthetics: An Agenda for the Future* (St. Louis: CEMREL, 1977), pp. 305–16; reprinted in the *Journal of Aesthetic Education* 11, no. 2 (April 1977), 117–32.

3   E. F. Kaelin, "Why Teach Art in the Public Schools?" *Journal of Aesthetic Education* 20, no. 4 (Winter 1986), 68.

4   Monroe C. Beardsley, "Aesthetic Welfare, Aesthetic Justice, and Educational Policy," *Journal of Aesthetic Education* 7, no. 4 (October 1973), 49–61; reprinted in Beardsley's *The Aesthetic Point of View*, ed., Wreen and Callen (Ithaca: Cornell University Press, 1982), 111–24.

5   Beardsley, *The Aesthetic Point of View*, p. 112.

6   Ibid.

7   Ibid., pp. 113–4.

8   For example, the publicized reactions to Richard Serra's *Twain* in St. Louis and his *Titled Arc* in Manhattan, and Carl Andre's *Stone Field* in Hartford.

9   For some remarks along these lines, see Arthur C. Danto's review of Gerald Nordland's book *Richard Diebenkorn* (New York: Rizzoli, 1988), in the *Times Literary Supplement*, 13–19 May 1988, 537.

10 The concept of criticism as a performance is central to Francis Sparshott's *The Concept of Criticism* (New York: Oxford University Press, 1967), especially chap. 9.

11 David Swanger, "The Band Triumphant," *Journal of Aesthetic Education* 20, no. 4 (Fall 1986), 31–37.

12 See, e.g., R. A. Smith, "The 'New' Appreciation of Art," in *Papers on Educational Reform* (LaSalle: Open Court, 1974), pp. 143–58.

13 Nelson Goodman, *Languages of Art*, 2nd ed. (Indianapolis: Hackett, 1976), pp. 261–62.

14 See Richard Hoggart, "Access and Excellence," in his *An English Temper* (New York: Oxford University Press, 1982), p. 160. Hoggart recalls for communitarians the tradition of British adult education. "Among its many great qualities," he writes, is "the belief that people should be able to stand up and reach for the best and the most demanding; that, given that opportunity (not watered down), a surprising number will so reach, and that when they do their grasp will reveal that they and many others have far more abilities than either a closed elitism or an ill-thought-through communitarianism had realised. So they have the right to the best; no less."

15 Roy Shaw, *The Arts and the People* (London: Johnathan Cape, 1987), p. 81. Sir Roy, an erstwhile Secretary-General of the British Arts Council, writes: "I believe that the task of education, broadcasting organisations and arts organisations (especially the Arts Council and the Regional Arts Associations) is to make excellence accessible. This is to make the eminently democratic assumption that people deserve the best and need it."

16 Janet Adshead, Valerie A. Briginshaw, Pauline Hodgens, and Michael Robert Huxley, "A Chart of Skills and Concepts for Dance," *Journal of Aesthetic Education* 16, no. 3 (Fall 1982), 51–61. Further developed in Janet Adshead, ed., *Dance Analysis: Theory and Practice* (London: Dance Books, forthcoming).

17 Thomas Goolsby, "Music Education as Aesthetic Education: Concepts and Skills for the Appreciation of Music," *Journal of Aesthetic Education* 18, no. 4 (Winter 1984), 15–33.

18 William Cadbury and Leland Poague, *Film Criticism: A Counter Theory* (Ames: The Iowa State University Press, 1982), p. ix. The authors write that they "share an instrumental theory of aesthetic value [Beardsley's], namely the theory that art objects are good (if they are) because it does people good to have aesthetic experience of them, and we share the belief that it is in their capacity to provide aesthetic experience to people who know how to have it that aesthetic objects are defined . . . [W]e believe in aesthetic experience as a primary and constitutive category of knowledge about films—particularly, of the knowledge we think one should want to have about film—and hence as a principal term in film criticism."

19 Perhaps the most comprehensive study of critical categories is Alan C. Purves, with Victoria Rippere, *Elements of Writing about a Literary Work: A Study of Response to Literature* (Champaign: National Council of Teachers of English, 1968), esp. chap. 2. Though generally approving of the study, Beardsley observes that critical discourse about literary objects is more complex and ambiguous than the authors suggest. See his review in the *Journal of Aesthetic Education* 3, no. 2 (April 1969), 165–7. A perusal of recent publication catalogues of the National Council of Teachers of

English reveals English educators today to be preoccupied with problems of writing and not response to literature.

20 E. D. Hirsch, Jr., *Cultural Literacy* (Boston: Houghton Mifflin, 1987), especially chap. 5. Cf. R. A. Smith, *Excellence in Art Education*, updated version (Reston: National Art Education Association, 1987), p. 99.

21 Virgil C. Aldrich, *Philosophy of Art* (Englewood Cliffs: Prentice-Hall, 1963), pp. 35–55.

22 John Hospers, *Understanding Art* (Englewood Cliffs: Prentice-Hall, 1982), pp. 100–01.

23 Harold Osborne, *Abstraction & Artifice in Twentieth-Century Art* (Oxford: Clarendon Press, 1979), pp. 6–21. Another rich source of aesthetic concepts is Osborne's *The Art of Appreciation* (New York: Oxford University Press, 1970).

24 H. Gene Blocker, *Philosophy of Art* (New York: Scribner's, 1979), pp. vii–viii, and passim.

25 Francis Sparshott, *The Theory of the Arts* (Princeton: Princeton University Press, 1982), pp. 187–91.

26 David Martin and Lee Jacobus, *The Humanities through the Arts*, 3rd ed. (New York: McGraw-Hill, 1983), especially chap. 2.

27 Harry S. Broudy, *The Role of Imagery in Learning* (Los Angeles: J. Paul Getty Trust, 1987), pp. 52–53.

28 John Hospers, *Understanding the Arts*, chap. 4.

29 Jacques Barzun, ed., *The Pleasures of Music* [1951] (New York: Viking Press, 1960), pp. 15–16. Barzun adds: "The test of all such comparisons, analogies, associations, and transfers of sense-perceptions is pragmatic: let them be subjective or objective, concrete or abstract, secular or religious, physical or metaphysical: those which, after repeated use and repeated reading, serve well because they fit—because they lead to significance—are good (p. 16)."

30 I suggest reading first Beardsley's *Aesthetics: Problems in the Philosophy of Criticism* (1958), 2nd ed. (Indianapolis: Hackett, 1981), both the relevant parts of the text and the Postscript 1980; then *The Possibility of Criticism* (Detroit: Wayne State University Press, 1970), a much shorter volume, and finally his most recent reflections in his *The Aesthetic Point of View: Selected Essays* (Ithaca: Cornell University Press, 1982), especially section 4.

31 Beardsley, *The Possibility of Criticism*, p. 88.

32 Francis Sparshott, *The Concept of Criticism* (Oxford: Clarendon Press, 1967), p. 213.

Index

Page numbers in italic indicate page on which the reproduction appears.

Abstract expressionists, 20
Adams, Henry, 11
Aesthetic, the term, 3, 4, 200
Aesthetic appreciation, 35–38, 107–11, *see also* Aesthetic experience, Percipience
Aesthetic argument, 57–61; *see also* Criticism
Aesthetic attitude, 4, 77–78
Aesthetic auxiliaries, 205
Aesthetic capacity, 34, 204
Aesthetic communication, 44
Aesthetic concepts, chart, 214–16
Aesthetic contemplation, 76
Aesthetic criticism, 51–52, 67–71, 89, 93; Eaton on, 54–56; Crittenden on, 57–61; Beardsley on, 61–68; examples of, Clark, 71–75, Schapiro, 75–78, Steinberg, 78–83, Kauffmann, 83–88, Kramer, 89–92, Wollheim, 93–98
Aesthetic delight, 199
Aesthetic education, 1–4, 30, 35, 37, 43, 46–47, 52, 55, 125, 133, 165–69, 181–82
Aesthetic experience, 3–5, Beardsley on, 31–35, 203–04; Osborne on, 35–37; Goodman on, 39–43; Kaelin on, 44–46; Eaton on, 55–56; 72, Aiken on, 100–04; and deconstruction, 178–79; Tatarkiewicz on, 184–91; dualities of, 200–1; 225–26
Aesthetic gratification, 34
Aesthetic institution, 46–47
Aesthetic judgment, 34, 53, 107; *see also* Evaluative criticism
Aesthetic justice, 34, 203–4

Aesthetic object concepts, 52, 69, 221–24
Aesthetic opportunity, 204
Aesthetic point of view, 35
Aesthetic qualities, 106, 224
Aesthetic rationality, 56, 57
Aesthetic reasons, 63; *see also* Language of critical evaluation
Aesthetic skills, 52,69; chart, 214–16
Aesthetic understanding, Goodman on, 39–43; Parsons on, 117–22
Aesthetic value, 3, 32, 55, 62, 77, 89, 125, 202–6
Aesthetic wealth, 34, 203
Aesthetic welfare, 34, 203
Aesthetic wisdom, 181
Aesthetically educated person, 68, 221
Aesthetics, 4, 30, 39, 130, 142, 149, 182, 184
Affective reasons, 63
Aiken, Henry, 78, 99–107, 125, 135, 137, 155, 161, 207
Alberti, Leon Battista, 180
Aldrich, Virgil, 92, 211
Alternative art education, 158
Amusement arts, 38
Analogues, 4
Analysis, categories of, 211–13
Anthropology, 24, 25–26
Anti-art, 13–14, 20, 70
Antonioni, Michelangelo, *Red Desert, 85*, 70, 83, 92, 93, 207
Apperceptive mass, 109
Appreciation, 35–38, 107–11; *see also* Aesthetic experience, Percipience
Aristotle, 151, 185, 186, 189

Arnheim, Rudolf, 66, 189
Arnold, Matthew, 3, 21, 58, 170, 178, 182
Arnoldian ideal, 178, 182
Art as anxious object, 17
Art as media package, 18; *see also* Art and media system
Art and cognition, 36, 39, 66–67
Art and cultural context, 23–27
Art and ideology, 164–65
Art and mass communications, 16–21, 21–23
Art and politics, 171, 175, 177
Art and science, 43, 100
Art and society, 9–13, 13–16, 27–29
Art critic, 106
Art museums, 18–19; *see also* Museums
Art world, 7–8, 12–13, 46–47, 208–9
Artistic goodness, 69
Artistic intention, 53, 63, 85–86, 98
Arts education, 3, 160
Arts of communication (languages and literature), 130–31
Arts of continuity (history), 132
Arts of creation and performance, 132
Arts of criticism (philosophy), 133
Assimilation theory, 112–17
Ausubel, David, 111
Autobiographical criticism, 66

Balanchine, George, 132
Balinese culture, 26
Barbaro, Umberto, 25
Barnes, Annette, 173, 174, 182–83
Bartók, Belá, 132
Barzun, Jacques, 4, 7, 9, 13–16, 21, 27, 28, 37, 99, 106, 115, 124, 147, 168, 179, 205, 213
Baumgarten, Alexander, 184, 185, 187
Beardsley, Monroe C., 9, 23–27, 31–35, 38, 41, 43, 44, 45, 52, 61–67, 69, 72, 75, 80, 122, 125, 139, 166, 180, 187, 191, 198–99, 202, 206, 208, 209, 210, 212, 213, 214–16, 217–18, 221–24

Beauty, 12, 185–86, 187, 194–95
Beethoven, *Eroica* 30, 34
Bellini, G., 105
Berenson, Bernard, 105
Bergman, Ingmar, 132
Bergson, Henri, 189
Bias in mass communications, 22
Binary opposites, 172
Biographical criticism, 66
Blocker, H. Gene, 49, 211
Bloom, Allan, 179–80
Blunt, Anthony, 94
Boethius, 185
Bonaventure, St., 186
Bonnard, P., *Compotier Blanc*, 232
Bremond, H., 189
Brinton, Crane, 151, 153, 154, 180
Bruckner, Anton, Fifth Symphony, 61
Broudy, Harry S., 67, 192, 197–98, 211
Brueghel, Pieter, 240–46; *The Peasant Wedding, 241; The Peasant Dance, 243; The Land of Cockaigne, 241–42; The Procession to Calvary, 244; The Massacre of the Innocents, 245; Magpie on the Gallows, 246.*
Bromwich, David, 176–77
Bullough, Edward, 189 '
Burke, Edmund, 187

Caravaggio, *The Martyrdom of St. Matthew*, 7
Cassirer, Ernst, 7, 8, 28, 39, 129, 133
Castagno, Andrea del, 234–36, *Last Supper, 235*
Cézanne, Paul, *Quarry and Mont Sainte-Victoire*, 75–77, 199–200, 77; *The Card Players, The Bathers*, 154, 164, *Mont Sainte-Victoire*, 199–200
Chartres Cathedral, 10
Chirico, Giorgio de, 80
Ciardi, John, 181
Cicero, 192
Civic humanism, 103
Clark, Kenneth, 9–13, 16, 27, 38,

69, 70, 71–75, 103, 124, 125, 190, 205, 213
Classification of critical reasons and judgments, 61–68; *see also* Language of critical evaluation
Cognitive value, 62
Cognitive reasons, 67
Cohen, Marshall, 198–99
Collingwood, R. G., 118
Collinson, Diané, 199
Complexity, 64, 76
Concepts, 11–17, 49–52
Connoisseurship, 109
Constable, J., 10
Copland, Aaron, 72,85
Creative activities, 110, 207–8
Cremin, Lawrence A., 3
Crews, Frederick, 176
Critical activity concepts, 52, 69
Critical redescription, 58–59, 97
Critical reasons, 54, 61–68; *see also* Language of critical evaluation
Criticism, Eaton on, 53
Crittenden, Brian, 52, 56–61, 63, 64, 125, 174
Cultural consumption, 12
Cultural criticism, 51
Cultural heritage, 48, 68
Cultural literacy, 139
Culture, definition, 24, 180–83
Curriculum, 124–27, 133, 134–42, 165–66
Curriculum, art world, 133–43
Curriculum as itinerary, 124–26

Dada, 84
Dante, *Divine Comedy*, 30
Danto, Arthur, 46, 67, 118
Darwin, Charles, 125, 147, 152, 195
De-aestheticization of art, 15
Deconstruction, Wilsmore on, 170–73, 174, 175; Barnes on, 173, 174; Shaw on, 175, 177; Margolis on, 175–76; Bruner on, 176; Kimball on, 170; Crews on, 176; Bromwich on, 176; Bloom on, 179–80; Steiner on, 180
Deconstructionism, 176

De-definition of art, 15, 18
Deep description, 58
Definition of art, 4, 34, 38, 40, 56, 203, 220
Dekooning, W., 79
Delacroix, E., 10
Democratic ethos, 8–9
DeJouvenel, Bertrand, 146–47, 148, 152, 153
Derrida, Jacques, 170–71, 182
Description and redescription, 57–61, 97
De-schooling, 158
DeTolnay, Charles, 247
Dewey, John, 15, 23, 25, 33, 118, 161, 178, 201
Dickie, George, 46
Diebenkorn, Richard, 207
Diffey, T. J., 185
Discovery learning, 115
Don't look back fallacy, 3
Doyle, Arthur Conan, "The Adventure of the Copper Beeches," 192–93
Dubos, J. B., 186
Ducasse, C. J., 189
Duccio, *Maestà*, 9–10
Duchamp, Marcel, *Mona Lisa*, 18; *Nude Descending a Staircase*, 78
Dworkin, Martin S., 86

Eagleton, Terry, 25
Eaton, Marcia M., 52–56, 63, 125, 174
Eclecticism, 5
Education, 60–61
Egalitarianism, 8, 9
Eisenstein, S. M. *Potemkin*, 199
Elsen, Albert, 140
El Greco, *Espolio*, 74
Elitism, 56, 121
Elitism versus populism, 11
Emotive criticism, 66
Enlightenment, the, 187–88
Erigena, John Scotus, 186
Ethnocentrism, 8
Evaluative criticism, 52, 53, 69, 76
Excellence, 1, 2, 8, 9, 19, 30, 54, 126, 209–10

Excellence in art, 2, 8, 9, 54, 141
Excellence in Art Education (R. Smith), 127
Excellence-in-education movement, 126–27
Existential phenomenology, 44
Exploratory criticism, 52, 53, 69, 72, 76, 87
Expression, 63, 212
Extra-aesthetic values, 161

Fadiman, Clifton, 9, 21–23, 28, 38, 124
Fantin-Latour, H., 230–232, *Still Life,231*
Fechner, G., 189
Ficino, M., 186
Fiedler, K., 189
Firstness, 72
Fischer, Ernst, 164, 165
Fisher, John, 180, 198
Fleming, John, 140
Form, 223
Formal qualities, 57
Formalist criticism, 93
Freedom, 46
Frisch, Max, 61, 64, 65
Fry, Roger, 71

Gardner, Howard, 39
Geertz, Clifford, 26
Genetic reasons, 63, 68
Genius, 14
Genre, 102–3
Giorgione, 100–105, *The Tempest, 101*, 132, 207
Giotto, 10, 79, 105, 141
Gluck, G., 246
Goddard, H. C., 53
Gombrich, E. H., 66
Goodlad, John, 7, 116, 208
Goodman, Nelson, 27, 31, 39–43, 44, 45, 66, 115, 122, 125, 146, 154, 156, 173, 176, 179, 191, 208, 209, 211
Gordon, David, 165, 168
Gowin, D. Bob, 114, 210
Gravina, Gian Vincenza, 186
Great art, 92

Gulliver's Travels, 22

Habermas, Jurgen, 118
Haezrahi, Pepita, 194
Hamann, R., 189
Hamlet, 174
Hartley, D., 187
Hartman, N., 189
Harvard Project Zero, 39
Haydn, F. J., 161
Heath, P. L. 50, 82
Hegel, G. W. F., 185
Heidegger, Martin, 44
Herbart, J. F., 185
High culture, 8, 11
Hirsch, E. D., Jr., 139, 146, 211
Historical criticism, 72, 93
Historical generalizations, 9–11
Hoggart, Richard, 210
Hokusai, 40
Holmes Group, 143
Holmes, Sherlock, 86, 192–93
Homer, *The Illiad*, 180
Honour, H., 140
Hospers, John, 4, 200, 211, 212
Howard, Vernon, 39
Human regional quality, 64
Humane literacy, 28
Humanism, 93, 182
Humanism versus positivism, 11
Humanistic complex, 182
Humanistic understanding, 237, 239–50
Humanists, 150–51
Humanitarianism, 11
Humanities, 127–32
Humanization of knowledge, 3, 178
Hume, David, 14, 187
Husserl, Edmund, 44

Ideology, 1, 163–69, Williams on, 164; Fischer on, 164; Marcuse on, 164; Trilling on, 165; Gordon on 165–66; Swanger on, 166–68;Schonau, 168
Ideological criticism, 51
If-then thinking, 14, 206–7
Impressionism, 20, 84, 85
Indocrination, 59

Ingarden, Roman, 190
Instrumental theory of aesthetic
   value, 32, 166; *see also* Aesthetic
   value
Instrumentalism, 161, 166
Intention, 53, 63, 85–86, 88, 229
Intentional understanding, 182
Intentionalistic criticism, 98
Intensity, 64, 76
Interpretation, 66, 82, Eaton on, 52–
   54; Wilsmore on, 171–73, 174,
   175; Barnes on, 173, 174, 183;
   Steiner on, 180

Jacobus, Lee, 140, 211
James, Henry, *The Turn of the
   Screw*, 53–54, 125, 196
Janson, H. W., 140, 141, 200
Johns, Jasper, *Target with Four
   Faces*, 70, 78–82, 89, 116, 121,
   207
Journal of Aesthetic Education, 61
Judge, Harry, 143
Justification of critical judgment, 55,
   60

Kaelin, E. F., 31, 44–47, 58, 68,
   122, 124, 125, 166, 173, 191–92,
   198, 202, 207, 208, 211
Kandinsky, W., 125, 196
Kant, Immanuel, 101, 118, 120,
   131, 185, 187, 188, 189, 191
Kauffmann, Stanley, 69, 70, 83–88,
   92, 93, 125, 207
Kaufmann, Walter, 151
Kerman, Joseph, 141
Kerr, Donna, 146, 156–57
Kiefer, Anselm, 70, 89–93,
   Midgard, 90
Kimball, Roger, 176
Kimball, Solon, 147
King Lear, 180
Kivy, Peter, 66
Kline, Franz, 79
Knowledge, 50, 51, 108, 151, 153
Kohlberg, Lawrence, 117–18
Kramer, Hilton, 20, 69
Kronenberger, Louis, 20
Kuhn, Thomas, 111

Lange, K., 189
Langer, Susanne, 27, 118
Language of critical evaluation,
   table, 217
Learning, Novak on, 111–17; phases
   of, 133–42
Leavis, F. R., 51, 58, 148, 149,
   170, 178, 181, 182
Leisure, 37–38
Leonardo, *Mona Lisa*, 30; *Last
   Supper*, 234–36, *236*
L'esprit de finesse and *l'esprit de
   geometrie*, 32
Levi, Albert William, 7, 92–93,
   103, 127–32, 137–38, 140, 145,
   146, 155, 164–65, 182, 193–
   94
Liberace, 20
Liberal education, 177–78, 220
Lipps, T., 189
Literary heritage, 173
Literary intellectuals, 150
Locke, John, 186–87

Magritte, *The Listening Chamber*,
   232
Maquet, Jacques, 141
Marcuse, Herbert, 164, 167
Margolis, Joseph, 175–76
Martin, F. David, 140, 211
Martin, Jane Roland, 165
Marx(ism), 24, 25, 87, 163, 164,
   175, 177, 179
Maslow, Abraham, 32
Master concepts, 2, 70, 81
Matisse, Henri, *Joy of Life*, 78
McClellan, James, 147
McLuhan, Marshall, 19
Media package, 18
Media system, 17
Meinong, A., 189
Merleau-Ponty, M., 155
Metaphor, 65
Michelangelo, Medici Chapel, 10;
   David, 30, 141
Mitias, Michael H., 185
Modernism, 20
Monty Python Flying Circus, 18
Moral criticism, 93

Moral value, 62
Morawski, Stefan, 25
Motherwell, Robert, 207
Mozart, *Marriage of Figaro*, 180
Multicultural education, 8, 83, 138–39
Munch, Edvard, *The Cry*, 61
Museums, 18
Museums without walls, 18
Music, 140–41

National Council of the Humanities, 127
New Criticism, 31
New Nihilism, 182
Ngal, M. A. M., 26
Nietzsche, F., 190
Nonjudgmentalism, 209
Non-Western civilizations, 81, 138, 141
Novak, Joseph, 67, 111–17, 122, 135

Objective reasons, 63
Originality, 63
Osborne, Harold, 3, 35–38, 43, 44, 45, 102, 107–11, 122, 124, 184, 191, 192, 208, 211

Panofsky, Erwin, 45, 101
Parsons, Michael J., 116, 117–23, 134, 190, 210
Pasolini, *The Gospel According to St. Matthew*, 61
Patterns of response to art: Clark, 71–72, 75, 80, 88, 91, 100, 102; Parsons, 119–21
Peirce, C. S., 72
Percipience, 35–38, 105, 107
Performing skills, 207–8
Perkins, D. H., 39, 154
Persuasion, 55
Peters, R. S., 48–49, 60
Phaedrus, 194
Phases of aesthetic learning, 133–42
Phenomenological analysis, 45
Philosophical aesthetics, 4
Piaget, Jean, 117
Picasso, *Guernica*, 36, 45, 198, 199; *Les Demoiselles d'Avignon*, 78

Plato, 21, 151, 167, 185, 186, 193
Pleasure, 53
Plight of the public, 78
Plotinus, 185
Podro, Michael, 94
Polanyi, Michael, 67, 108, 206
Policy, 8, 35, 156–62, 202–4
Policy questions, 162
Popular culture, 8, 11
Populists, 56
Postmodernism, 20, 169–70
Poussin, Nicholas, 71, 93–98; *The Ashes of Phocion Collected by His Widow, 96*; *Landscape with Diogenes, 95, 97*; *Rape of the Sabine Women, 97*
Positivism, 11
Professional's fallacy, 168
Propaganda, 59
Prosumption, 167, 168
Psychoanalytical aesthetic criticism, 71, 93
Pythagoras, 185, 189

Quality, 84; *see also* Excellence in art
Qualities, aesthetic, 106, 224; *see also* Aesthetic qualities

Raphael, 34
Rationality, 4, 56, 83; *see also* Aesthetic rationality
Reasons, 54, 62–67, 217; *see also* Language of critical evaluation
Redfern, H. B., 168
Reid, L. A., 196–97, 199
Reimer, Bennett, 141
Relevant aesthetic reasons, 63
Rembrandt, 79
Research, 116, 202–18
Rosenberg, Jakob, 54
Rosenberg, Harold, 9, 15, 16–21, 23, 27, 28, 83–84, 124
Rowland, Benjamin, 141
Rules, 206–07, 213
Ryle, Gilbert, 108

Santayana, George, 187, 189
Schapiro, Meyer, 69, 70, 75, 106, 125, 154, 164, 199

Scheffler, Israel, 5, 48, 55, 60, 155, 181
Schiller, F., 14, 181, 189
Schönau, D., 168, 169
Schopenhauer, A., 188–89, 191
Science, 11
Science and culture, 181
Scientific aesthetics, 4
Scientific chain of meaning, 128, 182
Scientific ideas, 147
Scientific institutions, 47
Scientific literacy, 149–50, 155, 160
Scientific understanding, 155–156, 182
Scientism in art, 15
Scruton, Roger, 149, 181–82
Seeing-as, 57, 58, 100
Semiotics, 24, 26–27
Sensuous plane of music, 72
Shakespeare, 131, 132; *King Lear*, 180; *Hamlet*, 30, 174
Shaw, Peter, 175, 177
Shaw, Roy, 210
Sibley, Frank, 59
Siena, 9–10
Sincerity, 63
Sircello, Guy, 194–95, 201
Skills, 49–51, 107–9, 206–211, table, 214–16
Smith, Ralph A., 127
Snow, C. P., 19, 99, 147–56, 181
Socrates, 194
Sparshott, Francis, 30, 39, 42, 87, 88, 101, 161, 211, 218
Stalinism, 163, 165
Steinberg, Leo, 69, 70, 78, 98, 116, 121, 125, 200, 207
Steiner, George, 28, 48, 55, 115, 180
Stella, Frank, *Thruxton 3X*, 17
Stocism, 94
Style, 223
Surrealism, 84
Swanger, David, 166–68
Synoptic vision, 102

Tacit knowing, 67, 108
Tatarkiewicz, W., 184–91

Taste, 186–87
Teacher as aesthetic critic, 56–61, 126
Teacher education, 143–44
Teaching aesthetic criticism, 219–52
Teaching art, 56, 61, 67–68, 99–111, 127–32, 115
Teaching art as a humanity, 127–32
Teaching and art criticism, 106–7
Technical criticism, 66
The two cultures debate, 146–56, 180, 181
Theoreticism, 176
Theory of aesthetic education, 1–2, 28
Thinking with, 67
Third American Revolution, 12
Thomas Acquinas, Saint, 185, 186, 189
Tintoretto, 236–38, 240, *Last Supper, 238*
Todorov, T., 178
Touchstones, 181
Toulmin, Stephen, 83, 111
Tormey, Alan, 55
Tradition of the new, 17
Travers, R. M. W., 111
Trilling, Lionel, 26, 38, 57–58, 82, 165, 167, 197
Types of reasons and judgments, table, 217; *see also* Language of critical evaluation

Unity, 67, 76
Unity of the arts, 4

Valéry, Paul, 189
Van Gogh, Vincent, 21, 125
Vermeer, 70, 72–75, *A Painter in His Studio, 73*, 132;
Veronese, 246–50; *Marriage at Cana, 248*; *The Feast in the House of Levi, 249*
Visual arts, elements of, 221–24
Vitruvius, 186
Vitti, Monica, 84

Warhol, Andy, 20
Watson, Dr., 86, 192–93
Weitz, Morris, 49, 50, 66
Western civilization, 8
Williams, Raymond, 23, 38, 63
Wilsmore, M. J., 170–72, 174–75, 177, 179
Wilson, John, 50

Woelfflin, Heinrich, 140
Wollheim, Richard, 69, 71, 93–98, 207
Wreen, M. J., 32
Wyeth, Andrew, 85

Ziff, Paul, 97
Zweig, Stefan, The Royal Game, 109